Military Struggle and Identity Formation in Latin America

UNIVERSITY PRESS OF FLORIDA

Florida A&M University, Tallahassee
Florida Atlantic University, Boca Raton
Florida Gulf Coast University, Ft. Myers
Florida International University, Miami
Florida State University, Tallahassee
New College of Florida, Sarasota
University of Central Florida, Orlando
University of Florida, Gainesville
University of North Florida, Jacksonville
University of South Florida, Tampa
University of West Florida, Pensacola

Military Struggle and Identity Formation in Latin America

Race, Nation, and Community During the Liberal Period

EDITED BY

NICOLA FOOTE AND RENÉ D. HARDER HORST

University Press of Florida

Gainesville/Tallahassee/Tampa/Boca Raton

Pensacola/Orlando/Miami/Jacksonville/Ft. Myers/Sarasota

We are grateful to the College of Arts and Sciences at Appalachian State
University for assistance with the reproduction of chapter 11.

First cloth printing, 2010
First paperback printing, 2012

Library of Congress Cataloging-in-Publication Data
Military struggle and identity formation in Latin America : race, nation,
and community during the liberal period / edited by Nicola Foote and
René D. Harder Horst.
p. cm.
Includes bibliographical references and index.
ISBN 978-0-8130-3487-4 (cloth: acid-free paper)
ISBN 978-0-8130-4483-5 (pbk.)
1. Latin America—History, Military—19th century. 2. Latin America—
History, Military—20th century. 3. Blacks—Latin America—History.
4. Indigenous peoples—Latin America—History. 5. Nationalism—Latin
America—History. 6. Community life—Latin America—History. 7. War
and society—Latin America—History. 8. Latin America—Race relations.
9. Liberalism—Latin America—History. 10. Latin America—Politics and
government—1830–1948. I. Foote, Nicola. II. Horst, René, Harder, 1967–
F1410.5.M55 2010
305.80098—dc22   2010015327

The University Press of Florida is the scholarly publishing agency for the State
University System of Florida, comprising Florida A&M University, Florida
Atlantic University, Florida Gulf Coast University, Florida International
University, Florida State University, New College of Florida, University of
Central Florida, University of Florida, University of North Florida, University
of South Florida, and University of West Florida.

University Press of Florida
15 Northwest 15th Street
Gainesville, FL 32611-2079
http://www.upf.com

Military Struggle and Identity Formation in Latin America

Race, Nation, and Community During the Liberal Period

EDITED BY

NICOLA FOOTE AND RENÉ D. HARDER HORST

University Press of Florida

Gainesville/Tallahassee/Tampa/Boca Raton

Pensacola/Orlando/Miami/Jacksonville/Ft. Myers/Sarasota

We are grateful to the College of Arts and Sciences at Appalachian State
University for assistance with the reproduction of chapter 11.

First cloth printing, 2010
First paperback printing, 2012

Library of Congress Cataloging-in-Publication Data
Military struggle and identity formation in Latin America : race, nation,
and community during the liberal period / edited by Nicola Foote and
René D. Harder Horst.
p. cm.
Includes bibliographical references and index.
ISBN 978-0-8130-3487-4 (cloth: acid-free paper)
ISBN 978-0-8130-4483-5 (pbk.)
1. Latin America—History, Military—19th century. 2. Latin America—
History, Military—20th century. 3. Blacks—Latin America—History.
4. Indigenous peoples—Latin America—History. 5. Nationalism—Latin
America—History. 6. Community life—Latin America—History. 7. War
and society—Latin America—History. 8. Latin America—Race relations.
9. Liberalism—Latin America—History. 10. Latin America—Politics and
government—1830–1948. I. Foote, Nicola. II. Horst, René, Harder, 1967–
F1410.5.M55 2010
305.80098—dc22   2010015327

The University Press of Florida is the scholarly publishing agency for the State
University System of Florida, comprising Florida A&M University, Florida
Atlantic University, Florida Gulf Coast University, Florida International
University, Florida State University, New College of Florida, University of
Central Florida, University of Florida, University of North Florida, University
of South Florida, and University of West Florida.

University Press of Florida
15 Northwest 15th Street
Gainesville, FL 32611-2079
http://www.upf.com

To Marlene, Tali, and Matías
and to Carlos
and to the Afro–Latin Americans and indigenous people
who made these histories possible

Contents

Part II. War and the Racing of National Boundaries and Imaginaries

Figures

Tables

Acknowledgments

As an edited volume, this book is a collaborative work by its very nature. However, the list of people who were essential to the success of this project extends far beyond the list of formal contributors.

The work initially emerged out of a panel at the 2006 Latin American Studies Association annual conference in Puerto Rico, and was further developed at the Southeast World History Association annual conference in Boone, North Carolina, in October 2006. Thanks to the participants and audiences of both panels for their enthusiasm, comments, and suggestions. The topic seemed such a pertinent one that we decided it would benefit from a wider and more rigorous examination. We sought to extend our investigation beyond the "comfort zone" of our specialty countries, and scholars from a wide range of disciplines were extremely generous with suggestions for potential contributors or topics. Thanks to Ariadna Acevedo Rodrigo, Reid Andrews, Keith Brewster, Matthew Brown, Avi Chomsky, Jerry Dávila, Darien Davis, Judith Ewell, Virginia Garrard-Burnett, David Howard, Claude Malary, Iván Molina, Jason McGraw, Lara Putnam, Kate Quinn, Joanne Rappaport, Thom Rath, Aldo Lauria Santiago, Jonathan Warren, Thomas Whigham, and Doug Yarrington for their help. Michael S. Cole, John Cox, Jo Crow, Jeffrey Gould, and Eric Strahorn provided valuable comments and feedback on earlier drafts of this manuscript. We of course accept responsibility for any errors in the final product.

Thanks to Rachael Huerta, a senior geography student at Appalachian State University, for carefully crafting the maps in this book. Thanks also to Alex Jordan and Adam Molloy, both graduate students at Florida Gulf Coast University (FGCU), for compiling the bibliography, to Bill Mack of FGCU for his help with tables and formatting, to Aaron Akey of ASU for his help with indexing, and to Terri Crowley of FGCU for her help with proofreading.

Funding was provided by Appalachian State University for copyright permissions and other costs associated with producing the manuscript.

René Harder Horst also benefitted from an ASU faculty off-campus scholarly assignment used to translate the Spanish chapters. Thanks to the Inter-Library loan department at FGCU, especially Kimberly Reycraft and Rachel Tait, for their help with ordering source material.

Thanks to Taylor and Francis Publishing Group for permission to reprint Vincent Peloso's article "Racial Crisis and Identity Crisis in Wartime Peru: Revisiting the Cañete Massacre of 1881." Thanks also to University of North Carolina Press for permission to reprint Aline Helg's chapter.

Amy Gorelick has been a wonderful editor, and we are so grateful for her enthusiasm (and patience!) and for the commitment she has shown to this project. Thanks also to Kara Schwartz of University Press of Florida for her help with imaging, and to our project editor, Michele Fiyak-Burkley.

We are grateful to the indigenous and Afro–Latin American people who graciously took time from their busy lives to answer questions posed by chapter contributors. In the Chaco, Byrdalene and Willis Horst, Verena Regeher, Miguel Fritz, Wilmar Stahl, and many others graciously assisted in Horst's interviews of indigenous people, going out of their way for yet another at times pushy scholar with too many questions.

Thanks finally and especially to our family members, who made our lives more joyful and meaningful during the completion of this manuscript: Jeff, Margaret, and Chris Foote; Marlene, Tali, and Matías Harder Horst; and Carlos King.

Guatemala

MEXICO

BELIZE

Caribbean
Sea

GUATEMALA

SAN MARCOS
Momostenango
San Marcos
Tecpán Comalapa
Patzicia Guatemala City
San Antonio Chimaltenango
Aguas Calientes

HONDURAS

North Pacific
Ocean

EL SALVADOR

Nicaragua

HONDURAS

EL SALVA-
DOR

NICARAGUA

León

Managua

North Pacific
Ocean

Masaya
Granada

Lake
Nicaragua

Rivas

APACHERÍA

USA
MEXICO

Agua
Prieta

Rio Grande

UNITED STATES

Sierra

CHIHUAHUA

SONORA

Tres Castillos

Tomóchi
Ariseachi
Chihuahua
City

Narárachi

Madre Mtns.

North
Pacific
Ocean

Gulf of California

Mexico

Legend

——— Country Border

–·–·–· Department Border

——— River

★ Capital City

● City/Town

N

Cartography by Rachael Huerta

Gulf of Mexico

Havana
LA HABANA

PINAR DEL
RIO

Pinar
del Río

MATANZAS

Santa
Clara

CIEN
FUEGOS

VILLA
CLARA

SANCTI
SPÍRITUS

CIEGO
DE
ÁVILA

Spanish Júcaro-Morón
Trench

Atlantic
Ocean

ISLE OF
PINES

Trinidad

Santa Lucía

CAMAGÜEY

Jimaguayú
LAS
TUNAS

Mountains
of Trinidad

Caribbean
Sea

HOLGUÍN

ORIENTE

MANZANILLO
REGION

GRANMA
El Cobre
Santiago
de Cuba

SANTIAGO
DE CUBA
La Mejorana

GUANTÁNAMO

Baracoa

Cuba

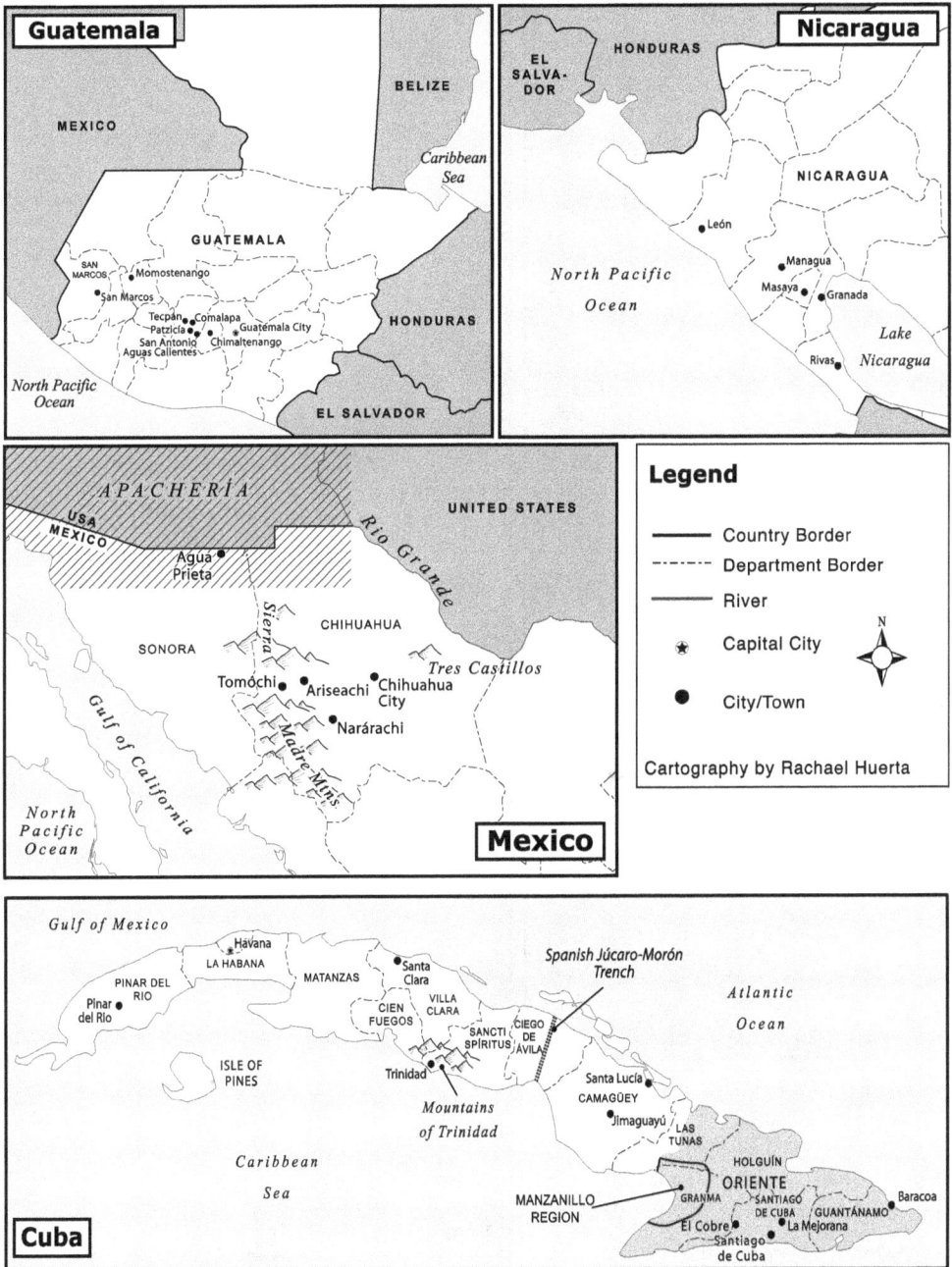

Map 1. Map of Central America, Cuba, and Mexico. Map original to this volume, created by Rachael Huerta, Appalachian State University.

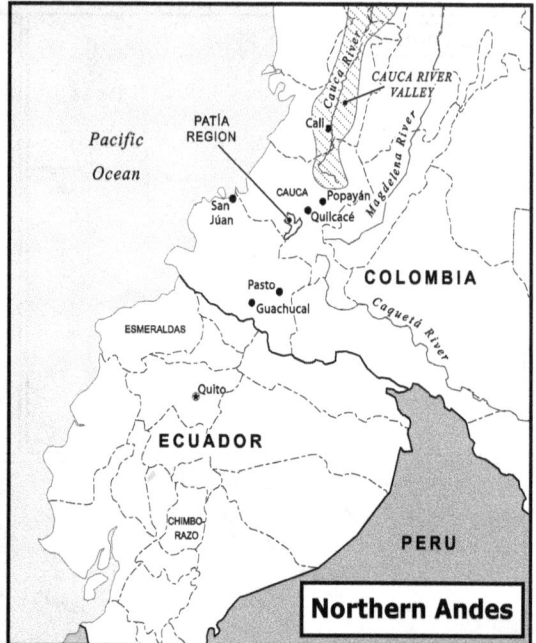

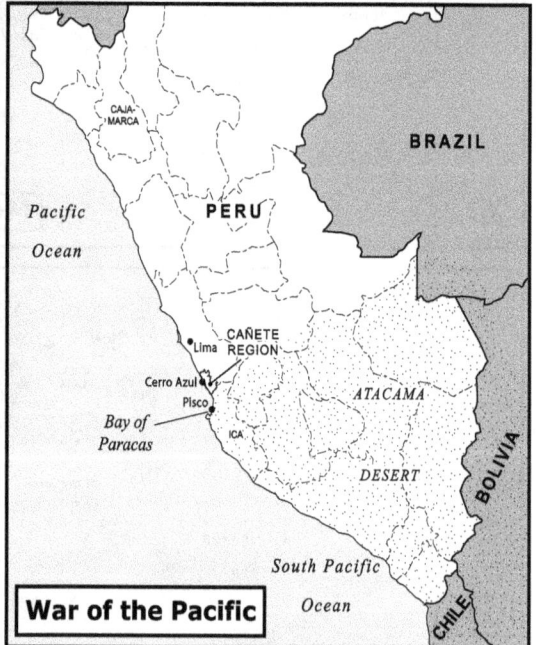

Chile

PERU
BOLIVIA
Tacna
Iquique
Territory Conquered
from Peru & Bolivia
Antofagasta
Pacific
Ocean
CHILE
ARGENTINA
Mapuche
Historic
Territory
Chol-Chol
Collipulli
Lebu
Victoria
Cañete
Traiguen
Lautaro
Carahue
Temuco
Imperial
Freire
Villarica

Legend

— Country Border   ✷ Capital City
---- Department Border
~~~~ River   N
• City/Town

Cartography by Rachael Huerta

CAUCA RIVER
VALLEY
Cauca River
PATÍA
REGION
Pacific
Ocean
Cali
CAUCA
Popayán
San
Juan
Quilcacé
Magdalena River
Pasto
COLOMBIA
Guachucal
Caquetá River
ESMERALDAS
Quito
ECUADOR
CHIMBO-
RAZO
PERU

Northern Andes

CAJA-
MARCA
BRAZIL
Pacific
Ocean
PERU
CAÑETE
REGION
Cerro Azul
Lima
ATACAMA
Pisco
Bay of
Paracas
ICA
DESERT
BOLIVIA
South Pacific
Ocean
CHILE

War of the Pacific

Map 2. Map of Chile, Ecuador, and Peru. Map original to this volume, created by Rachael Huerta, Appalachian State University.

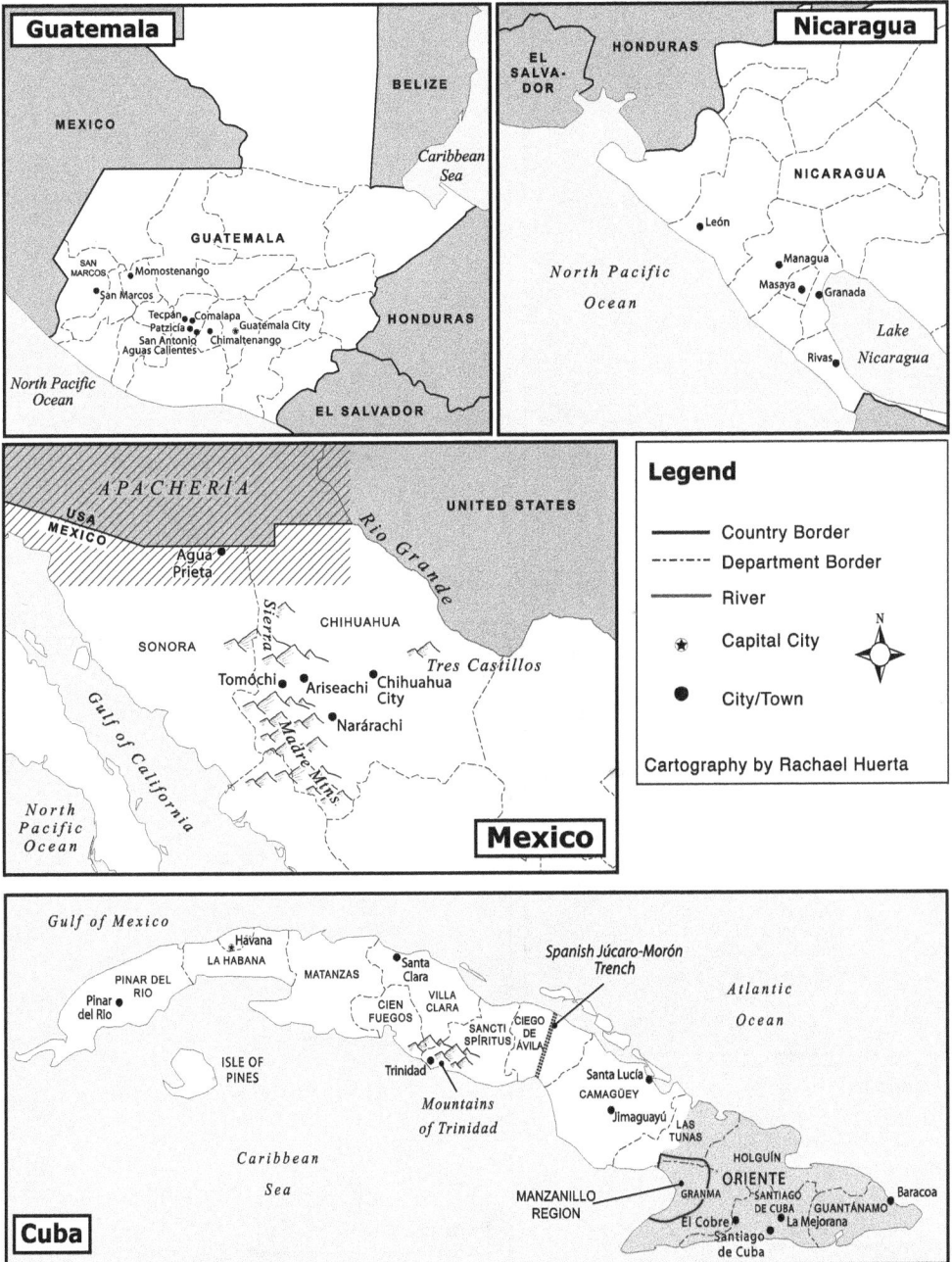

Guatemala

MEXICO

BELIZE

Caribbean Sea

GUATEMALA

SAN MARCOS
Momostenango
San Marcos
Tecpán Comalapa
Patzicía Guatemala City
San Antonio Chimaltenango
Aguas Calientes

HONDURAS

North Pacific Ocean

EL SALVADOR

Nicaragua

HONDURAS

EL SALVA-DOR

NICARAGUA

León

North Pacific Ocean

Managua
Masaya Granada

Lake Nicaragua

Rivas

APACHERÍA

USA
MEXICO

UNITED STATES

Rio Grande

Agua Prieta

Sierra

CHIHUAHUA

SONORA

Tres Castillos

Tomóchi
Ariseachi Chihuahua City

Madre Mtns.

Narárachi

Gulf of California

North Pacific Ocean

Mexico

Legend

———— Country Border
–·–·–· Department Border
———— River
★ Capital City
● City/Town

N

Cartography by Rachael Huerta

Cuba

Gulf of Mexico

Havana
LA HABANA
MATANZAS
Santa Clara

PINAR DEL RIO
Pinar del Río

CIEN FUEGOS
VILLA CLARA

Spanish Júcaro-Morón Trench

Atlantic Ocean

ISLE OF PINES

SANCTI SPÍRITUS
CIEGO DE ÁVILA

Trinidad

Mountains of Trinidad

Santa Lucía
CAMAGÜEY
Jimaguayú
LAS TUNAS

Caribbean Sea

HOLGUÍN

ORIENTE

MANZANILLO REGION

GRANMA SANTIAGO DE CUBA GUANTÁNAMO Baracoa
El Cobre La Mejorana
Santiago de Cuba

Map 1. Map of Central America, Cuba, and Mexico. Map original to this volume, created by Rachael Huerta, Appalachian State University.

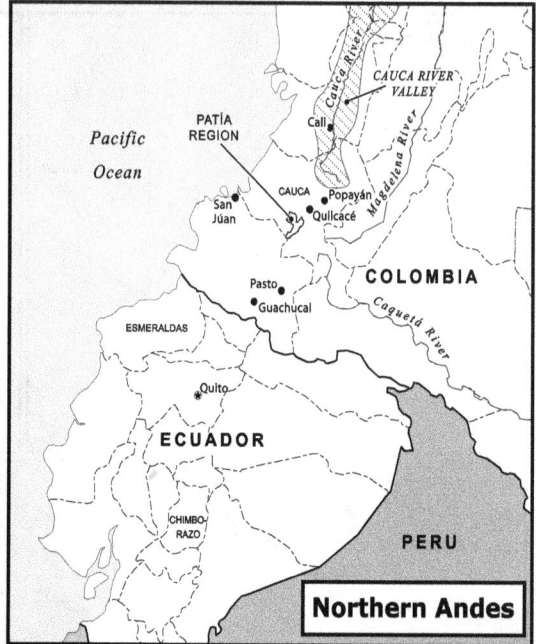

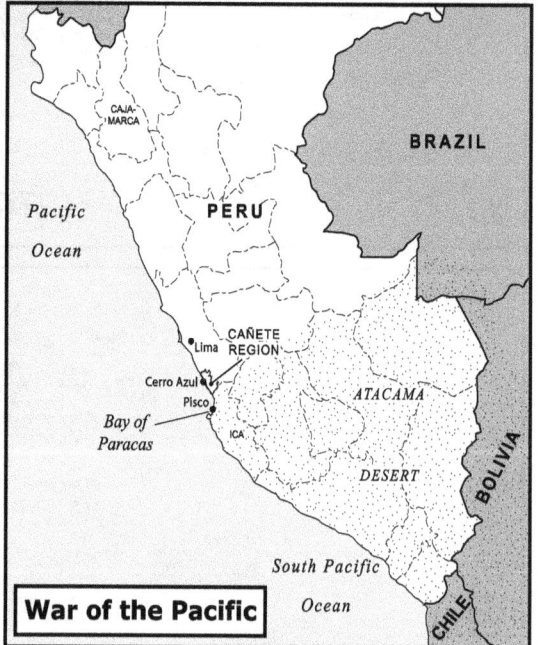

Chile

PERU
BOLIVIA
Tacna
Iquique

Territory Conquered
from Peru & Bolivia

Antofagasta

Pacific
Ocean

CHILE

ARGENTINA

Mapuche
Historic
Territory

Chol-Chol
Collipulli
Victoria
Lebu
Cañete
Lautaro
Traiguen
Carahue
Temuco
Imperial
Freire
Villarica

Northern Andes

Cauca River
CAUCA RIVER
VALLEY
Pacific
Ocean
PATÍA
REGION
Cali
Magdalena River
CAUCA
Popayán
San
Júan
Quilcacé

COLOMBIA
Pasto
Guachucal
Caquetá River
ESMERALDAS

Quito

ECUADOR

CHIMBO-
RAZO

PERU

War of the Pacific

CAJA-
MARCA
BRAZIL

Pacific
Ocean
PERU

CAÑETE
Lima
REGION
Cerro Azul
ATACAMA
Pisco
Bay of
Paracas
ICA
DESERT
BOLIVIA
South Pacific
Ocean
CHILE

Legend

—— Country Border   ☀ Capital City
--- Department Border
—— River
● City/Town

N

Cartography by Rachael Huerta

Map 2. Map of Chile, Ecuador, and Peru. Map original to this volume, created by Rachael Huerta, Appalachian State University.

Map 3. Map of Argentina and Paraguay. Map original to this volume, created by Rachael Huerta, Appalachian State University.

Introduction

Decentering War

Military Struggle, Nationalism, and Black and Indigenous Populations in Latin America, 1850–1950

NICOLA FOOTE AND RENÉ D. HARDER HORST

War dominates images of Latin America. Outsiders stereotype Latin America as a region of perpetual military struggle, a place of inexperienced and unstable nation states where elections are more often settled by coups and machine guns than by popular suffrage. In this picture, generals in dark glasses manage the destiny of the impoverished masses while sipping tequila amidst thick clouds of smoke, secret police torture dissidents, and soldiers head off in jeeps through the jungle to fight yet another war against their neighbors. Yet this image of political and military instability has been challenged, or at least nuanced, by scholars in recent years. A new wave of historical research into the nineteenth century has shown that violence was central to the operation of the political process but in ways much less disruptive to everyday life than has typically been imagined.[1] An influential study by sociologist Miguel Angel Centeno has suggested that the very reason for political instability—the fragility of the state—was itself the result of the relative absence of large-scale international warfare.[2] Meanwhile, an emerging body of work on the military as a social institution has suggested that far from being solely an agent of repression, the military has provided an important outlet of social mobility for many subordinate groups and has served as a medium for education and integration.[3]

Certainly, people in Latin America have been fortunate that none of the world wars were actively fought out in their region. While Latin Americans have struggled over land and resources, far fewer people there have lost their lives than in Asia, Africa, and Europe, and "total war" has been rare. Still, political changes, access to resources, and conflicts over borders have at times led to war. Violent conflicts were intimately tied to the nation-building process during the years 1850–1950, when new actors sought to dominate the political scene during the transition from the political chaos of independence to the relatively stable nation-states of the mid-twentieth century.

Prominent as soldiers and victims in this period's conflicts were those often-invisible groups, the Afro–Latin American and indigenous populations, who have too often been overlooked when significant national events are considered. In country after country, time after time, peoples typically presumed to be powerless and marginal played a central role in the outcome of critical national events as they sought to improve their living conditions, access political power, and change the course of their lives in ways that confound the stereotype that depicts them as passive victims. In recent decades there has been an outpouring of work on the histories of indigenous and Afro–Latin American peoples that has dramatically expanded our understanding of how economic development, political consolidation, and social transformations altered the lives of people outside the circles of power.[4] War and violence have provided an important backdrop to many of these studies, yet few works have rigorously examined how black and indigenous groups experienced and influenced military conflicts.[5] Certainly, no effort has been made to systematically examine within a comparative framework the extent to which war and military struggle permeated black and indigenous lives, or how this affected the process of race formation and the creation of national and community identities. Given the prevalence of such struggles and their importance to the nation-building process, this omission has impoverished Latin American history and perpetuated the exclusion of these people from our historical understanding of the continent. It has also deprived us of a valuable window into the intersection of race, community, and nation. The collection of chapters in this book addresses this omission by focusing on the indigenous and Afro–Latin American peoples' experiences during military conflicts and war. From Mexico's northern deserts to the southern tip of Chile's glaciers, these groups at times challenged state authority, other times fought in national armies, and always struggled to defend their lands, lives, and communities. In the process they forced their way into the plot of national histories in surprising and meaningful ways, with powerful reverberations for the formation of communal identities.

Frameworks and Backdrop: Liberalism, Race, War, and Nation-Building

There has been something of a renaissance recently in the study of warfare in Latin America. While the most important works have largely sidelined the issues of race and the popular classes, the emergence of both populist works apparently aimed at a general audience and of more rigorous and scholarly collections by specialist military historians have allowed us to obtain an overview of the major wars and conflicts of the nineteenth and twentieth centuries and their relationship to broader social, economic, and political trends.[6] From this spectrum of studies it becomes clear that two separate but equally important sets of pressures were at work in shaping ordinary peoples' experiences of war and militarized violence in the period 1850–1950: conflicting models of modernization and tensions over borders and resources.

When Latin Americans challenged former imperial structures in search of independence, they resorted to violence in their successful attempt to end Spanish hegemony. After achieving political freedom, though, the new nations of Latin America were seldom free from conflict. This was the case even in Brazil, where the relocation of the Portuguese crown to Rio de Janeiro served to sidestep much of the violence associated with Spanish American independence. Leaders found it difficult to contain the violence they had unleashed in the revolutionary process, and, as Brian Loveman has insisted, in the postindependence era "the habits of war became the habits of society, shaping attitudes and expectations, subverting respect for political principles and civility and cheapening human life."[7]

War was central both to the imagining and physical mapping of nation-states in Latin America. War created and defined territorial states. The mobilization of large sectors of society created long-standing partisan loyalties and in some cases undermined class differences and traditional relations of domination. This mobilization also created a political culture of participation and lower-class involvement in the struggles of the emerging nation.[8] The link between political power and military success was a strong one, and a large number of political actors won the presidency because of their success on the battlefield. War also profoundly altered the social structure of Latin America, pushing forward the creation of professional militaries and, with them, an option for social mobility for some members of subaltern groups.[9] The raising and maintaining of armies was typically the main state activity of the new republics.[10]

The centrality of war reflects the profound ideological and organizational issues that were at stake. People had to agree on how to govern their countries, turn a collective profit, and carefully manage the diverse groups of people left from the great colonial mixture that now composed the new nations. Certainly the political divisions between liberals and conservatives are crucial to understanding the violence associated with this period. Liberals stood for constitutionalism, equality before the law, the abolition of slavery, freedom from corporate and state control, and above all, free trade; conversely, the conservative focus was on Church and landowner rights and corporate privileges that had been central during the colonial period. While recent studies have stressed the overlap between the central goals and strategies of liberal and conservative modernization projects, the differences of expression were powerful and meaningful for many of the parties' subaltern constituents. Both liberals and conservatives needed subaltern electoral and military support, and black and indigenous groups were often able to capitalize on the situation to make demands of different political groups and regional governments, although always within a framework of uneven political and economic power relations.[11] Allegiances with different political factions have varied widely, depending on land tenure and the state's willingness to recognize them as minorities. Liberalism in particular became associated with popular concerns because of its ability to combine multiple ideological strands within a wider umbrella grouping.[12] Partly as a result, this ideology became ascendant in Latin America from the mid-nineteenth century and was displaced only by the populist currents of the mid-twentieth century.

The popular support that liberalism enjoyed obscured its pronounced racial dynamics. In its discourse of equality, the ideology presumed an unmarked, raceless, genderless individual, yet liberals typically presented idealized visions of nationalism and citizenship in racialized and gendered terms, and associated citizenship with whiteness and masculinity.[13]

Moreover, liberal economic development projects had markedly racialized undercurrents. Liberals considered slavery to be anathema to both ideals of liberty and economic modernization. However, the determination to expand commercial agriculture in order to facilitate integration into the world economy meant transforming indigenous communities from semiautonomous peasants into a wage-driven rural proletariat and opening their land to exploitation by the haciendas. Efforts to access and develop important raw materials on what had been the frontiers of Spanish colonization—the plains, deserts, and tropical forests—led to conflicts with indigenous residents, which in some notorious cases segued into wars of extermination. Global intellectual currents were also a factor, and the scientific racism that coalesced with the apogee of European imperialism encouraged a focus on whiteness as a marker of civilization and accelerated efforts to attract European immigration. These currents also affected the political engagement of racially subaltern groups. Blacks were more likely to support liberals, as chapters by Sanders, Helg, and Foote in this volume attest, while Indians occupied a more complex and ambiguous position. Meanwhile, groups that had previously possessed little knowledge or concern for national politics found their local, community-level interests dependent on much broader processes.

Thus race, war, and liberal ascendancy became powerfully intertwined in an at-times contradictory union in nineteenth and early twentieth century Latin America. Liberals needed to engage the popular classes but also to control them, and the ultimate unit of that control, the military, was paradoxically dependent on subaltern participation.

It must be noted that the fear of race war, inspired by the examples of the Haitian Revolution and the Tupac Amaru Revolt, was central to the formation of the armed forces in Latin America and underlay the nation-building process more generally. The duty of preventing or oppressing such movements was enshrined within the armed forces as an unwritten part of their historical mission.[14] As Centeno has argued: "Latin American elites lived in constant fear of the *enemy below*"[15]—the black and indigenous masses. Given the racialized nature of the Latin American class system, ethnically subaltern groups were invariably essential to the exercise of any military mission. Certainly they had been central to both colonial militias and the armies of the wars of independence.[16]

Yet there was always a fear among elites that subaltern agendas would burst through and overpower the wider alliance. Bolívar, for instance, became so concerned with the idea that black insurgents in the Venezuelan independence struggles were inspired by a spirit of "race vengeance" that he had the mulatto general Manuel Piar hunted down and executed for incitement of race war.[17] Popular liberalism became discredited and undermined because of its armed mobilization and subsequent association with race war.

This tension was a source of deep elite ambivalence about the army in the nineteenth and early twentieth century. Fear of armed blacks and Indians raised the specter not only of race war but also of the "perhaps more dangerous and insidious notion that participation in battle bestowed equality" on racially subordinate groups.[18]

This intersection hints at the profound and deep-rooted connection between military struggle and the racialization of citizenship. The "new military history" has conclusively demonstrated that military models have helped shape diverse forms of social action.[19] However, it is the link between military struggle and state formation that has been most extensively theorized. Scholars such as Richard Bean, Bruce Porter, and Charles Tilly have argued that a primary consequence of European warfare from the Renaissance to World War II was an increase in the size and power of the central government, and that war thus led to the rise of the nation-state.[20] This was adapted to the Latin American context by Miguel Angel Centeno, who argued that because Latin American nations have fought mainly limited wars, they have limited states.[21] If we accept that the economic and practical realities of war, based on the war technologies in use, led to the rise of the state, it is logical to assume by extension that war may have also led to the formation of other kinds of political entities and identities. However, an analysis of such links has been impeded by the fact that the causes of war have been much more thoroughly studied than its effects. Much more remains to be said about war's impact in the realm of imagination, emotion, and identity, and particularly about war's effect on the formation of racial, communal, and national identities.

Part of the problem is the way in which Latin America has been excluded from generalized theoretical frameworks pertaining to war and society—itself a reflection of the Eurocentric nature of mainstream military history. However, this is not an omission unique to Latin America. As far back as 1981, sociologist Anthony Smith lamented that although a vast literature exists on both ethnic groups and warfare, scholars have devoted little systematic attention to their interrelation.[22] It is still the case today that the link between ethnicity and war has been looked at mainly in terms of the relationship between ethnic cleavage and the outbreak of war, not how war shapes ethnicity and identity. As Smith then argued, "war has been a powerful factor in shaping, not society and ethnicity *per se*, but certain crucial aspects of ethnic community and nationhood."[23]

In Latin America, the connection between war, ethnicity, and nation has been obscured by the tendency to examine the conjunction of race and war mainly in the context of "race war," categorized in the historiography as a distinct and particular kind of war or cause for war. Such distinctions have served to imply that it is only if a struggle takes on the overt character of race war that war has important racial currents. As a result, the racialization of wars more generally is not taken up, nor is the way in which the experiences of war and militarism were themselves filtered through categories of race and ethnicity. This is despite the fact that movements classified as race war have been shown to be typically more complex and multifaceted than such simplified forms of analysis suggest.[24] The military as an institution has been proven to be of central importance to national identity and citizenship formation; this volume will demonstrate that the same can be said for war and military struggle more generally. Wars represented moments in which national identity could be contested and reimagined in a multiplicity of different ways as practical realities and ideological convictions crashed and converged. Because race was always so central to conceptions of national identity, and black and indigenous groups were invariably embroiled in the heart of national struggle, racial identities and ideologies were almost always up for negotiation.

Periodization and Definitions

The decision has been made to limit our study to the period 1850–1950 based on a consideration of the political and ethnic dynamics at stake. While some important work has recently been done on the issue of subaltern participation and agendas in the wars of independence, we felt that this time frame represented a separate era in which different questions were at stake.[25] There was also a series of wars during the period of 1820–50 that involved important black and indigenous engagement, but these mostly reflected the still-indeterminate nature of national boundaries as well as the ambitions of contending factions within each incipient nation-state.[26] Our concern lies with the period in which national boundaries were more solid and nations were no longer new but in which the physical and imagined limits were still being negotiated. We end in 1950, by which time a sociological developmentalist discourse had definitively eclipsed the civilizationist one associated with the high point of liberalism.[27] Military historian René de la Pedraja deems the period under consideration a central one to the history of Latin American warfare. The region was free of colonial rule but "not yet defined as it exists today."[28] Wars were fought to define national boundaries, to determine the composition of national governments, and to fend off European invaders and other Latin American states. These wars were always complex and simultaneously involved nation-building, territorial disputes, internal ideological and political conflicts, personalist and factional strife, and struggles over political power and government revenue. They involved coalitions of participants from different classes and regions, who held somewhat differing sets of motivations and concerns. Of course, in a brief work of this nature it is not possible to include all wars, and we have decided to focus on those in which black and indigenous engagement was most clear cut. There are many other examples, documented and undocumented, that are outside the realm of this volume. While we have tried to be as comprehensive as possible in our geographic reach and have included perspectives from Mexico, Central America, the Caribbean, Brazil, the Southern Cone, and the Andes, it was impossible to incorporate each individual nation, and in some cases our efforts to uncover historians working on subaltern engagements with the military proved futile. Equally, the cases of regional repetition—the two essays on Brazil and Guatemala—represent simply the richness of scholarly production on the topics that interested us rather than any country-specific "favoritism" on our part.

We are much less concerned with a formal definition of war than many of the scholars working on this topic because our interest is in military struggle more broadly; thus, any sustained violent movement that affected subaltern lives over an extended period is considered to fall within the orbit of this book. While in *Blood and Debt* Centeno focuses on international war to the exclusion of "internal strife"[29]—rebellions and revolutions—arguing that the former is key to state-building, we argue that it is the comparison between distinct forms of conflict that is central to understanding the broader meaning of armed struggle for identity formation. As Jeremy Black has insisted, there is limited value in viewing wars only as conflicts between states; internal eruptions of violence and state responses to them must also come under consideration.[30]

An Introduction to the Chapters

In this book, chapters are organized chronologically within two sections that reflect the two main divisions outlined earlier: internal development models, and boundaries and borders. Each section examines a major theme. The first looks at soldiering and military participation as they intersect with ideas from above and below about citizenship. The second compares international wars and internal wars of pacification or extermination and examines how both contributed to the racialization of national boundaries and imaginaries as well as the practical meaning of war for the subaltern peoples caught up in them. The chronological organization within each section allows us to examine the impact of liberal rise and decline as liberalism competed with a militarized conservatism and was gradually displaced by populism and *indigenismo*.

We begin by examining one of the classic and most-studied theaters of liberal-conservative military struggle: nineteenth century Colombia. In a summary of his prize-winning study of indigenous people and Afro-Colombians in Cauca, historian James Sanders explores the way in which Cauca's people took advantage of nineteenth-century civil wars to fulfill their own goals vis-à-vis the state. He notes a marked difference between how black and indigenous groups experienced and perceived soldiering. For Afro-Colombians, soldiering represented a real and viable means to claim citizenship and advance their political goals. Through engaging militarily in defense of liberalism they were able to push forward the abolition of slavery and defend against the conservative challenge that threatened their freedom. Many enriched themselves through war booty and gained access to land. In contrast, Cauca indigenous groups who had historical land rights granted by the Crown found it more important to protect their historical prerogatives than to advance new claims on the state through military service. Unlike blacks, Indians felt they did not have to "earn" citizenship militarily but rather that it should be based on their past rights and identities as Indians. Afro-Colombians, conversely, lacked resources or legal and historic rights and sought to create a new identity that was not dependent on an inherited identity. Sanders's chapter advances our understandings about subaltern agency and shows that, far from being used as pawns and cannon fodder, Afro-Colombians were literally fighting to become citizens and to overturn slavery and racism. However, their experience is also proof of the way in which black political conviction and engagement with liberalism was manipulated by conservatives who were able to shout "race war" to dismiss and marginalize liberalism. Sanders's chapter demonstrates the real meaning of colonial racial divisions in republican realities and underscores the insight to be gained from examining black and indigenous populations within a comparative framework.

The chapter by Justin Wolfe also finds soldiering to be an important but conflictive means of social advancement for people of African descent, this time in Nicaragua. Unlike other essays in this book that focus on larger groups of people and national dynamics, Wolfe takes a specific look at San Felipe, a neighborhood in the Nicaraguan city of León. Again, colonial racial divisions are important in understanding the national experiences of

Afro-Nicaraguans as Wolfe traces the political power of leaders from the city to their military heritage, which was itself a product of colonial efforts to maintain separation between black and indigenous groups through the creation of caste-specific militias.

During the civil wars that engulfed Nicaragua between 1837 and 1863, politicians came to depend on Felipeños as critical to political and military success. When the government subsequently regularized the army, however, it stabilized national politics but limited options for communities such as San Felipe. That blacks would fight at first on behalf of William Walker, typically characterized as a pro-slavery demagogue, underscores how subaltern mobilization reflected local needs, interests, and realities and defies easy assumptions about what marginalized groups "should" do.

Noted historian Aline Helg's chapter also addresses blackness and soldiering, this time during Cuba's struggle for independence from Spain (1895–98)—a war widely noted for its complicated racial dimensions. The island's large population of African descent provided the labor force for the important sugar industry. As Helg shows, the war with Spain in 1896 provoked a dilemma for elite Cuban patriots. How could they use the Afro-Cubans as soldiers in their war yet at the same time contain former slaves' aspirations for equality and freedom without endangering sugar production? Would arming blacks destine Cuba to become a second Haiti? Meanwhile, the ever-present threat of U.S. intervention and annexation presented an additional complication to the War for Independence. Based on archival and secondary records, this insightful essay explains the complex interplay between Afro-Cuban aspirations for freedom, military strategy, economic imperatives, and elite struggles for hegemony. The author demonstrates conclusively how central black soldiers were to the Cuban War for Independence. Yet their continued presence also led to the compromise of its goals through U.S. intervention because fears of Afro-Cuban insurrection were used by white leaders to jeopardize efforts and lobby for U.S. involvement.

Nicola Foote reinforces many of these findings in her study of the comparative relationship of black and indigenous groups to military service in Ecuador during the period of the Liberal Revolution of 1895. She shows that the participation of indigenous and, especially, Afro-Ecuadorian soldiers, was central to the liberal victory, but that dominant discourses about race mediated the ability of the respective groups to convert this activism into meaningful change. While Indian groups who were central to the liberal project of economic modernization were set on a (problematic) path to citizenship through cultural transformation, blacks continued to be neglected and marginalized. Paradoxically, their military contribution to liberalism was key to this exclusion. Afro-Ecuadorians were defined as "savage," "bloodthirsty," and inherently prone to revolt. Foote then examines how Afro-Ecuadorians responded to the failure of liberalism to usher in the transformation in their status they had desired, interpreting black participation in the Concha Revolution of 1913–16, typically understood in the historiography as a conflict between rival factions of liberal elites, as a subaltern attempt to attain citizenship. The failure of this movement led the black community to turn away from national society and to develop an Afro-centric local identity. Foote's chapter thus underscores how war can influence community, not just national, identity formation.

Two chapters on Guatemala that complete this first section assess the multifaceted meaning of the military as an outlet of race formation. Taken together the chapters demonstrate that the army is not a static institution but shifts and transforms with changing political regimes and shifting political currents and is also key to shaping this wider political climate. Distinguished ethnohistorian Richard Adams uses conscription records to study indigenous soldiers in Guatemala between 1871 and 1914. Based on a chance finding of a remarkable document—the 1914 internal census of recruits—the essay provides an intriguing and rare breakdown of how ethnic recruits were viewed by the military hierarchy and elucidates wider conceptions of indigenous people and the social meaning of the military. Leaders saw service in the army at the time as civilizing and educating "backward" indigenous people. Liberal president Justo Rufino Barrios needed a larger military force to face the eight military conflicts during the period and saw indigenous recruits as potentially docile soldiers with which to create a successful Ladino army, using images from the Mayan past. Adams skillfully teases out the conflict at the heart of the relationship between race and military service in Guatemala. While the military use of Indians has often been exploitative, abusive, and racist, it has been one of the few avenues to education and economic opportunity available to subaltern groups and has served as a primary arm of social policy. The shift in attitude that Adams traces toward Indian soldiers in the context of prolonged and endemic warfare with neighboring Central American countries and Mexico over territory likely paved the way for the indigenist reinterpretation of the army under the presidency of Gen. Jorge Ubico (1930–44) that David Carey documents in the following chapter.

Carey explores how during the rule of a president who celebrated native heritage at a time when *indigenismo* was in full swing through the Americas,

Kaqchikel youth were more able to celebrate the cultural markers that made them Mayan while participating in the army as soldiers. Carey underscores how Ubico's acceptance of Mayan ethnicity transformed the indigenous experience and understanding of military service, and the military became a place where Mayans could claim their citizenship without renouncing their claim to ethnic identity. For some, the military gained positive aspirations as a way and a place to earn respect and get an education. This venue represented an opening for rethinking the relationship between nation and indigenousness and opened up an avenue for national integration that was not based on the suppression of cultural attributes. Carey singles out the Ubico dictatorship as a high point in indigenous nationalism and argues that the army both reflected and constituted these feelings. This insightful chapter speaks to current debates as it suggests some ways in which ethnic distinctions need not necessarily impede national unity. It is also important in showing how in certain times and spaces the military could be an avenue for indigenous mobility much in the same way as scholars in the first half of this section identified in the case of blacks.

Part 2 deals with subaltern military participation in the moments of crisis precipitated by full-scale war. The section begins with two chapters on one of the most notorious of Latin American wars, the catastrophic War of the Triple Alliance, also called the Paraguayan War, which devastated the four countries involved and was responsible for the loss of 60 to 70 percent of the Paraguayan population.[31] While the importance of Afro-Brazilian soldiers, who—like Afro-Cubans—fought in exchange for liberation from slavery, is beginning to be understood, indigenous perspectives have been largely obscured. In the section's opening chapter, Brazilian historian Maria Fátima da Costa assesses indigenous participation in the war, focusing particularly on the little-known case of the Guaikurú indigenous people who lived in the Pantanal area between Brazil and Paraguay. Using archival and newspaper records as well as secondary studies created by anthropologists and oral historians, Costa helps to explain why the Guaikurú indigenous groups, long hostile to outsiders, surprisingly supported Brazilian troops throughout the war. She roots indigenous participation firmly in the history of native European relations, showing how indigenous action on behalf of the Brazilian effort stemmed from their historical enmity with Paraguayan settlers as well as from their own conceptions of their strategic best interests.

Peter Beattie takes a different but complementary approach, comparing how black and indigenous participation was represented during the war in political cartoons and literature. He looks at how the blackness and poverty of most Brazilian troops became a source of national embarrassment and shame, and he shows how Paraguayan propagandists used even the role of indigenous soldiers within the Triple Alliance as "proof" of Brazilian impurity and degradation.

Both chapters assess the impact of the war on the shaping of ethnic and community boundaries. Costa highlights the diversity of indigenous experiences and stresses how different groups were affected in different ways. For the Kadiwéu, the War of the Triple Alliance became the "definitive national event," the framework within which they worked for the recovery of territorial rights. For the Guaikurú, who had already been fighting frontier settlers from Paraguay, state and subaltern interests intersected as they fought to obtain recognition of their land rights from the Brazilian state. Beattie pinpoints the war as the major cause in the decline of Indianism within artistic and literary representations of the nation, and he suggests that the reality of fighting alongside Indians during the war shattered the mythology of the "noble savage." He also charts the impact of the shift from Indianism to Sertanism (the focus on mixed-race backwoods frontiersmen, widely seen as the "heroes" of the war, as the embodiment of national identity) on national politics, arguing that the collapse of the monarchy was hastened by Pedro II's continued association with Indianism, which was classified as "unmodern" in the aftermath of the war. Ultimately, both chapters remind us that black and indigenous participation, however marginalized within conventional historiographies, was central to the course of Brazilian victory.

We then turn to three "wars of extermination"—genocides perpetrated by national states against the plains tribes of Argentina, the Apache of Northern Mexico, and the Mapuche of Chile. While these chapters do not seek to minimize the immense human suffering inflicted, they do complicate and nuance our understanding of the meaning of these wars for the groups targeted, the communities surrounding them, and the wider structures of national identity.

Argentine historian Carlos Martínez Sarasola engages Argentine national stereotypes of whiteness and exceptionalism in his exploration of the wars that Argentina's government waged against its plains indigenous people in the late nineteenth century. Intellectual ideals of whitening at the time led politicians first to try to exclude natives from their frontier. When this plan failed, politicians resorted to wars of extermination. The military campaigns that Argentina waged against its indigenous population resulted in large-scale genocide of Argentina's native tribes and helped eliminate "unwanted" Afro-Argentines. However, Sarasola powerfully argues that even in the context of genocide, relationships between elites and subalterns are never straightforward. In Sarasola's account, the frontier of the 1850s appears as a place of mobility, fluidity, and coexistence. He shows that even as communities competing for land and resources mobilized to defend their resources, the wholesale destruction of the indigenous side was far from inevitable. Sarasola presents a pluralistic account of white Argentine society in this era and shows that not everyone agreed on a policy of extermination, and that indeed Rosas, who is typically characterized as the precursor of genocide, envisaged Indians as part of the Argentine nation. However, voices of opposition to the idea that Argentina could only be, and must be, wholly "white" have been silenced within the historical record. He also draws out how indigenous populations on the frontier used the national political process over a broad period to try to advance their own local and community interests. Thus, the so-called friendly Indians who have been viewed with such ambivalence within the historical literature represented an indigenous effort to engage white society. The idea that all Indians strenuously resisted white colonization is itself a false one and suggests rich avenues for future research.

Julia O'Hara's chapter deals with the so-called Apache Wars of the U.S.-Mexico border. These conflicts pitted multiple groups of indigenous people against two national armies, professional mercenaries, and civilian "bounty hunters." However, the focus of her chapter is on the meaning of this conflict to an indigenous group that was outside of the remit of the war but was hugely affected by it—the Tarahumara Indians of the northern Mexican province of Chihuahua. O'Hara traces the contradictory nature of Tarahumara agency as actors in the genocide against an indigenous group with whom they shared important cultural, linguistic, and economic ties by emphasizing the dynamics of intercommunity rivalry that had made the Tarahumara the victims of Apache violence. She also links this to national political processes, emphasizing how liberal land-reform legislation had led to the dispossession of the Tarahumara, and how land was offered as an incentive for indigenous military service. Thus, revenge against a long-standing enemy and the need for protection of resources coincided. Military service was also a path to white respect and prestige as Tarahumara fighting skills became mythologized and woven into nationalist mythologies, in particular their skill with a bow and arrow and their prowess and endurance as long-distance runners.

O'Hara also underscores the importance of the war for the process of race formation, which defined Mexico's national enemy as not just the United States but also the "Indians," an invented construct that incorporates multiple ethnic groups—many of whom were at odds with each other and would have rejected any common label. The Tarahumara were fitted into this narrative by means of characterizations that cast them as "tame" or "domesticated" Indians, in a categorization paralleling the "friendly" Indians of Argentina's and even the U.S.' frontiers at the time. For this classification to make sense, Tarahumara participation in the practice of scalp-hunting in the process of the war was obscured. The collaboration of the Tarahumara in the extermination of the Apache complicates assumptions about race war and the internalization of the enemy, and it qualifies the meaning of whiteness within national identity. As O'Hara demonstrates, the contradictions set in play by the complexities of the frontier wars are linked to the roots of the Mexican Revolution in Chihuahua.

Joanna Crow examines the Chilean war of "pacification" against the Mapuche in the context of the War of the Pacific with Peru (1879–83). Historians have long held Mapuche resistance in Southern Chile as a prime example of native defiance to European and, later, national settlement. Crow's study reveals, however, a multilayered history of Mapuche collaboration and negotiation with Chile's government as evidenced by indigenous responses to this national conflict. Crow demonstrates first that the Chilean occupation of Araucanía was not a one-sided story of oppression. Indians raided towns and exploited opportunities created by the withdrawal of troops to the Pacific front to their own advantage. Other Mapuche joined the Chilean army and fought in the War of the Pacific against their own presumed "group" interests, and did so to advance themselves against their local rivals and gain government support for the acquisition of land, analogous with O'Hara's findings about the Apache. Crow also examines how this contradictory and multilayered Mapuche engagement affected discourses of nationhood, challenging the long-held assumption that Chile won the war because of its unified national composition and the absence of competing peasant or indigenous loyalties.[32] Both official and popular nationalisms in this period were divided and ambiguous. Crow traces how the image of the Mapuche in elite discourse moved from that of heroic "founding fathers" and resistance to Spanish oppression, to barbarous "other" as the pacification campaign in Araucanía progressed. Yet as the War of the Pacific advanced, the heroic imagery of the Mapuche as unyielding warriors was resurrected as a symbol of Chileanness. Crucially, however, these shifting symbols and imageries created a space for the Mapuche to assert themselves as loyal citizens of the Chilean nation. As such, Crow pushes forward understandings of peasant nationalism by asserting something Florencia Mallon's (1995) groundbreaking work on this topic had only implied: that the formation of peasant nationalist sentiments occurred not *despite* class conflict and local loyalties but *because* of them; it was their understanding of their local, class-based interests that persuaded peasants of the advantage of defending the nation. The complexity of this story reveals insights to processes of accommodation and resistance, cooperation and struggle that together impart insightful lessons about the colonization process itself and its results for indigenous peoples of the Southern Cone.

We then move to the other side of the Pacific theater, with Vincent Peloso's examination of the meaning of the Chilean occupation for Afro-Peruvian peasants and indentured Chinese laborers, which he assesses through the lens of a notorious massacre in the coastal valley of Cañete. He examines how the attack by mainly Afro-Peruvian peasants on Chinese plantation workers created a racially charged conflict that sheds light on peasant loyalties, political allegiance, and economic rivalries during foreign occupation at the height of a major international war. Like Crow, Peloso engages the subtleties of the enduring debate over whether subalterns did or did not show nationalism during the war and how this contributed to Peru's defeat. On the surface the Cañete massacre appears as a classic example of what some have perceived as the breakdown of national ties, yet Peloso demonstrates that the uprising was informed by Afro-Peruvian visions of national identity and citizenship, mediated through local class interests. Black participants in the massacre sought to rid themselves of their debt burden to Chinese merchants, and to punish Chinese men for their sexual engagement with, and violence against, black women. Yet class interests were not all that was at stake. Afro-Peruvians feared racial and cultural pollution by a group they pathologized for their religious and cultural practices and their growing postindenture economic power. They heard ideas of Chinese "racial danger" reflected back to them in dominant nationalist discourses. Thus blacks sought to show their loyalty to the nation by removing a pernicious element. However, the massacre was itself used by elites as a symbol of the illegitimacy of Afro-Peruvian claims to inclusion in the nation. The idea that they took pleasure in killing was used to reinforce ideas of black savagery and backwardness, and the centrality of black women to the revolt—itself the result of the gendered dynamics of intercommunity tension—was used to present black men as effeminate and un-Peruvian.

Peloso also shows how the massacre was used by the Chilean army to gain the moral high ground in the conflict, and to present themselves as the "saviors" of the Chinese. He questions such interpretations and underscores the unnecessary slowness of their response, suggesting that the massacre served Chilean strategic interests by fomenting social unrest and the disintegration of national ties. The landowner cooperation with Chilean invaders, which has been central to the arguments made by Mallon that it was elites rather than peasants who repudiated nationalist loyalties in favor of class interests, is linked by Peloso to the massacre, which appeared to realize elite's worst fears of "race war" and black peasant vengeance.

The final chapter studies the 1932 Chaco War between Latin America's two poorest nations, Bolivia and Paraguay, who fought for control of the dry Chaco area between them. Historians have long puzzled over the causes of this war; oil speculation, access to waterways, and national pride all played a role. Using interviews with elderly Chaco indigenous people and military archives, René D. Harder Horst discovered that local native people shaped the conflict in the years immediately preceding the war. Bolivia relied on highland indigenous people for its fighting force, and both armies employed indigenous guides and used their languages for secret communications. The war dramatically altered native health, land tenure, and interaction with the nationals who settled the Chaco. Horst also draws out the gendered dynamics of this involvement, underscoring the rape and abuse of indigenous women. However, despite the centrality of indigenous knowledge and resources to the outcome of the war, indigenous participation did little to benefit and protect Chaco tribes. For indigenous people, the war led to epidemics, forced removals, and the loss of lands as settlers moved into the Chaco from both sides. Contact with the native tribes led to an *indigenista* movement in Paraguayan literature that glorified the nation's native heritage and resulted in the creation of a state agency to settle indigenous people. This parallels the findings of historians of Bolivia, where the loss of the war has been shown to contribute directly to a national crisis marked by rural turmoil and violence that culminated in the Revolution of 1952.[33]

Agency, Identity, and Struggle: Conclusions and Directions For Future Research

The traditional view of black and indigenous military struggle is that blacks and Indians possessed no sense of nationality, and joined armies or guerrilla bands out of "duress . . . habit, or to acquire arms, but rarely under individual initiative."[34] Such ideas about how the Latin American rural masses experienced war have been entwined with the historical perception of peasants as merely "reactive" political actors.[35] Just as this reductionist perspective has been roundly challenged in recent years, this volume underscores the need to reexamine the issue of peasant agency in military encounters. While it is undoubtedly the case that on many occasions peasants did find themselves caught up in military struggle against their will, we must also examine the political, economic, and intellectual currents through which subalterns negotiated the situation in which they found themselves. We must guard against a partial tendency being essentialized as the principle characteristic of subaltern military behavior and consciousness, but without over-romanticizing black and indigenous subaltern engagement. While war's destructive and dehumanizing consequences are well known, these chapters collectively show that war had different meanings and at times functioned as a way for peasants to improve their lot and as an opportunity to gain land, a political voice, specific policy demands, and in some cases, freedom itself.

Military engagement could stem from and could engender a sense of frustration with nationalist promises of inclusion. In virtually all of the cases discussed here, war created a space for debates over the national political potential of previously marginalized groups. This could, and often—but not always—did, create a space for marginal people to push forward their own agenda. One of the strengths of this volume is the nuance with which the chapters push forward our understanding of peasant nationalisms and show how multiple visions of nationalism could be encompassed within a single war or movement. Sometimes these conflicting visions of collective identity overlapped, but more typically elite visions surmounted and marginalized the popular.

Certainly the advance of popular agendas in wartime was used to justify renewed oppression and invariably aroused elite fears of the armed other, as we see in the way in which mobilization was equated with race war. There are parallels between the way that images of black and indigenous savagery in battle were used to suppress claims for more inclusive citizenship and recent findings about the connections between gender and war in the independence process: once the moment of crisis had passed, social conservatism emerged precisely in response to the currents generated by war, and efforts were made to reinstitute and reinstate traditional boundaries.

These cycles reflect the way in which subaltern experiences of war served as a fountain of material for elite-driven cultural constructions of race, which scholars have pinpointed as an increasingly important supplement to biological understandings of race in this period.[36] Ideas about the Afro-Ecuadorian Conchistas who would turn their white rivals into soup, or the plains Indians who "flew" on horseback, both drew from and fed into dominant stereotypes about blackness and Indianness and their lack of suitability for inclusion into "civilized" society. These cultural formulations created a limit to the racialized social mobility engendered by war. Witness, for example, the twin exclusions of famed Afro-Cuban Gen. Antonio Maceo and Afro-Ecuadorian commander Sergeant Lastre from ultimate command of their respective revolutionary movements, which occurred despite their clear suitability for the posts.

It also seems that war had different repercussions for Afro–Latin American and indigenous groups. Afro–Latin Americans, who lacked any historic claim to inclusion or resources, were more likely than Indians to seek to claim citizenship through military service. They were also more likely to see this path closed to them than were Indians, whose military exploits often became the basis for nationalist celebration rather than stigmatization, even if meaningful integration did not necessarily follow. How subalterns experienced war, then, reflected preexisting positioning within the racialized system and hierarchy. Modern racial ideas cannot be separated from colonial frameworks, and elites continued to manipulate these differences in a process of "divide and conquer."[37]

In its contemplation of the subtleties and divergences of group experiences, the volume also speaks to the complexity of the relationship between race and war, and pushes forward theoretical understandings of these intersections. The chapters show that the relationship between race and war can have multiple dynamics. War and military struggle could expand the power of the state over black and indigenous land and push racial subalterns toward closer engagement with the national unit, or could strengthen the ethnic self-consciousness and ethnic imagery advanced by marginalized communities and weaken the cohesion of already fragmentary alliances.

This collection provides more evidence of the complex and profound ways in which race, gender, and nation intersect, and further demonstrates that the direct comparison of black and indigenous populations is essential to understanding the nuances of these interactions. The volume also demonstrates that such processes—even ones as dependent on events as seemingly elite-driven as international warfare—cannot be understood only from above but must also assess how subordinate groups have understood race and contributed to the process of race formation.

The application of social and cultural perspectives to the study of war and the military augers many new directions for historians and social scientists, and there is still much work to be done in the Latin American context as to how war relates to ideas about gender and the role and status of the Church, among other compelling issues. Our hope is that this book will reinvigorate interest in this complex subject and suggest some tantalizing avenues for further research.

Notes

1. Earle, *Rumours of War*; Fowler, "Civil Conflict in Independent Mexico"; and Safford, "Reflections on Internal Wars."

2. Centeno, *Blood and Debt*.

3. Andrews, *Afro-Latin America*; and Beattie, *Tribute of Blood*.

4. Andrews, *Afro-Latin America*; Appelbaum, *Muddied Waters*; Appelbaum, Macpherson, and Rosemblatt, *Race and Nation*; Clark and Becker, *Highland Indians*; de la Cadena, *Indigenous Mestizos*; de la Fuente, *A Nation for All*; Horst, *Stroessner Regime*; Gould, *To Die in This Way*; Graham, *The Idea of Race*; Naro, *Blacks, Coloureds and National Identity*; O'Connor, *Gender, Indian, Nation*; Radcliffe and Westwood, *Remaking the Nation*; Thurner and Guerrero, *After Spanish Rule*; Sanders, *Contentious Republicans*; and Wade, *Music, Race, and Nation*.

5. For exceptions that have deeply influenced this work, see Mallon, *Peasant and Nation*; Brewster, *Militarism, Ethnicity and Politics*; and Thomson with LaFrance, *Patriotism, Politics and Popular Liberalism for Mexico*. For Cuba, see Helg, *Our Rightful Share*; and Ferrer, *Insurgent Cuba*. For Brazil, see Kraay, *Race, State, and Armed Forces*. For Peru, see Méndez, *The Plebian Republic*. For Colombia, see Lasso, "Race War and Nation"; and Helg, *Liberty and Eqaulity*. For Ecuador, see Ortiz, *Indios, Militares e Imaginarios*. See also special edition of *ICONOS*, Méndez, "Populismo Milítar y Etnicidad." The connection between military service and the racialization of citizenship is also being raised in the field of African American studies. See, for example, Berlin, Reidy, and Rowland, *Freedom's Soldiers*; and Kerr-Ritchie,"Rehearsal for War."

6. See de la Pedraja, *Wars of Latin America*; Scheina, *Latin America's Wars*, Vols. I and II; Centeno, *Warfare in Latin America*; and Santoni, *Daily Lives of Civilians*. The works of de la Pedraja and Scheina are comprehensive in their scope but rather unsophisticated and simplistic in their analysis and are more reflective of the old "drum-and-trumpet" tradition in military history than the "new military history" that has transformed other fields. Centeno's recent edited collection is much more scholarly and provides an insightful and cohesive overview of wars and battles from the Spanish Conquest to the present. However, he is only minimally interested in race, and only a handful of his book's chapters engage the topic. Santoni's collection makes an engaging effort to examine Latin American warfare from a subaltern perspective, but none of the contributors explicitly take race as a category of analysis, despite the preponderance of black and indigenous peoples among the civilians affected by war. It should be noted here that Latin American military historiography has been quite narrow in focus and concerned mainly with the military as

an institution and political actor, especially in the second half of the twentieth century, and has focused mainly on explaining and contextualizing authoritarian rule. The classic works are Loveman, *For la Patria*; Nunn, *Time of the Generals*; Roquie, *The Military and the State*; and Stepan, *Rethinking Military Politics*. Those works that do elucidate intersections of race and war probably would not consider themselves military history, e.g., Ferrer's *Insurgent Cuba*. Similarly, recent efforts to broaden the framework within which military actors are discussed, or to link military conflict explicitly to national identity formation, such as Pion-Berlin, *Civil-Military Relations in Latin America* or Fowler and Lambert, *Political Violence and the Construction of National Identity*, have not incorporated race as an analytical category.

7. Loveman, *For la Patria*, 27.

8. López-Alves, "Wars and the Formation of Political Parties"; and Earle, *Rumours of War*.

9. Scheina, *Latin America's Wars*, xiv–xv. We use the term subaltern here to refer to people without power, in this case the black and indigenous masses.

10. Deas, "The Man on Foot," 79.

11. Appelbaum, *Muddied Waters*; and Sanders, *Contentious Republicans*.

12. Charles A. Hale was one of the first scholars to sketch out the fissures within liberalism and elucidate its two different strains—the elitist "conservative liberalism" with its emphasis on order, and the more "Jacobin" popular liberalism. Hale, *The Transformation of Liberalism*. See also Thomson, "Popular Aspects of Liberalism."

13. Appelbaum, Macpherson, and Rosemblatt, *Race and Nation*, 4.

14. Loveman, *For la Patria*, 20, 37. Indeed this historical legacy is key to understanding the internalization of military power during the period of bureaucratic authoritarianism.

15. Centeno, *Blood and Debt*, 66. Emphasis in original.

16. Campbell, "The Army of Peru," 34; Vinson, *Bearing Arms*; Lasso, "Revisiting Independence Day"; and Lasso "Race War and Nation." See also Dominguez, *Insurrection or Loyalty*, 74–81 and 275–76; Lynch, *Caudillos in Spanish America*, 78; and Archer, "'La Causa Buena,'" 11–12.

17. Lynch, *Caudillos in Spanish America*, 57, 187.

18. Centeno, *Blood and Debt*, 149.

19. Black, *Rethinking Military History*; and Citino, "Military Histories Old and New."

20. Porter, *War and the Rise of the State*; Bean, "War and the Birth of the Nation-State"; and Tilly, especially "Reflections on the History of European State Making" in his edited volume *The Formation of National States in Western Europe*. See also Rasler and Thompson, *War and State Making*.

21. Centeno, *Blood and Debt*.

22. Smith, "War and Ethnicity."

23. Ibid, 375.

24. Gabbert, "Of Friends and Foes."

25. Lasso, "Revisiting Independence Day"; and Méndez, *The Plebian Republic*.

26. Safford, "Reflections on the Internal Wars," 8.

27. Appelbaum, *Race and Nation*.

28. De la Pedraja, *Wars of Latin America*, 1.

29. Centeno, *Blood and Debt*, 34.

30. Black, *War in the Modern World*, 14.

31. Whigham and Potthast, "The Paraguyan Rosetta Stone."

32. See especially Bonilla, "The War of the Pacific."

33. Albó, "From MNRistas to Kataristas to Katari," in Stern, *Resistance*, 381.

34. Lynch, *Caudillos in Spanish America*, 134.

35. This was typical of "first-generation" studies of peasant politics such as Wolf, *Peasant Wars*; and Popkin, *The Rational Peasant*. Steve Stern's *Resistance, Rebellion and Consciousness* overturned this paradigm in the Latin American context.

36. Appelbaum, *Race and Nation*, 8.

37. This fits with Peter Wade's argument that the divergent ways in which Afro and indigenous Latin Americans were racialized and othered is rooted in colonial hierarchies and legal classifications. See Wade, *Race and Ethnicity*.

I

Soldiering and Citizenship

1

Subaltern Strategies of Citizenship and Soldiering in Colombia's Civil Wars

Afro- and Indigenous Colombians' Experiences in the Cauca, 1851–1877

JAMES E. SANDERS

When Colombian Liberals and Conservatives confronted one another during the 1860–63 civil war, a conservative newspaper derisively described Liberal troops as "ferocious gangs of blacks."[1] By mid-century, Afro-Colombian volunteers, fiercely proud of their status as soldiers, formed the backbone of Liberal armies in the Cauca region of southwestern Colombia, ensuring Liberal victories in the 1851, 1860–63, and 1876–77 civil wars.[2] Years earlier, some Liberals had feared the Cauca's indigenous peoples might develop a similar relationship with Conservatives as Afro-Colombians had done with the Colombian Liberal Party. Liberals had complained that Conservatives were going from village to village among the indigenous peoples to gather support for the upcoming 1851 civil war, "preaching the defense of religion, their women, and their properties" against Liberal threats to reduce the influence of the Church, to enact secular marriage, and to privatize and divide Indians' *resguardos* (communal landholdings).[3] Given Liberal hostility to indigenous communal landholding and self-governance, an alliance with Conservatives seemed logical. Yet, in general, after 1854 Indians were rarely eager volunteers in Conservative ranks and did not tend to use soldiering as a strategy for improving their social or political status. This chapter explores why these two social groups' experiences with soldiering and civil war differed so much in the Cauca region of southwestern Colombia, one of the relatively few regions of Latin America where large numbers of both Indians and people of African descent lived in close proximity.[4]

I propose that Afro-Colombians embraced military service as a way to claim citizenship and increase their political voice as members of the Colombian Liberal Party. Saddled with a colonial identity marked by slavery and the lack of a public voice, and with few historical claims to the new republican nation in the form of past rights, privileges, or resources, Afro-Colombians saw military service in the defense of the Liberal Party as a path to citizenship. In addition, Afro-Colombians realized substantial gains (and hoped for more) via military service and bargaining with a receptive Colombian Liberal Party; soldiering helped them to ensure the abolition of slavery against a Conservative challenge, to acquire booty during the wars, to claim citizenship, and to open an opportunity to press for access to land.

Cauca's Indians took a different tack for claiming citizenship, focusing on their historical rights granted by the Crown and on their lasting place in Colombian society. Protecting their historical prerogatives to communal landholding and local self-government were always more important than making new claims on the state as a reward for military service. In addition, given the Colombian Liberal Party's hostility to corporate bodies within the nation and the Colombian Conservative Party's distaste for bargaining and openly negotiating with subaltern allies, Indians lacked a partisan faction they whole-heartedly could support and be supported by. Indians would fight in civil wars to protect their communities' rights, but they found more success in remaining neutral while threatening to join the adversaries of whichever party attacked their corporate rights.

Afro-Colombians' and Indians' choices about soldiering took place in the context of a series of civil wars that raged in Cauca. While the wars of 1851, 1854, 1860–63, and 1876–77 each had their particular causes and pretexts, all were also contests between the Liberal and Conservative parties (or factions thereof) for power. The parties emerged in the late 1840s and had surprisingly distinct ideological platforms, especially at the local level in the Cauca. Liberals, who tended to come from less established families in the region, opposed the power of the Catholic Church, supported an expanded citizen class, and pushed for the abolition of slavery, monopolies, and corporate landholding (both of Indians and of the Church). Conservatives, who emerged out of the region's most powerful clans, thought the Church was central to organizing society, argued citizenship should be limited to those of high rank, and supported property rights, including those of slavehold-ers and corporate bodies. These local partisan divisions mirrored national politics, although elsewhere differences between the parties may have been slightly less stark, and Cauca was a key battleground in the parties' efforts to control the national state.[5] Each party would need soldiers to fight for them in these civil wars—which involved both guerrilla-style smaller skirmishes and set battles involving thousands on each side—and thus turned to the general population, a population actively engaged in and knowledgeable about politics and the parties' positions as revealed by their petitions sent to state authorities and their actions recorded in newspapers and state documents.[6] Most of these potential soldiers lived in the broad and long Cauca River Valley, bounded by two mountain chains that met near the Ecuador border (see map 1). A census from 1851 recorded that Indians made up 7.9 percent of the region's population while blacks and mulattos composed 34.8 percent (out of a total population of approximately 324,000); a geographer from Cauca estimated Indians at 9.1 percent and Afro-Colombians at 60.4 percent.[7] Indians tended to live in villages higher in the cordilleras, especially around Popayán and Pasto; while Indians often spoke Spanish and practiced a culture similar to their neighbors, they maintained a separate legal identity from the colonial period that allowed communal landholding and local self-governance.[8] Afro-Colombians mostly resided along the coasts and in the valley proper, especially around Cali; most were free, but in 1843 there were still more than fifteen thousand slaves in the Cauca.[9]

By the time the Liberal and Conservative parties formed in the late 1840s, Afro-Colombians already had a long history of using military service, especially in the wars for independence and the War of the Supremos (1840–42), to push for greater inclusion in Colombian society.[10] Yet in spite of these efforts, by mid-century, slavery still existed, citizenship was limited by property and literacy requirements that excluded most people of African descent, and Cauca was dominated by large land- and slave-owning families who saw control of politics and public space as their right. In the Cauca Valley, Afro-Colombians mostly worked in mines and as day laborers or tenants on the large haciendas that controlled most of the arable land in the valley. By the time the Colombian Liberal Party came to power nationally in 1849, Afro-Caucanos had little to show for their past efforts in the independence period—even though most were free, slavery still defined their identity, most lacked citizenship, few held any land, and a conservative ruling class thought them racially unfit for public life.

When Conservatives revolted against the Liberal government in 1851, in part to halt the abolition of slavery promoted by the Liberal state, they expected success given their past dominance of the region. However, Liberals predicted that "manumitted blacks" would make the best national guard soldiers, and the war proved them correct.[11] Afro-Colombians quickly swelled the Liberals' ranks, marching to resoundingly defeat the Conservative rebellion. A Liberal politician noted that "the blacks knew that the revolution had, in part, the object of impeding their liberty and they let it be known that they were ready at any moment to go and fight for their freedom and that of their children."[12] Indeed, while many concerns motivated Afro-Colombians (and other poor subalterns with whom they formed a multiethnic alliance) to volunteer in 1851—including debates over the control of public lands, issues of social equality, and access to citizenship—the abolition of slavery clearly was the central factor.

In the subsequent civil wars (saving that of 1854 in which the Colombian Liberal Party was internally divided), Afro-Caucano soldiers and other popular liberals were a formidable military force, ensuring Liberal victories in the Cauca and nationally. Organized in peacetime in political clubs called Democratic Societies (which Conservatives claimed were populated entirely by "blacks," reflecting both the reality of the club's membership, and as we will see later, the confluence of liberalism and blackness in the Cauca[13]), in war the clubs quickly formed volunteer brigades. During the 1860–63 civil war, a conservative denigrated the liberal troops that would defeat his cause: "The majority of that army is composed of blacks, zambos and mulattos, assassins and thieves of the Cauca Valley."[14] During the war, Afro-Caucano popular liberal guerillas incited fear in Conservative landholders.[15] In the 1876–77 civil war, the clubs of popular liberals again volunteered, causing the Liberal state president to refer to his army as "the armed Democratic Society."[16] As in past wars, Liberal troops were disparagingly described as "multitudes of blacks and mulattos."[17] Afro-Colombians were active participants in the civil wars.

In contrast, indigenous peoples played much less of a role as volunteer soldiers. In 1851, while Afro-Caucanos established an alliance with Liberals, it appeared that Indians might do the same with Conservatives. In 1850, the national Liberal state had enacted legislation allowing the provinces to dispose of indigenous *resguardos*, assuming that most provinces would opt for division and sale of the communally held land; as a result, in eastern Colombia many Indian communities were losing their land at a rapid pace.[18] Conservatives were less bothered ideologically by the corporatism of *resguardos*, and some sought to recruit Indians to support their 1851 revolt.[19] Indians, as their petitions to state officials begging that the division be rescinded attest, deeply opposed the Liberals' proposed division of communal lands, and thus may have been willing to support the Conservatives' rebellion.

However, when Conservatives did rise in revolt, they relied on dragooning troops, even the Indians, who might have been more willing supporters if given the opportunity. As the vignette that opened this chapter suggests, inspired by Conservatives' efforts to vilify Liberals throughout the Cauca's villages and towns, some Indians feared Liberal intentions concerning secular marriage (indigenous officials used a gendered discourse of power and order to justify their local rule, which secular marriage might disrupt) and their *resguardos* enough that they voluntarily enlisted in Conservative ranks.[20] However, Conservatives failed to establish the same alliance with volunteer soldiers as Liberals had with Afro-Caucanos. Conservatives in the early 1850s regarded all plebeian mobilization not tightly controlled from above as a threat, and thought the social elite should rule. Conservatives relied more on wealthier mounted troops, and if they needed foot soldiers, they preferred the time-honored method of conscription.[21]

The distinction between volunteers and conscripts was very important in Cauca, belying the view of some that have considered nineteenth-century troops as cannon fodder, peons forced to fight without motivation of their own.[22] Generally, armies were made up of both volunteers and unwilling recruits. Both Conservatives (especially after their defeat in 1851) and Liberals made appeals for volunteers and claimed to enjoy popular support, although, of course, armies were not hesitant to conscript troops, often violently, when necessary.[23] For commanding officers, there was nothing embarrassing about forced recruitment, although volunteers seemed to have been preferred.[24] Commanders could not assume loyalty and had to concern themselves with the conditions of their troops, fretting over lacking money for pay or having enough food to prevent desertion.[25] One officer described his troops saying, "they do not acknowledge their duties and assert that they are free, recognizing nothing but their own will."[26] As we will see later, voluntary enlistment also served as the basis for establishing an alliance between elites and subalterns as well as the justification used by subalterns to press claims on the state in exchange for their service. Conservative preference for conscription in the 1850s doomed a possible alliance with Indians on the same level as that of Afro-Colombians with Liberals because forcible recruitment both alienated the soldiers and prevented bargaining between elites and subalterns that might have created a long-lasting relationship.

The Cauca's Indians generally did not volunteer in large numbers in the subsequent civil wars after 1851; thus, they never developed a strong association with either party due to military service, as Afro-Caucanos did with the Colombian Liberal Party. Since Liberals still threatened the existence of their *resguardos* in 1854, some Indians did ally with Conservatives (and constitutionalist Liberals) against the Melo military revolt (a Liberal revolt against their own party, which was in power).[27] However, when Tomás Mosquera was planning his military revolt against Conservative rule in 1860, he astutely maneuvered to convince the Cauca's Indians not to ally with Conservatives again. In 1859 the Liberal legislature passed Law 90, which ensured the *resguardos'* legal status, recognized the local authority of indigenous officials, set no timetable for division of communal lands, and even made provisions for return of lands illegally obtained by outsiders back to the indigenous communities.[28] Indians now had no reason to side with Conservatives, and generally tried to avoid the war, although some did serve on both sides as clients of powerful patrons (including Mosquera) and others suffered as conscripts (further alienating many Indians from Conservatives).[29] Indians' experiences of the war no doubt played a role in the 1860s and 1870s, as they developed a strategy of negotiated neutrality.

This was not the first time indigenous people had made open plays for protection of their *resguardos* in exchange for military support. In 1852 Indians from two small southern villages had begged the provincial governor not to support the *resguardos'* division, promising him "that all the Indians of this district are and will be ready to lend any services that the government demands of us."[30] Liberals ignored the Indians' offer in part because, unlike abolishing slavery, maintaining communal lands and corporate identities was ideologically antagonistic to Liberals' positions.[31] However, Mosquera's gamble that he could preempt Indians' support of Conservatives by assuring Indians that their *resguardos* would not be threatened created a new political calculus. Indians never embraced military service as did Afro-Caucanos, and when Liberals began to plot dividing the *resguardos* yet again in 1873, Indians responded not with offers to side with Liberals if they protected the *resguardos* but with threats of supporting Conservatives if Liberals attacked their lands. More than five hundred Indians from a coalition of villages across the southern Cauca demanded that Liberals cease their plans to divide the *resguardos* and warned the Liberals of the consequences of ignoring the Indians' concerns: "If the mentioned law is put into effect or practice, we would find ourselves by necessity standing with the first who gave the shout of rebellion, as long as they assured us the repeal of the aforementioned law."[32] Indians did not have to volunteer to fight; they only had to threaten to do so. That was enough, as Liberals grudgingly backed off their plan.[33] When Conservatives rebelled again in 1876, Indians again mostly stayed on the sidelines while Afro-Colombians saved the Colombian Liberal Party once again; Indians' strategic neutrality meant volunteering was not necessary, even if avoiding conscription was always difficult.[34]

So why did Indians mostly soldier as conscripts while Afro-Caucanos more readily volunteered? Blacks and mulattos fought in the civil wars as a way to claim citizenship and its rewards. Conservatives thought Afro-Caucanos had no place (beyond providing quiescent labor) in public society, one claiming that blacks were "ignorant men" who "hate our constitution," only seek to rebel, and "do not deserve the title of true Granadans."[35] Liberals were more open to allowing Afro-Caucanos some role, but Afro-Caucanos did not have any traditional standing with which to support the Colombian Liberal Party: little money, little land, little historical influence. Yet they could, and as we saw above did, offer their blood. Afro-Caucanos and other poor subalterns redefined citizenship as based on service in defense of the nation (or party) against those who would threaten it, mainly Conservatives.

In 1852 two men in Cali faced forced conscription for being vagrants, which they protested, claiming they had the right to volunteer when the government was threatened and would serve as "armed citizens in its defense."[36] When the residents of the village of Quilcacé, many former slaves or descendents of slaves, needed help from the Liberal state in a land dispute, they reminded the official what they were owed for the past military support, recalling "the services the village made to the cause of the federation [in the 1860–62 war] and due to the bloody sufferings that it endured because of its adherence to that cause."[37] After the 1876–77 civil war, former liberal soldiers (from the Afro-Caucano Patía area) stood accused of banditry. They wrote to the Liberal state president seeking help, justifying their pleas with claims to past service: "You know, Citizen President, what are the causes that motivate the said charges [of banditry], since one of them is having sustained in the civil war of '76 and '77 the dignity of the government, of the Cauca, and of the rule of the constitution of the republic."[38] Afro-Caucano boatmen who ferried goods and people between the Pacific Ocean and the Cauca Valley cited their service in the same war: "In our profession we have lent great services to the liberal cause, and more than a few times we have set aside the punting poles and oars in order to take up the gun."[39] Soldiers from the Democratic Society of Cali went further, demanding that the state distribute hacienda land to them for their past service: "How can one think it just that those who have come every time to defend this soil that saw them born, against the repeated and unjust invasions from Antioquia [a conservative bastion], invasions aided by those who call themselves the owners of the greater part of the Cauca's land, live without a home?"[40]

Afro-Caucanos used the justification of their armed service to claim citizenship, a new public and political identity to replace the "social death" of slavery. Residents of a former slave-holding hacienda claimed citizenship, identifying themselves as "inhabitants of the San Julián hacienda to which once we belonged as slaves, before you in the use of our rights as citizens."[41] From the coastal village of San Juan, ex-slaves wrote to the Liberal-dominated national Congress after abolition to thank them for "the precious possession of liberty, so long usurped, and with it all the other rights and prerogatives of citizens."[42] The boatmen mentioned earlier complained during a labor dispute that "we should be treated like citizens of a republic and not like the slaves of a sultan."[43] Liberal citizenship so appealed to the Afro-Caucanos because it demanded no special identity, history, or property beyond a willingness to support the liberal cause. A petition by one of the valley's Democratic Societies summed up how citizenship, its rewards, and service intertwined; the Society reminded the Colombian president that "the poor class" has made "the very valuable contribution of their blood in order to defend our institutions, public order, and national independence and integrity. . . . These individuals have, at the very least, an unquestionable right to be protected by a liberal government."[44] Thus the armed citizen became central to popular liberals as it gave them a new public identity that elite Liberals recognized.

In contrast, Liberals argued that Indians "will never be able to become free citizens and active members of the democratic republic" as long as they lived under the special laws of their *resguardos* and did not accept the "universal" identity of liberal citizenship.[45] While "universal" citizenship, with its connotations of abandoning other identities (be they racial, corporate, or regional) in favor of that of "citizen" appealed to Afro-Caucanos, whose past identity as slaves gave them no advantage, that definition of citizenship alienated Indians, who were devoted to their historical customs, identities, and properties. Afro-Caucanos, with the rarest of exceptions, never publicly described themselves in racial terms (and often acted in a multiethnic alliance with other poor popular liberals), only at times using the legal category of "ex-slaves." Indians, however, almost never failed to identify themselves as "*indígenas*" in any public document. Petitions from Indians usually began by identifying the petitioners as indigenous authorities (*gobernadores* and *regidores* [officers] of the *cabildo pequeño*, the locally chosen councils that governed Indians' *resguardos*), such as in an 1852 document in which petitioners opened by describing themselves as "the members of the cabildo pequeño de indíjenas of Guachucal parish and Muellamuez vice-parish."[46] Indians contrasted their racial/legal position as Indians with the Cauca's other groups; the same *cabildo pequeño* from Guachucal declared that "thousands of citizens of the indigenous class" are the "defenseless victims of the abuses and outrages of the whites" who were stealing *resguardo* land.[47] A village farther to the north of the valley implicitly implied they should not be treated as Afro-Caucanos, identifying themselves as "we Indians" who were "subjects of the government but not slaves of those mestizos."[48] Being an *indígena* was a racial and legal identity from the colonial period that still guaranteed certain privileges in the republican era, namely the right to local self-government and corporate landholding in the *resguardos*.[49]

Indians looked to their past traditions and rights based on their indigenous identity to protect their lifeways. Indians from Riosucio begged that the governor shield their *resguardos* from farmers who coveted their land, lands "granted by the king, and that until now have been respected, and which since the time of our ancestors have been cultivated freely."[50] Another indigenous village complained that a local *hacendado's* seizure of their land denied them the "enjoyment of our land that for the space of three centuries and with just titles we have possessed."[51] Yet another village noted that they possessed "our lands following the statutes, customs and uses that we have inherited from our ancestors."[52] Unlike Afro-Caucanos, Indians were not necessarily trying to establish new identities or gain new rights or economic resources from the state but rather were attempting to maintain their precarious local resources; therefore, they had less need to gain favor with the state or political parties through military service. Indians' conception of citizenship was based on their past rights and identity as Indians; they did not have to "earn" citizenship. Afro-Colombians, without resources, a favorable legal standing, or historic rights, attempted to create a new identity within liberalism based not on inherited identity and past or current standing in society but based on armed service to create a radically new public social position as armed citizens.[53] Indians would fight when they had to protect their standing as indigenous citizens; Afro-Caucanos had to fight to become citizens.

Those who had the least to lose were more willing to risk their lives as soldiers to improve their situations as citizens. Afro-Colombians had few resources and fewer historical claims to inclusion in society, but they did have the opportunity opened by elite Liberals who desperately needed soldiers to fight against Conservatives and whose program of abolishing slavery and promoting universal citizenship greatly appealed to popular liberals. Indians had resources and a vision of citizenship they needed to protect, at times by fighting in wars, but they had fewer claims to press and no political party willing to bargain for their support as liberals did with Afro-Caucanos, so soldiering was much less enticing.

Do these patterns hold beyond southwestern Colombia? In Cauca, liberal militias—and popular liberalism generally—become almost synonymous with blackness to such an extent that one Conservative thought his party opposed "the blacks and all that call themselves Liberals."[54] This was not a phenomenon unique to Colombia. Recent literature, especially George Reid Andrew's *Afro Latin-America*, shows the breadth of Afro-Latin American engagement with soldiering, first in the independence wars and then usually as popular liberals in civil wars to secure abolition, citizenship rights, social respect, and economic resources.[55] In at least Cuba, Brazil, Uruguay, Venezuela, Ecuador, Peru, and Mexico, Afro–Latin Americans supported popular liberal or republican movements (as, of course, did African Americans in the United States).[56]

Why were their struggles similar? They had the same goals: abolition, antiracism, citizenship rights, and usually struggles for economic independence in the form of land, which most Afro–Latin Americans emerging from slavery still lacked (although the particulars await more study in most areas). In addition to similar goals, they also faced similar challenges and tended to share similar resource bases, or lack thereof. All had to deal with the legacy of racism and all faced new nations with an at best an undefined identity, but usually one related to slavery that offered few resources or discourses with which to lay claim to the nation and call upon the state. Therefore, they had to create a new identity, which soldiering seemed to provide. It certainly did so in the Cauca. Liberalism seemed especially appealing with its calls to universalism, which would make liberalism and blackness synonymous, not just in the Cauca, but often in the wider Atlantic world as well, so much so that Joseph Conrad at the turn of the century incorporated the idea of "Negro liberals" into his novel *Nostromo*, even though he denigrated the black liberals' political understanding.[57]

Indians' situation was much more particular, even if this particularity was based on the common experience of having a powerful identity from the colonial period that many Indians (although certainly not all) were eager, if not desperate, to defend. Of course, many Indians adroitly combined this colonial identity with national citizenship. At least in the Cauca, they largely did not need to soldier to do this, although in other places, such as Mexico, soldiering could form the base of indigenous political identity. Therefore, it is much harder to generalize about the indigenous experience, which varied so much from place to place, especially based on how much land Indians possessed, whether the postcolonial state would acknowledge their identity and communal lands, the varying pressure from the state to abandon indigenous identity and indigenous peoples' own commitment to that identity, whether they sought inclusion in the state or sought to (re-) create independent indigenous societies such as in the Caste War of Yucatán, and whether their demographic superiority so threatened the state and the wealthy as to make elites reluctant and fearful to open up any space or turn to Indians for support in civil wars.[58] In some areas, such as Mexico, Indians became popular liberals, in spite of liberalism's often intense hostility to indigenous identity, because the potential for inclusion as citizens outweighed the risks of Liberals' intentions.[59] Other indigenous peoples became popular conservatives due to the threats of liberalism to indigenous identity, as in Guatemala, even if elite Conservatives tended to view them derisively.[60] Some indigenous movements sought to engage the state, others to overturn it, and still others hoped to escape the state's gaze. While indigenous peoples all faced some common threats (land loss and the intense Liberal hostility to indigenous identity that Brooke Larson has shown[61]), they had much more variation in their local situations than did many Afro–Latin Americans, who shared both a more common past and more common nineteenth-century challenges.

Although we must be careful not to overgeneralize, there does seem to be a strong link between Afro–Latin American politics and soldiering (acknowledging, of course, that the particulars will vary from place to place, especially the success of each movement). While many indigenous peoples certainly used soldiering in the nineteenth century, given that they had less common goals and more divergent histories, soldiering seems to have had less of a central role for many, and there was more variability in the use of military service and the political party given support among Latin America's Indians.

Both the Cauca's Indians and Afro-Colombians took advantage of nineteenth-century civil wars between Liberals and Conservatives to pursue their own agendas vis-à-vis the state and nation. However, each social group followed distinct strategies during the civil wars, based on their conceptions of citizenship, current resources, potential gains from the wars, and their relationships to the dominant political parties. War presented opportunities and challenges to all social groups in nineteenth- century Latin

America. The contrast between the soldiering decisions of Afro-Caucanos and Indians not only shows the need to go beyond looking at all subalterns as unthinking clients, pawns, or victims of civil wars but also to take seriously the political engagement as well as the political thought behind that engagement that determined when and why subaltern farmers, miners, or artisans put aside the plow, pick, or lathe to take up the machete or gun.

Notes

1. *El Espectador: Dios, Religion i Libertad* (Pasto), October 2, [1862] (the year is printed as 1852 on the paper, but this was an error).

2. This chapter is concerned with uncovering the differences between Afro-Colombians' and Indians' use of soldiering to press their own political and social agendas, not explaining the politics of particular civil wars. For an excellent general history of the Cauca, see Valencia Llano, *Estado Soberano del Cauca*.

3. J. N. Montero to Secretary of Government, Barbacoas, June 26, 1851, Archivo General de la Nación, Bogotá (hereafter AGN), Sección República, Fondo Gobernaciones Varias, Tomo 165, p. 706. See also, Arboleda, "El Misóforo," 336; and *Las Máscaras* (Pasto), November 21, 1850.

4. Recovering subaltern politics in nineteenth-century Colombia generally does not allow a focus on individual lower- class individuals because such sources are mostly lacking; it instead requires gathering strands of evidence to give voice to subaltern social groups. While I would of course much prefer to give individual subalterns agency and subjecthood, the evidence at least allows larger groups of subalterns to claim their historical role.

5. Palacios, *El café en Colombia*, 29; and Escorcia, *Sociedad y economía*.

6. For this political engagement, see Sanders, *Contentious Republicans*.

7. For the 1851 census see, Safford and Palacios, *Colombia*, 158, 261; for the geographer, see Mosquera, *Memoria sobre la geografía*, 96.

8. Rappaport, *Cumbe Reborn*, 26–28.

9. Urrutia M. and Arrubla, eds., *Compendio de estadísticas*, table 8.

10. Lasso, *Myths of Harmony*; Helg, *Liberty and Equality in Caribbean Colombia*; and Zuluaga Ramírez, *Guerrilla y sociedad en el Patía*. For party formation, see Uribe-Uran, *Honorable Lives*.

11. Alaix, *No sin desconfianza en mis propias fuerzas*, 54. As this and the following quotations reveal, both Liberals and Conservatives denoted some popular liberals as "black," although for Conservatives this was always a derogatory strategy. This does highlight a difficulty in identifying if some popular liberals were "really" Afro-Colombian (and clearly Afro-Colombians acted with mestizo and white subalterns because many of their concerns were the same). However, beyond elite descriptions, subalterns' own characterization of themselves as "ex-slaves" offers one clear indication. Another is to assess the village subalterns identify as their home, many of which are areas of Afro-Colombian demographic importance, sometimes even known sites of former slave-holding haciendas

or mines. Finally, of course, the demands made by subalterns, especially for the abolition of slavery, provide us with some clues.

12. J. N. Montero to Secretary of Government (national), Barbacoas, May 10, 1852, AGN, Sección República, Fondo Gobernaciones Varias, Tomo 179, p. 243 (the letter is out of order, with other pages interspersed within it).

13. J. M. Bustamante to Mariano Ospina, Cartago, September 15, 1859, Biblioteca Nacional (Bogotá) (hereafter BN), Fondo Manuscritos, Libro 210, p. 97.

14. A *zambo* was a person of both African and Indian descent. Anonymous, "Diario Histórico del Ejército Unido de Antioquia y Cauca," appears to have been written in 1861, Archivo Central del Cauca (Popayán) (hereafter ACC), Fondo Arboleda, Signatura 63, p. 235; see also, *La Voz de la Juventud* (Popayán), November 12, 1861; Cabal, *Contestación al inmundo pasquín*, 15; and Testimony of Juan Nepomuceno Molina, Cali, 11 December 1871, ACC, Fondo Arboleda, Signatura 633, p.1.

15. Daniel Mosquera to Provincial Governor, Tambo, August 18, 1861, ACC, Archivo Muerto, Paquete 82, Legajo 27, n.p.; and Unos Caucanos, *Los tratados con Mosquera*, 1.

16. César Conto, "Mensaje del Presidente del Estado Soberano del Cauca á la Legislatura de 1877," Popayán, July 1, 1877, ACC, Archivo Muerto, Paquete 137, Legajo 27, n.p.

17. Manuel María [Mosquera] to Tomás [Mosquera], Popayán, May 15, 1877, ACC, Sala Mosquera, Documento 57,555; see also, Carlos Holguín to Sergio Arboleda, Manizales, January 30, 1877, ACC, Fondo Arboleda, Signatura 1,515, n.p.; and Joaquín [Mosquera] to Tomás [Mosquera], no place on letter, May 1, 1877, ACC, Sala Mosquera, Documento 57,544.

18. Villegas and Restrepo, *Resguardos de indígenas,* 36–44; and Curry, "The Disappearance of the Resguardos Indígenas."

19. Alcaldes Mayores of Túqerres and Ipiales Cantones, along with all the pequeños cabildos de indígenas of the Province to President of the Provincial Legislature, Túquerres, September 17, 1848, ACC, Archivo Muerto, Paquete 44, Legajo 39, n.p.; and Alcalde Mayor de indígenas of Túquerres Cantón (and over 40 others, members of various cabildos) to President of the House of Representatives (national), Túquerres, December 30, 1848, Archivo del Congreso (Bogotá) (hereafter AC), 1849, Cámara, Informes de Comisiones IX, p. 184; The undersigned Regidores de indígenas of Guachucal Parish to President of the Provincial Legislature, Túquerres, September 21, 1849, ACC, Archivo Muerto, Paquete 46, Legajo 8, n.p.

20. The undersigned landowners to the President of the Provincial Legislature, Pasto, September 20, 1852, ACC, Archivo Muerto, Paquete 53, Legajo 70, n.p. The landowners noted how their labor force of Indians had abandoned their work to join the rebellious armies (and that the government had conscripted others); see also, *Boletín Político i Militar* (Pasto), July 20, 1851.

21. *Boletín Democrático* (Cali), July 12, 1851; see also, Mercado, *Memorias sobre los acontecimientos del sur,* lxxxvi.

22. Tirado Mejía, *Aspectos sociales de las guerras civiles*, 37–38; Bushnell, *Making of Modern Colombia*, 94; Jaramillo Castillo, "Guerras civiles y vida cotidiana." For an opinion closer to my own, see, Deas, "Poverty, Civil War and Politics."

23. Los Editores, *Documentos curiosos*, 15, 20–27.

24. Ibid., 19; *Los criminales, al presidio*, 1.

25. Commander of the First Army to Jefes and officials of the South, Chiribio, March 29, 1862, ACC, Archivo Muerto, Paquete 82, Legajo 42, n.p.; Cdr. Luis Acero to Secretary of Government, Palmira, April 28, 1863, ACC, Archivo Muerto, Paquete 98, Legajo 22, n.p.; and Anonymous, "Diario Histórico del Ejército Unido de Antioquia y Cauca," appears to have been written in 1861, ACC, Fondo Arboleda, Signatura 63, p. 235.

26. Tomás María Mosquera to Tomás C. de Mosquera, Santander, May 28, 1860, Biblioteca Luis Angel Arango (Bogotá) (hereafter BLAA), Sala de Manuscritos, Manuscript 558.

27. Constitutionalist troops came from Silvia, Totoró, Morales, Tunía, Paniquitá, and Cajibío. All of these towns except for Morales had Indian *resguardos*. Toribio María Malo to Provincial Governor, Silvia, May 12, 1854, ACC, Archivo Muerto, Paquete 58, Legajo 85, n.p.; Cenón Pombo, "Circular a los Señores Gobornadores del Cauca, la Buenaventura, Neiva i Pasto," no place listed, May 23, 1854, ACC, Archivo Muerto, Paquete 56, Legajo 1, p. 81; J. M. Caicedo to Provincial Governor, Bolívar, June 19, 1854, ACC, Archivo Muerto, Paquete 58, Legajo 84, n.p.; José de Obaldía to Tomás C. de Mosquera, Ibagué, September 11, 1854, ACC, Sala Mosquera, Documento 31,743; Manuel [Luna] to Sergio Arboleda, Popayán, October 25, 1854, ACC, Fondo Arboleda, Signatura 1518, n.p.; and José Tomás Diago to Tomás C. de Mosquera, Popayán, November 8, 1854, ACC, Sala Mosquera, Documento 29,852.

28. *Gaceta del Cauca* (Popayán), October 29, 1859; see also, Castro, *Informe*, 47–48; for a different interpretation of the law, see, Findji and Rojas, *Territorio, economía y sociedad Páez*, 68–69.

29. Mosquera, *T. C. de Mosquera*, 1; *Boletín Oficial* (Bogotá), January 20, 1862, July 24, 1862; No author listed [someone in the Centralist Army] to Reto A. Martínez, Inzá, August 31, 1860, ACC, Fondo Arboleda, Signatura 65, p. 1; Marcelino Rodríguez to Provincial Governor, Silvia, September 15, 1861, ACC, Archivo Muerto, Paquete 82, Legajo 27, n.p.; Anonymous, "Diario Histórico del Ejército Unido de Antioquia y Cauca," appears to have been written in 1861, ACC, Fondo Arboleda, Signatura 63, p. 235; *El Espectador: Dios, Relijion i Libertad* (Pasto), February 13, 1862, April 10, 1862; Governor of the Indians of Quichaya to Commander in Chief of the State militias, Popayán, October 5, 1860, ACC, Archivo Muerto, Paquete 78, Legajo 44, n.p.; The Indian bosses of the Aldea de Coconuco to Alcalde of Popayán district, Coconuco, August 1, 1860, ACC, Archivo Muerto, Paquete 129, Legajo 45, n.p.; District Alcalde to Provincial Governor, Cajibío, October 5, 1861, ACC, Archivo Muerto, Paquete 82, Legajo 26, n.p.; and Marcelino Rodríguez to Provincial Governor, Silvia, October 1, 1861, ACC, Archivo Muerto, Paquete 82, Legajo 26, n.p.

30. The Members of the cabildo pequeño de indígenas of Guachucal Parish and the vice-parish of Muellamuez to the Provincial Governor, Guachucal, October 4, 1852, ACC, Archivo Muerto, Paquete 53, Legajo 56, n.p.

31. Jaramillo Uribe, *El pensamiento colombiano*.

32. The petition was signed by members of the *cabildos* of Túquerres, Guaitarilla, Ospina, Mallama, Imués, Pasto, and Yascual as well as more than 525 other Indians, all names marked with a cross or a sign. Members or vocales of the pequeños cabildos de indígenas of Túquerres, Obando and Pasto to Citizen Deputies of the State Legislature, Pasto, July 29, 1873, ACC, Archivo Muerto, Paquete 124, Legajo 60, n.p.

33. *Registro Oficial (Organo del Gobierno del Cauca)* (Popayán), October 25, 1873, November 1, 1873, December 6, 1873.

34. Report of Jefe Municipal of Barbacoas, Barbacoas, August 10, 1876, BLAA, Sala de Manuscritos, MSS 1, p. 70; Commander of Santander Reserve Battalion to Commander in Chief of state militias, Santander, August 7, 1876, AGN, Sección República, Fondo Libros Manuscritos y Leyes Originales, Tomo 197, p. 423; Manuel Hurtado to Jefe Municipal, Silvia, September 14, 1876, ACC, Archivo Muerto, Paquete 132, Legajo 59, n.p; Rafael [Arboleda] to T. C. de Mosquera, Popayán, December 7, 1876, ACC, Sala Mosquera, Documento 56,932; Col. M. Muse to Vicente Guzmán, Calderas, January 8, 1877, ACC, Archivo Muerto, Paquete 118, Legajo 72, n.p.; Felipe Meléndez to T. C. de Mosquera, Popayán, November 24, 1876, ACC, Sala Mosquera, Documento 57,146; and José M. Sánchez O. to Tomás C. de Mosquera, Popayán, May 23, 1876, ACC, Sala Mosquera, Documento 57,318.

35. Francisco González to Governor, Santander, March 20, 1855, ACC, Archivo Muerto, Paquete 60, Legajo 60, n.p.

36. The race of the two is unclear, but since they were accused of vagrancy in Cali, there is a reasonable chance they would have been seen as Afro-Caucanos. Camilo Salamendro and Manuel María Rivero (written by another) to Provincial Governor, Cali, April 5, 1852, Archivo Histórico Municipal de Cali (Cali), Archivo del Concejo Municipal, Tomo 120, p. 419.

37. By the 1860s the cause of federalism was more or less synonymous with liberalism. Residents of Quilcacé Aldea (more than eighty names) to Municipal Vocales, Quilcacé, February 14, 1864, ACC, Archivo Muerto, Paquete 88, Legajo 54, n.p. For status as exslaves, see José M. Castro, Treasurer of the Colejio Mayor to Jefe Municipal, Popayán, September 14, 1867, ACC, Archivo Muerto, Paquete 97, Legajo 8, n.p.; and Daniel Mosquera, District Mayor to Governor of the Province, Tambo, August 18, 1861, ACC, Archivo Muerto, Paquete 82, Legajo 27, n.p.

38. Pioquinto Diago, for himself and in the name of his friends (nine others, written by someone else because the petitioners were illiterate) to Citizen President of the Sovereign State of Cauca, Popayán, February 7, 1878, ACC, Archivo Muerto, Paquete 144, Legajo 64, n.p.

39. The bogas of the Dagua River (more than 115 names, all but 7 signed for by others) to Citizen President of the State, Cali, May 15, 1878, ACC, Archivo Muerto, Paquete 144, Legajo 64, n.p.

40. The undersigned members of the Democratic Society of Cali (more than 180 names, many with very rough handwriting or signed for by others) to Citizen President of the State, Cali, June 1, 1877, ACC, Archivo Muerto, Paquete 137, Legajo 7, n.p.

41. Inhabitants of the San Julián hacienda (more than twenty-five names, all but a few signed for by another) to Governor of the Province, San Julián, October 15, 1853, ACC, Archivo Muerto, Paquete 55, Legajo 92, n.p.

42. Residents of San Juan (twenty-four names, all signed with an X) to Citizen Senators and Representatives (national), no place or date on letter, but 1852, AC, 1852, Senado, Proyectos Negados II, p. 19.

43. The bogas of the Dagua River (more than 115 names, all but 7 signed for by others)

to Citizen President of the State, Cali, May 15, 1878, ACC, Archivo Muerto, Paquete 144, Legajo 64, n.p.

44. The undersigned Colombian citizens and active members of the Sovereign State of Cauca and the Democratic Society of Palmira (more than sixty-five names) to Citizen President of the United States of Colombia, Palmira, June 21, 1868, Archivo del Instituto Colombiano de la Reforma Agraria (Bogotá), Bienes Nacionales, Tomo 7, p. 492.

45. Anselmo Soto Arana and E. León to Deputies, Popayán, September 9, 1871, ACC, Archivo Muerto, Paquete 112, Legajo 2, n.p.; see also The undersigned citizens and residents of Silvia parish (more than forty-five names) to Senators and Representatives (national), Silvia, March 19, 1852, AC, 1852, Senado, Informes de Comisiones IV, p. 155.

46. The Members of the cabildo pequeño de indígenas of Guachucal Parish and the vice-parish of Muellamuez to the Provincial Governor, Guachucal, October 4, 1852, ACC, Archivo Muerto, Paquete 53, Legajo 56, n.p. There are literally hundreds of similar petitions in the Archivo Central del Cauca in Popayán.

47. The cabildo de indígenas of Guachucal and Colimba to Honorable Legislators, Guachucal, August 12, 1873, ACC, Archivo Muerto, Paquete 124, Legajo 60, n.p.

48. The Indian bosses of the Aldea de Coconuco to Alcalde of Popayán district, Coconuco, August 1, 1860, ACC, Archivo Muerto, Paquete 80, Legajo 70, n.p.

49. For the colonial heritage, see Wade, *Race and Ethnicity*, 25–30.

50. Vocales of the pequeño cabildo of Riosucio District (more than three hundred names) to Governor of the State, Villa de Riosucio, August 1, 1869, ACC, Archivo Muerto, Paquete 105, Legajo 74, n.p.

51. Members of the pequeño cabildo of Cumbal to President of the Sovereign State of Cauca, Cumbal, July 29, 1871, AGN, Sección República, Fondo Ministerio de lo Interior y Relaciones Exteriores, Tomo 82, p. 986.

52. Members of the pequeño cabildo of Túquerres to President of the State Legislature, Túquerres, June 1869 (no day on letter), ACC, Archivo Muerto, Paquete 103, Legajo 3, n.p.; see also, Members of the pequeños cabildos of Cumbal, Muellamuez, Imués, and Túquerres to Deputies of the Caucano State Legislature, Túquerres, July 31, 1871, ACC, Archivo Muerto, Paquete 112, Legajo 14, n.p.; and Governors of the parcialidades of Riosucio, Anserma Vieja and Guática to Governor of the Province of the Sovereign State of Cauca [*sic*], Riosucio, March 29, 1869, ACC, Archivo Muerto, Paquete 105, Legajo 74, n.p.

53. For differences in the colonial identity of Indians and Afro-Colombians, see Wade, "Negros, indígenas e identidad nacional."

54. Manuel González to Mariano Ospina, Cali, December 21, 1859, BN, Fondo Manuscritos, Libro 210, p. 127; see also, Clemente Daza to Secretary of Government, Rosario, December 2, 1868 and Testimony of Estansilao Castro, November 18, 1868, ACC, Archivo Muerto, Paquete 99, Legajo 15, n.p.; Joaquin Prado and eleven others to Secretary of the Treasury, Santander, March 4, 1879, ACC, Archivo Muerto, Paquete 141, Legajo 16, n.p.; Alfonso [Arboleda] to Sergio Arboleda, Popayán, September 3, 1879, ACC, Fondo Arboleda, Signatura 447, p. 71; Pedro José Piedrahíta to T. C. de Mosquera, Cali, March 12, 1859, ACC, Sala Mosquera, Documento 36,922; and *El Democrática: Organo del Partido Liberal Independiente* (Palmira), March 13, 1879.

55. Andrews, *Afro-Latin America*, 92–100.

56. Scott, *Degrees of Freedom*; Kraay, *Race, State, and Armed Forces*; Souza, *A Sabinada*; Lasso, *Myths of Harmony*; Wright, *Café con Leche*; Aguirre, *Agentes de su propia libertad*; de Carvalho Neto, *Estudios afro*; McGuinness, *Path of Empire*; Guardino, *Peasants*; Ferrer, *Insurgent Cuba*; Foner, *Reconstruction*. For a more complete bibliography, see Andrews, *Afro-Latin America*.

57. Conrad, *Nostromo*, 174, 338.

58. For the Andes, a more complete bibliography may be found in Larson, *Trials of Nation Making*; see also Mallon, *Peasant and Nation*; Thomson, with LaFrance, *Patriotism, Politics, and Popular Liberalism*; Thurner, *From Two Republics to One Divided*; Walker, *Smoldering Ashes*; Grandin, *Blood of Guatemala*; Guardino, *The Time of Liberty*; Reed, *The Caste War of Yucatan*; and Méndez, *The Plebeian Republic*.

59. Mallon, *Peasant and Nation*; and Thomson, with LaFrance, *Patriotism, Politics, and Popular Liberalism*.

60. Grandin, *Blood of Guatemala*.

61. Larson, *Trials of Nation Making*.

2

Soldiers and Statesmen

Race, Liberalism, and the Paradoxes of Afro-Nicaraguan Military Service, 1844–1863

JUSTIN WOLFE

Service in racially segregated militias in Nicaragua during the colonial period provided a key institutional structure for both black community formation and claims to equal citizenship. Soldiering was one of the few open avenues for black social advancement during the colonial period, but by the 1840s politics and professions had also become fertile fields. After independence from Spain, Afro-Nicaraguans could be found in both Liberal and Conservative camps, but it was among the Liberals that they achieved their greatest prestige and power.[1] If military service connected Afro-Nicaraguans to their colonial past, it was a critique of that past that motivated their liberal ideals of equality and democratic republicanism, and their loathing of aristocratic conservatism. As both Afro-Nicaraguan military men and statesmen vied to expand their power into the national arena, they continued to draw—on the battlefield, in the streets, and at the ballot box—upon the communities from which they emerged. Popular support made this politics possible, but the popular performance of citizenship went far beyond blind loyalty to charismatic caudillos or mechanical allegiance to wealthy, powerful patrons.[2]

This chapter traces the struggles to define the parameters of popular liberalism, particularly in the Liberal stronghold of León, in the face of Conservative oligarchic exclusion and in relation to the popular rebellions and civil wars that engulfed Nicaragua between 1844 and 1863. Unlike early republican Colombia where white elites controlled liberal politics, in Nicaragua politics was dominated by Afro-Nicaraguan men from León.[3] For soldiers, the colonial militia had provided the means to organize the black community and demand political inclusion. Liberal statesmen, by contrast, dismissed the colonial past in favor of a democratic future that promised equal opportunity. Afro-Nicaraguan soldiers and statesmen needed one another to imagine these larger political projects, but their contradictions constantly pulled them apart and left the popular communities that supported them with difficult choices. For Afro-Nicaraguan military men of ambition, the extension of their power inevitably distanced them from their home communities and required developing a politics that spoke beyond local needs. This tested the loyalty of the communities that originally stoked their ambitions. For León's Afro-Nicaraguan statesmen, by contrast, until the late 1850s, the center of their local power was home to the institutions and leaders of national politics. This shared urban space enabled these statesmen to leverage popular support for their national agenda while remaining attentive to local needs and responsive to local demands.

Racial conflict had simmered beneath the seemingly tranquil surface of late-colonial Nicaragua. As the Spanish empire faltered in the early years of the nineteenth century, colonial officials worried about the size of Nicaragua's African descended population, which accounted for upward of 50 percent of the province's inhabitants. León and Rivas, from which would hail the period's most ardent Liberal voices, had even larger black populations, constituting 56 and 72 percent, respectively, in 1778. These figures hardly changed according to the census of 1883, with León's black population rising to 57 percent and Rivas's declining to 71 percent.[4] Within this context, perhaps no place better illuminates the conflict between soldiers and statesmen than San Felipe, a barrio of the provincial capital of León, which had been created as a racially segregated black neighborhood and had housed the city's *pardo* militia. After independence, San Felipe produced some of Nicaragua's most influential Liberal political and military leaders.

Scholars of Nicaragua have tended to view military participation as anathema to popular communities, but I argue that such conclusions stem from twentieth century nationalist historiography, which imagined Nicaraguan subalterns as homogeneously mestizo and politically disengaged.[5] In other words, race is seen as irrelevant and communities as essentially reactive. Analysis of these issues is further weakened by the limited scholarship on the military in Nicaragua.[6] As historian Hendrik Kraay has argued, although in Latin America "military institutions touched the lives of thousands of men and women, while their reform preoccupied liberals and conservatives alike," their investigation has been relegated to the "historiographical back burner."[7] This chapter, by contrast, argues not only for the complexity of Nicaragua's racial politics but also for the activism of subaltern communities like San Felipe.

The Community of San Felipe

In the mid-seventeenth century the Spanish Crown decreed the creation of a separate barrio in León for "mulatos, negros y mestizos."[8] Called San Felipe, this barrio marked an effort to keep non-Indian *castas* out of the neighboring indigenous community of Subtiava and from living in the center of León, the capital of the colonial province of Nicaragua. The decree was part of a wider effort by the Spanish Crown to map the logic of the *sistema de castas* onto the urban geography. Walling off indigenous communities from outside influences while also cementing Crown control over Indian labor was the policy's primary goal, but in some cities a number of black barrios were also created.[9]

San Felipe might have devolved into a heterogeneous plebeian neighborhood had it not been for the creation of a *pardo* militia in León and the erection of the Church of San Felipe. Drafted mostly from the barrio's residents, the militia became the de facto political leadership of San Felipe and increasingly worked for political independence from the Spanish leadership of León. Together the church and the militia served as key markers of Felipeño identity. While the barrio was also home to other *castas*, the link to the militia ended up racializing the barrio as black. Between 1730 and independence, conflicts between the barrio and Spanish authorities laid the foundation for deep divisions.[10] Despite these struggles and the Spanish ambivalence about arming men of African descent, the Spanish Crown recognized the service of San Felipe's militiamen and rewarded the barrio with its own communal lands, which further cemented the barrio's distinct identity.[11]

Independence from Spain threw established social relations into disarray, yielding political struggles that quickly evolved into regional rebellions and civil war. Afro-Nicaraguans and mestizos engaged in pitched battles with mostly white, aristocratic factions. While these battles took place throughout the country, León bore much of the destruction. By the end of the 1820s, German traveler Jacobo Haefkens described the city as composed, "only of the humble classes, since the wealthy people escaped or were robbed of their fortune."[12] The result was the emergence of a new generation of Liberals, mostly Afro-Nicaraguans, who increasingly took control of local politics. As Haefkens reported, with the weakened position of the local oligarchy, "the mulattoes have taken over the greater part of the city."[13] Many, if not most, of these emerged from San Felipe's approximately seven thousand inhabitants (about 30 percent of León's population of approximately twenty-four thousand).[14] The ideological tide favored the Liberals and so did the surging power of the plebeian communities.

Liberal victories enabled a generation of university-educated professionals and politicians to emerge from the poorer barrios of Nicaragua's major cities in the years after independence. Gone were the colonial restrictions on men of African descent, and they leapt at these new opportunities.[15] Among the most famous of these were Francisco Castellón, Rosalío Cortés, Gregorio Júarez, and the brothers Sebastián and Basilio Salinas, who all graduated from the Universidad de León.[16] Many of these, including Júarez and the Salinas brothers, hailed from San Felipe and marked a shift in the barrio's politics as they chose careers in the professions and politics over the military. Education and military service were hardly opposed, of course, but given the discrimination faced by Felipeños in the colonial period, many of these men saw themselves first and foremost as legislators, jurists, and diplomats in the vanguard of republican values. While a few of them had access to modest economic resources or social connections through elite white fathers, all were born to a plebeian status that would have made these opportunities and their rapid achievements all but impossible before independence.

Despite these advances, Felipeños faced serious political and economic challenges. During the colonial period, Felipeños had used their service in the *pardo* militia as a bargaining chip—playing factions of local, provincial, and imperial officials off one another. Enabling the militiamen as well as all blacks and mulattoes in Nicaragua to refuse paying tribute was just one their achievements.[17] The militia also successfully petitioned for common lands for the barrio, freeing its inhabitants from the city council of León's control of *ejidos*.[18] With independence, however, León's *pardo* militia was disbanded and León claimed San Felipe's common lands. The Church of San Felipe remained one of the few institutional links to the community's past. Felipeños had gained political opportunity but at the expense of corporate autonomy. Over the next four decades they worked to use the former to reclaim the latter.

Race and Deracialization in Postcolonial Nicaragua

The earliest postindependence conflicts in Nicaragua were frequently tinged with the language of caste war and the fear of social upheaval reminiscent of the Haitian Revolution. That more than a hundred "negros franceses" from Saint Domingue—albeit ones who had sided with the Spanish—swelled the ranks of the Nicaraguan military at the end of the eighteenth century only intensified these feelings.[19] In this context, Central Americans abolished slavery, the official use of racialized caste terms, and honorific titles such as "excellency" and "don."[20] What might seem like paper changes became frighteningly real for Nicaragua's white oligarchs when crowds in the barrios turned the legislative prohibition on titles into chants of "the dons are finished!"[21]

The abolition of slavery transformed the rhetorical landscape in Nicaragua in ways that distinguished it from other Latin American countries with significant African descent populations, such as Colombia, Venezuela, and Argentina, where slavery continued into the 1850s.[22] Slavery's explicit links to blackness meant that racialized language flourished in these countries in everyday social encounter and struggle. At the same time it highlighted the failure to fulfill the promises of Enlightenment, liberalism, and republicanism, a failure that animated black soldiering and political activism on behalf of emancipation, citizenship, and social equality.

For Nicaraguans, the deracialization of public discourse meant a contentious unsettling of postindependence relationships. If blacks could aspire to the same ranks of political leadership and social advancement as whites, if they could not be publicly disparaged and categorized in the language of race, if slavery could only be held up as a symbol of colonial shame, rather than a sign of enduring racial ignominy, how could distinctions of wealth and social distance be reestablished? In Colombia, Venezuela, and Argentina, by contrast, race remained a viable and volatile symbol precisely because slavery and public racism lasted so long into the republican era.[23]

While race played a limited role in public discourse in Nicaragua, Afro-Nicaraguans developed a constellation of rhetorical devices that both outlined and critiqued racism and racial thinking without invoking this language itself. Terms such as "odious distinctions," "oligarchy," "humble origins," "blood," "merit," and "social equality" provided the contours of debate, evoked collective memory, and warned of the convulsive anger beneath the surface. By the same token, for Conservatives the name "Felipeño" came to stand in the for the worst excesses of liberalism and the consequences of undoing colonial hierarchy and distinctions, although in private Conservative discourse could be virulently racist.

Controlling the "Military Spirit," 1844–1853

Nicaragua's secession from the Central American Federation in 1838 marked a turning point in Nicaraguan national politics and signaled the emergence of a new generation of Liberal statesmen whose politics seemed increasingly rooted in local communities like San Felipe rather than under the umbrella of federalist liberalism. While the *patria grande* remained attractive in concept, treaties and alliances over the next decade tended to favor local sovereignty.[24] This political shift, including the new prominence of Afro-Nicaraguan statesmen, coincided with an expansion of local military power. The Afro-Nicaraguan community reacted with an ambivalence that mirrored the uneasy alliance between Liberal Afro-Nicaraguan statesmen and soldiers. During the colonial period, the black militia had, like its counterparts throughout the Americas, engaged in short-lived and sporadic actions, from repelling pirates to patrolling frontier zones to controlling riots.[25] The civil wars of the postindependence period, by contrast, lasted years, with each side feeling compelled not just to bring the other side to heel militarily but also to subordinate the other to its political will. The physical and emotional toll of military service began to diminish its appeal.

Ambivalence turned to dissension in 1844 when the growing militarism of Liberal commandant Gen. Casto Fonseca provoked criticism by his erstwhile allies, particular Liberal Felipeño statesmen. Fonseca responded by having Felipeño Basilio Salinas publically flogged, an act that resonated with Felipeño collective memory of slavery and colonial abuse. Forced into exile, Salinas and his compatriots fled into the uneasy embrace of Salvadoran Conservative Francisco Malespín, who planned to invade Nicaragua to depose Fonseca. Most Felipeños, however, remained behind, ready to defend León—if not Fonseca—from Malespín's mostly Conservative forces.

Despite the overwhelming size of Malespín's army and his advantage in firepower, Fonseca refused to surrender. Malespín responded with savagery—summary executions, rape, arson—meant to force Liberal capitulation.[26] In the midst of the brutality, the Felipeños within Malespín's forces rushed into the city to protect the barrio from Malespín's depredations.[27] That the Hondurans and Salvadorans under Malespín's command would fail to distinguish San Felipe from the rest of León confronted Felipeño statesmen with the importance of loyalty to community and community autonomy.

Liberal weakness after Fonseca's defeat led to the election of Conservative José León Sandoval, who moved the government to Masaya and began implementing state-building reforms that were facilitated by the military and its new commandant general, José Trinidad Muñoz. Although born in Nicaragua, Muñoz built his military career in Mexico and elsewhere in Central America. He returned to Nicaragua soldiering with General Malespín. Muñoz's ascendancy along with Sandoval's conservative policies led to revolts by military men who had defended León against Malespín, notably Casto Fonseca's lieutenants José María Valle and Bernabé Somoza.[28]

José Trinidad Muñoz brought military professionalism to Nicaragua when he started a modest military academy in León. He also began to reorganize the Nicaraguan military, which was still localist and unprofessional.[29] The academy's students came mostly from Leon's leading Liberals, including Sebastián Salinas, Máximo Jerez, Mariano and Trinidad Salazar, Mateo Pineda, and Felix and Santos Ramirez Madregil. This more formalized education in the art of war appealed particularly to the university-trained *licenciados*. Their support, however, was qualified and constantly being negotiated. Thus, while numerous Felipeños trained and fought under Muñoz in León, they generally did so as "patriots"—volunteers not officially under the command of the state.[30] Nonetheless, when Muñoz had to give chase to rebels outside of León, he left the plaza of León "in the care of the students of the military academy, particularly of those courageous ones from San Felipe who had cooperated in the ranks of the allied armies . . . against Casto Fonseca."[31] The Felipeños rewarded this confidence with their public support "to defend the fatherland [*patria*], the Government, and the just cause."[32] Still, one of the most profound lessons for Felipeños caught in the war with Malespín was the importance of political autonomy. The attraction of republican politics was the representation of community will; the military by contrast seemed to subjugate that will to the dictates of a vertical hierarchy embodied in a single leader.

Felipeños and their leaders, especially the Salinas brothers and José Guerrero, walked a fine line in supporting the government. In turning against the soldiers who had defended the plaza of León, Felipeños demanded greater Leonese control over the government and a Liberal shift in government and policies, including the promotion of social equality—what one voice called "distributive justice."[33] While one of the most moderate and respected Afro-Nicaraguan statesmen, Gregorio Juárez, saw "bright and productive" possibilities in "all these dissensions," José Trinidad Muñoz feared they would spark "an interminable civil war."[34] General Muñoz's assertion, made in a pronouncement known as the "Acta de Limay," demanded that political debates be subsumed to political stability. As he concluded, although the constitution "imposes on the armed forces the duty to be essentially obedient," attacks on the sovereignty of the state from within would nullify such a limitation. Moreover, civil unrest was now to face military justice.

This shift in policy, questions about the conservative drift of the Sandoval government, and ambivalence about Muñoz's political motives brought Afro-Nicaraguans back to the street. Both San Felipe's military service and its outspoken liberalism developed in relation to its history of racialized exclusion. Strategic engagements with both civil and military law were central to Felipeño collective memory. During the colonial period they made claims to military service and the *fuero militar* to divide the white elite and navigate colonial power structures. After independence, however, Felipeños took to the street as citizens in a show of popular, democratic political power. That one could face military justice without benefiting from membership within the military, or conversely, be stripped of civilian rights, raised fears about the promise of democratic politics and the unaccountable power of the military.

In November of 1846, a pamphlet authored under the pseudonym Las Sombras spoke directly to Afro-Nicaraguan fears of an oligarchic restoration and the prohibition against popular protest. Acknowledging the Afro-Nicaraguan base of Leon's most radical democrats, Las Sombras spoke not of the yoke of Spanish colonialism—a frequent trope for both Liberals and Conservatives—but rather of a feared return of the "idiotic situation of Haiti in its days of slavery!"[35] Haiti possessed a charged and freighted symbolic power, one rarely used in Central America except as a way to raise questions of race without resorting to overtly racialized language.

Felipeño statesmen and the wider San Felipe community struggled to balance Muñoz's zeal for power with his function as a counterweight to Conservative influence in the Sandoval administration. In late 1846, Sandoval called a constituent assembly to replace the liberal constitution of 1838 with one that would reign in popular politics *and* military leaders such as Muñoz.[36] Liberals feared these provisions would privilege the wealthier Conservatives of Granada and place overly broad coercive power in their hands.[37] Debates over the constitution spilled into the streets and countryside as supporters of popular republicanism registered their disenchantment and scuttled the assembly. Felipeños certainly worried about Muñoz's power but refused to exchange their own political power for his removal.

Conservative anger over both Muñoz and Liberal power continued to build, and that anger found expression in increasingly racist terms. Discourse that had remained commonplace in Venezuela and Colombia now reared its head in Nicaragua.[38] Felipeño ally José Guerrero, whom Sandoval originally called a "worthy successor" now found himself described in a Conservative pamphlet as "the *negrito* Guerrero, the inveterate revolutionary of Nicaragua."[39] And while some euphemistically referred to Felipeños as "vulgar democrats," in private they easily became "Hottentots."[40]

Civil War and William Walker, 1853–1856

A short-lived coup led by Muñoz toward the end of 1851 split Liberals in the run up to the national elections of 1853.[41] When no one achieved a majority of the vote, the decision went to the legislature, which awarded the position to Conservative Fruto Chamorro over Liberal Afro-Nicaraguan Francisco Castellón. Chamorro viewed Liberal republicanism as a threat to the social order and began maneuvering to push aside his Liberal rivals and undermine their supporters' access to political institutions. In the most forceful public expression of Conservative racism since Nicaraguan independence, Chamorro lamented Nicaragua's "racial heterogeneity" and "the desire to establish the absolute equality between the races."[42] For Afro-Nicaraguan liberals, this equality gave republicanism its meaning; for Chamorro, it was a social illness. Chamorro argued that the Liberal constitution of 1838 had infected the body politic, resulting in an anemic executive, an overly representative legislature, and a propensity to social disorder. He ordered a new constituent assembly to remedy these failings by curtailing suffrage rights, access to political office, and the republican structure of the legislature.[43]

Just weeks before the assembly was to be seated, Chamorro claimed to have uncovered a plot to overthrow his government and ordered the arrest of leading Liberal figures.[44] Faced with exile, political exclusion, and an attack on the constitutional foundations of liberal republicanism, the Liberals rebelled. In May of 1854 they established a provisional government under the presidency of Castellón and then took their fight to Granada, entrenching themselves in the Liberal indigenous barrio of Jalteva.

The Liberal ranks were joined by a number of foreign fighters, mostly travelers who were passing through as customers of Cornelius Vanderbilt's transit route on their way to or from California.[45] Despite these reinforcements, the tide appeared to be turning against the Liberals. So when Byron Cole, one of these early sympathizers, offered to help contract a group of seasoned fighters under the command of William Walker, Castellón leapt at the chance.[46] Castellón hoped to add not just well-trained and well-equipped forces to the Liberal cause but also partisans of Liberal republican values.

The Conservatives viewed Walker's arrival with fear and disdain, arguing that North Americans were "declared enemies of our race" bent on
Americanizing Nicaragua.[47] In many ways this response charged the North
Americans with the racism that in fact animated U.S. Manifest Destiny.[48]
But North American attitudes were hardly homogeneous, and—at least
through 1840s and mid-1850s—Nicaraguans of varying political stripes
and classes found much to admire in the cultural, economic, and political
path of the United States.[49] Although William Walker would come to be remembered as a proslavery demagogue, he was initially embraced by a wide
array of Nicaraguan Liberals, especially Afro-Nicaraguans such as Francisco
Castellón, Sebastián Salinas, and Cleto Mayorga, who would not part ways
with Walker until the summer of 1856, a full year after his arrival.[50]

Not all Liberals greeted Walker and his troops so enthusiastically, particularly the more moderate white Liberals of León such as Nazario Escoto
and Jose Maria Sarria, who descended from León's colonial oligarchy. Escoto, who became provisional president in September 1855 after Castellón's
untimely death from cholera, hoped to ally with the Conservatives to expel
Walker. But it was Felipeño statesmen such as Sebastián Salinas and his
supporters—what one contemporary euphemistically referred to as "the
vulgar democrats"—who held the reins of Liberal power. Walker's victory
over the Conservatives in Granada, however, made the question moot.[51]
Fighting continued, but it was concentrated in the regions over which
Walker had greatest control—around Granada, Rivas, and the border with
Costa Rica—leaving the Liberal provisional authorities in León nearly independent of Walker's machinations.

Felipeño statesmen played a central role in the Liberal government—
prior to Walker's arrival, during his military ascendancy, and after they broke
with Walker to ally with the Conservatives against him. Sebastián Salinas,
who had been minister of government and foreign relations in Francisco
Castellón's provisional government, retained this position throughout the
entire episode.[52] By June 1856, however, Afro-Nicaraguans realized their
faith in Walker was misplaced. In that month, Walker came to León and
began to assert himself over the city. Informed that Walker wanted the
presidency of Nicaragua, Sebastián Salinas declared, "We have maintained
in good faith that that man [Walker] has not wanted to usurp power or
dominate the country." Within a week, Salinas and his fellow Liberals had
abandoned Walker and the Americans. Mariano Salazar (Francisco Castellón's brother-in-law) rode through the streets of San Felipe, which Walker
termed "one of the most turbulent quarters," denouncing Walker's betrayal

and calling the Felipeños to arms.[53] The troops Walker had stationed in León were forced to abandon the city. San Felipe's military tradition and its adherence to radical republicanism were in full display even though Felipeños had not been significant participants in combat, either in the 1854 civil war or in support of Walker, until now. Indeed, since the disastrous siege of León in 1844, the Felipeños had tended to participate in war as "patriots" for the cause but not as soldiers within the formal military structure. It was their ability to mobilize quickly and en masse that gave Felipeños their sway and allowed their leaders such influence within Liberal political circles.

A Farewell to Arms, 1856–1863

Within a week of their break with Walker, the Liberals sought to join forces with the Conservatives against the Americans. Both sides spoke in the language of unity but a unity built on the understanding that each side bore the blame for Nicaragua's woes.[54] This compromise required a political moderation not easily accepted by the hardliners of either group.[55] One might imagine that Felipeños like Sebastián Salinas would have been tainted by their close alliance with Walker. It had been, after all, the established white families of León who first sought to ally with Granada's Conservatives against Walker nearly a year beforehand. Yet when Liberals and Conservatives negotiated a joint government, the position of minister of government remained in Salinas's hands.[56] As in the past, the backing of San Felipe provided Salinas with political leverage that was hard to ignore. These supporters had forced Conservative José León Sandoval to dismiss his Conservative cabinet in 1846; now they worked to ensure a place at the table in the allied war against Walker and subsequent political developments.

Starting in the late 1840s, Felipeños had increasingly shifted their support from the military men who had dominated local politics to the statesmen. Felipeños chose the path of political compromise not simply out of a desire to avoid war but with expectations that long-held demands for local power and political and economic autonomy would be fulfilled. On October 6, 1856, just weeks after Liberals and Conservatives joined forces against Walker, the provisional government responded to Felipeño requests for greater political autonomy by establishing a *junta de mejoras* for the barrio. The decree hearkened back to the barrio's military service on behalf of the Spanish Crown and the common lands with which the barrio had been rewarded. Questions over municipal control of commons had proved vexing with indigenous communities, and clearly they rankled Felipeños too.[57]

The barrio's lands had served as a terrestrial tie to its collective memory of military service, racial exclusion, and distinguished merit. As Liberals and Conservatives began to negotiate a new national unity as well as the incumbent forgetting of historical claims and conflicts, Felipeños wanted to ensure their stake in the future. The junta began this process by allowing Felipeños to elect their own representatives; administer policing, governance, and taxation within the barrio; and control their commons.[58]

The united Nicaraguan and Central American armies forced Walker to surrender on May 1, 1857, but Walker's scorched earth retreat created little jubilation. The dissent that Gregorio Júarez had seen as so productive ten years before now augured the end of Nicaraguan sovereignty. Even Sebastián Salinas, one of the most stalwart republicans, came to support "the intimate union of the sons of the Republic, like individuals in a single family, irrespective of their opinions."[59] Difficult financial, political, and military questions remained unresolved. Who would pay for the war? How would soldiers be demobilized? And how could these goals be achieved without risking peace and union? One of the earliest answers came two months after Walker's defeat, when the provisional government decreed a series of privileges for soldiers and officers in the united army who served through the end of the campaign. Most notably, these men would be enjoy the *fuero militar* for life, a privilege that the new militia regulation of 1858 would normally grant only after twenty years of regular service.[60] Initially this excluded the Felipeños who drove Walker's troops from León; few of them had continued as soldiers in the allied forces, preferring the independence of fighting as "patriots." Within a month, however, Felipeños had jockeyed to expand these privileges to everyone who fought against the filibusters at any time.[61] Twenty years later, the state continued to pay the price of this political choice. As Conservative president Joaquín Zavala noted in 1880, in León few cases came before the criminal court since "the better part of the accused belong to the *fuero militar*."[62]

Felipeños continued to push for greater autonomy and privilege in the wake of the war. In 1859 they received a double favor: a decree that suspended the militia duty for any Felipeño who worked on repairs to the Church of San Felipe.[63] Those who worked for free would earn double their time off. The Church of San Felipe had stood since the barrio's founding and had formed, along with the *pardo* militia, the center of community life. A horrendous earthquake had destroyed the church in 1835 and the subsequent wars made rebuilding impossible.[64] The decree thus served to revive a vital symbol of Felipeño identity while also offering Felipeños a way to avoid unwanted military service. The rebuilding process lasted more than a decade.[65]

Oddly enough, as Felipeños worked to escape the militia service that had helped forge local identity, they called upon the collective memory of both that service and the institutional racism faced by Afro-Nicaraguans to make claims that blurred the line between colonial privilege and postcolonial citizenship. On the one hand, Felipeños demanded the lands they had won through bravery and loyalty to the Spanish Crown. On the other, they wanted the political sovereignty of an independent municipality and the rights of voice and vote that formed the foundation of liberal republicanism, rights that colonial law consistently refused them.[66]

In 1862 a crisis in postwar governance offered Felipeños an opportunity to renew their demands. President Tomás Martínez, a moderate Conservative from León, had presided over the most politically stable period in Nicaragua's postcolonial history. Popular both as a war hero in the fight against Walker and as a conciliatory politician, Martínez sought another four-year term despite the new post-Walker constitution's prohibition against reelection. Martínez argued that since the constitution was enacted during his presidency, his reelection would actually be to a first term under the new charter. Liberals split over the issue with Afro-Nicaraguans throwing their support to Martínez.[67] To give their vote more weight and counterbalance Leonese Liberals who planned to vote against Martínez, his supporters in the legislature voted to establish San Felipe as a municipality. More than just an electoral voice, the decree confirmed Felipeño authority over their own common lands and enabled them thereafter to claim half of the *tierras baldíos* (unclaimed state lands) that would otherwise have been given to León.[68] Just before Martínez left office in 1867, he repaid Felipeño support with a revised electoral law that carved San Felipe out of León's electoral district. In this new configuration, San Felipe would have its own congressional deputy and sixty electors, giving it the same influence as Managua (by then capital of Nicaragua for nearly a decade) and Masaya.[69]

Conclusion

Liberal Afro-Nicaraguans found themselves caught between competing visions of national politics: one driven by a Liberal militarism, the other by democratic republicanism. Both met resistance from the oligarchic conservatism embodied in the elite of Granada. Because Conservatives proved unable to limit popular political participation through political means, these conflicts inevitably turned violent, transforming political struggles into military ones. Despite this, the participation of Liberal Felipeños in the Guerra de Malespín and their ambivalent relationship to Gen. José Trinidad Muñoz brought faith in an authoritarian approach to the breaking point.

The opportunity to contract with William Walker and his Americans fighters in the Liberal cause during the civil war of 1854 opened up the possibility for a way out of this conundrum. A limited number of foreign fighters—Liberals whose politics lay outside the geography of Central America—could turn the tide and help solidify the cultural foundations for democracy. Unfortunately for the Liberals, Walker and his swelling army of compatriots proved as open to dictatorial and demagogic means as local military men.

The fight to expel Walker, however, created a new balance of power. The unification of Liberals and Conservatives made clear that the popular support of Liberals, especially Felipeños, would be fundamental to any success. So, too, however, would be the subjugation of the radical promises of democratic liberalism to a more conservative republicanism. The new post-Walker constitution of 1858 expressed this compromise, keeping the franchise nearly as accessible as the 1838 Liberal constitution while limiting, like the 1854 proposal, senate seats and the presidency to those with two thousand and four thousand pesos in wealth, respectively. While this ensured the institutionalization of political participation for Felipeños and other Liberals, it did so at the expense of a more democratic leadership and more radical Liberal demands for social equality. Concomitant with this shift was the nationalization and regularization of the military, a project that stabilized national politics but left communities such as San Felipe to pursue their goals within the more limited confines of postwar politics.

Acknowledgments

I would like to thank Miguel Centeno, Hendrik Kraay, René D. Harder Horst, and Nicola Foote for their comments. The research for this essay was supported by the Fulbright Scholar Program, the Department of History and the Stone Center for Latin American Studies at Tulane University, and the David Rockefeller Center for Latin American Studies at Harvard University.

Notes

1. Throughout this essay, I use the terms "black" and "Afro-Nicaraguan" to refer to people and communities understood to be of African descent. Although this oversimplifies the social history of African descent communities in Nicaragua, it is not my intention to suggest a "one-drop" rule or that race and racism function in Nicaragua as they do in the United States but rather to underscore the importance of race and of blackness as a discursive repertoire in colonial and early republican Nicaragua.

2. For more traditional interpretations of early republican politics, see Lynch, *Caudillos in Spanish America*; and Hamill, *Caudillos*. More recently, scholars have begun to take popular politics more seriously and to engage traditional interpretations with new, often highly detailed local sources of evidence. See, e.g., Chambers, *From Subjects to Citizens;* Sanders, *Contentious Republicans*; and Guardino, *Time of Liberty*.

3. Sanders, "'Citizens of a Free People,'" 277, 311.

4. The figures for 1778 and 1883 are calculated from Archivo General de Centro América (hereafter AGCA) A3.29, leg. 1749, exp. 28130 (1778); and Nicaragua, Ministerio de Fomento, *Memoria* (Managua, 1884), respectively. While the figure for León in 1778 does not include the indigenous barrio of Subtiava, this is likely compensated for by the absence of the mostly black shipbuilding port town of Realejo.

5. See, e.g., Coronel Urtecho, "Introducción a la Época de Anarquía en Nicaragua."

6. Alvarez Montalván, *Las fuerzas armadas en Nicaragua*; and Zambrana Fonseca, *Civiles y militares*. See, also, Holden, *Armies without Nations*, 80–95.

7. Kraay, *Race, State, and Armed Forces*, 1.

8. Buitrago Matus, *León*, vol. 2, 134–39. See, also, AGCA A1.10 (5), leg. 21, exp. 142 (1663).

9. Mörner and Gibson, "Diego Muñoz Camargo"; and Molina Argüello, "Poblaciones fundadas en Nicaragua."

10. AGCA, A1 (5), leg. 97, exp. 746 (1730).

11. For a recounting of this service, see *Boletín Oficial* (León), October 10, 1856.

12. Haefkens, "Viaje a Guatemala y Centroamérica," 56.

13. Ibid, 45.

14. *Boletín Oficial* (León), October 10, 1856; and Lévy, *Notas geográficas y económicas*, 403.

15. See, e.g., Konetzke, *Colección de documentos para la historia*, 3: 265–66, 340–41, 821–29.

16. See Meléndez Obando, "Presencia africana en familias nicaragüenses," 341–60.

17. Konetzke, *Colección de documentos*, 3: 628–21.

18. *Boletín Oficial* (León), October 10, 1856.

19. AGCA, A2 (5), leg. 42, exp. 239 (1797); AGCA, A1 (5), leg. 42, exp. 242 (1818); Houdaille, "Negros francéses en América Central," 65–67; and Geggus, *Haitian Revolutionary Studies*, esp. ch. 12., "Slave Leaders in Exile," 179–203.

20. Kinloch Tijerino, *Nicaragua*, 41.

21. Cuadra Pasos, "Don Anselmo H. Rivas," iii.

22. Andrews, *Afro-Latin America*, 57.

23. Andrews, *Afro-Argentines of Buenos Aires*; Wright, *Café con Leche*, 31–38; Helg, *Liberty and Equality in Caribbean Colombia*; and Sanders, *Contentious Republicans*.

24. See, e.g., Montes, *Morazán y la Federación Centroamericana*, 233–36.

25. Romero Vargas, *Las estructuras sociales*, 324–42; and Voelz, *Slave and Soldier*.

26. Gámez, *Historia de Nicaragua desde los tiempos prehistóricos hasta 1860*, 515–17.

27. de la Rocha, *Revista política sobre la historia de la Revolución de Nicaragua*, 31.

28. Casanova Fuertes, "Orden o Anarquía."

29. "Decreto," *Alcance del Registro Oficial* (San Fernando), June 23, 1845, 98.

30. See "Estado soberano de Nicaragua," *Registro Oficial* (San Fernando), July 12, 1845, 109; José Trinidad Muñoz, "Parte Oficial. Ejército del Estado, General en Gefe," *Registro Oficial* (San Fernando), August 23, 1845, 133.

31. Ortega Arancibia, *Cuarenta años*, 79.

32. Los Felipences, "Rasgo de lealtad," *Registro Oficial* (León), October 18, 1845, 126.

33. Juan Antonio Bravo, "Director Supremo, ajentes gubernativos, ilustres militares, respetables corporaciones, y honrados Ciudadanos," *Registro Oficial* (León), September 20, 1845, 108–9.

34. Gregorio Júarez, "Discurso que el S. Senador Lic. G. Juares pronunció al abrirse las conferencias á que se refieron los documentos anteriores," *Registro Oficial* (León), March 21, 1846, 256; and José Trinidad Muñoz, "El Acta de Limay (23 de marzo de 1846)," *Revista de la Academia de Geografía e Historia de Nicaragua* 7, no. 3 (1945): 51.

35. Las Sombras, *Documento para la historia del estado de Nicaragua* (Masaya, Nicaragua: Imprenta de la Fraternidad, 1846), 5, Latin American Library, Tulane University.

36. "El Proyecto de Constitución Política de 1848," in Esgueva Gómez, ed. *Las constituciones políticas*, 1: 287, 295.

37. On these debates, see *Al público: Una cuestión grave*.

38. Wright, *Café con Leche*, 31–38; and Sanders, *Contentious Republicans*, 139–42.

39. Sandoval, "Discurso pronunciado por el Sr. Director Supremo José Leon Sandoval, 30; and Los Defensores del Orden, "Diálogo entre Pastracio y Liborio," August 9, 1854, in Cerutti, "Documentos para la historia," 70.

40. Ortega Arancibia, *Cuarenta años*, 202; Bishop Jorge Viteri (León) to Agustín Vijil, October 20, 1852, in Vijil, "El Licenciado don Francisco Castellón," 297.

41. Gámez, *Historia de Nicaragua*, 568–69.

42. Chamorro, "Mensaje de S. E. el general director," 109.

43. "El Proyecto de Constitución Política de 1854," in Esgueva Gómez, ed., *Las constituciones políticas*, 1: 305–26.

44. Gámez, *Historia de Nicaragua*, 582; Chamorro Zelaya, *Fruto Chamorro*, 266–70.

45. See Doubleday, *Reminiscences of the "Filibuster" War in Nicaragua*; and Wells, *Explorations and Adventures in Honduras*. Doubleday and Wells were among the earliest American supporters of the Liberals. They also detail the arrivals of so many others.

46. Wells, *Walker's Expedition to Nicaragua*, 42–43.

47. *El Defensor del Orden* (Granada), September 15, 1855.

48. Horsman, *Race and Manifest Destiny*; and Greenberg, *Manifest Manhood and the Antebellum American Empire*, 91–96.

49. Gobat, *Confronting the American Dream*, 21–41; and Kinloch Tijerino, *Nicaragua*, 201–13.

50. For a review of the historiography on William Walker and the Central American campaign against him, see Aguilar Piedra, "La guerra Centroamericana."

51. Walker, *War in Nicaragua*; and Montúfar, *Walker en Centro-América*.

52. "Oficial," *Boletín Oficial* (León), April 9, 1856; and Rivas, "El Presidente provisorio."

53. Walker, *War in Nicaragua*, 224.

54. "El Pacto Providencial del 12 de septiembre de 1856," in Esgueva Gómez, ed., *Documentos de la historia*, 190–92; 185.

55. Díaz Lacayo, *Nicaragua, acuerdos políticos: 1*.

56. Rivas, "El Presidente provisorio."

57. Wolfe, *Everyday Nation-State*, 80–121; and Dore, *Myths of Modernity*, 69–96.

58. *Boletín Oficial* (León), October 10, 1856.

59. Sebastián Salinas to Máximo Jerez, June 15, 1857, in "Documentos relativos a la Guerra Nacional," 101.

60. Jesús de la Rocha, ed. *Código de la legislación de la República de Nicaragua en Centro América*, (Managua: Imprenta de "El Centro-Americano," 1873–74), 1:217–18. See, also, Nicaragua, *Código de la legislación de la República de Nicaragua: Ramo Militar i disposiciones sueltas, 1821 a 1863* (Managua: Imprenta de "El Centro-Americano," 1872), 1:47.

61. de la Rocha and Castillo, eds., *Código de la legislación*, 1:219.

62. Joaquín Zavala to Francisco Morazán, April 20, 1881, Box 6, Folder 4, Joaquin Zavala Solís Collection (hereafter JZS), Tulane University, Latin American Library. See, also, Joaquín Zavala to Joaquín Elizondo, October 18, 1880, Box 6, Folder 2, JZS; Joaquín Zavala to Vicente Navas, October 18, 1880, Box 6, Folder 2, JZS.

63. de la Rocha, ed., *Código de la lejislación*, 2:124.

64. Wells, *Explorations and Adventures in Honduras*, 38.

65. Nicaragua, *Colección de acuerdos y decretos gubernativos, emitidos de enero a diciembre de 1864*, 116–17; and "Decreto legislativo mandando dar $500 á la Junta de edificación de la parroquia de San Felipe," *Gaceta de Nicaragua* (Managua), April 10, 1869, 116.

66. The Cortes of Cádiz offered an opportunity to undo, or at least mitigate, the institutional discrimination against people of African descent found scattered throughout royal *cedulas* and edicts of the colonial period. Instead the Spanish Constitution of 1812 distilled these prejudices into a single document. See, King, "Colored Castes and American Representation"; and Rodríguez, *Cádiz Experiment in Central America*, 60–62.

67. Ortega Arancibia, *Cuarenta años*, 327. See also, "Remitido. Justificación," *Gaceta de Nicaragua* (Managua), June 13, 1863, 2, which lists members of the León's "Clubs Central" supporting Tomás Martínez's reelection.

68. de la Rocha and Castillo, eds., *Código de la lejislación*, vol. 1, book 3, title 1, law 26; vol. 2, book 4, title 1, law 14; Nicaragua, *Colección de acuerdos y decretos gubernativos, emitidos de enero a diciembre de 1865* (Managua: Imprenta del Gobierno, 1866), 95–96.

69. "Decreto, reformando la ley electoral y sus adiciones de Supremas Autoridades de la República (30 de Enero de 1867)," in Esgueva Gómez, ed., *Las leyes electorales en la historia de Nicaragua*, 1:493–97.

3

Afro-Cubans in Cuba's War for Independence, 1895–1898

ALINE HELG

Liberty has to be conquered with the blade of the machete, it cannot be begged for.
—Antonio Maceo

When Cuban patriots launched the War for Independence against Spain on February 24, 1895, the rebellion succeeded fully only in Oriente, the region with a significant population of African descent and a tradition of struggle against Spanish colonialism.[1] From the insurgency's beginning, blacks and mulattos joined en masse for a variety of reasons, ranging from the need to flee from Spanish repression to the possibility of improving their personal lives, following the leadership of mulatto general Antonio Maceo, or contributing to the fight for a just Cuba. In the process, many of them experienced increased expectations for better positions once independence was achieved, although, not surprisingly, racism did not vanish from social relations among rebels. This chapter explores Afro-Cubans' contribution to the war and some dimensions of their military experiences. It also discusses the concerns their massive participation raised among certain white separatist leaders who did not hesitate to jeopardize Cuba Libre's most decisive victory against Spain—Maceo's invasion of the western part of the island—and to lobby for U.S. intervention in order to limit the revolutionary potential of the war and to keep Afro-Cubans marginalized in postindependence Cuba.

Until 1895, white Cuban's fears of a black takeover similar to the Haitian Revolution hampered the nation's struggle against Spanish colonialism. No doubt Cuba's two first wars for independence, the Ten Years' War (1868–1878) and the Guerra Chiquita (Little War, 1879–1880), had weakened Spain and contributed to the abolition of slavery in 1886. But with about a third of its population being of African descent, Cuban society was pervaded by racial and social prejudice, which held back the independence movement. From his exile in the United States, white intellectual José Martí, head of the Partido Revolucionario Cubano, campaigned to stress the bonds of fraternity built by black, mulatto, and white Cubans in the previous wars and to dismiss the possibility of another Haiti in Cuba.[2] Simultaneously, mulatto journalist Juan Gualberto Gómez spread the same message in Cuba to his Afro-Cuban readers in his newspaper *La Igualdad*.[3]

Yet the specter of the 1804 victory of the Haitian Revolution was still very much alive among separatist leaders. Significantly, in 1895 the supreme military command of the Liberation Army was entrusted to the white Dominican general Máximo Gómez rather than to the Afro-Cuban general Antonio Maceo. In addition, the *Manifiesto de Montecristi* signed by Martí and Máximo Gómez, which officially launched hostilities against Spain, addressed the risk of a race war in Cuba with troubling ambiguity. On the one hand, it denied such a possibility and claimed that the fear of the "black race" was "foolish and never justified in Cuba." On the other hand, it contemplated the very possibility of a race war. It ventured that during the struggle against Spain "a still invisible minority of malcontent freedmen" could turn lazy and arrogant and prematurely aspire "to the social respect they will only gain securely once they have proven their equality in virtues and talents." If "[black] infamous demagogues or greedy souls" instigated such a movement, "the race [of color] itself would extirpate the black menace in Cuba, without the need for raising a single white hand," it prophesied.[4]

In Cuba itself, with the very aim of preventing the mislabeling of the new insurgency as a race war, the leadership in Oriente was divided right from the start between two separatist veterans: the white Bartolomé Masó, a wealthy planter of Catalan origin from Manzanillo, in western and northern Oriente, and the black Guillermón Moncada (who died in early April 1895) in southern and eastern Oriente. Among the chieftains who rose in arms that day, in addition to Masó, some major figures were white, such as Perequito Pérez in Guantánamo and José Miró Argenter in Holguín. But mass support for the rebellion came mostly from the following that Afro-Cuban veteran leaders Guillermón Moncada, Quintín Banderas, Jesús Rabí, and others had among peasants, day laborers, and some city youth of Oriente. This following was largely Afro-Cuban, founded on camaraderie in the previous struggles, family ties, and labor relationships. Lt. Col. Eduardo

Rosell wrote in his diary shortly after he joined the rebels in March 1895: "I understand perfectly that the Spaniards say that this movement is racist, of the race of color."[5] Moreover, it was clear to everyone in Oriente that the real spirit of the rebellion, the uncontested leader of the people rising in arms, was Gen. Antonio Maceo, still in exile in Costa Rica.[6]

Until Maceo, José Martí (who died in May 1895), and Máximo Gómez landed in Oriente, however, there was little coordination in the uprising. Although united by a common will to sever ties with Spain, "each group had rebelled in its respective district, each fraction in its own way, and each *cabecilla* (rebel leader) at the head of his own supporters."[7] Although few *orientales* were able to leave written testimony of their motivation to join the insurgency, their goal was probably not only independence from Spain but also the creation of a new society in which they would fully participate.[8] Blacks rebelled against racism and inequality, landless peasants regardless of race stood up for land, popular *cabecillas* wanted political power, and *orientales* in general hoped to gain control of their region's destiny. The potential for the war to become a social revolution was strong indeed.

After the landing near Baracoa on April 1, 1895, of Antonio and José Maceo, Flor Crombet, Agustín Cebreco, and other exiles, the insurgency entered a new phase. The news that Maceo, the incorruptible *caudillo* of all past independence struggles, had arrived to lead the movement rapidly spread to the cities and the countryside of Oriente. As Maceo's small group proceeded into the interior of the province, veteran chieftains placed themselves under his command, rebel bands united with his group, and new recruits left families and *bohíos* (palm huts) to follow him, often with no arms other than old machetes and no uniforms other than rags and sandals. Country people gave what they had to help the cause, from food to their best horse. Even "whole families desert their homes and place themselves under our command," José Maceo wrote to his wife.[9] From a little over two thousand in late March, the estimated number of insurgents in Oriente reached five thousand one month later, eight thousand by mid-May, and sixteen thousand by the end of August.[10] As the British consul at Santiago later reported, "Had Maceo not effected a landing, the insurrection would never have assumed its present proportions. Should anything, however, happen to him, it would completely disconcert the negro element, which is the powerful one here."[11]

Simultaneously, in neighboring Camagüey, the insurgency was gaining ground, as Máximo Gómez proceeded with a two-hundred-man escort into the province. The social makeup of the *camagüeyano* rebels, however, differed from that of Oriente rebels. At the head of the small movement that took arms in June was the sixty-seven-year-old marquis of Santa Lucía, Salvador Cisneros Betancourt, a white aristocrat veteran of the Ten Years' War, "some young men of distinguished families," and their countrymen, who swelled Gómez's troops.[12] Although there were Afro-Cubans among the two thousand *camagüeyano* insurgents reported in August 1895, the predominance of whites in their ranks and of men of the "better class" in their leadership limited the revolutionary potential of the movement in Camagüey. In addition, throughout the war *camagüeyanos* pitted themselves against *orientales* at the expense of rebel unity.

In the central province of Santa Clara, insurgent bands formed around white and Afro-Cuban *cabecillas* in late April 1895. After the landing of the expedition of Carlos Roloff and Serafín Sánchez, the separatist movement gained strength in the region, totaling about twenty-five hundred by August 1895. Rebels were of very diverse social origin, with a predominance of Afro-Cubans.[13] The movement in Santa Clara comprised *hacendados* as well as *colonos* (cane farmers), day laborers and freedmen as well as some bandits who roamed the mountainous area of Trinidad.[14]

The province of Matanzas rebelled only in late 1895, after a first attempted uprising led by Juan Gualberto Gómez ended in total failure on February 24. In this former stronghold of slavery, the U.S. journalist Grover Flint estimated that "half of the enlisted men . . . were negroes, with here and there a Chinaman," but "a trifling percentage of negroes and mulattoes" were officers. Most chieftains were white peasants of some means, professionals, or planters who sometimes went to the war with their own workers. In fact, the stricter social hierarchy in Matanzas (as compared to Oriente) reflected on the organization of rebel units. In addition, as elsewhere, regionalism was strong, and insurgents preferred to follow local leaders rather than *orientales*. But many, especially among Afro-Cubans, also joined the rebel movement because of Juan Gualberto Gómez's previous leadership.[15]

In the provinces of Havana and Pinar del Río, where people had supported Spain rather than independence during the Ten Years' War, the rebellion was put down right at its beginning in February 1895. It revived only in early 1896 after the troops led by Maceo and Gómez crossed the Spanish Júcaro-Morón trench and completed the invasion of the western part of the island. In Pinar del Río, with a population of Spanish and white Cubans in the majority, peasants discovered with surprise that Maceo and his men were not the "head cutters" they expected but were polite and merciful.

They received them with white flags and sometimes with full support. The inhabitants of the province of Havana, busily cultivating and trading in spite of the war, showed less hospitality at the sight of the invaders. To many of them, with exceptions that included wealthy young *habaneros*, the *orientales* hardly distinguished themselves from bandits.[16]

In general, the war against Spain brought men of completely different social backgrounds together. Blacks and whites, poor and rich joined forces to free Cuba. As the American continental armies that fought for independence from Spain in the 1810s, Cuba's Liberation Army was an integrated body in the sense that there were no distinct black or white battalions. Some claimed that it was color-blind. According to Bernabé Boza, Máximo Gómez's white chief of staff, "Here nobody cares about the color of a man, but about his talents and his self-respect."[17] The Afro-Cuban general Agustín Cebreco was more circumspect: "Here we are putting the principles of democracy into practice, because the hazards of war purify and unify, and will enrich our people who despite everything tend to the better."[18]

Afro-Cubans participated en masse in the struggle against Spain. That many among them were willing to fight and die for the freedom of Cuba indicates the high hopes they placed in the revolution. Afro-Cuban *mambises* (fighters of the Liberation Army) cherished dreams of a better place for themselves in independent Cuba, based partially on their war experience. As one white army surgeon noted, "Of course, these deluded men imagined a state of things founded on social equality, on the supremacy of military men, of the *guapos* [braggarts], without the distinctions that forcibly impose themselves in any society."[19] Others were less hopeful and sensed that racism was deeply rooted in Cuban society. Among them was Col. Enrique Fournier, an educated *orientale* of French and African descent, who reportedly predicted to his Afro-Cuban comrades: "The race of color, which is the nerve of this war, is going to sacrifice itself so that white Cubans continue to exploit their superiority [over blacks]."[20]

Indeed, the war offered new opportunities to Afro-Cubans on which they built expectations. Above all, there were unquestionably times of true fraternity in the army. One of them was in November 1895, when Antonio Maceo crossed the Spanish trench at Morón with seventeen hundred cavalry, seven hundred infantry, and members of the provisional government and was welcomed by Gómez and all his forces. "We merged together, *orientales*, *centrales*, and *occidentales*, blacks and whites," exulted Boza.[21] Some white leaders openly fought racism in the army. They spoke in favor of Afro-Cuban commanders when these were discriminated against. They stood up in defense of Antonio and José Maceo when the two were accused of black racism. This was clearly the position of Lt. Col. Eduardo Rosell and Fermín Valdés Domínguez (delegate to Cuba Libre's Constituent Assembly and vice-secretary of Foreign Relations in 1895), who consistently sided with José Maceo and transferred racist white military men to civil posts to avoid problems with the troops.[22] Such support coming from whites brought to several Afro-Cubans hopes of justice for the future.

On a more mundane level, Afro-Cubans had some good times in the war. A real meal with barbecued meat and starchy food, a gulp of rum, a cup of coffee, or a cigar were all sources of joy. Sometimes dances were organized with the participation of women of the region. Cockfights were held with roosters found or stolen along the way. These moments of shared fun allowed people to imagine a simple but fraternal life when the war was over.[23]

Afro-Cubans under the command of mulatto or black *cabecillas*, especially Antonio Maceo, experienced the pride of serving under famous leaders who were of African descent and lower-class origin like themselves. To them "[Antonio] Maceo was an idol," but not an inaccessible one. They could identify with him and emulate him without having to question their heritage. Moreover, although hierarchy was strict, there was a climate of camaraderie in Maceo's units. Most positions were based on courage, intelligence, and merit, and everyone felt that he had a chance to be upgraded— and downgraded—because Antonio Maceo did not keep in high positions those he called "figureheads." Officers fought alongside their men and each had been wounded several times. In fact, during the battles, all faced the enemy in the same condition. In special circumstances, hierarchies vanished: Antonio Maceo jumped off his horse and acted like a simple soldier.[24] No doubt such experiences affected soldiers and made some of them believe that class and race distinctions would be banned in the new Cuba for which they were fighting.

Among Afro-Cuban soldiers, the positions with the highest prestige were in the personal escort of the Maceo brothers. Several rebels risked their lives to join the divisions headed by the Maceos and to be noticed by them. The first step was often to secure a gun, and men did not hesitate to fight unarmed against Spanish soldiers in order to seize one of their Mausers. These Afro-Cubans then continuously participated in battles until they acquired a reputation of bravery, strength, and intelligence. The fifty or so men in Antonio Maceo's escort continued to endeavor to become his chief of guard.[25] In addition, few in the escort lived long because they were always on the battle front line with Maceo. From April 1895 to October 1896, a succession of five chiefs of his guard died in combat. The last one, Julio Morales, was a rough old black man with a white beard who had been on Maceo's side since 1868 and had finally fulfilled his life dream: "to be the chief of the escort of his intrepid and beloved caudillo."[26]

The poor and little-educated Afro-Cubans who reached officer rank acquired a new self-esteem. They sensed that they were valued for their merits and talents, something unknown to most of them. If Cuba Libre rewarded them rightfully, they doubtless thought, they would be treated similarly after independence. Although other Afro-Cubans were less dedicated to the struggle against Spain, they too were optimistic for their future. According to Esteban Montejo, the former runaway slave recorded by writer Miguel Barnet in the early 1960s, many believed the war was a "fair to collect honors" but they were not ready to fight; some were attracted by the prospect of pay. A number of rebels in fact ignored the aims of the insurgency. "One got involved because it just happened," Montejo recalled. "Myself I did not know much of the future. The only thing I said was 'Cuba Libre!'"[27] For their part, freedmen and African-born reportedly partook in order to eliminate Spanish domination and the kind of life that was imposed upon them: "No one wanted to see oneself in the stocks again, or eating salt meat, or cutting cane at dawn. So they went to the war," Montejo remembered.[28] Yet, although motivations were sometimes selfish, most Afro-Cuban rebels shared the sense that they were united in a struggle that would lead to better conditions for all.

To join the Liberation Army and become a soldier often meant to have a gun—the ultimate symbol of power. This partly explains why numerous rebels did not hesitate to put their lives in peril to grab a weapon from a Spanish soldier. According to Boza, they then developed "a kind of indescribable love for their arms."[29] Few, in fact, would surrender their guns after the armistice, and many kept them forever, as evidence of their commitment to the republic.

To a certain extent, even those in rags and armed only with machetes, even those in the *impedimenta* (the men, women, and children accompanying the Liberation Army) chose their side in the struggle. By following the rebels, they signified that they refused continuing repression under Spanish rule and wanted their condition to change. Among the men were many freedmen accustomed to work on sugar plantations and with little experience of the world beyond the *central*. While most were "moved by the only hope to acquire a gun in order to take an active part in the campaign,"[30] some reportedly thought that to join the Liberation Army meant "to do what one wants."[31]

In many aspects the war gave blacks a new pride in themselves and their African origin. Traditional Afro-Cuban skills gained some respectability in the ranks of Cuba Libre. Musicians and storytellers provided entertainment. Previously in peacetime, most people had turned to Afro-Cuban healers for medical assistance because scientific medicine hardly existed in rural Cuba. During the war, the services of traditional healers became all the more indispensable. The army lacked doctors, and units had their self-appointed healers, mostly charismatic Afro-Cubans who brought comfort, if not recovery, to the wounded. Several women, in particular, became famous even among officers. Such was La Rosa, of Camagüey, an "independent, masterful negress, profoundly confident in her own methods," who had a wide knowledge of medicinal plants that cured fevers, wounds, and illnesses.[32] Other women, contacted by a relative, managed to get to the *manigua* (the insurgent-held territories) to take care of their recovering husbands, sons, or nephews.[33]

Like scientific medicine, the Catholic Church had little presence in rural Cuba, especially in Oriente where it was perceived as an instrument of Spanish domination and was resisted. People filled their religious needs in their own ways, often founded on beliefs of African origin. Amulets provided by leaders of Afro-Cuban cults were popular among rebels, a practice that surprised more than one educated white insurgent who came to discover the reality of lower-class Cuba in the *manigua*.[34] In the upper strata of Cuba Libre, however, many rebels were Freemasons: Antonio and José Maceo, José Martí, Máximo Gómez, and Bartolomé Masó, to name only a few. While in exile in the United States, some had been initiated as Odd Fellows; others had joined Cuban lodges in Florida and New York. Most belonged to the Grand Orient of Cuba and the Antilles, an irregular masonry that professed independence and racial equality. Although Spain banned masonic activities in Cuba in June 1895, masonry continued to attract members in the battlefields. More lodges were created and many insurgent officers were initiated, making the Grand Orient of Cuba and the Antilles an institution of more political influence at the armistice than the Catholic Church.[35]

The war provided many blacks with a new pride, not only in their traditions but also in their skin color. The Maceos became the symbols of the intelligence and strength of the *raza de color*, with whom all could identify. More trivially, to be black also meant to be imperceptible at night, a marvelous military artifice that made many Afro-Cuban soldiers famous throughout Cuba. Commanders Agustín Cebreco and Vicente García, in particular, notoriously used their blackness and that of their men, often choosing to fight at night. They disrobed from the waist up so they were almost invisible to the Spaniards but could distinguish themselves from the enemy.[36]

Some old former slaves went through a sort of regeneration during the insurgency. Elder African-born who followed their sons or nephews in the war found a new dimension to duties that they had been fulfilling as slaves. They volunteered to do essential but commonplace tasks such as washing clothes, cleaning arms, or doing night watches. They became most resourceful cooks in the scarcity of the *manigua*.[37] Included in the *impedimenta*, they participated in a process that transformed them into full Cuban citizens.

Although the war produced the dissolution of many families, a few rebels managed to maintain ties with their loved ones through messengers and new recruits who brought letters and tobacco to the *manigua*.[38] Other men and women succeeded in creating new bonds during the insurgency. With the exception of the invading army of Antonio Maceo, most units included numerous women in the *impedimenta*, who sometimes became companions of soldiers. Banderas's division, for example, included Afro-Cuban women "who squatted about, doing the cooking for their husbands and their particular friends."[39] There were also refugee camps of women and children in the liberated territories. When rebel troops camped out in their vicinity, people got together, and men and women met.[40]

Although only a handful of women took part in combat, those who went with the rebels shared their lives, contributed to the maintenance of the troops, and broadened their life experience; a few probably set new goals for their future.[41] Some women lived with commanding officers. This was notoriously the case with Quintín Banderas, who since 1897 lived "an immoral life" with several women in the mountains of Trinidad. Less publicized were the cases of women living with officers of "the better classes," such as José María (Mayía) Rodríguez and Enrique Loynaz del Castillo.[42] José Maceo also reportedly was in the war "with his women, two or three *mulaticas* that he calls his nieces."[43] Agripina Barroso Lazo, a fourteen-year-old *orientale* nicknamed "La Negra," followed the general long enough to give birth to his son.[44]

The portion of Cuba under rebel control (Oriente, Camagüey, and part of Santa Clara, with the exception of the large cities) was divided into districts and administered by prefects appointed by the provisional government. Although white prefects prevailed, some were Afro-Cubans. According to

Grover Flint, Oriente had schools to which parents were required to send children. Revolutionary newspapers were printed in presses hidden in the forest. Also located in inaccessible places, workshops kept busy rebels who were unfit for the army. Some men repaired arms and machetes; others made shoes, saddles, belts, and ammunition pouches; still others made clothes and straw hats.[45] People in Cuba Libre also took care of concealed herds of cows, horses, and mules, as well as gardens planted with vegetables and starchy roots. Although far from a paradise, the freed territories fulfilled many basic needs of the population. On this sharing basis, Afro-Cubans, poor, and landless peasants envisioned a better life after independence than the one they had had under Spanish rule.

In sum, participation in the war enabled many blacks in particular to build expectations regarding their future based on new notions of justice and equality. Such change happened despite the fact that, not surprisingly, the Liberation Army did not eliminate deeply rooted race and class differences. As in most armies of the time, discipline was harsh and physical punishment was frequent. Troops were often taught with the flat of the machete, especially during marches. A throwback to slavery, wooden stocks served to punish disobedient soldiers.[46] Military justice was merciless toward traitors, robbers, and rapists: they were always hanged, even if they were officers—in order to secure popular support and internal discipline but also to counter Spanish accusations that rebels were black rapists and bandits.[47]

In addition, racial equality in the Liberation Army was hampered by the reproduction of paternalist work relations in military life. Officers had assistants, very often black or mulatto teenagers, who served simultaneously as scouts, hut-builders, food providers, cooks, messengers, and porters. Domingo Gómez, who served the future dictator Gerardo Machado, was called "el negro de Gerardito."[48] Eduardo Rosell, who owned an *ingenio* in Pinar del Río, had at his service the "*negrito* Alfonso," a childhood playmate and family domestic.[49]

Race and class differences were sustained by increasing emphasis on education rather than military performance in the appointment of new officers after 1895. This made promotion all the more difficult for Afro-Cubans and country people, who had had little access to schooling. As one white commander observed, "While those who could not read and write became only exceptionally more than simple soldiers, those who had instruction, from the moment of their entry in the Army of the Revolution, were singled out with the rank of lieutenant."[50] Medical doctors, engineers, and lawyers were assigned to nonfighting units, such as the sanitary and the judiciary corps. All were white, except a handful of Afro-Cubans such as Martín Morúa Delgado, who joined the rebellion only in June 1898 to become "lieutenant without having held the machete . . . and [to spend] his life in the camp's archives."[51] The few illiterates who gained promotion did so either because of their outstanding contribution to the war or because their example boosted the morale of the troops.[52]

Such a man was Quintín Banderas. Born a free black in 1834, Banderas was a mason in El Cobre (Oriente) when he left his family in December 1868 to join the rebels in the Ten Years' War. Like many Afro-Cuban *orientales*, his aim had been to free not only Cuba from Spain but also blacks from slavery. In 1878 Lieutenant Colonel Banderas had been among those who rejected the Pact of Zanjón ending the Ten Years' War and launched the Guerra Chiquita. In 1880 he and his companions had been arrested and deported to a Spanish penitentiary off the coast of Africa for six years. Back in Cuba, he had resumed underground revolutionary activities. Arrested again in 1893, he was imprisoned for eight months in Santiago de Cuba. At the outbreak of the war in 1895, Banderas was in command of the one-thousand-man infantry of mostly Afro-Cuban *orientales* who undertook the invasion of the west with Maceo. He spent the second part of the war in the region of Trinidad with the task of diverting, through sabotage and fighting, the attention of the Spanish army.[53] Based on his military achievements and an entire life dedicated to Cuba's independence, Banderas was promoted division general.

The case of Banderas was unique. Foreign journalists noted the racial imbalance in the army between troops, among whom Afro-Cubans were overrepresented, and officers, among whom whites predominated.[54] Most Afro-Cuban *mambises* received few rewards for their courage. Thus the automatic promotion of men with some education concerned them. "Chigüí," the mulatto scout and servant of a white officer, for example, reportedly complained to his superior that he always had to take risks and walk point on reconnaissance missions while "for the city dandies it was enough to join the war in order to immediately become colonel and lieutenant colonel."[55]

Regardless of the number of stripes they wore, Afro-Cuban generals and officers faced racism in their relations with civilians throughout the war. Banderas, for example, was refused a dance in Holguín by a white young woman solely because he was black. Only the tactful intervention of Antonio Maceo prevented him from creating a public disturbance. Such incidents were not isolated and showed that prejudice still ran high in some sectors of Cuba Libre society.[56] Afro-Cuban officers who were strong leaders were ridiculed or distrusted for allegedly being arrogant, ambitious, and racist. This was especially true of Antonio and José Maceo, against whom accusations of dictatorial or racist ambitions multiplied in proportion to their military successes.[57]

Conversely, other Afro-Cuban leaders were praised for their modesty. This was the case with generals Jesús Rabí and Pedro Díaz Molina. Rabí, the chief of one of two divisions in Oriente in 1896, was reputed to be highly professional, nonauthoritarian, and kind to his men.[58] Díaz became the head of the army in Pinar del Río in 1897, after the death of Antonio Maceo and the capture of his successor, Juan Rius Rivera, by the Spanish. An Afro-Cuban from Santa Clara and a veteran of the two previous wars for independence, Díaz returned from exile in New York in the early 1890s to be a sugar workers' contractor and a *colono* near Remedios; he joined the insurrection with a small group of rebels recruited in his area. A competent general, he was held up by whites as an example of the "good black" who did not seek prestige and popularity.[59]

Accusations of black racism forced Antonio and José Maceo to appoint whites to positions of command in the territories under their control. José Miró Argenter, Antonio Maceo's chief of staff, recalled that when Maceo completed the western invasion with overwhelmingly black troops in early 1896, he chose to appoint the white Rius Rivera rather than Pedro Díaz as commander of Pinar del Río in order "to silence the venomous tongues and to undo the prejudices, suspicions, mistrusts, and false slanders of the Caucasian group."[60] When Lino D'Ou and two other Afro-Cubans asked José Maceo to include in his staff a fourth nonwhite officer who had a broad cultural background and spoke English, Maceo refused on the basis that it would increase accusations of racism against him: "I know the value of [the candidate], but here, on my side, I do not want anymore of color than those who are now. You should know the war from the inside," he reportedly told them.[61]

Afro-Cuban officers who headed mostly black troops confronted discrimination. Although the existence of almost all-black units was the natural product of the mode of recruitment in the Liberation Army, through which local *cabecillas* raised troops among parents, dependents, friends, and neighbors, it nevertheless caused concern among the white leadership.[62] Predictably enough, therefore, the Liberation Army did not fully eliminate the double standard that ruled the lives of whites and blacks in colonial Cuba. Afro-Cubans needed to accomplish more than whites to be rewarded.

White commanders were praised for their ambition and popularity, but black commanders with the same qualities were called racist and dictatorial. Afro-Cuban leaders were under special white scrutiny that reinforced continuing prejudice and fear of a black takeover reminiscent of the Haitian Revolution. Yet continuing racism coexisted with limited Afro-Cuban upward mobility in the Liberation Army. This contradiction indicated a real potential for thorough social change on which many Afro-Cubans built hope of a fair share in the future Cuban republic.

At the same time, however, some white Cubans used racism as a means of limiting the revolutionary potential of the movement for independence. Especially active among them were some nonfighting sectors of Cuba Libre that were united around the president of the provisional government; the marquis of Santa Lucía, Salvador Cisneros Betancourt; and the all-white leadership of the separatists in the United States. At stake was the nature of the new Cuban society. Schematically, on one side the rebels in the troops and the military commanders fought for the destruction of the colonial order with its strict racial and social hierarchy. When they burned the countryside, they targeted the epitome of colonial exploitation: the sugar industry. Their war was one without concessions until Spain's full defeat. On the other side, both the provisional government and separatists in the United States had a more political agenda: the end of Spanish rule without a complete reversal of the socioeconomic order.[63] The struggle between the two projects of society expressed itself primarily in rivalries between the civil and the military powers.

Contradictions within Cuba Libre were already visible in the contrast between the lifestyle of the Liberation Army and that of the provisional government. Little discipline existed in Cisneros's encampment. "There were a number of lusty young aides with the Government, occupying positions one would expect to find filled only by rheumatic veterans," Flint reported.[64] Valdés Domínguez also had few kind words for "this cave full of vipers" consisting of young, vain men who spent their time criticizing friends and comrades and had no respect for "the old soldier" or "the good patriot who has sacrificed everything in the name of honor."[65]

In fact, the question of the civil versus the military dated back to the meeting of Maceo, Máximo Gómez, and Martí at La Mejorana, near Santiago de Cuba, in early May 1895. Maceo, looking back at his experience, insisted that the failure of the Ten Years' War and the Pact of Zanjón were due to the supremacy of the civil power; he argued the need for a strong military *junta* until independence had been won from Spain. Martí, on the contrary, looked at the future of independent Cuba and at ways to avoid the establishment of a military dictatorship; with the support of Gómez, he argued in favor of civil control over the military and the election of a civil government during the war. The three leaders had been unable to reach an agreement.[66]

After Martí's death in a skirmish in mid-May 1895, Maceo's military successes and wide popularity in Oriente began to raise suspicion among other leaders that he planned to promote himself as a dictator. Personal jealousies also developed against him and his brother José, because "it is undeniable that [the troops] adore the Maceos."[67] Especially opposed to them was Bartolomé Masó, chief of northwestern Oriente, who took increasing offense at his rivals' influence in the army and over the *oriental* population.[68]

Open confrontation between the separatist leaders erupted at the meeting of the delegates to the Constituent Assembly in Jimaguayú in September 1895. The issue of civil versus military predominance resurfaced. Moreover, before the meeting, Masó, Cisneros, and others renewed accusations that Antonio Maceo had ambitions to become the military and political dictator of the revolution. They claimed that Maceo had advanced himself to chief of the army in Oriente (a function he had already assumed in 1878 after most separatist generals had subscribed to the Pact of Zanjón). Although a majority of delegates for Oriente were white and acted independently of Maceo, Masó and Cisneros accused them of serving the racist and regionalist interests of the Afro-Cuban leader.[69]

Clearly, the onslaught against Antonio Maceo was a personal feud, but it also had a social and racial basis. Coming from such men as Cisneros and Masó—who could claim nobility, "pure" Spanish origin, wealth, and land—it aimed at asserting that part of the old order would be maintained after independence, with Afro-Cubans and whites of popular origin being excluded from power. By attacking Maceo, Cisneros and Masó targeted all who had rebelled against Spain to build up a society in which poor and blacks would have their rightful share. The onslaught also had a regional significance. It showed that although less numerous and slower to rise in arms, the insurgents of the whiter northwest Oriente and Camagüey refused to let the revolution be led by predominantly black southern *orientales*.

Maceo's response to the attacks by Cisneros was unequivocal. He had never sought favors, only positions based on his own merits, he disdainfully wrote to the marquis. Moreover, he knew that his darker skin and humble origins would not be overlooked in the light of his achievements: "From the beginning the humbleness of my birth prevented me from placing myself at the level of others who were born [with the right] to be leaders of the revolution. Perhaps this explains why you feel entitled to suppose that I will be flattered by what you say will be my share in the [power] distribution."[70] The provisional government installed by the Constituent Assembly of Jimaguayú further showed that prejudice had not disappeared from Cuba Libre. Cisneros was elected president of the republic, Bartolomé Masó, vice president. Tomás Estrada Palma became delegate plenipotenciary and foreign representative in the United States. The provisional government's four secretaries were also white, like all the vice-secretaries. Only three out of eleven were from south Oriente.[71] The Dominican Máximo Gómez was elected general-in-chief of the army. The position of lieutenant-general, or second in command, was created for Antonio Maceo under the pretext that it was inappropriate to have a man of color in a higher position "because of the judgment of those abroad."[72]

The provisional government reorganized the army to keep Maceo and the southern *orientales* in check. The province of Oriente continued to be divided into two military corps, one under Maceo, the other under Masó. There were three additional divisions, Camagüey, Santa Clara, and Matanzas, all under the command of white officers.[73] The civilians hastily demanded allegiance from the military. Chieftains and officers had to incorporate their forces into the restructured Liberation Army within two months. All new promotions in the five army corps had to be approved by the government.

As already mentioned, new rules ensured preferential positions to men with education. In fall of 1895 the provisional government decided that students joining the insurgency were automatically promoted to places above those of soldiers. Two years of secondary schooling in a *colegio* led to an appointment of corporal, the title of *bachillerato* (secondary school diploma) to an appointment of second lieutenant, and a university title to an appointment at least of captain. Higher rank also meant higher pay after independence: 30 pesos per month for a soldier, 40 for a corporal, 130 for a captain, and up to 500 for a general.[74] Because Afro-Cubans had been traditionally excluded from secondary and higher education, the measure favored urban whites. Such "privilege" annoyed Antonio Maceo, who worried that "the preference granted to some while others with less instruction but more merits and military talents to ascend in the career are disregarded" would cause "general discontent." He recommended that Gómez follow the new rules "with discretion" to respect the "acquired rights" of the majority in the Liberation Army.[75] Although bravery and military achievements were still rewarded with promotion in combat units, the new demand for education intensified the "whitening" process of Cuba Libre's officer corps.[76]

It was in this difficult context of social change in the officer corps and tensions with the civil power that Antonio Maceo undertook the most successful campaign of the war: the invasion of western Cuba. About seventeen hundred men left Baraguá in Oriente on October 22, 1895. Most were cavalrymen, followed by infantrymen led by Quintín Banderas. Exactly three months later, on January 22, 1896, they reached Mantua in Pinar del Río, at the other end of the island. Simultaneously, the forces under Gómez that accompanied Maceo's column from Santa Clara to Havana had established a stronghold in the province of Havana.[77] The western invasion represented a double victory. First, it was a military success. Although Maceo and his troops dramatically lacked arms and ammunition and proceeded into regions (mostly in open country) they knew little about, they won over Spanish forces that were well armed and tenfold more numerous. Second, it was a political achievement. The invading column carried the revolution to a portion of the island where support for Spain was strong. At the same time, it broke the localism of *orientales* who had not envisioned their struggle beyond the limit of their home area. As a result, in January 1896 the independence struggle had acquired a truly national dimension.[78]

Instead of rejoicing at such success, however, the provisional government saw in the western invasion a threat to their political aims and further evidence of Antonio Maceo's supposed dictatorial plan. In a letter to Estrada Palma, Cisneros expressed his distrust of the general "who considers himself as the unique chief, not only of Oriente but perhaps of all Cuba. Oh human miseries and ambitions!"[79] He thus attempted to limit the impact of the invasion by various means—just when in February 1896 Spain appointed the ruthless Gen. Valeriano Weyler as the new governor general of Cuba.

In the beginning, the provisional government hampered the actions of the military by getting increasingly involved in army affairs, to the great dissatisfaction of Antonio Maceo and Máximo Gómez. The civilian leaders opposed or imposed new officers, appointments, and strategies. They disregarded demands for arms and reinforcements made by the two generals fighting the bulk of the Spanish troops in western and central Cuba. They ignored Maceo's conviction that, with supplies and fresh troops from the east, the Liberation Army could soon beat the Spaniards. On the contrary, Cisneros repeatedly countered the general-in-chief's orders for eastern reinforcements and kept men and arms in Oriente and Camagüey. The provisional government justified this position with obscure reasons of "high politics" that aimed, in fact, at limiting the power of the military and keeping Maceo's troops isolated in Pinar del Río.[80] As a result, it jeopardized the most decisive insurgent victory over Spain. As Maceo bitterly noted, "with the Council of Government . . . will rest, before history, the responsibility for this event that has prevented us from directing our triumphs to a Cuban Ayacucho."[81]

Simultaneously, the provisional government encouraged regionalism and racism within the independence movement. Cisneros made no secret of his racist and classist views. To Flint, who asked him if he feared a race war after independence, Cisneros answered: "Our negroes are far superior to the colored race of the United States. They are naturally peaceful and orderly, and they desire to be white, like the whites."[82]

Cisneros attempted to remove other prestigious Afro-Cuban field officers from positions of command. Since December 1895, he had plotted to depose the recently appointed division generals in Oriente, José Maceo and Jesús Rabí, because "these chiefs were not the legitimate ones for such high positions." He urged Estrada Palma to recall from exile Calixto García and other white veteran officers "of good condition" to replace them.[83] In March 1896 leaders from Camagüey renewed attacks against *orientales*, especially Antonio and José Maceo, for allegedly being black racists. Cisneros repeated such denigrations and hinted that the Maceo brothers planned to control the revolution, with Antonio in the west and José in the east. "It is necessary to cut this evil from the root with an astute and expert hand, to cut this evil in its origin and to cut it from its root . . . here [in Oriente] Valdés Domínguez united to [José] Maceo and two or three others could form their schism, but I hope to cut it at its source," Cisneros wrote to a penfriend.[84]

On the pretext of bringing order to Oriente, Cisneros bypassed Máximo Gómez's authority in the spring of 1896 and continuously sought to depose José Maceo from the command of Oriente. He eventually managed to install Calixto García in the position, although the latter had just joined the rebellion from exile (almost a year after the Maceos) and had few men behind him. In June José Maceo resigned, claiming that for him "it was a question of dignity . . . not to accept any of these generals as [his] superiors, because they did not have the merits justifying the position."[85] Calixto García further humiliated him by refusing to allot new guns and ammunition to his already poorly armed unit.[86] In this very tense atmosphere, a disillusioned José Maceo died in combat against Spanish soldiers, on July

5, 1896. Understandably, the rumor spread among his troops that he had been assassinated by García's men. The death of José Maceo, however, did not satisfy García. Not accepted as the undisputed leader of Oriente as he had expected, he accused all *orientale* forces of black racism and charged José Maceo's lieutenants with corruption, apparently to disarm the southeastern troops in favor of his contingency in Holguín. As one officer opined, García's "hatred for the Maceos led him to hate all men of their race." The officer feared that such an attitude could jeopardize not only García's leadership in Oriente but the revolution as a whole.[87]

For their part, Cuban representatives in the United States also did not view the western invasion and the destruction of the sugar industry favorably. They increasingly tried to halt a process that was all too revolutionary in their eyes. Estrada Palma showed clear signs of being more interested in U.S. recognition of the Cuban belligerency than in providing the rebels in Cuba with arms and ammunition. He played down the participation of blacks in the insurgency and used the "whitening" of the leadership of Cuba Libre as an argument in favor of U.S. recognition. He neglected to send armaments to the invading army in the west, although Maceo had asked for "30,000 rifles and 1,000,000 shots" from abroad and reinforcement from the east "to finish up the war."[88]

Discontent among military leaders against Estrada Palma increased. Some began to suspect that he favored U.S. annexation of Cuba.[89] Maceo in particular opposed the delegate's insistence on obtaining U.S. recognition of the insurgency. He reacted angrily to the fact that arms and ammunition were not sent to his forces in the west but to Oriente and Camagüey where most commanding officers did little to distract the Spanish general Valeriano Weyler from his offensive against the invading army. Only in September 1896 did an expedition, led by Rius Rivera, finally bring arms to Maceo's units.[90]

By November 1896 distrust between the military and the civil power had reached a climax. Máximo Gómez planned a coup to exclude Cisneros as president of the government. He ordered Maceo to cross the western trench guarded by the Spanish and to back him in Santa Clara. As a result, Antonio Maceo was killed near Havana on December 7, 1896.[91]

Antonio Maceo's death was devastating to the morale of the Liberation Army. "Sadness was in everyone, but even more pronounced, naturally, in the people of color," noted Rosell in his diary.[92] Another *mambí* recalled that he had never witnessed such deep sorrow in strong men used to danger and death. When the news reached Gómez's camp, "the entire staff . . . hats in their hands, silent and their eyes fixed on [the general-in-chief] seemed possessed by a religious emotion." Even the tough Gómez cried.[93] Conversely, the news was received with joy in Madrid and in the Spanish ranks. The general feeling was that Maceo was a man of unique talents and popularity in Cuba equaled by no other rebel leader. With his death, Spaniards thought, Afro-Cubans would lose their readiness to fight, and white Cubans would predominate in the insurgency, opening the way for conciliation.[94]

No doubt the killing of Maceo marked a turning point in the war. For many, especially among Afro-Cubans, Maceo embodied the revolution itself: continuous struggle until the victory, refusal to compromise, combined with humanitarianism. He had acquired a supranatural prestige among the rank and file for the numerous life-threatening wounds that he had survived. He had also become the standard-bearer of Afro-Cuban hopes for full participation after independence. With him dead, every soldier felt more vulnerable, and every Afro-Cuban less secure of a better future. The shock was so great that the Liberation Army was paralyzed for several days.[95]

The loss of Maceo gave a free hand to the civil faction and the delegates in the United States. The Dominican-born Máximo Gómez could not face them alone and developed doubts about the meaning of his struggle for the Cubans. Many of his generals had lost stamina and entered a dissolute life.[96] Meanwhile, Weyler progressively reconquered most of the western provinces, but he appeared unable to restore peace on the island despite systematic repression. Most of Santa Clara, Camagüey, and Oriente remained under separatist control. The Liberation Army, poorly armed and facing a Spanish army several times its size, could not achieve any major military breakthrough and focused mostly on destroying sugar plantations. Powerful sectors of the Partido Revolucionario Cubano, rather than encouraging the war, increasingly sought a negotiated solution with the participation of the United States.[97]

The civil branch of Cuba Libre continued to show attachment to colonial hierarchies. The new assembly of representatives elected in October 1897 had not a single Afro-Cuban member, and was composed of "men of refinement," many who were graduates from U.S. colleges. The new provisional government was all white as well, with Bartolomé Masó as president, replacing Cisneros. Máximo Gómez was reelected general-in-chief. Antonio Maceo's position of lieutenant general went to Calixto García.[98] Tomás Estrada Palma remained delegate plenipotentiary in the United States and now secretly maneuvered for U.S. annexation.[99] He assured the U.S. government that should it intervene in the war, it could count on the collaboration and obedience of the Liberation Army. In March 1898 the provisional government confirmed such assurance.[100]

Like the marquis of Santa Lucía one year earlier, Masó portrayed Afro-Cubans as obedient and faithful to whites. He had no progressive views on the destiny of blacks in independent Cuba.

> Our negroes . . . are mostly uneducated laborers, quite unfitted [sic] for holding positions. They will have the citizen rights, as given in the United States, and with sufficient employment will give no trouble. The population of Cuba is composed of one third colored, either mulatto or negro. Yet some gravely predict Cuba's future as a second Hayti [sic] or Liberia—a negro republic. This idea is manifestly absurd. Cuba is much under-populated, and one of our first measures will be to induce a restricted immigration of those likely to assist in developing our immense resources. Our negroes will work as before in the cane-fields, and I see no reason to anticipate trouble from them. We have no colored officials in this government, and very few of our officers are black, though the slaves we freed by the last war are fighting faithfully in this.[101]

Masó did not sense that many Afro-Cubans had joined the revolution to ensure a better future for themselves. In fact, he envisioned them only as sugar workers, as in slavery. In addition, he announced one of the most important policies designed by the first independent government of Cuba to reduce the proportion of blacks in the island's population: subsidized white immigration. Because the position of presidents Cisneros and Masó on the "black problem" paralleled their attitude toward the Maceos, it cannot be attributed to a need to reassure a foreign audience. In reality, it indicated that prejudice still ran high in some white separatist sectors that opposed social revolution.

When the *Maine* exploded in Havana harbor on February 15, 1898, the intervention of the United States in the war was sealed, although no evidence implied Spanish involvement in the explosion. Champions of U.S. expansion in the hemisphere within the McKinley administration had found the opportunity to carry out their program.[102] Few Afro-Cubans in the *manigua* understood the full impact of the event. They had spent the last years fighting and struggling to survive and to make their dreams come true. Only when the first U.S. troops landed on Cuban soil in June did some realize that the revolution was over.[103]

For most Afro-Cuban insurgents, the experience of the War for Independence had a long-lasting effect. They had joined the Liberation Army to signify their rejection of a colonial past in which they had been slaves and were discriminated against. The war had allowed them to show their force. It had also permitted some of them to assert their vision of a new Cuba in which they would be equal citizens and have their rightful share in all levels and spheres of power. Life in the *manigua* had taken them beyond the limits of their region and had broadened their horizons. It had increased the range of their experience and given them new skills and knowledge. While most had remained in the subordinate position of soldiers, a few had enjoyed influence and admiration. In an army that was somewhat unconventional, in which individual initiative and resourcefulness were praised, they had gained greater control of their destiny and new self-respect. For many, "independence" meant not only Cuba's independence from Spain but their own independence as well. They would be free to defend their rights in the new society toward the creation of which they had so powerfully contributed. In reality, however, a new, more complex struggle lay ahead: that for equal rights and opportunities for blacks in an independent Cuba.[104]

Notes

Abbreviations

ANC, DR: Archivo Nacional de Cuba (La Habana), Fondo Donativos y Remisiones.
PRO, FO: Public Record Office (London), Foreign Office Papers.

Editors' note: We are grateful to the University of North Carolina Press for permission to reprint this article, which was originally published as chapter 2 of Aline Helg, *Our Rightful Share: The Afro-Cuban Struggle for Equality, 1886–1912* (Chapel Hill: University of North Carolina Press, 1995).

1. On the Cuban War for Independence of 1895–98, see Dirección política de las F.A.R., ed., *Historia de Cuba*, 334–513; Pérez, *Cuba between Empires*, 39–227; Thomas, *Cuba*, 310–414; Ferrer, *Insurgent Cuba*, 141–94.

2. See particularly Martí, "Discurso en el Liceo cubano," Tampa (1891), in Martí, *Obras completas*, vol. 4, 269–79; Martí, "Mi raza" (1893), in *Obras completas*, vol. 2, 298–300; and Martí, "Los cubanos de Jamaica y los revolucionarios de Haití" (1894), in *Obras completas*, vol. 3, 103–6.

3. *La Igualdad*, November 6, 1894.

4. Martí and Gómez, "Manifiesto de Montecristi," in Martí, *Obras completas*, vol. 4, 91–101.

5. Rosell y Malpica, *Diario*, vol. 2, 19.

6. J. W. Ramsden to Earl of Kimberley, Santiago de Cuba, February 28, 1895, PRO, FO 72/1991.

7. Miró Argenter, *Cuba*, 17.

8. Few Afro-Cuban *orientales* have left written testimony of their participation in the War for Independence: see Maceo, *Ideología política*. On José Maceo, see Padrón Valdés, *El general José*. Some white participants have reconstructed the voices of Afro-Cuban *orientales* in their war reminiscences, notably Miró, *Cuba*; Valdés Domínguez, *Diario de un soldado*; Rosell, *Diario*; and Arbelo, *Recuerdos de la última guerra*.

9. José Maceo to Elena González Núñez, July 1895, quoted in Padrón, *El general José*, 99.

10. Ramsden to Earl of Kimberley, April 6, 1895, PRO, FO 72/1991; idem, May 25, 1895, PRO, FO 72/1991; Woodward, *"El Diablo Americano,"* 51; and *London Times*, September 17, 1895.

11. Ramsden to Marquis of Salisbury, October 16, 1895, PRO, FO 72/1991.

12. Miró, *Cuba*, 90; and Gómez, *Diario de campaña*, 288.

13. For the view of an Afro-Cuban from Santa Clara, see the oral history of Esteban Montejo, in Barnet, *Biografía de un cimarrón*.

14. *Times* (London), September 17, 1895; *Diario de Zayas*, April 25, 1895, to July 30, 1896 (typed copy), ANC, DR, leg. 73, no. 56, fols. 1, 3, 4; and Atkins, *Sixty Years in Cuba*, 186.

15. Flint, *Marching with Gómez*, 52. For the war reminiscences of an Afro-Cuban from Matanzas, see Batrell, *Para la historia*.

16. Miró, *Cuba*, 39, 259, 278, 280; and Rosell, *Diario*, vol. 2, 118. For the war reminiscences of a rural Afro-Cuban from the province of Havana, see Herrera, *Impresiones de la guerra*.

17. Boza, *Mi diario de la guerra*, 35.

18. Cebreco to Serra (April 7, 1897), in *La Doctrina de Martí* (New York), June 30, 1897.

19. Arbelo, *Recuerdos de la última guerra*, 55–56.

20. Ibid., 56.

21. Boza, *Mi diario*, 59.

22. Valdés Domínguez, *Diario de un soldado*, vol. 1, 229; and Rosell, *Diario*, vol. 2, 36.

23. Valdés Domínguez, *Diario de un soldado*, vol. 1, 141, 293.

24. Miró, *Cuba*, 424, 481, 443, 657.

25. Woodward, *"El Diablo Americano,"* 51, 93.

26. Miró, *Cuba*, 626.

27. Barnet, *Biografía de un cimarrón*, 161. See also Herrera, *Impresiones de la guerra*, 77.

28. Barnet, *Biografía de un cimarrón*, 159.

29. Boza, *Mi diario*, 11.

30. Miró, *Cuba*, 394.

31. Arbelo, *Recuerdos de la última guerra*, 184.

32. Flint, *Marching with Gómez*, 216–17; and Woodward, *"El Diablo Americano,"* 43, 107–8, 113.

33. Valdés Domínguez, *Diario de un soldado*, vol. 1, 164–65.

34. Arbelo, *Recuerdos de la última guerra*, 139–40; and Woodward, *"El Diablo Americano,"* 43.

35. Torres Cuevas, *Antonio Maceo*.

36. Cabrera, *¡A Sitio Herrera!*, 173; and Burguete, *¡La Guerra!*, 135.

37. Barnet, *Biografía de un cimarrón*, 160.

38. Valdés Domínguez, *Diario de un soldado*, vol. 1, 122.

39. Flint, *Marching with Gómez*, 20.

40. Arbelo, *Recuerdos de la última guerra*, 54.

41. Flint, *Marching with Gómez*, 85–88.

42. Gómez, *Diario de campaña*, 329, 332; and Valdés Domínguez, *Diario de un soldado*, vol. 4, 50, 52, 57–58.

43. Ibid., vol. 1, 115.

44. Padrón, *El general José*, 178–80.

45. Valdés Domínguez, *Diario de un soldado*, vol. 1, 267–69; Flint, *Marching with Gómez*, 237, 239, 244–52; and Manuel Corral, *¡El Desastre!*, 81.

46. Barnet, *Biografía de un cimarrón*, 181–82.

47. Boza, *Mi diario*, 72, 85; Valdés Domínguez, *Diario de un soldado*, vol. 1, 308; Cabrera, *¡A Sitio Herrera!*, 160–61; and Flint, *Marching with Gómez*, 47–48.

48. Herrera, *Impresiones de la guerra*, 16; and Flint, *Marching with Gómez*, 15, 130–31.

49. Rosell, *Diario*, vol. 2, 113.

50. Arbelo, *Recuerdos de la última guerra*, 36.

51. Barnet, *Biografía de un cimarrón*, 195.

52. Arbelo, *Recuerdos de la última guerra*, 36; and Herrera, *Impresiones de la guerra*, 77.

53. See in particular, Foner, *Antonio Maceo*, 95, 102–3, 118–23, 135, 185–86, 201–2.

54. Flint, *Marching with Gómez*, 52.

55. Espinosa y Ramos, *Al trote y sin estribos*, 78.

56. Fernández Mascaró, *Ecos de la manigua*, 11.

57. For example, Salvador Cisneros to Tomás Estrada Palma, December 6, 1895, in Primelles, *La revolución del 95*, vol. 2, 144; and Cisneros to Miguel Betancourt Guerra, May 16, 1896, in *ibid.*, vol. 4, 178.

58. Rosell, *Diario*, vol. 2, 46; and Valdés Domínguez, *Diario de un soldado*, vol. 1, 287–88.

59. Serra, *La Doctrina de Martí*, November 15, 1897; Boza, *Mi diario*, 46; and Rosell, *Diario*, vol. 2, 145.

60. Miró, *Cuba*, 656.

61. Quoted in Franco, *Antonio Maceo*, vol. 3, 194.

62. Batrell, *Para la historia*, 12, 22, 68.

63. Pérez, *Cuba between Empires*, 91–98, 103–8.

64. Flint, *Marching with Gómez*, 233–34.

65. Valdés Domínguez, *Diario de un soldado*, vol. 1, 93.

66. Helg, "La Mejorana Revisited."

67. Rosell, *Diario*, vol. 2, 35.

68. Valdés Domínguez, *Diario de un soldado*, vol. 1, 110; and Miró, *Cuba*, 50.

69. Antonio Maceo to Salvador Cisneros Betancourt (September 8, 1895), in Miró, *Cuba*, 289–92; and Franco, *Antonio Maceo*, vol. 2, 157–63.

70. Maceo to Cisneros, September 8. 1895, in Miró, *Cuba*, 290.

71. Estrada Palma to Olney (December 7, 1895), *Congressional Record*, 55th Cong., 2d sess., 1896, 29, pt. 1, 343.

72. Fernández, *Ecos de la manigua*, 12–13; and Rosell, *Diario*, vol. 1, 84.

73. Estrada Palma to Olney, *Congressional Record*, 55th Cong., 2d sess., 1896, 29, pt. 1, 343.

74. Llaverías and Santovenia, *Actas de las asambleas*, vol. 1, 68, 72. The men in the Liberation Army received their pay only after independence.

75. Antonio Maceo to Máximo Gómez, December 4, 1895, in Maceo, *Ideología*, vol. 2, 176–77.

76. Arbelo, *Recuerdos de la última guerra*, 56.

77. Miró, *Cuba*, 77–79.

78. José Maceo to Tomás Estrada Palma, October 9, 1895, quoted in Padrón, *El general José*, 106; Diario de Zayas, ANC, DR, leg. 73, no. 56, fol. 5; and Miró, *Cuba*, 100–101, 116–17, 280–81.

79. Cisneros to Estrada Palma, December 6, 1895, in Primelles, *La revolución del 95*, vol. 2, 144. See also Miró, *Cuba*, 546.

80. Antonio Maceo to Manuel Sanguily, Camagüey, November 21, 1895, in Miró, *Cuba*, 294–95; Gómez, *Diario de campaña*, 304–10; Llaverías and Santovenia, *Actas de las asambleas, vol.* 1, 83; and Miró, *Cuba*, 545–49.

81. Antonio Maceo to José M. Rodríguez, July 17, 1896, in Maceo, *Ideología*, vol. 2, 308. Maceo alludes to the battle of Ayacucho in Peru in 1824 that signified the final victory of South American patriots over the Spanish army.

82. Flint, *Marching with Gómez*, 226.

83. Cisneros to Estrada Palma, December 6, 1895, in Primelles, *La revolución del 95*, vol. 2, 152; and Cisneros to Betancourt, May 16, 1896, in ibid., vol. 4, 180.

84. Ibid., vol. 4, 177–78, 180–81.

85. José Maceo, quoted in Franco, *Antonio Maceo*, vol. 3, 197.

86. Padrón, *El general José*, 120.

87. Valdés Domínguez, *Diario de un soldado*, vol. 2, 40.

88. Miró, *Cuba*, 513, 545–49.

89. Valdés Domínguez, *Diario de un soldado*, vol. 1, 320–21.

90. Miró, *Cuba*, 509–10, 545–49, 590; and Franco, *Antonio Maceo*, vol. 3, 82.

91. Miró, *Cuba*, 714–17.

92. Rosell, *Diario*, vol. 2, 144.

93. Arbelo, *Recuerdos de la última guerra*, 238.

94. *Times* (London), December 12, 1896.

95. Arbelo, *Recuerdos de la última guerra*, 33, 238–39; and Miró, *Cuba*, 721–23.

96. Gómez, *Diario de campaña*, 329, 332.

97. Pérez, *Cuba between Empires*, 137.

98. Musgrave, *Under Three Flags in Cuba*. 165.

99. Drummond Wolff to Marquis of Salisbury, October 17, 1897, PRO, FO 414/152.

100. Dirección política de las F.A.R., ed., *Historia de Cuba*, 468, 494–96.

101. Musgrave, *Under Three Flags*, 162–63.

102. Thomas, *Cuba*, 379.

103. Herrera, *Impresiones de la guerra*, 130.

104. See Helg, *Our Rightful Share*; and de la Fuente, *A Nation for All*.

4

Monteneros and *Macheteros*

Afro-Ecuadorian and Indigenous Experiences of Military Struggle in Liberal Ecuador, 1895–1930

NICOLA FOOTE

The Liberal Revolution that came to power in 1895 and maintained ideological hegemony until 1944 represented a crucial period in the development of Ecuador as a nation-state. The Liberal state sought to impose far-reaching political and economic change, centered around the development of a secular state, integration into the world economy, the development of a more fluid national labor market, and the expansion of citizenship. Military struggle was central to the politics of this period. The victory of the Liberal Revolution represented the culmination of several decades of guerilla activity headed by the charismatic caudillo Eloy Alfaro. Black and indigenous troops were crucial to this military victory, and their role had an important impact on how racial ideas were created and entwined with national identity within the new regime. Yet this role has been largely written out of histories of the period, and where it has been noted, it has been seen as the result of coercion rather than genuine conviction. Moreover, military instability did not end with the Liberal victory. Instead interfactional disputes flowed over into civil war in the Concha Rebellion of 1913–1916. Black and indigenous troops also played an important role within this movement and in government responses to it, while the rebellion's failure had significant consequences for the development of a collective ethnic consciousness within the two communities. This chapter explores black and indigenous participation in both the 1895 Revolution and the Concha Rebellion of 1913–1916, analyzing the racial transcript that lay behind subaltern participation as well as the subsequent impact on nationalist racial ideologies and the collective consciousness of the two groups.

The Liberal Revolution and the Popular Classes

The participation of black and indigenous troops in the civil war of 1895 was absolutely central to the Liberal victory, yet this popular effort has largely been marginalized within histories of the period, which make almost no mention of the racial composition of revolutionary leader Eloy Alfaro's armies. This is true even of primary documentation: government records, such as the reports of the minister for war, mention the bravery of various columns and name individuals, but the ethnic origin of individuals is not specified. This pattern is mirrored in first hand testimonies—an account of the 1900 campaign in Tulcan, for example, emphasizes the courage and leadership of the "Alfaro" column but makes no mention of the fact that this section consisted mainly of blacks from the coastal province of Esmeraldas.[1] In view of the regional concentration of ethnic minority populations, however, it is possible to deduce the ethnicity of soldiers from the information provided in Ministry of War files on the locality from which individual columns were drawn. Ethnic populations in early twentieth century Ecuador were strongly regionalized. Civil registry data for 1930 divided the nation's population as follows: 10 percent white, 41 percent mestizo, 39 percent Indian, 5 percent black and mulatto, and 5 percent other.[2] Approximately 95 percent of the indigenous population lived in the highland provinces while blacks were concentrated in the coastal provinces of Esmeraldas, Manabi, Guyayas, and El Oro, in particular Esmeraldas, where approximately 85 percent of the population was Afro-Ecuadorian.[3] Using the reported demography in conjunction with photographic evidence and oral histories, it becomes clear that Afro-Ecuadorians formed the core of Eloy Alfaro's army.[4] Black troops fought in all Liberal battles and showed a strong sense of loyalty to Alfaro. The coastal provinces of Esmeraldas and Manabi had been the base of Liberal guerilla activities since the 1880s, and it seems that their activities served to radicalize local black and mixed-race peasants. These populations listened to the discourse of Liberal orators and suffered personally from the consequences of state repression directed at the guerillas; as a result they became convinced of the possibilities that liberalism offered for a radical democratic transformation. Of particular importance was Alfaro's focus on land redistribution and the abolition of debt peonage, an important and repressive institution in the region.

Certainly there is evidence that during the anti-Conservative struggles of the 1880s, ordinary black peasants repeatedly fought in the streets with sticks and stones, protesting against political abuses and electoral fraud.

One anecdote recounted by a historian of Esmeraldas describes how Roege-
lio Escobar, a "big, strapping black man," charged with a machete at the sergeant in charge of government troops who were regulating (and believed to
be defrauding) the elections and cut off his head.[5] The victory of the Liberal
Revolution in 1895 was declared first in the central plaza of Esmeraldas,
and an account of this victory by one of the main protagonists, Comandante Enrique Torres, tells of the important role played by young blacks
from the town:

> The first to jump, like tigers, on the guards of the army barracks and
> to dominate them in no time at all, were a group of 23 conspirators,
> armed with shining and sharpened machetes. The rest burst immedi-
> ately after like an avalanche, which left the soldiers paralysed, scarcely
> able to recover from the shock and surprise . . . the majority of these
> conspirators were young black Esmeraldans, who had proven them-
> selves among the Alfarista monteneros. . . . The cries of ¡Viva Alfaro!
> awakened the recognition: *Alfarismo* was triumphant.[6]

Indigenous people had less of a longstanding involvement with *Alfarismo*
than Afro-Esmeraldans, but they played a key role in the battle of August
1895 in Guamote, Chimborazo, which represented the decisive victory of
the civil war, and from whence Alfaro's troops marched into Quito. More
than ten thousand local Indians were convened, without outside involvement, by the leaders of the major surrounding Indian communities—Pedro
Guaman, Pablo Morocho, and Alejandro Saenz. Their knowledge of the local
terrain and their aid with the transportation of arms, munitions, food and
water to troops across the mountain range was vital to the course of the
battle.[7] The same Indian communities later turned out to cheer and fete "el
indio Alfaro" as he left for Quito. The name had been imposed on him by his
enemies in attempt to discredit him; however, it was adopted by Indians to
show their acceptance of him as a leader.[8]

So strong was this subaltern support for the Liberal Revolution in this
early period that Ecuadorian historian Enrique Ayala has suggested the
need to characterize the liberalism of 1895 as defined by two political projects: that of the peasants who fought for the redistribution of land and
the suppression of servile institutions such as *concertaje*, and that of the
coastal bourgeoisie who sought to consolidate their control over the export
economy. Alfaro himself was the link between the two: indeed, the bourgeoisie accepted his leadership largely because he guaranteed the popular
support necessary for military triumph.[9] This political consciousness and

belief in ideologies of liberty, equality, peace, and progress reflects recent findings regarding subaltern participation in political movements in other Latin American countries.[10]

Military Participation, Race, and the Nationalist Project

Black and indigenous people, then, fought for the Liberal Revolution out of genuine conviction, not coercion or clientilism. This important military role had an impact on the development of national identity but in conflicting and often contradictory ways. For Indians it formed the basis for the beginnings of political inclusion. As a result of his gratitude for indigenous support in the Battle of Guamote, Alfaro named the three prominent indigenous leaders—Guaman, Morocho, and Saenz—as colonels of his army and pronounced on the spot new rights for Indians, repudiating the territorial taxes and the forced labor programs.[11] In practice, these rights were not guaranteed by law until much later; however, the key point is that rights for subordinate racial groups were placed onto the agenda of the Liberal Revolution from its very outset. The power of this alliance from an indigenous perspective is reflected in popular memory. Indigenous oral testimonies recall that it was specifically Eloy Alfaro who confiscated Church-owned haciendas and implemented other favorable Liberal policies. In a collection of testimonies by Indians from Cayambe, Alfaro was remembered as a *"runa who desired that we all lived equally."*[12] This description of Alfaro as a *runa* is especially significant: he was considered by Indians to be one of them.[13]

Yet popular pressure for ethnic rights coexisted with other important influences, in particular social Darwinist ideas, which presented the racial composition of nation states as the determining factor in their success or failure. Liberal discourse was also affected by the particular goals of the state project, which was aimed primarily at political and economic modernization. Crucially, the Liberal Revolution represented a regional transformation of power, with the coastal mercantile and banking elite seeking to assert a political power commensurate with their economic status. As such, the revolution's aims were to transfer state resources away from the highlands toward the coast, secularize the state, and facilitate the integration of Ecuador into the world economy. The status of Indians was relevant to each of these goals. Indians were perceived to be under the control of the Church and the highland landowners while the exploitation of their labor—essential to the development of an effective market economy—was constrained by the institution of debt peonage. Moreover, indigenous culture was generally presented as being anticapitalist: it was asserted that Indians had few needs and were concerned only with the lowest level of subsistence. Thus, policy toward Indians reflected these perceived realities.

The result was that in Liberal discourse Indians became classified as future potential citizens but also as childlike and in need of patriarchal protection in the interim. It was argued that Indians were incapable of participating fully in the nation because of their history—a history of oppression by the Catholic Church, highland landowners, and local officials. Therefore liberal discourse on Indians focused on the need to free them from abuse and transform them into beings capable of participating in national life, and the policies formulated to ameliorate the situation of indigenous peoples were centered around the idea of "fitting" them for integration. Debt peonage and Church-based taxes and labor requirements were abolished to free Indians from the control of the Church; Indian schools were established in rural villages and haciendas to transform indigenous "psychology," and sanitation and hygiene programs were enacted to eradicate and modernize cultural traditions.[14]

One of the most paradoxical embodiments of the idea of Indians as suitable for citizenship, but at some unspecified point in the future after cultural and moral transformation had occurred, was the institution of military service. Despite Alfaro's early recognition of the key role played by indigenous soldiers in bringing the Liberal Revolution to victory, Indians continued to be listed alongside the clergy and the physically and mentally disabled as the only adult males to be exempted from military service.[15] Military service is one of the key mechanisms by which the state asserts its authority over marginal populations and instills in them a sense of national identity. In Ecuador, however, Indians were excluded because they were considered bad soldiers. They were held to be too short in stature to make a good fighting force, and to lack initiative, intelligence, and fierceness of character. Leonardo Chiriboga, the minister for the armed forces, argued that Indians were too small and weak to carry even the same loads as the average European; that their muscles had been selectively developed for agricultural work, not marching and carrying weapons; and that their circulatory and respiratory systems prevented them from working quickly, citing indigenous music, dance, and song as reflections of their slow and monotonous physiological state.[16] Other commentators opposed indigenous military service on more paternalistic grounds, arguing that Indians were too weak and childlike to withstand the rigors of military activity.[17] Even after the military reform of 1938, officers in the armed forces remained extremely reluctant to recruit Indians, despite the shortage of soldiers, repeatedly arguing that indigenous people should keep doing their agricultural jobs to ensure the economic health of the country during times of war. This stood in contrast to the pattern in most other Andean nations, where Indians formed the core of military squadrons throughout the nineteenth and early twentieth centuries.

The marginalization of Indians from the military also contrasts strongly with the prevalence of Afro-Ecuadorians within the institution. A North American musicologist traveling in Ecuador during the 1920s recounted seeing black boys as young as eight or nine in Esmeraldas dressed in soldiers' uniforms and carrying rifles.[18] Soldiers could earn much more than ordinary laborers, and the military provided a key opportunity for social mobility for coastal blacks; indeed, many of the officers in Alfaro's army were known to have had black or mixed race blood. During the 1941 war with Peru, black *macheteros* from Esmeraldas were considered to be Ecuador's "secret weapon" and were sent in large numbers to fight when it became clear that the regular Ecuadorian forces were no match for the Peruvian army. So mythologized had black fighting skills become that it was imagined (hoped) by the government that a few hundred men with machetes could overcome a modern military force armed with machine guns and a trained air force squadron.[19] The contrast highlights the ambiguity created by the "nonimagining" of blacks within the national community: that because of their lack of status as a particular legal or sociological group they could be more easily be grouped into the generalized classification of "the masses."[20] One of the key ways in which the nation is constructed is through military service—in other words, through the pact that all men must be prepared to go out and fight and be prepared to die on the nation's behalf.[21] The exclusion of Indians from the service must be read as part of the feminization of the indigenous population, an attempt to construct them as subjects, not citizens, under the paternalistic, benevolent wing of the state.[22]

Yet military service was perhaps the only way in which blacks were included in the nation; moreover, this perceived military prowess also became part of the basis for their wider exclusion. Despite the importance of blacks to the Liberal Revolution, blackness became constructed within liberal discourse as a source of "racial danger." Writers and politicians pontificated on the laziness and indolence of blacks and emphasized their alleged tendencies toward criminality as a source of racial danger. Blacks were presented as a corrupting influence on the indigenous population and described as stealing indigenous land and possessions and instilling in them magical religions and antimissionary beliefs.[23] A particular part of this classification of blackness as a source of racial danger was the idea that blacks and mulattos were to blame for the country's political instability. It was posited that the importation of African slaves in the colonial era had "disrupted the course" of Ecuadorian history because of the "bloody and war-like ways" of the blacks.[24] Constant military struggle was classified as an inalienable racial characteristic and used to classify blacks as "unredeemable" and thus unsuitable for citizenship.[25] Indeed, efforts were consistently made to negate the national identity of Ecuadorian blacks in government and media discourse through the construction of blacks as Colombians, not Ecuadorians, whenever they appeared in discussions of policy or local events. While the "Indian problem," as it was conceived, was recognized by elites, who devised strategies to tackle it, blacks were simply ignored, and as a result social and infrastructural policy provisions essentially stopped at the provincial borders of Esmeraldas. Schools and hospitals were not established in the region until the 1930s, and plans to establish a road or rail route to the capital were repeatedly sidelined. The region was simply not part of the national imaginary, and race was central in informing this negation.[26]

Blackness and the Concha Rebellion

Despite this exclusion, Afro-Ecuadorians did not lose faith in liberalism. Rather, they believed that the values and ideals of Eloy Alfaro (whose presidential terms spanned from 1895–1901 and 1906–11) had been subverted by corrupters of liberalism, and they mobilized to defend what they believed was its true embodiment. This can be seen most clearly and most famously in the Concha Rebellion of 1913 to 1916. The Concha Rebellion was essentially a civil war between two liberal factions that followed the deposition and murder of Eloy Alfaro in 1911. The followers of Alfaro blamed the supporters of Gen. Leonidas Plaza, leader of the more moderate mercantilist sector of the Liberals, for the assassination, and what had been an interparty schism degenerated into a bloody civil war that ravaged the province of Esmeraldas for more than four years. While the majority of the troops were black—and a large part of the movement's notoriety within Ecuadorian history has centered on the prominent participation of blacks— the movement has normally been analyzed principally as a factionalized guerrilla uprising, with no effort made to read the potential racial transcript. Oscar Efrén Reyes's summary of the revolution is typical of the way in which the movement has been perceived by orthodox histories as a movement of criminals and mercenaries motivated by personal gain:

> As in every bloody revolt, true criminals were able to cover up their lawless tendencies under the pretext of political belief, and mere criminal types became, in that way, "revolutionary" captains and majors. . . . Agriculture in the battle zone was wiped out altogether because farm hands had been recruited into bands entrusted with the task of cutting off the heads of *serranos* with machetes. . . . This is one of the darkest and most detestable episodes in the history of our turbulent politics of claims.[27]

Attempts to revise this interpretation have centered on efforts to restore the reputation of Concha himself.[28] There has been almost no effort to reexamine the motives of the black popular groups involved in the movement who have been seen, at best, as coerced or duped into fighting by political elites bent on power and revenge.[29] Yet an overfocus on the hostility between Concha and Plaza has undermined the dynamic of social struggle and the principles of subversion that motivated many Esmeraldan blacks. The loyalty and conviction that had motivated blacks in their engagement with the Revolution of 1895 did not wane throughout the first two decades of Liberal rule. As a result many blacks fought for the Conchistas out of loyalty to Alfaro and a belief that the victory of his ideals would lead to the implementation of greater rights for them.

Alfaro was remembered with real affection among Esmeraldan blacks. Throughout his two presidencies, Afro-Ecuadorians looked to Alfaro to uphold and implement their rights. Black peons addressed their solicitudes and petitions to local and national governments directly to Alfaro; they were convinced that he must be unaware of their situation, and expressed the belief that if only he could be made aware of their problems he would be able to make things better. Certainly the name Alfaro possessed tremendous prestige among blacks, a legacy of his immense personal charisma and his ability to convince subaltern groups of the power of his project. Thus his name was an effective tool for recruiters, and appeals made in the name of Alfaro were extremely effective in convincing black recruits that enlisting in the Conchista army would serve their own political ends.[30] Blacks could easily be convinced that it was a particular faction that had corrupted the ideals of Alfaro and was to blame for the failure of the Liberal government

Figure 4.1. Funeral of Colonel Carlos Concha, Esmeraldas, 1919. Photograph courtesy of Archivo Historico del Banco Central, Quito, Fondo Fotografías.

to fulfill its promises to them.[31] The rebel leader, Col. Carlos Concha, was from a prominent but progressive Esmeraldan landholding family and had been governor of the province under Alfaro. Concha had his own black support base as a result of his campaigns against debt peonage and his efforts to establish schools and public works in the region, which although largely unsuccessful had earned him the respect and affection of the local people, reinforcing the appeal of the movement. Indeed, the support he engendered can be seen quite movingly in photos of Concha's funeral of 1919, which show local blacks sitting in the tops of trees that overlooked the burial site, determined to pay their last respects (see figure 4.1).[32]

But Afro-Ecuadorians were not moved only by leadership appeals. Many also saw in the movement a chance to advance their own economic and social goals. Most of the insurgents were impoverished peasants who were suffering from the expansion of agro-export industries and the expansion of haciendas, which were forcing them in increasing numbers to become *conciertos*, or debt peons, where they were subject to harsh and often violent conditions. Many peasants had turned to *tagua* collection as an alternative to enserfment on the haciendas, but by the 1910s this industry was in crisis. Thus the economic conditions were ripe for a black peasant rebellion.

Certainly, as the movement developed it took on its own economic logic. Many blacks saw the Concha Revolution as a means of self-ascension and social mobility, inspired by the black sergeants and lieutenants among the

Conchista ranks. The armed forces had long been used as a means of social mobility by blacks, and the Concha Revolution was able to tap into this tradition. Many blacks were freed from debt-peonage by their recruiters. Others were inspired by their ill-treatment at the hands of government troops, the rape and ill-treatment of their wives, or the theft of their livestock. There was also a general sense of anger and a feeling that the poor state of the province was a result of racism on the part of the central authorities, and many people were keen to express their anger at the government that had neglected them.

The fact that this was a local, Esmeraldan movement also inspired many blacks to join because it fed into the values of rebellion and freedom that were so central to the self-identification of Esmeraldan blacks. The power of this discourse can be seen in the oral history and popular literature of the region, which centers on the foundational shipwreck and the story of how blacks liberated themselves and forged inland from the coast, forming the "Zambo Republic" through their encounters with indigenous peoples and vigorously protecting their freedom, allying with the Spanish crown on their own terms only after years of armed struggle.[33] The twin sentiments of resentment and cultural pride as a driving force in the movement are captured by Afro-Ecuadorian writer Nelson Estupiñan Bass in his 1954 novel about the Concha Revolution, *Cuando los Guayacanes Florecian*:

[The] *Conchistas* belonged to their class, they were from their province, or other coastal provinces. . . . As children they had played with the *Conchistas* in the river. . . . They were their people. They were the courageous, indomitable people, with Carlos Concha as their leader, fighting sincerely to avenge an infamous act and to secure the endangered freedom. They were the people of the rivers, of the immense and depopulated plains at the foot of the mountains, completely separated from the rest of the *Patria*, fighting face to face with the government. And what great pride for a man of the woods, whatever his class may be, to fight against the government! Because, throughout history, the governments only remembered the "wild niggers" (*negros salvajes*) when it came to the collection of taxes and the recruitment of "rebellious and courageous men"—now no longer "wild niggers"—when the Boundaries of the Fatherland were threatened by the Peruvian invader. It was Eloy Alfaro, it was Carlos Concha, it was Esmeraldas, it was freedom.[34]

The movement provided an outlet for the resentments many Afro-

Esmeraldans felt at what they perceived as the racist neglect of the province, and tapped into local and cultural pride. While doubtless some blacks were press-ganged unwillingly (and there is certainly plenty of visual evidence of child soldiers being used by the Conchistas), to suggest that this was universally true would be to undermine the very real personal and political motivations that factored into black support for the Concha Revolution, and to ignore the desire for racial equality and freedom from oppression that was manifested within it.

Whatever the motivation of blacks, there is no denying that they played a crucial role in the Concha Revolution. The movement was dependent on and famous for its black militia, and blacks appear in key roles in the narratives of the Concha Revolution. In the first act of the revolution, the capture of the police barracks of Esmeraldas at 3 a.m. on September 24, 1913, thirty blacks from Tianoe armed with pistols and machetes carried out the raid and took possession of the barracks. These thirty men were the sole revolutionaries at this point.[35] After they had successfully taken the barracks, an additional thirty men, whose ethnicity was not specified in the accounts of this event, arrived from Tachina. Even if all of the men in the second group were white or mestizo, at least half the revolutionaries at this stage would have been black. This group of sixty men then proceeded to attack the military barracks that garrisoned the 4th Company of Manabi. These soldiers had been relieved for the evening by Afro-Esmeraldans to allow the regular soldiers to celebrate the day of the Virgin of Mercedes, the patron saint of the Ecuadorian army, and it seems that an agreement had already been made between these black stand-ins and the revolutionaries. Segundo Luis Moreno, an officer with the government army who later wrote a memoir of his experiences in the war, describes how as the first shots were fired, the Esmeraldan soldiers, having thrown their arms into the streets, jumped from the garrison to receive the revolutionaries, and, "conforming to what had previously been agreed," fled to the back parts of the building.[36] Photographs of the Conchistas show that most were black peasants in their everyday clothes, all armed with machetes. Many photos also grant clear visibility to women, showing that black women were also participants in the war, occupying roles as nurses, cooks, and guerrillas.

Blacks remained important right to the end of the war. When Concha was captured in 1915, one of his black attendants, Patricio, who had been assisting in nursing him, was taken prisoner alongside him. Patricio managed to break open his bindings on the march from Concha's hacienda and escape into the forest, where he ran to give the information on the capture

Figure 4.2. Handover of weapons at the negotiated end of Concha Revolution, Rioverde, November 1916. Photograph courtesy of Archivo Historico del Banco Central, Quito, Fondo Fotografías.

to the rebel command.[37] This underscores the loyalty and commitment of black troops and auxiliaries to the Concha cause and to Concha himself. On November 7, 1916, the last four hundred guerrillas handed over their arms. Photos taken in Rioverde on this occasion show that blacks participated right to the end (see figure 4.2).

Many blacks rose through the Concha ranks to become sergeants and lieutenants. Sergeant Lastre in particular became a legendary figure, revered for his exploits on the battlefield. Even government forces recognized the leadership skills of Lastre. Moreno, who fought against him, showed a remarkable level of respect and admiration for his military skills and valor, describing Lastre as an exemplary leader who managed to maintain order and discipline among the troops "in a form worthy of imitation and just applause."[38] Lastre became a true hero to blacks in the region, who recognized in his ascension the validation of their culture and who had the pride of serving under a famous leader of the same race as themselves.[39] When the revolutionary forces entered the city of Esmeraldas on December 15, 1913, Lastre was named Jefe Superior of the Central Plaza and rode through the entrance to the city mounted on a white horse.[40] This would have had a tremendously powerful racial symbolism for local blacks, representing their entry into the political domain and the inversion of traditional racial hierarchies. According to Esmeraldan popular tradition, Lastre was said to have declared as he entered the city: "I be ridin' top o' the whole white race."[41] In spite of the difficult conditions and shortages arising from the government blockade of the port, Lastre was able to maintain order and discipline in the city, and Moreno argued that "there remained a true fraternity between the soldiers of the revolution and the civil element in a way which has almost never been seen in the Ecuadorian army, especially not in times of war."[42] Certainly Lastre exercised an iron discipline over his soldiers. Anecdotes recounted his refusal to accept civil disobedience among his troops; offenders who failed to pay for the services of a brothel or cantina or who raped a local woman were punished and humiliated.[43]

The pathologization of the Concha Revolution centered on the issue of black involvement. Newspapers in particular noticed the fact that the majority of the fighters were blacks and used this as shorthand to symbolize their brutality and barbarism. In descriptions of particularly violent acts of war, the guerrillas were described simply as blacks, as opposed to soldiers or rebels. This went in tandem with accusations that the principal characteristic that distinguished the guerrillas was violence, and that they lacked political goals, ideals, or principals. *El Guante* described the Conchistas as "something less than a faction, a little bit more than a gang of rebels," with "neither flag, nor program; neither ideas, nor resources; neither illusions, nor hopes; neither honourable proposals, nor honorable people."[44] The minister of the interior went a step further, insisting that the rebels were "simply gangs of outlaws, headed by criminals, who enter into the sacking of innocent populations, and commit outrages against private property and the honor of families, and kill those who resist."[45] The rebels were regularly accused of banditry and crimes against property. It is possible that such activities reflected the anger of black rebels at white elites and landlords. However, these actions were interpreted by many elites as representing a lack of ideology and a desire on the part of the black masses simply to rabble-rouse. The blackness of the soldiers was central to such accusations. *El Guante* described the Conchistas as "black hordes that prowl in the thicket like jackals congregated in a general ambush," using race as a shorthand to challenge the social standing and morality of the rebels: "The lost, the broken, the drunk, the indigent, the men of the gambling houses and brothels, the criminal underworlds of some pueblos of the coast, the outcasts of the city. Is this a guerrilla? No, it is a horde."[46] The specter of cannibalism was also raised, with Concha rebels said to have revived the "African tradition" of consuming the flesh of those killed in battle.[47]

This highlights how existing stereotypes of blacks as brutal, bloodthirsty and barbaric—themselves emerging in part from previous military involvement—were attached to the Conchistas. President Plaza accused the rebels of failing to recognize any of the normal rules of combat, assassinating prisoners and the injured without mercy, mutilating bodies and victimizing civilian landowners.[48] The notoriety of the black soldiers became a source of terror for government troops already afraid of the hostile environment. Moreno describes the "epidemic of fear" that spread among government forces intimidated by what they had heard about the *macheteros*—"the title acquired by blacks fond of death and desolation." He describes his friend, an army captain, losing his mind with fear, unable to walk even a step without "looking crazily left to right, sure that he would be assaulted by a *machetero*." He ended up a victim of *"mieditis"*—that is, he died of fear, apparently not an uncommon fate.[49] Some government soldiers had scarcely disembarked when they were sent to hospital, using all kinds of illicit measures to get themselves medically discharged and sent back to the sierra. "They would leave the hospital by night, and return to the boat triumphant, free of the *"negritos"* who wanted to make them into soup."[50] This fear could be used to the strategic advantage of the Conchistas. The Concha victory at the battle at Camarones in April 1914, in which government troops were attacked simultaneously on several fronts by Lastre's forces was facilitated by the panic of government troops at the cry *"los macheteros."* When the troops heard this, they began to flee toward the beach where they were met by other rebel forces and ended up trapped between the forest and the sea.[51] *El Telegrafo* expressed sympathy with their fear. "The very figure of such naked blacks, with red turban and brandishing a machete is enough to set on edge the nerves of even the toughest soldier."[52]

Sergeant Lastre was often singled out in these efforts to construct a negative imagery of the black Conchista soldiers. He was regularly described in press accounts as a scoundrel and a womanizer who would "give his life for a white woman" and who would resort to any means to possess a woman in whom he had an interest. In *Cuando los Guayacanes Florecían* the rumor circulates around Esmeraldas that Sergeant Lastre had announced that as soon as the Conchistas were victorious they would take hold of all the white women and distribute them among black men.[53] This reflects, of course, the other major stereotype of black men—that of insatiable sexual desire and prowess—and echoes the imagery of the black rapist so common in slave societies throughout the Americas.

In his presidential message of 1914, Gen. Leonidas Plaza drew on these fears, interpreting the Concha Revolution as a race war, with Esmeraldan whites on the side of the government against blacks full of "murderous hatred." He stated that the revolution in Esmeraldas formed its army from the black inhabitants of the surrounding area, who had in their favor the "sinister complicity" of the land. While the constitutional troops had enjoyed "the support and adhesion of the totality of the scarce white people of this territorial zone," they had been forced to struggle "distressingly against the climate, the impenetrable forest, sickness, and the murderous hatred of the black race, which inhabits and dominates the Esmeraldan forests."[54] Likewise, in concluding his presidential message of 1915, Plaza repeatedly drew a distinction between the rebels and the "Ecuadorian race."[55] At one level this can be read as a simple attempt to discredit the patriotism of the rebels, but it can also be read as the exclusion of *black* rebels in particular from the national imaginary because black rebels epitomized everything considered to be dangerous about the inclusion of Afro-Ecuadorians in the nation.

Ideas about blackness were also used in different ways to represent the negative impact that the Concha Revolution was having on the nation. The national press would regularly print graphic accounts of peasants killed and injured in the war in order to undermine the idea of the rebellion as a popular movement and to present it as something with negative consequences for popular groups. A particularly striking example of this can be found in an edition of *El Ecuatoriano* that described in detail the case of a "Herculean negro" who received a bullet in "the most secret part of his organism," and had to walk on foot for two miles in search of a doctor before "ending his brief journey dying amid horrific contortions." Witnesses stated that his cadaver was the most horrible thing they had ever seen.[56] The use of a black man injured in his "intimate parts" as an example of the brutality and violence of the war is telling, focusing on that which was most mythologized about the Afro-Ecuadorian physique—male sexual prowess and power—to imply that fighting the war would strip this virility away, a metaphor perhaps, for its impact on the nation.

However, it is important to emphasize that it was not just blacks who took part in and suffered from the Concha Revolution. Soldiers passing through the northern highlands on their way to Esmeraldas also wreaked havoc on Indian communities. A U.S. Army officer sent to assess the uprising described riding in a train with government soldiers on their way to Esmeraldas, who drunkenly fired their rifles out of the windows, hitting several indigenous laborers working in the fields.[57] Indigenous oral testimonies recall the Conchista movement with horror, remembering how government soldiers passing through ransacked their houses and stole or killed their animals. Others described Indians from their villages who had left to fight the Conchistas and never returned.[58] Many of the government forces were indigenous peons, despite the ban on using Indians within the national army. This reflected the enormous difficulty in recruiting soldiers in view of the hysteria surrounding the alleged savagery of the black soldiers, compounded by fear of the Esmeraldan climate. The only loyalist soldier to be fleshed out as a character in *Cuando los Guayacanes Florecían* was Gabriel Simbana, an Indian who had enlisted as a soldier to escape the miserable life of debt peonage, highlighting the fact that troops on both sides were using the war to escape slavery and submission. In the novel, Simbana cries before going into battle, aware that he faced certain death on the battlefield.

> The patron's pitiless whip was preferable he thought to certain death at the hands of an Esmeraldan black, emerging from a dense thicket, with his eyes bulging, bursting with an insatiable thirst for blood. . . . He wouldn't be able to return to his land he thought. Now, between his village, distant and unreachable, and him, there stood, blocking his way, a thick wall of blacks, thirsty for blood, with sharpened machetes, ready to cut off his head at the first movement and to pursue him if he tried to escape across the plains.[59]

Simbana was indeed killed by one of the three black peons who are the main characters in the book. The group of friends was shocked when they discovered from letters found in Simbana's pocket that the loyalist soldier they had killed was also a debt peon, fleeing the life into which he was born. While this is merely a fictional account, it is likely that the gradual realization that the men they were fighting against were not the "rich Serrano oppressors" of elite discourse but rather poor peasants and debt peons like themselves would have had a disillusioning effect on the black rebel forces.

By 1916 troop morale was low. Conditions in the rebel camps—and, indeed, in the province as a whole—were desperate. Food and medical supplies were scarce. Many men, after spending long periods in the trenches, were now victims of beriberi, and children were emaciated through severe malnutrition. In the countryside, fields were completely ruined, and many abandoned houses had been completely covered by brush. Mental and physical exhaustion was compounded by growing evidence of corruption on the part of Conchista elites, who were using the revolution to conduct land seizures and the theft of livestock, and on the part of blacks, dizzied by their rank. Moreover, after the capture of Concha, no leader could emulate his universal prestige. Lastre was not accepted by white Alfarista elites, and other leaders more acceptable to these groups did not find favor with the black masses. Thus the movement gradually petered out before coming to a negotiated cease-fire in November 1916.

After the revolution was over, elite members of the movement were let off with a pardon in the name of promoting "a spirit of harmony and toler-ance."[60] Many of them had made significant financial gains because of their cattle raiding activities during the revolution, and the official pardon meant that there was minimal effect on their political standing. In contrast, the majority of the peasants who had fought in the revolution found their liv-ing conditions worsened. Many haciendas took advantage of the confusion generated by the war to expand their boundaries, and many peasants found themselves dispossessed and pushed off the land. In Estupiñán Bass's novel, the peasants' efforts to gain freedom through participation in the rebellion end in disaster, with one peon imprisoned, another returned to *concertaje* on the same hacienda he had left at the start of the novel, and the third killed attempting to escape this same fate.[61]

The revolution was defeated in part because of its limited social reach. To triumph, it needed to find solutions to the needs most strongly felt by the peasants who were a fundamental component of the guerrillas, and to reach out not only to Afro-Ecuadorians but also to the indigenous population. Yet this was never part of the movement's agenda. That this was the case un-derscores the continued power of the state's "divide-and-rule" strategy as applied to black and indigenous groups. While the two racially subordinate groups had come together in a cross-regional, cross-ethnic alliance in the early stages of Alfarismo, they were united only by his immediate persona, and it appears that leaders from neither sector realized the profundity of their common interests. This speaks to the ways in which the resistance of the masses could be politically disarmed because fissured identities made sustained challenges to power much more difficult. In many respects the traditional negative interpretations of the Concha Revolution are correct. It represented the bankruptcy of liberal political philosophy, especially vis-à-vis the masses, for whom the revolution offered no direct appeal other than an ironic call to defend a freedom they had not yet received. For the *Alfarista* elites, perhaps "revolution" simply meant gaining armed revenge against those responsible for Alfaro's death. However, many of the black peasants who became involved in the revolution read different meanings within it, and their support for it manifested their desire for a better future and a rejection of their present circumstances. The enduring legacy of the movement can be seen in the permanent place that the Concha Revolution has achieved within Esmeraldan folklore. Work songs dedicated to Carlos Concha continued to be sung in the fields of Esmeraldas into the 1980s; one includes the lines: "Carlos Concha es mi papa/ bajando del infinito/ si Carlos Concha se muere/ el negro quedo solito."[62]

Revolutionary Disappointments: The Rejection of Liberalism and the Development of Collective Consciousness

For both black and indigenous populations, then, military involvement based on a desire to be part of the nation did not result in the kinds of transformation and inclusion they had hoped for and on which their participation was based. This recognition ushered in both a period of disconnect from the state and an emerging sense of ethnic-based collective consciousness among both communities.

The failure of the Concha Rebellion represented a watershed in Afro-Esmeraldan engagement with the state. It generated powerful resentment and a feeling that the government would not help blacks; as a result, the community turned inward, apparently concluding that only community agency and cooperation would lead to development and prosperity for the region. It was argued that if Esmeraldans wanted schools, hospitals, and other services, then they must create them themselves. Thus a local political movement emphasizing solidarity and collaboration developed from the mid-1930s. This was strongly tied to the development of a cultural literary movement through which Afro-Esmeraldan intellectuals began to channel their protest toward the creation of an explicitly black local identity. This included the promotion of the *decima* based on traditional African poetry, and the development of black consciousness poetry and prose, which dealt with the economic problems black people faced and emphasized Africa as a source of inspiration and pride. This movement was of course influenced by the wider current of Afro-Americanism and *negritude/negrismo*, which was emerging throughout the Americas in this period, and especially by the work of black Caribbean poets such as Nicolas Guillén and Luis Pales Matos. However, it should be emphasized that this self-conscious articulation of a black identity occurred much earlier than in other mainland Latin American countries, where such ideas and movements typically did not begin to occur until the 1960s and '70s. This chronological difference is directly related to the exclusion of Afro-Ecuadorians from the national state, despite their efforts to be engaged, and the failure of earlier military movements to challenge this marginalization.

Post-1895 indigenous mobilization followed a different pattern from that of Afro-Ecuadorians but also had a significant impact in terms of the emergence of an indigenous collective consciousness. In common with Peru and Bolivia, Ecuadorian indigenous people went through what Silvia Rivera Cusicanqui and Alberto Flores Galindo have described as a "rebel cycle" during the 1920s and '30s.[63] Indigenous uprising in this period represented a protest against a parasitic state and the gap between the favorable legislation passed on behalf of the Indians and the absence of any real reform. Rebellions in Azauy, Chimborazo, and Cañar protested the new taxes and labor obligations imposed by the Liberal state, as well as land policies that had confiscated Church holdings but failed to undertake any kind of redistribution toward the indigenous population.[64] The demands of indigenous insurgents touched on the fundamentals of social organization in the countryside; for example, Indians insisted that the state comply with all the promises made in the Liberal laws proclaimed by distinct governments since 1895, in a direct critique of state authority.

Significantly, through these movements Indians developed and articulated a sense of local consciousness and ethnic identity. In these uprisings, protest spread from hamlet to hamlet and from town to town, and as it passed away from its initial starting point, protest was based less on concrete demands and specific grievances than on a sense of solidarity and commitment to their indigenous neighbors. Different indigenous groups launched carefully cocoordinated joint attacks and they shared leadership, strategy, and communication networks. In Chimborazo, indigenous rebels sought to establish an Indian army and to name an Indian president, in an apparent parallel with the Inca revivalist movements that were occurring in Bolivia and Peru at this time. Many elites became convinced as a result of this solidarity that they were experiencing the first stages of a "race war," and that the Indians were set upon a war of "reconquest."[65] The same intercommunity solidarity and alliances were seen in the emerging leftist-influenced movements of the 1920s and '30s in the northern province of Cayambe, where efforts were made to establish an Indian congress where representatives from communities across the entire country could come together (a development that was prevented only by police intervention and persecution of activists), and in efforts to create a national Indian party, which became a forerunner to the Federation of Ecuadorian Indians, finally established in 1944.[66] While it may be a stretch to suggest that this collaboration and cross-community solidarity emerged because of the experience of military activity in support of the Liberal state, it does seem that the gap between the Liberal rhetoric of inclusion—itself partly generated by indigenous military participation—and the reality of continued exclusion pushed forward a shared sense of grievance and resentment that went significantly beyond the localized, particularized "rebellions" that had characterized indigenous protest during the nineteenth century.

Conclusion

For both black and indigenous groups, citizenship was the underlying focus both of military engagement on behalf of the Liberal Revolution and their physical and cultural protest in its aftermath. Racially subaltern groups believed in the transformative power of liberalism. When the state did not extend the rights they felt had been promised to them, black and indigenous groups mobilized to demand their citizenship rights. In this they manifested an understanding of themselves as part of the nation as well as a desire to play a fuller role within it.

Black participation in the Concha Rebellion, in particular, could be classified as representing "popular liberalism" in the sense advanced by Mallon, Sanders, and Thompson.[67] Afro- Esmeraldans joined the movement out of a determination to defend and enforce the Alfarista ideals that they viewed as offering them freedom from debt peonage and hacienda oppression, and as presenting a foundation on which the rights of black people could be advanced. But indigenous rebellions also reflected an engagement with the ideals projected by liberalism, particularly as these were articulated (and embodied) by Eloy Alfaro, as well as a desire to reorder their relationship with the state. The experiences of both communities underscore the power of their experience in helping to shape the emerging nation-state and demonstrate that an analysis of military experience is essential to understanding both subaltern demands for citizenship and the formation of collective consciousness.

Acknowledgments

The research on which this article was based would not have been possible without financial support from an Arts and Humanities Board doctoral studentship, an Institute of Historical Research Scouloudi fellowship, as well as travel grants from the Royal Historical Society, the Society for Latin American Studies, the Hale Bellot Fund, the University College London Graduate School, the University of London Central Research Fund, and the Florida Gulf Coast University Faculty Senate Professional Development Fund. Thanks also to Christopher Abel, Jeff Gould, René D. Harder Horst, Anatoly Isaenko, Nicola Miller, and Shawn Smallman for their comments on earlier versions of this paper.

Notes

1. Elías Troncoso Barba, *La Campana de 1900 de Tulcán*.

2. Ecuador, Dirección Nacional de Estadística, *Ecuador en cifras*, 55.

3. Penaherra de Costales and Costales Sanmiego, *Historia Social del Ecuador*, 395; Rodriguez, *Search for Public Policy*, 26; and Whitten and Quiroga, "Ecuador," 294. Certainly, ideas about race have given a particular slant to the historical consolidation of regional divisions in Ecuador, with racialized idioms framing discussions of regional differentiation.

4. Available group photographs from the 1880s and '90s depicting the Alfarista military struggles of this period almost always include black soldiers. See Archivo Histórico del Banco Central, *Fondo Fotográfico*. Many biographies of Alfaro also include group photos of his military supporters. See especially Troncoso, *Vida anecdótica*.

5. Muñoz Vicuña, *Primero entre iguales*, 56.

6. Torres, cited in Pérez Concha, *Carlos Concha Torres*, 34.

7. Granizo Romero, "Lideres de pies des calzos."

8. Goncharovo, "Los indígenas en la revolución liberal," 197.

9. Ayala, "De la revolución alfarista al régimen oligárquico liberal," 119, 122–23. Ayala, however, takes a class-based analysis of this division; he has not analyzed the possible racial transcript.

10. See Helg, *Our Rightful Share*; Lasso, "Revisiting Independence Day"; and Wright, *Café con Leche*.

11. Granizo Romero, "Lideres de pies des calzos."

12. *Runa* is the Quichua term used to describe themselves as a communal group. Literally translated it means "person."

13. Del Pozo, *Yo declaro con franqueza*, 62. It is significant that Ecuadorian Indians supported Liberals, in contrast to the pattern Sanders notes for Colombia in chapter 1 of this book. This was largely due to the leadership of Alfaro, who adapted liberal politics to subaltern ideas about landholding and community and expressly reached out to black and indigenous communities. As a result, Ecuadorian liberalism in the early twentieth century was much less interested than its nineteenth century counterparts elsewhere in the privatization of communal land. Arguably, with land rights protected, Indians had something to gain from the pursuit of citizenship.

14. Foote, "Race, State and Nation."

15. Ley de Reclutas y Reemplazos, Ministro de Relaciones Exteriores, Cultos, Justicia

etc., 1903, Mensajes e Informes, 1903, ABFL; Código Militar, 1905, Mensajes e Informes, 1905, ABFL.

16. Chiriboga, *El problema del Indio*, 590–91, 594, 598, 601–10.

17. *El Comercio*, Quito, March 10, 1925.

18. Lhevinne, *Enchanted Jungle*, 23.

19. For a fictionalized account of the role of black Esmeraldans in the 1941 war see Ortiz, *Juyungo*, 189–211.

20. In regard to contemporary Colombia, Peter Wade has argued that the black civil rights movement has suffered from a tendency to regard blacks as citizens, but second-class ones. Wade, *Blackness and Race Mixture in Colombia*.

21. Anthias and Yuval-Davis, *Woman-Nation-State*.

22. Efforts to emasculate racially subordinated males have been a regular part of gendered social stratification in all racially divided societies, and the sexual abuse and rape of black and indigenous women by white men in colonial Latin America and the Caribbean can be read in this way.

23. Informe del Gobernación de la Provincia de Esmeraldas al Ministro de lo Interior, Policía, Obras Publicas, etc., 1902, Mensajes e Informes, 1902, ABFL; and Metallí, "A civilizar la cayapa."

24. Guzmán, *Los inmigrantes en el Ecuador*, 50.

25. Foote, "Race, State and Nation," 265.

26. This political and economic neglect has strong parallels with the experiences of black provinces on the Atlantic Coast of Central America. See Chomsky, *West Indian Workers*; and Sharman, "The Caribbean *Carretara*."

27. Reyes, *Breve historia general del Ecuador*, 277.

28. See Muñoz Vicuña, *Primero entre iguales*; and Pérez Concha, *Carlos Concha torres*.

29. One exception is Alfonso Castro Chiriboga, who has called for an analysis of the insurrection as a "local ethnic phenomenon." See Castro Chiriboga, "Revolución de Concha," 86. His article, however, provides only a very general outline of the movement and does not advance the analysis he himself has demanded.

30. This is highlighted by the recruitment scene in Nelson Estupiñán Bass's novel, *Cuando los Guayacanes Florecian* (1954), 3–7, where the captain in charge of recruiting implores the debt peons in his audience: "You . . . all . . . have to help us avenge the death of General Alfaro, the idol of the nation, the man who gave us this freedom that all of us, regardless of race, now enjoy."

31. There is evidence that the assassination of Alfaro had a similarly emotional impact on indigenous people. An oral testimony from Cayambe recalls that on hearing the news of the assassination, the Indians of Pesillo declared their refusal to work for those who had killed "el indio Alfaro." del Pozo, *Yo declare con franqueza*, 68. Likewise, Whitten and Corr describe how, in the festival of Caporal held by the Salasca Quechua, the "good president" Eloy Alfaro was represented as besieged by "devils" in the person of high-ranking bureaucrats and wealthy politicians who wanted to ensnare and dislodge him. Whitten and Corr, "Imagery of Blackness," 221–23.

32. Archivo Banco Central del Ecuador, Fondo Fotográfico.

33. See Cabello de Balboa, *Descripción de la Provincia de Esmeraldas*; Estupiñán Tello, *Esmeraldas de ayer*; Garcia-Barrio, "Blacks in Ecuadorian Literature"; and Rueda Novoa,

Zambaje y Autonomia. This can be seen too in the themes emphasized by the black writers of the 1940s. The main character in Adalberto Ortiz's *Juyungo*, for example, is a black man who constantly speaks in the language of freedom, and who all observers agree would never have submitted to slavery.

34. Estupiñán Bass, *Cuando lo Guayacanes Florecían*, 21–22.

35. Moreno, *La campana de Esmeraldas*, 2. Moreno's account is one of the most balanced and detailed firsthand accounts available. Although he fought on the side of the Plazista government against Concha, he was deeply angry at the way the government conducted their response to the rebellion and was critical of its actions while he admired many elements of peasant conduct.

36. Ibid.

37. Pérez Concha, *Carlos Concha Torres*, 180. See also Adalberto Ortiz, "Captura de un caudillo."

38. Moreno, *La campana de Esmeraldas*, 28.

39. In many respects the imagery of Sergeant Lastre parallels that of Antonio Maceo during the Cuban War of Independence.

40. Moreno, *La campana de Esmeraldas*, 28.

41. Ortiz, *Juyungo*, 38.

42. Ibid, 29. The occasionally rose-tinted nature of Moreno's account of Lastre's administration of the city of Esmeraldas, at odds with his position on the opposing forces, reflects his anger and disillusionment with how the government ran its campaign against the Conchistas.

43. Ibid, 29.

44. *El Guante*, Guayaquil, November 1, 1913.

45. Informe que Modesto A. Peñaherrera, Ministro de lo Interior, Municipalidades, Policía, Obras Publicas, etc. Presenta a la Nación en 1915, Mensajes e Informes, 1915. ABFL.

46. *El Guante*, October 31, 1913.

47. Maloney, "El Negro y la cuestión nacional," 65.

48. Mensaje del Presidente de la República al Congreso Ordinario de 1915, Mensajes e Informes, 1915, ABFL.

49. Moreno, *La campaña de Esmeraldas*, 36–37. It has been estimated that six to eight government soldiers were killed for every day of the combat. See Muñoz Vicuña, *Primero entre iguales*, 151.

50. Moreno, *La campaña de Esmeraldas*, 44.

51. Ibid, 40.

52. *El Telégrafo*, April 26, 1914. This obsession with black barbarity was paralleled in Cuba, where blacks in the Liberation Army were stereotyped as headcutters. See Helg, *Our Rightful Share*, 58.

53. Estupiñán Bass, *Cuando los Guayacanes Florecían*, 100.

54. Mensaje del Presidente de la República al Congreso Ordinario de 1914, Mensajes e Informes 1914, ABFL.

55. Mensaje del Presidente de la República al Congreso Ordinario de 1915, Mensajes e Informes 1915, ABFL.

56. *El Ecuatoriano*, January 30, 1914.

57. Captain Gardien, 26th Infantry Military Attaché, on board USS *Maryland*, Ecuador, to Young, February 11, 1912. National Archive of the United States, Records of the Department of State Relating to Internal Affairs of Ecuador, 1910–1920, Decimal File 822. As replicated in University of Texas at Austin Nettie Lee Benson Latin America Collection Microfilm Collection, Film 22, 623 1-26, 1910–1929.

58. del Pozo, *Yo declaro con franqueza*, 71, 73.

59. Estupiñán Bass, *Cuando los Guayacanes Florecían*, 15–16.

60. Informe que el Ministro de lo Interior, Policía, Obras Publicas, Municipalidades, etc. Presenta a la Nación, 1920, Mensajes e Informes, 1920, ABFL.

61. Estupiñán Bass, *Cuando los Guayacanes Florecían*.

62. Estupiñán Bass, "Artistas Negras," 74.

63. Flores Galindo, *Buscando un Inca*, 308–43; and Rivera Cusicanqui, *Oppressed but not Defeated*, 36–37.

64. For details on these rebellions see Baud, "Campesinos indigenas contra el estado"; and Foote, "Race, Gender and Nation in Ecuador," chap. 5.

65. *El Comercio*, May 22, 1921; and Informe del Ministro de lo Interior, 1921, Mensajes e Informes 1921, ABFL.

66. Becker, *Indians and Leftists*.

67. Mallon, *Peasant and Nation*; Sanders, "'Citizens of a Free People'"; and Thomson, with LaFrance, *Patriotism, Politics, and Popular Liberalism*.

5

Race and Ethnicity in the Guatemalan Army, 1914

RICHARD N. ADAMS

The relationship that holds, and has held, between the Guatemalan Mayan Indian population and the military establishment of the Guatemalan state is complex and has been the subject of little social research.[1] The principle reason is that the military establishment of Guatemala has long blocked almost any effort to explore its past. This chapter originated in the discovery, among the governor's (Jefe Político) papers of the Department of San Marcos,[2] of a document labeled simply "Filiación," a register of soldiers. It comprises a list of 259 recruits from January through April of 1914 in the departmental capital of San Marcos. Because it provides an intriguing series of descriptions of the recruits, it may be useful for better understanding the roles that the Indians, Ladinos, and ethnicity may have played in development of the military in early twentieth century Guatemala.

Army–Indian Relationship, 1871–1914

The Liberal reforms introduced in the 1870s opened a new era in Guatemalan history. While ramifications were felt in all sectors of the society, the new Liberal government early decreed changes in the military. Of particular concern was to create a military establishment of national loyalty in order to centralize power in the state. Since liberal political economic philosophy required controlling the labor of the peasants, overwhelmingly an Indian population, it was critical that the country's military forces should serve the central government and not regional interests. The plan was first to set up some core battalions, followed by universal obligatory military service, a full-scale voluntary service, and an elite military academy to produce officers for the new professional service.

The first core battalions were decreed in December of 1871; officials were directed to travel through "all the ladino communities in each department,"[3] and to seek recruits younger than thirty years of age who were also literate. The notion of a voluntary army was further consolidated a year later in a decree that stipulated that recruits be from the "ladino populations of the respective departments." It would appear that if the literacy requirement were not enough to discourage Indian participation in the new volunteer battalions, the specific orders to seek out Ladinos made it clear.

In the end, it appeared that a volunteer army apparently could not provide sufficient military force to meet the demands of the era. On June 8, 1872, Decree No. 65 established obligatory military service.[4] This document stated that "the principles of equality and justice on which political association ought to be based requires that, without regard to the class of persons, all should participate in accord with their aptitudes." It was further argued that formerly "an abusive system whereby the sacrifice of blood, the most onerous of all sacrifices, fell exclusively on the destitute class, and provided no way for a counterbalancing service by the superior classes who, receiving the major advantages of the society, are most interested in the maintenance of order and peace." In this decree the clause concerning "aptitudes" seemed only to refer to excusing the physically defective from obligatory service, or those who would pay fifteen pesos for each year of service to be excused.[5]

The first plan for obligatory service evidently did not work well, and in January 1873 a further decree reiterated that "it is just and convenient, as far as possible, to relieve the proletarian class, which has for so long alone borne the sacrifice of blood which all citizens are equally obliged to bear."[6] More specifically, Article 5 inserted an additional exception apparently based on "aptitudes": "To be excepted are the Indians who have not been accustomed to this service and, instead, shall lend other services of a different nature."

The liberal leaders were convinced that they needed a national army that would draw on individuals who might be hoped to have a broader, national vision—hence, the emphases on literate voluntary recruits and that both conscripted and voluntary members should be Ladinos. The argument that the "destitute class" (Decree No. 65) or the "proletarian class" (Decree No. 85) had unfairly borne the entire burden of the "contribution of blood" gave logic to the demand for a broader social base for the army but did not exclude the Indians from giving further service. The Escuela Politécnica (the National Military Academy)—also central to the national vision—initially involved only sons of better families, and the possibility of Indian participation apparently did not arise.[7]

Justo Rufino Barrios' vision of a well-trained and educated Ladino army, loyal to the central government and under the command of professionally trained officers, proved unrealistic. Indian labor, increasingly in demand for the export economy, was also needed for the army. Indians were, after all, more likely to be a military object than to be a subject. By 1894 the Barrios experiment had gone far enough to expose its weaknesses: (a) assuming that educated Ladinos would flock to the service; (b) allowing people to purchase their way out of the service; (c) thinking that rural ladinos would make better soldiers than Indians; (d) believing that Indians could not be trusted to control other Indians; and (e) trying to do so much with so little available manpower. Also, *indigenismo* was appearing in newspapers and intellectuals were showing concern about the condition of the Indian and what should be done about it.[8] The harsh and oppressive forced labor decreed by Barrios in 1877 was not compatible with a world where republicanism, liberty, justice, and equality were increasingly thrust forward as touchstones of the future.

By the turn of the century, the problems of a clearly defective system were being discussed openly in the military press. The papers of the governor of the department of San Marcos in the first decade of the century contains often conflicting requests for men for one or another of these efforts, and the policy that farms had priority over the army for these purposes led to a constant problem on the part of the military to keep itself well staffed. But nothing seemed to work. The universal, obligatory military service did not provide enough recruits, agricultural labor was still short in many regions, and justice and equality existed only in print.[9] The *Revista Militar Ilustrada* (1900) reported:

> Today, our military service is nourished by the poorer classes, whose education, moral and intellectual, leaves much to be desired. Today, the individual entering the Service suffers much more than elsewhere, his sacrifice is greater and his rewards are less. Today the man who takes up the gun instead of the plow, the bayonet in place of the machete, suffers a radical shock to his customs, to his entire being.[10]

This was a period filled with wars, or threats thereof, with neighboring Central American countries and Mexico. Besides the 1885 conflict in which Barrios lost his life, Manuel Lisandro Barrillas declared war on El Salvador in 1889, and there were invasions of Guatemala, principally by Guatemalan exiles in combination with Salvadoran and or Honduran troops, in 1898, 1899, 1903, 1906, 1915, and 1916.[11] Thus the expansion of the military was seen as a matter of singular national importance.

Reinterpreting the Role of the Indian in the Army

The failed strategy to create a literate Ladino army led to discussions rein-terpreting the nature of the Indian and what that might in turn mean to the military service. One element of these ideas rationalized that the ancient Maya had been notable warriors, and that this ancestry was an important component in the contemporary soldier. An anonymous romantic waxed enthusiastic in 1904:

> Easily aroused by noble ideas, and tenacious to defend them are Guatemalan soldiers, as in them are combined the contrary ethnic conditions that permit a combination of all that was good in their ancestors. . . . Valiant and inured to war were the Indian tribes that populated ancient Guatemala; on the other side, the Spaniards came preceded by great fame as the vanguard of the Roman legions, now having fought for centuries against the Arabs, then for having shaken Europe through victorious campaigns in Flanders and Italy. The Gua-temalan soldier, heir to both, has glorious antecedents."[12]

Zamora Castellanos proposed a somewhat different twist some years later, referring to the late colonial era:

> Little by little, in spite of Spanish laws, the indigenous and Iberian races were mixed, and it became necessary to call upon the "*criollo ladino*" and the mixtures to lend themselves for military service. The new race, mixture of conqueror and conquered, was an amalgam that embodied the value, joy and intelligence of the Spanish adventurer, and the wisdom, the passionate character and skills of the Indian sol-dier, fallen at the feet of his idols. . . . Races of heterogeneous blood, are united for unity, for discipline, and they initiate civil wars that destroy peoples.[13]

The enthusiasm for the heroic contribution that the Indian component lent to the army did not reflect an unalloyed ardor for the Indians as such. The *Revista Militar Ilustrada* provided a more common view in an essay ti-tled "The Indian":

> There he comes, hunchbacked, a bundle on his shoulders, sweating, panting, half naked, filthy . . . apparently forever condemned to look downwards, to focus on the things small; always looking at the earth. Has he once seen the majestic flight of the eagles? smiled with the

dawn? felt God in his soul when watching the stars? . . . Impoverished race! with routine and almost stupid simplicity, tells the truth.[14]

In contrast, Guillermo Kuhsiek A. saw the Indian to be the product of centuries of oppression:

> The Guatemalan Indian, descendent of the warlike K'iche' and Kaq-chikel, whose iron valor shown against the armor and cannons of the Spanish invader, is today a patient and humble peasant. . . . The great mass of the Indians continues being patient and docile labor. The spirit of his arrogant ancestors has not been resuscitated.[15]

He then stated that until now the Indian had formed only a small part of the army; the majority were Ladinos, so poor and uneducated that the Escuela Politécnica graduates had to instruct them in the search for line officers. However, the fact that Indians constituted two-thirds of the population means they are potentially a major source for the army.[16] Although the Indians' moral condition was not promising, his physical state was more auspicious: "although he is extremely self-denying, malnourished and badly clothed, he works with the same endurance in the heat of the coast as in the cold of the mountains, in the summer sun and the winter rains."[17]

These essays also addressed one final advantage the Indian had as a soldier: his food consumption was minimal: "Our army does not need heavy food convoys to follow them. To be without food for some time or without water is not something that holds anyone back. . . . The food of most of the country's inhabitants is essentially vegetal—the supreme aspiration of advanced peoples because it is seen as a way to reduce conflict between capital and labor—so the Guatemalan troops spend very little on their food.[18] Physiologists may say what they will, the fact is that our soldiers, fed with legumes, can place cannons high in the mountains with awesome facility."[19] Kuhsiek specifically mentions the military advantage of the Indian diet: "For all of them in the most difficult day's march they carry no more than . . . 'totoposte,' toasted corn tortillas."[20]

During this period of intense military turmoil under consideration the army did include Indians, but we are far from knowing just how many, either relatively or absolutely. Moreover, whatever may have been the opinions about the use of Indians in the army, it is clear that in time of war, obligatory service was often employed, both formally and informally.[21]

Regionally, the goal of creating a Ladino army was sometimes ignored. Carmack describes how the Ladinos of Momostenango used the developing

Ladino army to ensure their local dominance but combined it with the use of Indian militia:

> From the end of the century on, they could draw upon the full force of arms from the military wing of the state, as well as the various police agencies, to back them in both their personal and national political agendas. What made the system so effective, far more than the one established by Barrios, was the way the caudillos co-opted local Indian leaders. . . . The militia, almost exclusively ladino under Barrios, became the primary vehicle in this process. Indians were given not only a place in it, but also the opportunity to prove themselves and even become officers. The traditional native social divisions were respected, as with the equestrian squadron of caciques . . . and the artillery squadron of San Bartolo . . . and the Indians' traditional religion was "rationalized" in such a way that it provided ritual support for all things military.[22]

In 1920, when Estrada Cabrera realized that the movement against him was indeed serious, he called in to defend his residence, La Palma, "troops of San Marcos, Sija, Momostenango and Canales, the last famous as being well seasoned."[23]

In the half century that followed the Liberal decrees to create a Ladino professional army, the army that emerged was far from what had been originally conceived. The officer corps, increasingly a product of the elite Escuela Politécnica, was concerned that the army represent the country and that it be of quality. Given the nature of the Guatemalan people, the two goals were not readily reconcilable. Because those with wealth could afford to purchase their way out of service, only the poorer Ladinos, of whom there were not enough, became soldiers. So it was necessary to recruit Indians as well, in spite of the ideological and legal obstacles that stood in the way. Precisely because of this, however, we find the Indians were being used in some instances, and a literature began to put forth arguments, both practical and ideological, as to why more Indians needed to be incorporated into the military service.

Indians and Ladinos in 1914 San Marcos Recruitment

The 1914 list of 259 San Marcos recruits may be, for the moment, the only document available to scholars describing the composition of the Guatemalan army in this era. Because the recruits are identified as to their ethnic and racial characteristics, this document offers an unusual opportunity to gain an idea of how the two ethnic groups were perceived at the time, and to perhaps evaluate how some assumptions and assertions made by military essayists of the era accord with a real case.

It seems reasonable to assume that one reason for these detailed descriptions of the recruits was for information necessary in the case of desertion, although this is not specified. Such descriptions were sent out from time to time.

Recruit Background

There are a number of reasons for uncertainties about ethnic relations in this era and region. Since most San Marcos Indians had surnames of Spanish origin, it is impossible to be sure of ethnic identification in a great many of the documents of the era. Moreover, even when ethnic identification is provided, detailed somatic and sociocultural information on indigenous individuals were of little interest to those who were literate enough to record observations.

While the 1914 list is uneven in information, it provides data on both sociocultural and somatic characteristics of a large enough number of both Indians and Ladinos to allow an initial picture of the two populations. Included for each recruit are data deemed important for identification, the signature of the recruit (or if he was illiterate, that of a witness), and the signature of an official, all written by hand in paragraph form. Descriptions varied somewhat both as to the order in which the data were given and as to completeness.

Most recruits were identified as being *indígena*, or Ladino. (See table 5.1.) Generally I assumed that the soldier's ethnicity followed that of both parents. However, in one case, #64, Reyes, the soldier is listed as Ladino. His mother is parenthetically listed as an *indígena* while his father has no ethnic listing and so was probably Ladino. This is interesting because it suggests that ethnicity may have been seen to be inherited though it does not involve *identity*—that is, it ignores how an individual may seem himself and reflects only the view of the person who is bestowing it. We presume in the present case that the terms are being applied by Ladinos who were in charge of the recruiting. While we do not know whether they made the classifications independently, it is unlikely that they asked the recruits to tell them, so it is probably best to take these designations as "external" labeling.[24]

Recruiting in San Marcos City drew principally on neighboring *municipios*. A precise comparison cannot be made between the recruiting sample

Table 5.1. Ladino and Indian Recruits (1914) Relative to the Total Population (1921)

Municipality	Population Census, 1921				Recruit Ethnicity, 1914			
	Indian		Ladino		Indians		Ladinos	
	No.	%	No.	%	No.	%	No.	%
San Marcos	1,680	27.9	4,349	72.1	7	30.4	17	69.6
Esquipulas Palo Gordo	535	29.3	1,292	70.7	1	7.7	12	92.3
San Lorenzo	1,250	60.1	829	39.9	3	42.9	4	57.1
Rio Blanco	1,016	65.4	538	34.6	3	27.3	8	72.7
Tejutla	4,643	75.9	1,473	24.1	27	87.1	4	12.9
San Jose Ojetenám	2,725	85.4	467	14.6	15	88.2	2	11.8
San Cristobal Cucho	2,825	89	350	11	22	95.7	1	4.3
San Antonio Sacatepequez	3,189	89.4	378	10.6	21	95.5	1	4.5
Tacana	10,928	89.9	1,231	10.1	13	100	0	0
San Pedro Sacatepequez	11,972	91.5	1,116	8.5	62	93.9	4	6.1
Tajumulco	9,103	97.9	197	2.1	1	100	0	0
Ixtahuacán	5,350	98.8	110	1.2	0	0	1	100
Comitancillo	10,372	99.6	44	0.4	2	100	0	0
Other municipalities	1,680	27.9	4,349	72.1	0	0	2	100
Total	67,268	80.1	16,723	19.9	177	76.0	56	24.0

and total population for a number of reasons: Data is not complete in all cases and we have no dependable demographic data for 1914.[25] Table 5.1 compares the 1914 recruitment figures with the 1921 census figures for those *municipios* for which data were available.[26] There is no question that the *municipios* individually contributed quite differently to the army's needs. The four municipios with the greatest Ladino percentage also gave the largest proportion of Ladino recruits. The situation was essentially parallel in the Indian *municipios* if we omit those that only sent one or two people. The principle geographical basis for recruiting, however, was the proximity of the *municipios* to the city of San Marcos (see map). In both ethnic groups, the major part of the recruits were drawn from six *municipios*; Tejutla and San Pedro Sacatepequez were important for both, but otherwise the distribution was complementary.

Ethnic Variations

This section will treat each of the characteristics provided in the descriptions. Before taking up the individual traits, however, there are two issues of cultural bias that need to be discussed.

The Recruiters

A question immediately arises as to what ethnic perspectives were used in observing the recruits and recording these features (see table 5.2). While the ethnicity of the recruiters is not given, it is possible to make a guess.

Table 5.2. Possible Ethnicity of Signatories of Recruitment Entries, 1914

Surnames of Signatories	Ethnic Identification of Name		Number of Entries Signed By	
	Ladino	Indian	Ladino	Indian
Barrios	14	2	89	0
Bautista	0	2	0	19
Castillo[a]	0	0	26	0
de Leon	12	1	1	0
Fuentes	1	12	0	13
Lopéz	10	35	0	16
Maldonado	6	0	130	0
Mendez	2	6	0	31
Ruiz	2	0	84	0
Total	47	58	330	79

a. The name "Castillo" does not appear in this list but is a well-known Ladino name in San Marcos.

Each entry apparently was supposed to be followed by two different signa-tures. One with no designation was either the recruit or a substitute (we will call him the "signatory") and one marked as a witness. In addition to those recruits who signed their own names, ten individuals participated in signing the entries, four of whom acted as both signatories and witnesses but not for the same entries. In all, signatories signed 204 of the entries, and 227 were signed by witnesses. Six entries had no signatory, and 13 had no witness. There is some basis for guessing the ethnicity of these recruit-ers. First, since only 5.3 percent of the Indian recruits were literate as com-pared with 32.8 percent of the Ladinos, it is likely that these literate signa-tories also would be Ladino. Second, if army personnel served these roles, we might assume them to have been Ladinos if officers but Indians if they were noncommissioned officers. In the present recruitment sample, there are seven non-commissioned officers (all corporals) and only one of them is a Ladino (to be discussed later). And third, if we go by the surnames, our best indication at present is that five (possibly six) were Ladino and four were Indian. This is derived from comparing the surnames with those on a list of surnames from San Marcos in this era where the ethnicity of indi-viduals is known.[27] Fourteen known Ladinos and two known Indians use the name Barrios. This suggests that the signatory Barrios was probably La-dino. Table 5.2, then, is a guess based on the hypothesis that the individuals whose surname is most used by people of one or the other ethnicity, will be of that ethnicity. The last two columns give the numbers of recruiting entries signed by individual of the supposed ethnicity.

While it appears from table 5.2 that both Ladinos and Indians could have been both signatories and witnesses in the recruiting process, it must be remembered that the Spanish surnames used by San Marcos Indians are used by non-Indians somewhere in the world. So it is always possible that none of the signatories or witnesses were Indian. Whatever the situation, the Ladinos were responsible either for signing for many more recruits than were the Indians, or for signing all of them. We may tentatively conclude that a Ladino perspective dominated the formulating of the descriptions.

From this analysis, it is clear that caution must be exercised in inter-preting the recruitment list's descriptive terms and their application. In the main, however, I think that it is reasonable to treat these descriptions as relatively reliable representations of the recruits as seen by the society of the period.[28] While there is surely ethnic stereotyping, there are also conditions that would have interfered with systematic biases. First, each set of observations were made on individuals and not applied collectively to a group. We can assume that direct observation of each recruit was at least an important basis for the description. Second, the presence of the ten different signatories and witnesses suggest different individual biases are present, which may reflect both Indian and Ladino perspectives, although we assume the latter predominates. Third, the observations were made over a period of some four months, which suggests that factors that may have biased some descriptions at one time need not have carried over later into others. And fourth, because the features described here were probably intended in great part for individual identification, it is likely that more attention was paid to features useful for that purpose and less to others that might have yielded greater ethnic variety. From the point of view of an expression of ethnic bias, however, the focus on the individual is advantageous because the persons making the descriptions would not necessarily have been trying to make an Indian or Ladino appear more Indian or more Ladino.

Genetics and Constitutional, or Culture

Most of the traits described in the *filiación* (military files) are fairly clearly of either a cultural derivation or of a genetic or constitutional derivation (see table 5.3). All the classifications, of course, are culturally devised. Phenotypic features are the product of genetics but can also often be further modified by cultural and social action. Because there are differences attached to the genetic–cultural issue, we will discuss the traits under those two categories. However, it must be repeated that genetically derived traits are inevitably subject to environmental modification, and some of this may be cultural. And culturally derived traits are often constructed out of genetically derived products.

Table 5.3. Genetic and Cultural Classification of Traits of Recruits

Genetically Derived	Socioculturally Derived and Selected
Beard and mustache	Age
Bodily identification marks	Army rank
Cheeks	Civil status
Eyes	Legitimacy
Face	Literacy
Forehead	Municipality of origin
Lips	Occupation
Mouth	Stature
Nose	Surname
Skin color	Use of shoes

Table 5.4. Ethnic Similarities of Genetically Derived Features

Feature	Characteristic	Indian %	Ladino %
Hair	Black	100.0	100.0
Eyebrows	Black	100.0	97.4
Eyes	Black	94.1	80.4
Cheeks	No differences reported	76.2	84.2
Skin color	Brown	74.2	75.4
Nose	Straight	71.9	69.2
Face	Long	50.6	67.3
Lips	Thick, distinguished, protruding	76.5	50.0
Mouth	"Regular"	48.5	55.8
Forehead	Narrow	64.0	40.0

Genetically or Constitutionally Derived Phenotypic Features

With respect to genetically derived traits, the two groups are more similar than different. Before exploring this issue, however, let us review the separate cases. Table 5.4 shows the percentage of each ethnic group that shares given traits; 50 percent or more members of the two groups are similar in six of the eight traits. I have included, simply for the argument, both hair and eyebrow color although they manifest no real ethnic difference.

Eyes

The terms used here were black, large, olive-shaped, and nut brown, while small, sunken, and with clouds, are bunched in "other." Almost everyone (94.1 percent of Indians and 80.4 percent of Ladinos) had dark eyes, the major divergence being that some 17.4 percent of the Ladinos were reported to have eyes of a green or light brown color, but even this was shared by 8 percent of the Indians.

Cheeks

Because no observation was made on more than 75 percent of the individuals, cheeks were not usually a feature of distinction. Of the remainder, 26 percent of the Indians and about 16 percent of the Ladinos were said to have high cheekbones, which were variously described as protruding. There is little to suggest any significant difference in the two populations in this matter.

Skin Color

Skin color was given as white or pale, brown, and dark. Both ethnic groups showed a strong similarity in basic skin color. While the term for brown

Table 5.5. Recruits by Shape of Nose and Ethnicity

	Number		Percent	
Description	Indian	Ladino	Indian	Ladino
Straight	135	43	74.2	75.4
Flat, flattened, somewhat flattened	40	8	22.0	14.0
Regular	4	3	2.2	5.3
Aquiline, somewhat curved	3	0	1.6	.0
Large	0	1	.0	1.8
Oblique	0	2	.0	3.5
Total	182	57	100.0	100.0

(*trigeño*) is probably not as widely used today as it apparently was in 1914, the high consistency of its use by the various reporters is striking. Although three-quarters of both groups are the same, with 74.2 percent of Indians and 75.4 percent of Ladinos described as brown, the remainder contrasts markedly. Of the Indians, 22.6 percent were called dark compared with 5.8 percent of the Ladinos, while 25 percent of the Ladinos were labeled as white or pale as compared to 5.5 percent of the Indians. Skin color is thus one of the few physical features that suggest a clear ethnic divergence, even though most individuals share the same color.

Nose

The terminology for describing the nose is somewhat exaggerated, and I have bunched certain of them for purposes of the analysis: straight, little, flat, regular, aquiline, slightly curved, and oblique. The shape of the nose was basically similar for both groups, being described as "straight" for approximately 75 percent of both groups. However, as with skin color, but not to the same degree, the remaining tended to diverge (see table 5.5). Almost all the rest of the Indians as well as more than half of the remaining Ladinos were described as having small and flat noses. As with the case of the cheeks and the eyes, the two groups are basically similar.

Face

Descriptions of the face were given as long, long with big cheeks, medium, olive shaped, round, and regular; here as elsewhere, I am not sure what to do with "regular." While Indian face shapes are roughly equally divided between "long" and "round or oval," only one-third of Ladinos have "round" or "oval" faces; almost all the rest are classified as "long."

Table 5.6. Recruits by Shape of Forehead and Ethnicity

	Number		Percent	
Description	Indian	Ladino	Indian	Ladino
Broad	27	13	16.4	26.0
Regular	31	17	18.8	34.0
Narrow	99	20	60.0	40.0
Long	4	0	2.4	0
Small	4	0	2.4	0
Total	165	50	100.0	100.0

Lips

The principal contrast in describing lips is between thin and thick. A few were labeled as protruding and fewer yet were labeled with the problematic "regular." About half the Indians and Ladinos are similar, but the divergence among the remainder is much more marked. Almost 45 percent of the Ladinos, compared with only about 18 percent of the Indians are described as having thin lips. In contrast, proportionally, half again as many Indians as Ladinos are described as having thick lips, under a number of different descriptive terms. Observations concerning lips were made on less than half the recruits, for reasons that are unclear.

Mouth

The terms used for the mouth were large, long, small, and regular, the last again being problematic. About one half of each of the two ethnic groups are credited with "regular" mouths, whatever that may be, and another third with "small" mouths. The difference comes in that of the remaining, 22.5 percent of the Indians but only 7.7 percent of the Ladinos are described as having "long" mouths.

Forehead

Forehead descriptions were given as wide, wide and flat, big, small, and regular (see table 5.6). This is the single genetically related feature in which differences are clearly more pronounced than similarities. Half again as many Indian are described as having a narrow forehead while the majority of the Ladinos are described as having "broad" or "regular" shaped foreheads.

Stature

This was a straightforward measurement given in meters and centimeters. The two ethnic populations manifest a small difference in stature. The documents examined show a tendency for Ladinos to predominate among the higher figures, and that they have both an average and a median height of about two centimeters greater than that of the Indians. It is unlikely, however, that if one could physically mingle with these populations that the Ladinos' higher average stature would be clearly in evidence. Indeed, at the upper end of the scale, 163 cm to 172 cm, there were more than twice as many Indians as Ladinos (thirty-three Indians compared to fifteen Ladinos), and the two tallest recruits in the group were Indians.

Difference in stature is probably more of academic interest than it was of real ethnic significance at the time. Because this recruit sample is drawn from the national population long before there was a general public health concern with nutrition and child care, there is no reason to think that either ethnic group suffered disproportionately from the absence of such services. The differences, then, are presumed to be related to existing domestic nutritional practices and to the genetic predispositions of the two populations. To the degree that the latter were operative, it appears that as has been the case in many other traits, the two populations were more similar than they were different.

Beards and Mustaches

In most societies the arrangement of hair carries cultural messages.[29] While the abundance, quality, and locus of facial hair are determined by both genetic and individual factors, social norms dictate how it shall be modified and how it is read culturally. The fact that, in the present case, the majority of both ethnic groups are without beards and mustaches may be due to one or more of three reasons: (a) the individuals were too young to display much facial hair; (b) they had little or no genetic potential for growing hair; and (c) the beard or mustache had been shaved off. Youth seems to be the principal issue with the Ladinos described as beardless and having little facial hair. Because the Ladinos were in general younger, it would also explain why half of them fell into this category. It surely also applies to many of the Indians described as beardless, but there are also many older Indians in that category. Classically and genetically, however, the native peoples of the Western Hemisphere tend to have little facial hair, so it is not surprising that more than 30 percent of the Ladinos are described as bearded, regular, and thick; inversely, while Indians have higher average ages, they still are reported as having less facial hair. (See tables 5.7, 5.8, and 5.9.)

Beards were described in three general and two marginal categories: scarce, beardless, and regular. In addition, three were red and one thick. A

Table 5.7. Recruits by Beard and Ethnicity

	Number		Percent	
Description	Indian	Ladino	Indian	Ladino
Bearded and Regular	20	13	14.0	28.9
Beardless	85	27	59.4	60.0
Scarce, thin	38	5	26.6	11.1
Total	143	45	100.0	100.0

Table 5.8. Recruits by Shape of Mustache and Ethnicity

	Number		Percent	
Description	Indian	Ladino	Indian	Ladino
Small, sparse, scarce	40	5	69.0	26.3
"Regular," bearded, thick	15	8	25.9	42.1
Just beginning	0	3	0.0	15.8
Nothing, beardless	1	2	1.7	10.5
Blond, slightly blond	2	1	3.4	5.3
Total	58	19	100.0	100.0

Table 5.9. Comparison of Use of Beards and Mustaches by Recruits

	Beards				Mustaches			
	No.		%		No.		%	
	Indian	Ladino	Indian	Ladino	Indian	Ladino	Indian	Ladino
Bearded, regular, thick	22	15	31.9	65.2	15	8	26.3	50
Small, sparse, none, without, lacking	47	8	68.1	34.8	42	8	73.7	50
Total	69	23	100	100	57	16	100.0	100.0

comparison among those in these top three categories (bearded, regular, and thick) gives the Indians less than half the percentage of the Ladinos. There is no way from this list to know what role shaving may have played.

The mustache was described as hairy, regular, thick, little, thin, none, blond, slightly blond, beardless, beginning, scarce. The most striking thing about mustaches is that only seventy-seven individuals are described at all. The proportion of each ethnic group represented in the mustache list, however, is almost identical to that of the total population of recruits. The omission of almost 70 percent of the total is probably because when the beard was marked as beardless or none, it was intended to be applied also to the mustache. If this is true, then mustaches and beards have similar distributions. In table 5.9, the beardless, blond, and beginning—all the individuals who were said to be beardless or for whom nothing was reported—are removed, and just those for whom facial hair is reported are compared. Table 5.9 shows 73.7 percent of the Indians as compared with 50.0 percent of the Ladinos had mustaches classified as little, thin, none, without, or scarce. In contrast, 50.0 percent of the Ladinos, as contrasted to 26.3 percent of the Indians, are described as having mustaches that are hairy, regular, or thick. This not surprising based on the genetic expectations.

Bodily Identification Marks

The broad category of bodily identification marks included distinctive scars and marks on exposed body parts (birthmarks, cicatrizes, pox marked), and dysfunctional limbs. (Some of these may be, and others clearly are, of social or cultural derivation, but I deal with them collectively simply because there are not enough to treat them separately.) I have included the absence of data together with "none." Table 5.10 shows that items that might be considered congenital, i.e., spots, moles, birthmarks, have a slightly higher incidence among Ladinos than among Indians. Ladinos are also reported to have a higher incidence of scars, which may suggest they were somewhat more subject to wounds from fights. The Indians have a much higher incidence of smallpox scars, suggesting a greater vulnerability to that disease, or inferior medical care, or both. Since vaccinations were given in this era, it implies that fewer Indians received them. They also have a higher incidence of immobilized fingers, probably due to more machete accidents without effective treatment.

Table 5.10. Recruits by Bodily Identity Marks and Ethnicity

Description	Number		Percent	
	Indians	Ladinos	Indians	Ladinos
Spots, moles, birthmarks	27	14	14.2	23.0
Scars	45	19	23.7	31.1
None	88	25	46.3	41.0
Smallpox scars	23	2	12.1	3.3
Immobile fingers	5	0	2.6	.0
Other	2	1	1.1	1.6
Total	190	61	100.0	100.0

Sociocultural Traits

The traits of concern here are those that are entirely due to cultural or social factors and can claim no genetic determination. It is interesting at the out-set, then, to observe that most of these eight traits show some divergence, in contrast to most biological features, which demonstrated that the two ethnicities were generally more similar.

Age Distribution

The age distributions are biased by the fact that the dates registered tend to prefer years ending in 5 and 0 (see table 5.11). The high numbers re-corded for 18- and 19-year-olds are presumably due to trying to recruit not only young men but also to recruiting boys under 18, a practice still used today. There is a significant difference among the recruits of the two ethnic groups. While 65.6 percent of the Ladino recruits were under 25 years old and none were over 44, less than 50 percent of the Indians were under 25, and 9 percent were over 45. The average Ladino age was 23.21 years, while that of the Indians was 27.38. It was striking that there were individual Indians recorded as being 60, 68, and 75 years old. The disproportionately high incidence of Ladinos in the lowest age brackets, and the extension of Indians into higher brackets, replicates a phenomenon found among labor-ers in the department of San Marcos in the same era. Data from ten early twentieth century San Marcos coffee *fincas* showed that while 39 percent of the Indian laborers were under 30 years old, 57 percent of the Ladinos were below this age.[30]

Table 5.11. Recruit Age and Ethnicity

	Numbers		Percent	
Ages	Indians	Ladinos	Indians	Ladinos
18–19	33	19	18.8	32.8
20–24	51	19	29.0	32.8
25–29	37	9	21.0	15.5
30–34	19	6	10.8	10.3
35–39	15	3	8.5	5.2
40–44	5	2	2.8	3.4
45–49	8	0	4.5	0.0
50–54	2	0	1.1	0.0
55–59	3	0	1.7	0.0
60–75	3	0	1.7	0.0
Total	176	58	100.0	100.0

One can only speculate on the social significance of these differences, but it seems clear that the burden of military duty could weigh more heavily in the lives of Indians than of Ladinos. For the latter, the obligations of military service could be met and put aside in one's youth, whereas Indians were apparently more vulnerable to being conscripted, being kept on in the service, or possibly deciding on the army as a career. To what degree this accorded with the individual's own wishes is not clear from the present material.

Army Rank

All individuals were called soldier except seven corporals, six of whom were Indian. They appear to have been mature individuals, with an average age of thirty-seven, and all but one (a twenty-nine-year-old) was married. All were of legitimate birth. They came principally from three towns, San Pedro Sacatepequez, San Cristobal Cucho, and Rio Blanco. This apparently heavy dependence on Indians may be due to the fact that there were many more older Indians in the service and possibly that they remained in the army for longer periods. It is also possible that it was preferred to use Indian noncommissioned officers for the same reason that Indians were preferred for auxiliary municipal officers and as foremen on the *fincas*; they had better communication with their subordinates. The commissioned positions, however, probably went to Ladinos, for reasons such as were proposed by Kuhsiek: "The Indian does not have the conditions needed by officers: his lack of initiative and decision, and even greater lack of education than is found in ladino ranks, make him inept to command troops."[31] Kuhsiek made no comment on Indians as noncommissioned officers.

Marital Status

Almost all recruits were listed as single or married, with only one individual listed as living in free union and one widower. The stability implied for the Indian population in the list of corporals seems at first glance to be further supported by the marital status of the recruits. Here the percent of Indians who were married was three times as high as that for Ladinos. However, on closer examination, it appears that the difference in age distribution of the two groups may account for this difference. The percentage of single Indians and single Ladinos is very similar in each age group (see table 5.12). Moreover, even though the small absolute numbers of married Ladinos casts doubt on any observation, it should be noted that married men under 24 years of age is 12.8 percent for Indians and 12.5 percent for Ladinos. Also,

Table 5.12. Recruits by Civil Status and Ethnicity

Civil Status	Number		Percent	
	Indian	Ladino	Indian	Ladino
Single	94	48	54.3	84.2
Married	78	8	45.1	14.0
Free union	0	1	0	1.8
Widowed	1	0	0.6	0
Total	173	57	100.0	100.0
Average age				
of single men	22.52	21.71		
of married men	33.04	33.63		

the average ages for both single men (Ladinos, 21.71; Indians, 22.52) and for the married (Ladinos, 33.63; Indians, 33.04) are similar.

However, the similarities may not be indicative of the Indian and Ladino societies in general, since the main body of older Ladinos were simply not represented in the army. A low incidence of marriage among Ladinos is a fairly well-known characteristic in more recent years, and contemporary data from the archives of the Catholic Church suggests that Ladinos in this era did not observe formal marriage very much either.[32] It is puzzling, however, that other materials suggest that while Indian domestic units tend to be more stable than those of rural Ladinos, free unions are much more common among the former than the latter. Yet in these records, only one recruit, an Indian, was recorded as having been in a free union.

Legitimacy

In spite of the difference in marriage patterns, both ethnic groups are reported to have very high legitimacy rates, the Ladinos being slightly higher than the Indians with 94.7 percent as opposed to 92.3 percent for Indians. How the Ladinos turn up with such a high rate of legitimacy when they manifest such a high incidence of lack of marriage is not clear. The conventional ways the child of unmarried parents is legitimized is either for the parents to get married or for the father to legally recognize the child. The latter is not an uncommon practice, although I have little data at present to suggest how common it may have been.[33]

Use of Shoes

Although reporting on this was absent from half the entries, the recorded material is suggestive. The reports were simple: shod or unshod. Although very few used shoes at all, of the 127 recorded, 9, or 30 percent of the Ladinos, and 2, or 2.1 percent of the Indians used shoes. All the shod were farmers and between nineteen and thirty years of age (average age, twenty-four; median, twenty-two). While 4 came from San Marcos, the rest were scattered from Rio Blanco, San Antonio Sacatepequez, San Diego, San Sebastian, Tajumulco, and Tejutla. All but 2 are literate, and all but 2 are single.

One of our anonymous essayists was enthusiastic about the unshod quality of the recruits: "As for their clothing, it is simple; and the shoes, simpler still; and yet there are no instances of swollen feet or of any discomfort that hindered extended marches or climbing the lofty mountains."[34] The 1903 comments of Pedro Castañeda C., an infantry captain, are a little more down to earth:

> We have to discard use of shoes by our soldiers, as much because of the economic condition of the county as because they are a positive hindrance; it is well known that it is the disinherited class of the society that gives their service, and they are not accustomed to use them, it just doesn't work, they have deformed their feet and they have created swellings and protuberances that makes them suffer and do not cut a very good military figure. I believe that it would be better to give them sandals, preferably the Spanish *alpargatas*, economizing because they are very cheap; it also frees them to march with ease.[35]

Literacy

In most records, this information was given as "schooled" or "not schooled"; in a few cases, it was given as "reads and writes," or "does not read or write." Claims to literacy received some support in that all so listed signed the document; all others were signed by a witness. A third of the Ladinos, but only 5 percent of the Indians could read and write. Twenty-five percent of the literate recruits came from San Marcos, and two-thirds of the total came from San Marcos, San Pedro Sacatepequez, Rio Blanco, and Tejutla. While four of the nineteen Ladinos were artisans (carpenters, sawyers, tanners, tailors), most of the remainder were farmers. Among the nine literate Indians, three were laborers and six were farmers. It is of more than passing interest that even though the total number of literate Indians was low, that a third of them were day laborers.

It will be recalled that an 1899 article in the *Revista Militar Ilustrada* declared that less than half the men in the army were literate.[36] The San Marcos recruit figures cast some doubt on this claim because much less than

Table 5.13. Recruits by Occupation and Ethnicity

	Number		Percent	
Occupation	Indians	Ladinos	Indians	Ladinos
Farmer	81	35	46.3	60.3
peasant and day laborer	89	12	50.9	20.7
Subtotal	*170*	*47*	*97.1*	*81.0*
Sawyer	1	4	.6	6.9
Mason	1	2	.6	3.4
Tailor	0	2	.0	3.4
Carpenter	0	1	.0	1.7
Tanner	0	1	.0	1.7
Weaver	0	1	.0	1.7
Merchant	1	0	.6	.0
Spinner	1	0	.6	.0
Shoemaker	1	0	.6	.0
Subtotal	*5*	*11*	*2.9*	*19.0*
Total	**175**	**58**	**100.0**	**100.0**

half—indeed, barely one-eighth—were recorded as able to read and write. Clearly there were real reasons for the despair expressed by those authors who still retained a grain of hope for a literate Ladino army. Moreover, the fact that there was little choice but to seek to incorporate more Indians in the army meant that the literacy rate would decline further.

Occupation

The twelve occupations are all fairly straightforward, except for farmer, skilled laborer, and laborer. Our analysis reduces this to two categories, farmer and laborer. This decision is because elsewhere the terms of skilled and unskilled laborer often appear in complementary distribution. From this data we assume that they are more or less equivalent.

The fact that most Indians were day labors becomes clear from the data on occupation. Table 5.13 shows that only 20.7 percent of the Ladinos but more than half of the Indians were laborers. While agriculture was important to both, less than half the Indians were farmers and 60 percent of the Ladinos made their living this way. More impressive is that while 19 percent of the Ladinos made their living in occupations other than agriculture, only 3 percent of the Indians did this. However, one might question this data concerning the heavy dependence of Indians on wage labor. It is clear from many sources that the state regime and export farmers of this era forced

Indians into wage labor. There was a shortage of hand labor in almost all regions, and especially during the time of the coffee harvest. It was necessary to use both debt peonage and government-sponsored forced labor to meet the combined demands of the export farmers, the government requirements for development work (roads, bridges, telegraph lines, etc.), and the army's requirements for recruits. The question that cannot be answered is whether the Indians labeled as skilled or unskilled labor were so designated by the recruiter or by themselves. Because Indians were forced to work regardless of whether they owned land, the question must remain open as to whether the occupations of these individuals are correctly labeled. There is nothing in the descriptive material to suggest the economic or income level of the recruits. Also, the term *"agricultor"* could refer to both landowners and renters.

Surname

The data that was provided in a complete description included the recruit's first name, father's surname, and mother's surname. Of these, we took only the father's surname for analysis because that was the first surname of the recruit. Also given were the father's first name and two surnames, and the mother's first name and two surnames, but the rest of these were not recorded for analysis.

As was noted earlier, San Marcos Indians surnames are predominantly of Spanish origin. It seems to be the case, however, that there is some differentiation in the use of Spanish surnames: some are mainly or exclusively used by one ethnic group or the other. Because the recruit list is limited, and to gain a better understanding of the use of surnames in this region, I have listed all the ethnically identifiable surnames that I have thus far run across in my research on San Marcos for the period 1901–14, together with the names that appeared on the *filiación*.[37]

What is particularly interesting is that on the 1907–14 list, the names tend to be strongly one ethnic group or the other. Of all the names on the list, only López is shared by more than two individuals of the two groups. Of the 105 surnames that appear on this list, 61 are exclusively used by Indians and 17 exclusively by Ladinos while the remaining 27 are used by both; and of the last, 13 are predominantly one or the other. This means that more than 85 percent of the names tend to be ethnic specific. Of the names on the recruiting list, 46 of the 72 (64 percent) are used either by Ladinos or Indians but not by both. While the recruiting list is obviously a very small sample from these municipalities, the more inclusive list suggests

Table 5.14. Recruits by Municipality of Origin and Ethnicity

Indians	No.	%	Ladinos	No.	%
San Pedro Sacatepequez	62	35.0	San Marcos	15	27.3
Tejutla	27	15.3	Palo Gordo	12	21.8
San Cristobal Cucho	22	12.4	Rio Blanco	8	14.5
San Antonio Sacatepequez	21	11.9	San Pedro Sacatepequez	4	7.3
San José Ojetenam	15	8.5	Tejutla	4	7.3
Tacana	13	7.3	San Lorenzo	4	7.3
San Marcos	5	2.8	San José Ojetenam	2	3.7
Rio Blanco	3	1.7	San Cristobal Cucho	1	1.8
San Lorenzo	3	1.7	San Antonio Sacatepequez	1	1.8
Comitancillo	2	1.1	Serchil	1	1.8
Serchil	2	1.1	Ixtahuacán	1	1.8
Palo Gordo	1	0.6	San Diego	1	1.8
Tajumulco	1	0.6	San Sebastian	1	1.8
Ixtahuacán	0	0	Tacana	0	0
San Diego	0	0	Comitancillo	0	0
San Sebastian	0	0	Tajumulco	0	0
Total	177	100.0	Total	55	100.0

that there may be a greater differentiation of surnames along ethnic lines than the recruiting list suggests.

Origins

One of the most distinctive features of the recruits was the fact that their ethnicity was closely related to their community of origin. This data is expanded in table 5.14 to show the really extraordinary differences that hold here.

In general, the sociocultural features are much more indicative of ethnic differences than was the case with genetically derived characteristics. Table 5.15 summarizes the situation. In general, the contrasting features seem to reflect a socially distinct population. Unfortunately, few culturally descriptive traits, such as clothing and language, were given in the list. The places of residence are clearly differentiated, the major occupational orientations indicate a rather different place in the economic structure, the age differences indicate a different degree of dependence or involvement with the army, and the difference in literacy obviously suggests a different access to the benefits of a literate society. The data on the use of shoes is, perhaps, more of a curious artifact because only eleven individuals in the entire sample were recorded as using them at all and observations were made on less than half the total number.

Table 5.15. Sharing of Social and Cultural Features and Ethnicity

	Indian %	Ladino %
COMMON FEATURES		
Legitimacy	92.3	94.7
Average age of single men	22.76	21.71
Average age of married men	33.04	33.63
CONTRASTING FEATURES		
Origins: San Pedro Sacatepequez, San Cristobal Cucho, Tejutla or San Antonio Sacatepequez	76.4	18.2
Origins: San Lorenzo, Rio Blanco, Esquipulas Palo Gordo, San Marcos	5.1	70.9
Use of shoes	2.1	30.0
Literate	5.2	32.8
Use surname common to own ethnic group	74.4	40.4
Occupation: Agriculturist	46.3	60.3
Occupation: Wage laborer	50.9	20.7
Younger than twenty-four years old	47.8	65.6
Older than twenty-five years old	52.3	34.4

Conclusions

The fact that there was little evidence for any major phenotypical biological differences between these two populations suggests that any serious racially based arguments concerning the two populations could be readily countered insofar as physical evidence mattered. While this may sound familiar to readers who favor a cultural bias, it may have significance for the present context. If one recalls the arguments reviewed earlier for the inclusion of Indians in the army, it will be clear that there is almost no recourse to racist reasoning. The inferiority that was universally ascribed to Indians was explained by some as the result of centuries of oppression that had converted previously heroic warrior peoples (the pre-Columbian Maya) into downtrodden peasants. The argument was that if biological differences were a defect for military needs, then it could be countered with education, and with the civilizing process. As was suggested earlier, this was an important current in the evolving *indigenista* philosophy of the times. There were many racist *indigenistas*, but it would have been hard to argue that civilizing can counter an inferiority that is biologically based.[38]

One may speculate that the officers confronted with the need for a larger reservoir of potential recruits had to reflect ruefully that the Ladino army they had created was already at best half-shod, predominantly illiterate, and far from the elite, literate voluntary professional army envisioned by

Barrios. Their ideal of a universal service drawing on all sectors of the population did not materialize because those who were best equipped simply purchased their way out. Given this picture, the vision of the Momostecos who were credited with killing the Salvadoran president, Tomás Regalado, in 1906, and the qualities of the Totonicapán soldiers that warranted Kushiek's favorable observations concerning them must have appeared very positive.

In short, from the perspective of a service that needed them, the Indians looked very good indeed. The fact that many Ladinos were indistinguishable from Indians physically would have materially eased the decision to opt for more Indians.

In hindsight, the events under discussion were part of a long development that began with the Liberal decision to create a professional army of Ladinos, and that has evolved today into an army made up heavily of Indians. The turn-of-the-century discussions favoring Indian participation were couched in terms of the specific virtues of Indian soldiers—obedience, docility, endurance, subordination, loyalty, cheap food, no shoes, tenacious fighter, and so on. There is no mention made in any of the essays cited of the kinds of reasons for the prevalence of Indians in the army that we have just discussed—the failure to create an effective Ladino army, the continuing need for troops, and the lack of much difference between poor Ladino and Indian recruits.

In fact, of course, Indians were already conscripted before the end of the century. In some cases, such as with the Momostecos described by Carmack, Indians were formed into regional militia reminiscent of those that existed earlier in the century. But more important, Indians were being recruited into the army that was being created by the central government, an army that was supposed to be Ladino. Liberal labor policies and permissive exemptions almost guaranteed that the Ladino army would be poor and undermanned. The essays in the early twentieth century give us an ideology legitimizing the fact that Indians were being used, and sanctioning an expansion of the practice.

If one turns to the late twentieth century, the picture has changed, but many of the details are far from clear. The Indian is still very much the follower and rarely the leader. But the culturalist (as opposed to racist) arguments of the officers writing at the time have been borne out, at least to an important degree. No one now questions whether Indians can learn to be as effective soldiers. The role of the army as a "civilizing" agent has been widely accepted, not the least among rural Ladinos and Indians. This evolution also saw another phase that we cannot pursue here but that also well deserves more historical attention, the indigenous community battalions that so pleased Ubico. Federico Hernandez de Leon enthusiastically describes a number of these colorful troops in his accounts of Ubico's travels.[39] Ubico's own view was that Indians were destined to be food producers, agricultural laborers, or soldiers—nothing else.

Another phase of the changing image of the Indian soldier emerged as an anachronistic repetition of the army's early twentieth-century experience. The outbreak of insurgency in the early 1960s repeated the same pattern of learning. While it took the Guatemalan army, beginning in the 1870s, more than half a century to learn that a Guatemalan military force ultimately would have to depend on Indians, the lesson was apparently lost on Marco Antonio Yon Sosa, Augusto Turcios Lima, and the other early guerrilla commanders of the 1960s. Their effort to initiate a revolution in the eastern part of the country was ultimately smashed by the more effective military action of Carlos Arana. The survivors of this failure then moved to the northwest, over the Mexican border, to rethink their strategy. Perhaps the most important element in the revision was to realize the importance of the Indian in the development of a serious revolutionary struggle. There are, however, differences. The army at the turn of the century sought out the Indian because of his docility; six decades later the insurgents turned to the Indian because he was seen to have perhaps the most deep-seated motivation for seeking social change. In both cases, the decision was the right one from the point of view of those trying to improve their military situation.

In summary, the ethnicity of the troops that were recruited in San Marcos in 1914 were roughly proportional to the numbers of Indians and Ladinos in the national population and in San Marcos at that time. Unlike the more famous Momostecos, or the more picturesque Indian community battalions developed later, the San Marcos troops probably came closer to representing a national mix, more representative of an army of Guatemala, than Barrios could have imagined. At the end of both the nineteenth and twentieth centuries, military planners choose to omit Indians from their strategies of military development. In both cases they would recognize their error and change their policies.

Notes

Author's note: This is a much reduced version of a Spanish language study that appeared in 1995. Many details and more historical background will be found in the Spanish version. See Adams, "Etnicidad en el ejército."

1. See works by Santiago Bastos, José Luis Cruz Salazar ("El ejercito como una fuerza politica" and *Escritos de José Luis Cruz Salazar*), Mario Monteforte Toledo (*Guatemala: Monografía sociológica*), Hector Rosada Granados (*Soldados en el poder*), Schirmer (*Guatemalan Military Project*), and Adams (*Crucifixion by Power*, "Development of the Guatemala Military," "Ethnic Images and Strategies in 1944," and "Etnicidad en el ejército.")

2. The Jefe Político papers are in the Archivo General de Centro América (AGCA), and I am indebted to the service provided by the personnel of that institution for making this study possible. The historical archives of the ministry of defense remain closed. Other such lists may be found in military archives, but these are unavailable to civilian scholars. When I had finished this essay, I inquired of the military whether they would release other recruiting data from the nineteenth and early twentieth century and was advised that they could not for reasons of national security.

3. Translated: "todas las poblaciones ladinas del departamento respectivo."

4. It required eight years of service from all males between eighteen and fifty years of age; the upper limit was reduced to forty by Decree No. 99 of June 26, 1873.

5. Allowing the purchasing of escape, which would seem at the outset designed not to achieve its goal of broad social participation, was raised by Decree No. 99, June 26, 1873, to 50 pesos a year, and on December 24, 1885, was reduced to 25 pesos a year. It was changed subsequently, by Decree No. 603 in 1901, and then raised to 100 pesos (150 for those who did not participate in military practices) on July 31, 1905, Decree No. 561.

6. Decree No. 83, January 11, 1873.

7. The entering class of cadets came from the better families, some of them clearly of the Liberal persuasion. The surnames included Springmühl, Herrarte, Garcia Granados, Tejada, Arzú, Arevalo, Samayoa, Solórzano, Castellanos, Mayén, and Taracena. See Valdés Oliva, *Fundación de la Escuela Politécnica*.

8. Indigenismo was an emerging nineteenth century ideology that sought to rescue Indians from their apparently depraved situation by education and more humane treatment than was current in the society of the time.

9. See Anonymous, *Revista Militar Illustrada*, 1900b.

10. García Aguilar, *Revista Militar Ilustrada*, "El Recluta," Cuadro III, 1900.

11. Gramajo, *Las revoluciones exteriores*.

12. Anonymous, *Revista Militar Ilustrada*, 1904, 66.

13. Zamora Castellanos, *Vida Militar de Centro América*, 553.

14. Anonymous, *Revista Militar Ilustrada*, 1900a, 68–69.

15. Kuhsiek A., "La importancia del indio," 3–4.

16. It may be noted that Kuhsiek, as well as most other writers of the period, refers to "the Indian" and often "the ladino" in the singular, as if they constituted a singular mass rather than diverse populations.

17. Kuhsiek A., "La importancia del indio," 4.

18. This allusion escapes me.

19. Anonymous, *Revista Militar Ilustrada*, 1904, 66.

20. Kuhsiek A., "La importancia del indio," 4.

21. Arevalo Martinez, *Ecce pericles*, 191.

22. Carmack, "State and Community in Nineteenth-Century Guatemala," 121.

23. Arevalo Martinez, *Ecce pericles*, 578.

24. See Adams, "Ethnic Images and Strategies in 1944."

25. There is a set of municipal level figures for 1914 in the American consular papers. Unfortunately, the figures are extremely high, and I am uncomfortable in using them. Hence I prefer to make the simple comparison with 1921, even though there is a seven-year interval between the two sets of data.

26. Serchil and Las Barrancas are aldeas of San Marcos, San Diego had been split up, and San Sebastian probably refers to a municipality in Huehuetenanto. Collectively they account for eight individuals in the sample.

27. This list was compiled as part of my research in this area. It currently contains the names with ethnic identification of 68 Ladinos and 139 Indians and is based on the names in the 1914 recruitment list and from *mozo* lists from six San Marcos *fincas* dated between 1900 and 1904.

28. Since it is possible that there is some variation by ethnicity of the signatory, I counted the number of times signatories of each (potential) ethnicity signed for the use of the term "regular." The comparison revealed no clear variation in terms of the different features except possibly for the beard and mustache.

29. Hair color was given as black in all cases. Color of the eyebrows was recorded as black in all but two cases. "*Rubio*" (blond) was ascribed to an Indian whose beard and mustache were called "*poco rubio*" (a little blond); "*Mechas*" (blond) was used for one individual of unknown ethnicity.

30. Data from AGCA, Jefe Political papers, 1900–1911.

31. Kuhsiek A., "La importancia del indio," 6.

32. See Adams, "Ethnic Images and Strategies," 30–49. This is based on data from the archbishopric visits to the dioceses and parishes in 1899–1903; data in the Archivo Historico Arquidiocesano "Francisco de Paula García Pelaez," Guatemala City.

33. In a preliminary study of La Reforma, San Marcos, in 1899, only 30 percent of births registered "natural" were recognized by the father at the time of the registration.

34. Anonymous, *El amigo del soldado*.

35. Castañeda, *Trabajo Técnico Militar*, 15–16.

36. Anonymous, *Revista Militar Ilustrada*, 1899, 232–33.

37. It should be emphasized that the larger list is a project in process, which will be expanded as I find other lists where surnames are directly associated with ethnic identification. It is my hope that eventually it may be possible to identify the ethnicity of some individuals based merely on their surname and community of origin.

38. Perhaps the best known *indigenista* was Miguel Angel Asturias.

39. Hernández de León, *Viajes presidenciales*.

6

Mayan Soldier-Citizens

Ethnic Pride in the Guatemalan Military, 1925–1945

DAVID CAREY JR.

When in 1944 a drill sergeant at the Matamoros military barracks in Guatemala City asked Waqxaqi' Imox and his compatriots, "Do you want to serve?," they replied, "*Ja* [yes]." Whether these Mayan recruits responded in their language to a Ladino (nonindigenous Guatemalan) superior is not as important as Waqxaqi' Imox's memory that they did. Despite a long history in Guatemala of government and elite efforts to compel Maya to acculturate to Ladino norms, many Maya recall Gen. Jorge Ubico y Casteñeda's dictatorship (1931–44) as a time when they could openly express their ethnicity. For this reason, even though the state conscripted Mayan males, military service was not as daunting as it had been previously (or has been since).

Unlike most of his peers, Waqxaqi' Imox enlisted voluntarily. In fact, he sold his machete to pay for his bus fare from San Antonio Aguas Calientes to the capital. Although few Maya were eager to serve, in other ways Waqxaqi' Imox's experience reflects that of other indigenous conscripts. After passing the physical examination, he served eight months in the military before returning to his hometown to get married. Because he preferred to farm in the hills surrounding his town, Waqxaqi' Imox insists he never wanted to stay in the capital.[1] Few Maya, even those who appreciated their military experience, felt attracted enough to military or Ladino culture to want to extend their service. Since military service was compulsory, it became a rite of passage for Mayan males. "When you leave the military, you have changed from a boy to a man," observed one elder.[2] While significant, these were not the changes liberal Ladinos had wanted to inculcate. Even though the military's Ladino urban experience was the antithesis of Mayan rural life, during the Ubico regime, Kaqchikel-Maya (the third largest Mayan language group in Guatemala) negotiated and then performed broad notions of national belonging and thus became more vested in the nation. This chapter argues that despite seeming an unlikely refuge for Maya, the military became a vehicle through which Kaqchikel conscripts could claim their citizenship without renouncing their ethnic identity. Though short lived, this opening augured a potential symbiosis between nation and indigeneity.

The relationship between Maya and the military had been an uneasy one since the 1870s when Liberal leaders began expanding the size of the army and the role of militias. Since militias were intended to reinforce state authority and uphold Ladino interests, initially Maya were excluded from them. Conversely, the military's mission was to defend the nation from foreign threats, and for that Maya were suitable.[3] As historian Lowell Gudmundson demonstrates for nineteenth- and early twentieth-century citizens of San Gerónimo, participation in the military or militia conferred citizenship upon soldiers in ways that the "Federation-era, republican formula of literate male propertied voter" had not.[4] Nonetheless, citizenship still hinged upon renouncing Mayan culture, language, and worldviews, and many Ladinos viewed the military as a place to "civilize *indios*." As one of the first Liberal leaders to create a space for ethnic expressions, Ubico made citizenship and ethnicity more compatible. Taking advantage of this opening to wear their traditional clothing during military exercises, Kaqchikel soldiers reconstituted citizenship and thus defied the vision of nation formation set forth by Ladino (and other Latin American) intellectuals who presumed the integration of indigenous people as citizens necessitated their marginalization as ethnic groups.[5]

As individual recruits made gains, Ubico cultivated support among Mayan conscripts. In addition to allowing new forms of dress uniforms, Ubico's motorcycle trips to Mayan communities never before visited by heads of state; the instant brand of justice in which he castigated abusive authorities, *patrones* (landowners), or Ladinos on the spot; and his willingness to receive Mayan delegations in the capital all contributed to a sense among Maya that at least the dictator, if not the state, was responsive to them.[6] Instead of integrating Maya into the nation, Ubico's manifestations of tolerance for Maya sought to bolster his dictatorship by securing their loyalty. To a certain extent, it worked.[7] But as an institution, the military went beyond the whims of a single dictator. It provided a more permanent sense of equality and inclusiveness than Ubico's ephemeral personal interactions. In the military, Maya acquired skills—Spanish, literacy, trades—and enjoyed more egalitarian relations than in broader society. These experiences helped them to advocate for themselves when the dictator was not around to intervene on their behalf, which of course was most of the time.

By affirming Mayan conscripts' sense of nationalism while respecting ethnic distinctions, Ubico's military was a venue where Ladino goals of a more modern nation dovetailed (to the chagrin of Ladino state-builders) with the perseverance of Mayan ethnicity and community identity. In this way, the military modeled the potential for national integration in an otherwise divided nation.

Ladino Nation Building and Alternative Nationalisms, 1871–1931

Following independence in 1821, the national government controlled by Creole (American-born pure-blooded Spaniards) and Ladino elites tried desperately to create a nation that would identify with its European influences and circumscribe its Mayan heritage.[8] Unlike Mexico, Guatemala refused to recognize *mestizaje* (racial mixing)—an attitude reflected in Creoles' vigilant protection of their racial purity. But because Creoles were a tiny, insular minority, by the late nineteenth century two competing national possibilities emerged: autochthonous Maya and Hispanicized Ladinos.[9] Since Maya resisted acculturation, only Ladinos were welcomed as national citizens who enjoyed the privileges and conditions associated with the elite.

According to most Creole and Ladino Liberal elites who controlled Guatemala from 1871 to 1944, Maya were poor, dirty, ignorant, lazy, uncivilized, and susceptible to disease. In turn, blaming Maya for Guatemala's backward condition justified efforts to assimilate them. To reify their power, Ladino leaders sought to normalize Ladino conventions, worldviews, and values. As a result, the construction of citizenship excluded indigenous people. This marginalization not only undermined opportunities for alliances between Ladinos and Maya who shared class positions, it also precluded the possibility of a united coherent nation.

Along with public education, by the beginning of the twentieth century, the military was one of the main vehicles for *Ladinoization* (the process of becoming Ladino.) "The Indian in the army will have to abandon his primitive outfit to dress in uniform . . . sleep in a bed, in a room that is much better than the home he left, eat at a table and bathe in a bathroom . . . acquire the habits of an exterior that better conforms to civilization," noted one journalist in 1911.[10] By offering courses in reading, writing, mathematics, grammar, geography, and other subjects, the military hoped to create a "new Indian."[11]

Of course, the goal of this transformation was not to welcome Maya as equal citizens but to mold them into subjects that would conform to Ladino norms and acquiesce to Ladino demands. Put bluntly, military discipline ensured that Maya would, in the words of Jorge García Granados, "execute always what the authorities or *patrón* ordered."[12] Like García Granados, most intellectuals writing in the 1920s doubted that military service could turn Maya into full citizens or could even impart a sense of nationalism.[13]

With such uninviting prospects, few Maya were eager to enter the military. Once enlisted however, they sought to benefit from the experience and acquire skills that would improve their opportunities and status. In this sense, Mayan conscripts facilitated a connection to the nation according to their own nationalist visions and understanding of citizenship.

Although not isolated from Ladinos or intent on establishing a separate nation, Maya maintained an autonomous ethnic ideological system. Their pride in being Maya contributed to local alternative nationalisms. Unlike Ladinos who attempted to establish a national identity grounded in European influences, Kaqchikel perceived the nation as inherently Mayan. By defining the nation as indigenous, Kaqchikel rejected the nationalist project of Ladinoization. For many Maya, assimilating indigenous people would undermine the very essence of the nation. Unlike Ladino intellectuals and leaders who believed that ethnic distinctions hindered Guatemala's development, Maya believed their ethnicity strengthened the nation. On the periphery of state power, Maya communities were well situated to resist *Ladinoization* and in some cases even invert it. Some highland Ladinos practiced Mayan customs, spoke Mayan languages, and incorporated Mayan epistemologies.[14] Even in the quintessentially masculine Ladino institution of the military, neither Ladino nor state power were omnipotent.

Transformation without Acculturation, 1931–1944

Throughout the 1930s, Ladino nation-builders contradicted themselves by extolling Maya as exotic symbols that could attract international tourists and thereby contribute to Guatemala's development on the one hand and insisting that the very process of modernization necessitated Mayan assimilation on the other. Yet Ubico's perspective was distinct from elites who denigrated contemporary *indios* even while they profited from traditional Mayan culture. With a 1938 decree establishing bilingual education in rural areas, Ubico demonstrated that his interest in Maya was not just economic. As reflected in his insistence that Maya be permitted to wear their traditional dress in schools and barracks, Ubico championed the right to publicly express indigeneity.[15] His validation of Mayan ethnic markers helps to explain laudatory descriptions of him in Kaqchikel and other Mayan historical narratives.[16]

His efforts to ease discrimination notwithstanding, Ubico never identified Guatemala as an indigenous nation. The tension between portraying Maya as a people clinging to a halcyon past and Guatemala as a nation poised to enter the modern world plagued government officials.[17] For Ubico, the military was perhaps the best place to reconcile these contradictions. Despite encouraging the maintenance of some Mayan cultural traits, Ubico believed that Maya went through a metamorphosis in the military: "They come [to the military] rude, brutish, and with a primitive nature, but they return learned, *desnados* [transformed from a donkey-like condition] with good manners and in a condition to face life with improved personal faculties."[18] According to the national press, by the late 1930s and early 1940s Ubico's efforts had been successful. *El Imparcial* noted "the obvious transformation" of Mayan participants among whom "a beneficial change is reflected in their customs, clothing and self identity."[19] Similarly, *El Liberal Progresista* asserted that Maya "conduct themselves better in society" after their military experience.[20]

From Mayan perspectives, it was not so much that they were conducting themselves better in society but that society was conducting itself better toward them. Once Kaqchikel conscripts experienced more egalitarian relations in the military, they refused to allow local Ladinos to exploit them when they returned to their communities. "When studies and military service came, they gave value to our people. We fought Ladinos and then we could read. There was no more *ixto*," remarked one elder.[21] Knowing the soldiers had received combat training, Ladinos were reluctant to act on their racist tendencies. Oxi' Tz'ikin explained:

> In those days, the Ladinos did not like *qawinäq* [our people] and they did not treat us well. You always had to walk on the side of the road. If you got in the Ladinos' way, or even if not, they would push you or hit you. You let them have the middle. . . . My dad got people together and told them it was wrong what the Ladinos do to us. They kill us. We are dumb. Back in those days, there was no school. He told them not to be afraid. He said they should go to the military because it makes you tough. That is how we can rise up.[22]

As Oxi' Tz'ikin's father had predicted, military service empowered Kaqchikel men vis-à-vis Ladinos.[23] "During the time of Ubico, it [the military] helped our people. For example, when a young man went to the army, he gained self-esteem. He had never been to school, but they taught him things, like how to write and speak Spanish. So he no longer was afraid of the Ladinos. During Ubico's time, Ladinos had to perform military service also," recalled B'eleje' K'at.[24] According to one general, Ladino and Mayan soldiers were "battalion brothers and *compañeros*."[25] By bringing Ladinos and Maya together in an egalitarian environment and instilling Maya with the confidence to confront Ladinos, the military helped to reduce racial separation in Guatemala. Recognizing that military service had both positive and negative aspects, Waqi' K'at explained that Maya gained a sense of value and respect because in the military, "they [Kaqchikel conscripts] could do whatever Ladinos did."[26] Of course, Kaqchikel conscript's confidence was a product of their aptitudes. Chimaltenango second sergeant Pedro Ajquij's second place in a shooting contest during the 1936 national military ceremony is but one example of Kaqchikel achievements that matched or bested their Ladino counterparts.[27] More important, immersed in a Ladino institution, Maya learned more about Ladino culture, which in turn made Ladinos less foreign and intimidating to them.[28] Like other Central American indigenous groups, Maya approached the military as "a space in the State that would permit them to improve the[ir] conditions."[29]

For many, the military was their only opportunity to get an education. Although reading was especially valuable for farmers who needed to apply for, alter, or defend their land titles, understanding Spanish also connected them to the nation by providing access to national media outlets such as newspapers and radio. But as Ka'i' Imox confided, it was not simply learning Spanish but knowing *how* to speak that boosted their confidence: "My boss in the military told me to talk tough."[30] Taking advantage of this education and the opportunity to develop leadership skills, some former privates served in public posts after returning to their communities.[31] In addition to increasing their sense of efficacy in their communities, these former soldiers had a sense that they were connected to the nation in ways that monolingualism and illiteracy had precluded. Instead of eschewing nationalism in favor of local loyalties, Kaqchikel cared deeply about the nation.[32]

By offering the opportunity to experience the nation beyond each conscripts' community, the military expanded their worldviews. Those who traveled throughout Guatemala in the military gained a broader sense of their nation.[33] Even if they returned to their villages for much of the remainder of their lives, as many of them did, they had a more profound notion of their country based on personal experience. Along with long-distance merchants, former conscripts shared this knowledge with other community members. Although not in the way nineteenth- and twentieth-century state-builders had envisioned, the military helped to create a more united nation.

When Ubico respected Mayan ethnic markers and entrusted Maya with leadership positions, the military experience of Maya changed significantly. Only Ubico allowed Maya to wear their *xerkas* (knee-length cloth) over their uniforms.[34] This concession was a radical departure from the military's goal of compelling "the Indian . . . to abandon his primitive outfit to dress in uniform."[35] When they wore their traditional clothes in the annual June 30 Military Day parades in Guatemala City, Kaqchikel soldiers showcased their ethnicity in a broader national setting and at times earned the respect of Ladino onlookers and authorities. According to the *Diario de Centro América*, the volunteer companies that "wore their regional *traje* [traditional clothing] and who, just like the soldiers from the capital, demonstrated great practice in their maneuvers," were crowd favorites "receiving great and prolonged applause."[36] At least on this day, they were celebrated as citizens who contributed to "the health and greatness of our *patria*."[37] One Kaqchikel elder explained, "I was in the military for one and a half years during the time of Ubico and I liked it. They formed a military company here [in San Juan Comalapa] and in the parade on June 30th, we won first place. We had beautiful uniforms with our jackets and hats; we even wore our *xerkas*. The governor of Chimaltenago thanked us for winning."[38] If at the center of state power in one of the nation's most venerable institutions, Kaqchikel could openly express their ethnicity and still receive praise from authorities, including the dictator, then their sense of national belonging was not simply imagined.

By expanding the public spaces where it was acceptable to wear *traje*, Ubico facilitated expressions of alternative nationalisms and citizenship. When Gen. Eduardo Villagrán Ariza welcomed the "*soldados de la patria*" with the "fraternal hug that you deserve" at the 1936 Military Day ceremony, he specifically referred to the Kaqchikel volunteer companies.[39] Further cementing their connection to the nation, some conscripts spoke with the president during these ceremonies. "I knew Ubico. I met him. He thanked us for serving the country. He said that if we ever had any problems, we should come to him: 'I will wait for you.' He had a good spirit," noted a Kaqchikel carpenter.[40] As one former soldier who participated in Ubico's volunteer companies for eight years and marched in front of the president in *traje* a number of times recalled: "I liked it. They gave us lessons and respect. We marched and learned how to use arms. And we were directed by experts. . . . The best thing was that he [Ubico] recognized us as *indígenas*. [He said], 'They are *indígenas*. We have twenty-six companies of *indígenas* in this country and we are happy about it.' . . . But at the same time, it was difficult."[41] With foot soldiers donning their traditional clothing of *xerkas*, corduroy jackets, white pants and hats, the circa 1940 photograph of a company formation in the Kaqchikel town of San Martín Jilotepeque that graces this book's cover projects an image of a military that was as much Mayan as Ladino.[42] The photo reveals one of the few state institutions where ethnic and national identities could coalesce. Perhaps for this reason more than any other, many Kaqchikel appreciated their military service under Ubico.

Ubico's aperture and Kaqchikel displays of ethnicity notwithstanding, national discourse purported that Maya became citizens in the military because it "civilized" (i.e., assimilated) them. In the context of a national narrative that sought to normalize Ladino conventions, expressing ethnic difference through material culture was subversive. Since *traje* evoked images of community, Kaqchikel conscripts who donned it during national military parades and ceremonies compelled the nation to include distinct indigenous influences as part of its master narrative. As historian Florencia Mallon has shown for nineteenth-century Mexico and Diane Nelson has shown for twentieth-century Guatemala, the construction of national identity and citizenship was a negotiated process.[43] Even though Ladinos and the state held the upper hand, dialogues within society ultimately determined what it meant to belong to the nation. With its parades and ceremonies, the military provided the most public and powerful forum to which Maya had access; Kaqchikel soldiers used it to inject ethnicity into nationalism.

The Military's Role and Reputation

Throughout Ubico's rule, his goal was to centralize authority by removing it from local officials and squelching popular organizations. He replaced rural *alcaldes* (mayors) with *intendente* loyalists. Since more than 90 percent of the population lived in rural communities of fewer than ten thousand people (and two-thirds of these residents were Maya), he established laws to concentrate power in the capital. As ethnohistorian Richard Adams notes, "The kind of power exercised by Ubico relied on a scattered population, lack of communication, and lack of knowledge of political activities."[44]

Of course, the military, volunteer companies, and an effective network of spies also were instrumental in maintaining control.[45]

Through the schools, media, forced labor, and intendentes, Ubico militarized Guatemalan society. The military had a physical presence in many highland towns. When planning a new municipal building in the Kaqchikel town of San Juan Comalapa (hereafter Comalapa) in 1943, for example, local leaders reserved part of it for the military headquarters. By 1944 the goal was to provide a separate building to house the military and communications office. Indeed, it was considered one of municipality's "most urgent public works" and of "vital importance."[46]

When Ubico extended the military's control into the countryside, he did so with the intent of restricting the power of local leaders and controlling Mayan revolts.[47] Despite efforts to eviscerate local power and decision making, oral histories and archival documents indicate that in many communities, Kaqchikel leaders maintained significant control. Except for issues dealing directly with the national government, *alcaldes* and other local leaders had the authority to settle disputes. Because Ubico likely would have considered such competing spheres of sovereignty subversive, Mayan authorities were fortunate that he was largely unaware of the extent of their power.[48] Seen from this perspective, instead of interpreting the increased military presence as an imposition, many Kaqchikel welcomed it as a means to maintain order without significantly undermining their local control.

Faced with capricious *patrones*, labor brokers, and officials who sought to conscript their labor through spurious legislation, corruption, debt peonage, and intimidation, Maya appreciated knowing that the rules of the game in the military were consistent and fair. And many Kaqchikel valued military discipline. "I did not have a mother or father, but the Ubico government taught me discipline and that is important. If you do not have discipline then you are screwed [*fregado*]," exclaimed one rural farmer.[49] During the Ubico dictatorship, many Kaqchikel had a profound respect for the military as an institution and for its leaders. When Domingo Avila Mejía, an *encargado militar* in San Martín Jilotepeque, and his assistant went house to house asking for signatures and a ten-cent donation to remove the *comandante local* (local military commissioner) in 1937, not a single Kaqchikel man signed the petition or contributed to the fund. Whether residents refused the overture because they were "extremely poor and barely made enough to subsist," as the thirty-year-old bachelor Ciriaco Pec testified, or whether they respected or feared the *comandante local* (some terrorized the population and were seen as "Ubiquitos"[50]) is unclear, but none of them spoke ill of the Ladino *comandante*. On the contrary, most questioned Mejía's motives. As Cecilio Corominal, a twenty-year-old Kaqchikel *jornalero* (day laborer) said, "I do not get involved in any of these affairs, if it is demanding, or more accurately wanting to compel removing the '*jefe*.'"[51] Whatever his behavior, the *comandante's* authority in the community had become normalized.

To modernize the military, Ubico professionalized the officer class and improved soldiers' living and working conditions.[52] Already by 1933, the military's international image had blossomed in some circles. During his travels to Guatemala, Aldous Huxley noted, "The Guatemalan army is reputed to be efficient."[53] Other observers remained less impressed, however. Eleven years later, a U.S. Federal Bureau of Investigation report considered the Guatemalan military "poorly trained and poorly equipped." "It is doubtful," the report continued, "that many of the soldiers have ever shot their rifles."[54] But most importantly, at least in terms of national identity, Guatemalans took pride in their military. After observing the annual military exercises in 1936, the *Diario de Centro América* noted: "The soldiers demonstrated a solid preparation in military material."[55]

Although military formations in the highlands were intended for a local audience, when the military paraded through Guatemala City, the goal—at least in part—was to demonstrate Guatemala's strength, progress, orderliness, and discipline to Ladinos and foreigners alike. That Ubico permitted Maya to wear their *traje* indicates that he did not see their ethnicity and national pride as mutually exclusive. Perplexingly, whereas Ubico juxtaposed a Mayan past against a technological future in such venues as the national fair, in the military—an institution he was "modernizing"—Mayan ethnicity coexisted with national progress. By demonstrating that Maya could be part of Guatemala's transformation into a developed nation, indigenous soldiers wearing their *traje* complicated images of premodern exoticized Maya.[56] For Mayan soldiers who later returned to their highland communities, the message was an affirming departure from that of previous governments: Maya could maintain, even celebrate, their ethnicity and could be productive citizens of Guatemala. Not only was there a place for Maya in Guatemala's march toward progress, they would be an integral part of it.

During the Ubico dictatorship, rural Kaqchikel conscripts were redefining what it meant to be Guatemalan. As ex-soldiers returned to their remote communities with new skills, experiences, and perspectives, they increasingly connected their communities to national life. Instead of encouraging separatist notions as some Ladinos feared, allowing Maya to wear *traje* facilitated their integration into the nation. Although it was not as Ladinos desired, Mayan conscripts who maintained their material culture modeled the potential for a more functional, coherent nation. In contrast to Erna Fergusson's observation during her travels in the early 1930s that through military conscription Maya gained a sense of nationalism that subsumed their ancient tribal allegiance, Kaqchikel demonstrated that national and ethnic identities were not at odds with each other but were interdependent.[57] By allowing for this possibility in a highly public, respected institution, Ubico contradicted intellectuals such as the Nobel Prize laureate Miguel Angel Asturias, who posited, "He [the Indian] does not understand the existence of the republic. The concept of his native country is an enigma to him, and he does not even know about municipal government, but he loves his village deeply."[58] Guatemala's challenge lay not in cajoling Maya into being more patriotic but rather in convincing Ladinos to embrace a nation infused with Mayan identities.

Mayan Experiences and Expectations in the Military

Despite the benefits of military service, most Maya were ambivalent at best about it, even during the Ubico years. "I served in the army for one year. The lieutenant instructed us. We had to carry arms and we also learned Spanish. I liked the military, but it was also a loss of my own time," noted one elder.[59] In Momostenango, for example, K'ichee'-Maya were "involved in almost constant militia and active duty service."[60] Because it interrupted their agricultural responsibilities, many men considered their military service detrimental to their livelihood.[61] For these reasons, unlike Waqxaqi' Imox who sold his machete to join the military, most young men were conscripted. Often military recruiters would arrive unannounced at community festivities to shanghai young men into military service. When the military grabbed men in less dramatic fashion, families often were unsure of what happened to their sons.

After arriving at the barracks, Maya endured squalid living conditions, poor and inadequate food, physical abuse, and the knowledge that they would be separated from their families for at least a year. For the most part, conscripts bore the burden of the military's lack of resources: if Mayan soldiers were paid, it was often a paltry sum (and always less than Ladinos) and they had to provide their own footwear and clothing.[62] In the words of an official who served under Ubico, "to the soldiers they gave a very bad treatment."[63] One Ch'orti'-Maya elder said he would rather die than return to the military.[64] Yet according to many Kaqchikel conscripts, conditions improved under Ubico. The dictator constructed new barracks, burned infested uniforms and ordered new ones, and paid conscripts for their service. To achieve these goals, Ubico dedicated 17 percent of the national budget to the military.[65] Though many Kaqchikel praised Ubico for these changes, others insisted that the goal remained the same: "Ubico sent men to the military to fuck [*joder*] them, threaten them."[66] Even as Kaqchikel soldiers were deepening a sense of belonging to the nation via the military, they understood that their participation was intended to keep them in line. Citizenship was conditional. For all his commitment to allowing expressions of ethnic identity, Ubico maintained a sense of Ladino superiority.[67]

Even with the improved physical and social conditions in the 1930s and 1940s, few Maya pursued a career in the military. One elder recalled: "I liked the military because here [Comalapa] there were many problems. Ladinos fucked us. They fought us. They looked down upon us. [Then] I learned Spanish in the military. I did it for two and a half years. I was a first sergeant. I became literate. They wanted to promote me, but I did not want to stay. I wanted to come back to Comalapa. It is better that I work in the fields."[68] Despite (or perhaps because of) their immersion into Ladino mores and national culture, most Kaqchikel soldiers retained a strong connection to their natal communities. As a result, even though the military was one of the few institutions in Guatemala that facilitated social mobility, few Maya availed themselves of this opportunity even when encouraged to by their superiors.[69] Another ex-soldier who left the military partly because of the excessive consumption of alcohol recalls: "I did not like the barracks. I went to school and graduated from third grade. The army liked that I knew how to read and write so I gave classes to others. A long time ago Ladinos and *indígenas* were not civilized. I was a second sergeant and eighteen years old when I left in 1929."[70]

Their reluctance to pursue advancement through the military speaks to Kaqchikel conscripts' alternative nationalisms and rejection of Ladinoization. For them, moving up through the military where they would have been increasingly exposed to Ladino norms and isolated from their communities did not resonate with their idea of progress. Because their conceptions of national identity were rooted in a valuation of Maya, forfeiting their Kaqchikel identity and community ties to improve their social position would have been counterproductive.

Aware of such powerful community connections, Ubico established "volunteer" companies in the highlands to continue military training after Maya had left the barracks. For four to five hours each Sunday morning, Mayan males performed military exercises. Like conscripts, these groups too marched in the annual military parades.[71] "The volunteer companies were not good. They took away our work and time. Every Sunday we would just walk around," lamented one elder.[72] As Wo'o Kawoq pointed out, the companies were volunteer in name only: "I did the military and the volunteer company when I was eighteen to twenty years old. There was no joy in it, no freedom in it. Everyone had to do it. They called it volunteer, [but] Ubico himself grabbed men over the age of eighteen."[73] For those who avoided the military, the volunteer companies seemed a reasonable compromise. "I was never in the military, but I was part of the company in Comalapa that Ubico set up. He gave them arms. . . . They never left town. It was only to prepare soldiers and there were about 150 of them. My uncle was a captain. The company taught him a lot, including how to speak Spanish," recalled one elder.[74]

A sense of ambivalence also permeates Kaqchikel historical narratives regarding the volunteer companies. A few appreciated the instruction they received and skills they honed, but most resented the infringement upon their personal time (without compensation). One rural farmer remarked, "I participated in the volunteer company for four years beginning in 1936 during Ubico's time. It was pure instruction and mobilization of arms. We did not get paid, but I was good at it. I never went to school, but I learned how to read in the military, but just on machines. I learned Spanish by hearing it here in the village. Then I bought a dictionary to improve."[75]

Because they were making sacrifices for the nation, Kaqchikel who participated in the volunteer companies came to expect certain privileges in return. In one crucial example of how tangible these expectations became, when the municipal secretary of Patzicía did not attend to him immediately on a September morning in 1943, Mateo Muj caused a raucous in the central plaza. In his defense, Muj explained to the judge that as a soldier who participated in a volunteer company, the secretary "should put aside all his work to attend to him."[76] Although the nation may have been an imagined community, the benefits Kaqchikel soldiers felt they earned were real. By the following year, however, this social contract would be shattered.

Altered States

Of course Maya did not necessarily have to ally with Ubico to partake in a growing sense of national identity. In the days and weeks immediately following the 1944 October Revolution that overthrew the dictatorship, a group of Kaqchikel men from Tecpán distributed a flyer encouraging "the indigenous class" to cooperate with both Ladinos and other Maya because "united we can work to make a great nation (*una patria grande*)."[77] Developed prior to the revolutionary movement, their connection to the nation inspired them to advocate for the new government.

In contrast, for Kaqchikel such as those from Patzicía who were the victims of a Ladino massacre during the 1944 October Revolution, national identity lost the appeal it had under Ubico. Although the violence in Patzicía erupted partly because many Kaqchikel there were loyal to Ubico, the massacre also can be read as a Ladino response to increased Kaqchikel control over the municipality, schools, and natural resources, particularly land. Not coincidentally, many of the members of this increasingly efficacious group of Kaqchikel Patzicianos had served in the military. Seen against the backdrop of Maya demonstrating their skills in military ceremonies year after year and then marching, machetes in hand, through the streets of Guatemala City in support of the liberal party on the eve of the overthrow in 1944, the Patzicía massacre also appears deeply embedded in Ladino resentments of Ubico's arming of Indians.[78] The Ladino perpetrators of the massacre, which claimed between sixty and nine hundred lives, intended to intimidate Kaqchikel via exemplary murders and put them back in their place.[79] Ironically, the democratic opening provided an opportunity to wipe out Mayan gains made during the Ubico dictatorship and reinforce Ladino superiority.

With such a haunting end to the security, stability, and relative empowerment enjoyed during Ubico's reign, it is not surprising that Patzicianos, in particular, and Kaqchikel, more broadly, identify 1944 as a fateful historical marker for very different reasons than Ladinos do. For the most part, Kaqchikel knew the rules of the game under Ubico. Although still constrained as working class indigenous people, they could improve both their communities and individual lives. Like most radical political changes, the October Revolution destabilized the nation. Whereas some Kaqchikel welcomed the changes, they all had to learn a new system. Yet since Juan José Arévalo Bermejo's government (1945–51) did not understand rural or indigenous politics the way Ubico's did, Maya were largely excluded from the new political coalition. Memories of the Patzicía massacre underscore this exclusion. In some Kaqchikel communities such as Sololá, municipal officials whose practices continued to reflect those common under the Ubico regime were rebuked by a democratic government intent on extirpating any vestiges of the dictatorship.[80]

More problematically, according to some Kaqchikel, the new democracy created the conditions for its own demise in 1954 and the subsequent civil war (1960–96) during which Maya were both conscripts and targets of the military. Reminiscing about his service, one K'ichee'-Maya elder drew a sharp contrast with the military in the 1980s: "I was a soldier in the time of Ubico. . . . We always went out to inspect something for the head of our unit, but they were always watching us so that we did not do anything against others. But now it appears that those in the army have no discipline, because they no longer respect our rights as campesino *indígenas*."[81] For some, the Patzicía massacre was a harbinger of the violence that reached genocidal proportions in the late 1970s and early 1980s.

Looking back on the past through the lens of Guatemala's thirty-six-year civil war reinforces Kaqchikel historical reconstructions of the Ubico years as a halcyon era when Kaqchikel soldiers felt both part and proud of the nation. Because the capricious and wanton violence that followed the Ubico regime made the dictatorship look good, Kaqchikel soldiers reflecting on their experience in the late 1990s were more likely to dwell on positive attributes than they would have been had these interviews been conducted prior to 1944. Yet in an indication that their memories are lucid, they also critiqued aspects of their military service. And because people act on the way they remember the past, whether distorted or not, these memories reveal how Mayan soldiers perceived (and continue to perceive) their place in the nation.

Conclusion

Since the early twentieth century, Mayan men had a shared experience of military service that exposed them to Maya, Ladinos, and other Guatemalans beyond their communities. In this way, the military encouraged a sense of nationalism. Significantly, what changed during the Ubico regime was that Maya could celebrate instead of suppress their ethnic markers as part of their military experience and by extension their national identity. This effect should not be overstated however. After the overthrow of Ubico, Arévalo and Col. Jacobo Arbenz Guzmán (1951–54) ushered in democratic reforms that ultimately encouraged assimilation. With the 1954 coup and subsequent return to military dictatorships, repression skyrocketed. For Kaqchikel raconteurs looking back on Guatemala's otherwise assimilationist twentieth-century history, the space Ubico opened for ethnic expression mitigated his repressive reputation.

With early twentieth-century intellectuals and leaders attempting to define Guatemala as a Ladino nation that excluded, if not erased, contemporary Maya, efforts to celebrate or even simply maintain Maya culture were targets of denigration and were often singled out as a source of the nation's inability to modernize. By permitting displays of community identity in an institution that was pivotal to his politics and administration, Ubico radically transformed national material culture.[82] Building on this transformation by responding in their language to a military officer who addressed them in Spanish, Kaqchikel conscripts literally altered, however briefly, the language of hegemony.[83] In a nation that was at war with indigenous ethnicity, and in an institution that Ladinos hoped would "civilize *indios*," accepting and at times even celebrating ethnic markers was a dramatic departure from the national narrative and identity.

Conscripts who introduced their material culture to the military redefined citizenship. In so doing, they not only included themselves in the national imaginary on at least one of their own terms but they also broadened perceptions of the nation. The extent to which these community narratives entered into and altered the national narrative can be seen in contemporary newspaper reports that celebrated Mayan soldiers in their traditional clothing.[84] According to one journalist present at the 1936 annual military parade, "Everyone applauded enthusiastically" for both the military and volunteer companies. He was particularly impressed by "the martialism and gracefulness with which the troops marched and also *los trajes* of the indigenous Volunteer Companies." According to General Villagrán Ariza, these "soldiers of *la patria* . . . honored the citizenship."[85] Without saying a word, Kaqchikel soldiers thrust themselves into national political life and offered a social critique. By representing community-oriented Maya as legitimate citizens, Kaqchikel conscripts modeled the potential for a more inclusive national imaginary.

Sadly, the marriage of Mayan ethnicity and national identity was the exception to the rule in postcolonial Guatemala; thus, to claim that Kaqchikel conscripts enjoyed some sort of heroic subaltern purity or even self-determination would be disingenuous. Since accepting the validity of Mayan claims to citizenship delegitimized Ladino power, Guatemala continued to portray itself as a Ladino nation. Notwithstanding the brief reprieve during the Ubico regime, Maya continued to live in a nation bent on assimilating them. Kaqchikel most efficaciously constructed and owned their meanings of citizenship, legitimacy, and community when they enjoyed an alliance with Ubico. Yet because their community narratives seldom penetrated the national narrative, acting on their meanings generally marginalized them. In her study of twentieth-century Mapuche history in Chile, Mallon found that although the state "sets the rules of the game . . . the poor and oppressed push at the boundaries of these discourses, structures, and institutions." "The result," she concluded, "is neither the system that those in power originally conceptualized and hoped for, nor the way of life desired by subalterns."[86]

Writing in 1966, the Kaqchikel teacher from Comalapa Cayetano Ottzoy Apenn [sic] lamented that Guatemala was not like "Mexico, El Salvador and other countries that were authentic nationalists [who] appreciated and looked for their regional values." He continued, "If we want to be nationalists, we [must] extend by all means the personality of our simple aborigines who dignify the pages of our history, forgetting for a moment the concepts of superiority, vanity, and racial indifference. *Vanitas vanitatum, et omnia vanitas* [Vanity of vanities; all is vanity]"[87] Like Kaqchikel conscripts before him, Ottzoy demonstrated what citizenship and nationalism meant to him by calling for a national narrative that included regional values. That hegemony and racism continued to thwart these alternative nationalisms speaks to Ladinos' refusal to negotiate with Maya to construct a more united, coherent nation. By opening up an alternative to Ladino state-building, Ubico's military demonstrated that ethnic distinctions need not impede national unity. Silencing this history normalizes the belief that ethnicity is incompatible with nationalism. Perhaps broader dissemination of the ways community and national narratives reinforced each other in Ubico's military could erode *vanitas* and serve as a foundation for a new national narrative.

Acknowledgments

I wish to thank Lowell Gudmundson, René D. Harder Horst, Nicola Foote, Miguel Centeno, and Hendrik Kraay for their comments on earlier drafts of this essay.

Notes

1. Waqxaqi' Imox interview, November 28, 1997, San Antonio Aguas Calientes (hereafter Aguas Calientes). I conducted the oral history interviews, which date from 1996 to 2005, in Kaqchikel. Due to Guatemala's continued political volatility and recurrent human rights abuses, I have preserved the anonymity of my sources. For the most part, I have used names that derive from the Mayan calendar. Female informants can be recognized by the "Ix" prefix to their one-word names; male names have two words.

2. Oxi' Tz'ikin, August 5, 1998, San Juan Comalapa (hereafter Comalapa).

3. McCreery, *Rural Guatemala*, 180–81; and Reeves, *Ladinos with Ladinos*, 166. Robert Carmack argues that late nineteenth- and early twentieth-century militias in Momostenango were intended to co-opt local Mayan leaders; see Carmack, "State and Community," 121.

4. Gudmundson, "Firewater, Desire," 276. In fact, during the 1870s, Liberals eased literacy and land ownership as conditions for citizenship, settling upon gainful employment; see Reeves, *Ladinos with Ladinos*, 237–38, 55.

5. For an excellent study of the dialectic between national and ethnic identity, see Gould, *To Die in This Way.*

6. Carey, *Our Elders Teach Us*, 195–219; Grieb, *Guatemalan Caudillo*, 115; and Tax, "Problem of Democracy," 196. While Kaqchikel had some success meeting with Ubico, an expanding state bureaucracy frustrated other Maya, such as the K'ichee' leaders from Quetzaltenango; see Grandin, *Blood of Guatemala*, 195–96.

7. For Kaqchikel perceptions of Ubico's rule, see Carey, *Our Elders Teach Us*, chap. 7.

8. A united Central America declared its independence from Spain on the tails of Mexico's independence in 1821. In 1823, the Central American Federation declared its independence from Mexico, and in 1839 Guatemala became an independent nation. See Handy, *Gift of the Devil*, 36–53.

9. Knight, "Racism, Revolution, and Indigenismo," 71–113; Smith, "Race-Class-Gender Ideology," 725; and Casaús Arzú, *La metamorfosis del racismo*, 34–35.

10. Anónimo, "El Ejército y los indios," *Revista Militar Ilustrada*, September 15, 1911, 9–11.

11. Gaitán, Herrera, Durán, and Sobral, "Contribución al estudio," 34; Anónimo, "El Ejército y los indios," 9–11; Adams, "Etnicidad en el ejército," 26.

12. García Granados, *Evolución Sociológica de Guatemala*, 25.

13. See, for example, Asturias, *Sociologia Guatemalteco*, 79–80.

14. Carey, *Engendering Mayan History*, 49–52, 221–24; and Carey, *Our Elders Teach Us*, 166–67.

15. Maxwell, "The Path Back to Literacy."

16. Carey, *Our Elders Teach Us*, 195–219; and Warren, *Symbolism of Subordination*, 148–51.

17. *El Imparcial*, June 8 and 12, 1932, as cited in Little, "A Visual Political Economy."

18. Hernández de León, *Viajes presidenciales*, 17.

19. *El Imparcial*, January 2, 1940; July 10, 1940. See also *Diario de Centro América* (hereafter *Diario*), December 19, 1936.

20. *El Liberal Progresista*, February 14, 1941.

21. Waqi' K'at, September 6, 1998, Comalapa. "*Ixto*" is a derogatory term Ladinos use for Maya.

22. Oxi' Tz'ikin, August 5, 1998, Comalapa.

23. B'eleje Imox, September 20, 1997, Comalapa. At the same time military service emboldened Mayan males, it also exacerbated gender inequality in highland communities where men had greater mobility and access to resources than women.

24. B'eleje' K'at, November 5, 1997, Comalapa.

25. *Diario*, July 1, 1936.

26. Waqi' K'at, September 6, 1998, Comalapa.

27. *Diario*, July 1, 1936. Although not officers, other Maya such as Macario Tecum and Lorenzo Yac also placed in competitions.

28. Carmack, *Historia social de los Quiches*, 278.

29. Alvarenga, *Cultura y ética*, 36.

30. Ka'i' Imox, January 21, 1998, Panabajal, Comalapa.

31. Oxi' Tz'ikin, August 5, 1998, Comalapa; Carmack, *Historia social de los Quiches*, 278.

32. In her study of Peru and Mexico, Florencia Mallon also demonstrates indigenous peoples' national imaginings; see *Peasant and Nation* and "Constructing Mestizaje in Latin America."

33. B'eleje' Imox, September 20, 1997, Comalapa; Lajuj Imox, December 20, 1997, Comalapa; Kaji' Imox, August 2, 1998, Comalapa; and Lajuj Kan, October 16, 1997, Pachitur, Comalapa.

34. Wuqu' K'at, April 5, 1998, Comalapa; Waqxaki' K'at, November 8, 1997, Aguas Calientes.

35. Anónimo, "El Ejército y los indios," *Revista Militar Ilustrada*, September 15, 1911.

36. *Diario*, July 1, 1936.

37. *Ibid.*

38. Wuqu' K'at, April 5, 1998, Comalapa

39. *Diario*, July 1, 1936.

40. Jun Iq,' April 18, 1998, Comalapa.

41. Waqxaki' K'at, November 8, 1997, Aguas Calientes.

42. See also the contrasting images from the 1936 Military Day Parade of the San Antonio Aguas Calientes volunteer company and the Escuela Politécnica cadets in *Diario*, July 1, 1936.

43. Mallon, *Peasant and Nation*; and Nelson, *Finger in the Wound*.

44. Adams, *Crucifixion by Power*, 265.

45. Handy, "Resurgent Democracy," 395; and Gleijeses, "La aldea de Ubico," 42.

46. Archivo Municipal de San Juan Comalapa, (hereafter AMC), "Libro para actas de sesiones ordinaries y extraordinarias, comenzando 13 de 1942 terminado al 21 de 1945" (hereafter "Libro, 1942–1945"), 30 de enero 1943 (56): 66; 11 de enero y 12 de febrero 1944 (quote).

47. Gleijeses, "La aldea de Ubico," 36; and Handy, "Resurgent Democracy," 388.

48. For examples of such informal power in other Mayan communities, see Wagley, *Economics of a Guatemalan Village*.

49. Ka'i' Imox, January 21, 1998, Panabajal, Comalapa.

50. Gleijeses, "La aldea de Ubico," 39–40; and Metz, *Ch'orti'-Maya Survival in Eastern Guatemala*, 59.

51. AGCA, Jefe Político, Chimaltenango 1937, Diligencias seguidas sobre establecer si Domingo Avila Mejía, Encargado Militar de Estancia de Virgen, recogía dinero y firmas para quitar al Comandante Local, San Martín J., dic. 1937.

52. Jun Kawoq, May 1, 1998, Agua Caliente, Comalapa; *Diario*, October 24, 1936; and Cruz Salazar, "El ejercito," 77. For evidence of barrack improvements in Guatemala City and El Quiché, see *Diario*, October 20–November 5, 1936; *El Liberal Progresista*, February 14, 1941; Adams, *Crucifixion by Power*, 254; Gleijeses, "La aldea de Ubico," 37–38; and Cruz Salazar, "El ejercito," 77, 78.

53. Huxley, *Beyond the Mexique Bay*, 67.

54. Federal Bureau of Investigation, *Guatemala Today* (July 1944), 77.

55. *Diario*, December 19, 1936.

56. Little, *Mayas in the Marketplace*.

57. Fergusson, *Guatemala*, 317.

58. Asturias, *Sociología Guatemalteco*, 80.

59. Kab'lajuj Imox, November 5, 1997, Comalapa.

60. Carmack, "Spanish-Indian Relations," 243.

61. Waqxaqi' Kawoq, November 8, 1997, Aguas Calientes; Lajuj Kan, October 16, 1997, Pachitur, Comalapa; B'eleje' Kan, November 9, 1997, Aguas Calientes; Jun Iq,' April 18, 1998, Comalapa; Oxi' Imox, February 10, 1998, Comalapa; Kab'lajuj Imox, November 5, 1997, Comalapa; and Waqxaqi' Kan, March 18, 1998, Poaquil.

62. Waqxaqi' Kawoq, November 8, 1997, Aguas Calientes; McCreery,*Rural Guatemala*, 181; Adams, "Etnicidad en el ejército," 11; and Gleijeses, "La aldea de Ubico," 37.

63. Gleijeses,"La aldea de Ubico," 37.

64. Metz, "Without Nation, Without Community," 339.

65. Jun Kawoq, May 1, 1998, Agua Caliente, Comalapa; Ka'i' Kawoq, February 8, 1998, Aguas Calientes; Wo'o Kawoq and Waqi' Kawoq, March 3, 1998, Kojol Juyú, Comalapa; Oxi' Kawoq, October 31, 1997, Pamumus, Comalapa; Ixkawoq, April 17, 1998, Pamumus, Comalapa; and Woodward, *Central America*, 237.

66. Ka'i' Kan, November 24, 1997, Chuwatz'unuj, Tecpán.

67. Carey, *Our Elders*, 195–96.

68. Junlajuj Imox, May 23, 1998, Comalapa.

69. Jun Iq,' April 18, 1998, Comalapa.

70. Junlajuj Ajpu,' August 2, 1998, Comalapa.

71. AMC, "Libro, 1942–1945," 56; Ka'i' Kawoq, February 8, 1998, Aguas Calientes; B'eleje' Kan, November 9, 1997, Aguas Calientes.

72. Waqxaqi' Kan, March 18, 1998, Poaquil.

73. Wo'o Kawoq, March 3, 1998, Kojol Juyu,' Comalapa.

74. Oxi' Kawoq, October 31, 1997, Pamumus, Comalapa.

75. Oxlajuj Ajpu,' January 19, 1998, Panabajal, Comalapa.

76. Archivo Municipal de Patzicía, paquete 20, Libro de sentencias economicas 1943, Juzgado de paz, 29 de septiembre 1943.

77. *Nuestro Diario* November 18, 1944.

78. Woodward, *Central America*, 231.

79. Rodas and Esquit, *Élite Ladina-vanguardia indígena*; Carey, *Engendering Mayan History*, 129–58; and Carey, "A Democracy Born in Violence."

80. Archivo Municipal de Sololá, "Libro Numero 01" de acuerdos y sesiones municipals del 1/03/37 al 28/11/50. See especially 1945–50.

81. Stoll, *Rigoberta Menchú*, 119.

82. Cruz Salazar, "El ejercito," 96.

83. Roseberry, "Hegemony and the Language of Contention," 360–61.

84. See for example, *Diario*, July 1, 1936.

85. *Diario*, July 1, 1936.

86. Mallon, *Courage Tastes of Blood*, 237–38.

87. *Comalapan*, October 1966. I thank Peter Aicher for the Latin translation.

II

War and the Racing
of National Boundaries
and Imaginaries

7

Indigenous Peoples of Brazil and the War of the Triple Alliance, 1864–1870

MARIA DE FÁTIMA COSTA

The War of the Triple Alliance, in which the Brazilian Empire allied with Argentina and Uruguay against Paraguay, has been the subject of much scholarly interest since the nineteenth century.[1] However, traditional works are often highly partisan and influenced by the author's nationality. Most emphasize heroic military events or focus on political and economic issues related to the conflict. More recent studies have broken with this trend by focusing attention on the actors in the conflict. Scholars have analyzed, for instance, the role of blacks and women in the war. Yet the experiences of the indigenous people who were involved in or were enveloped by both sides of the war have been the subject of less attention.

On the Brazilian side, the constant presence of indigenous people as soldiers for the empire was well known at the time of the conflict and is documented in several firsthand accounts of the war. Prussian officer Max von Versen, for example, commented that while in the Argentine city of Corrientes, he witnessed hundreds of natives of different tribes who arrived in their classic canoes made out of hollowed logs—bringing along women and children—who had come to join the Brazilian navy.[2] Although he referred to "diverse tribes," Versen was unable to distinguish their ethnic identities; in his view, they "were all low in stature and very ugly. . . . Their bodies were ornamented with different hues, and they used only a species of thong to cover their private parts."[3] Such dismissive descriptions were typical of the attitude of contemporary elites toward indigenous populations.

Nevertheless, other printed and manuscript sources reveal more information about the participation in the war of the different indigenous groups whose territories were located in the Brazilian region called Pantanal. The most notable tribes in the area included the Txané-Guaná (Guaná, Terena, Kinikinawa, and Layano) and the Mbayá-Guaikurú (Guaikurú,[4] and Kadiwéu). In addition, the documentation reveals a few scarce mentions of the Guató. This chapter will reveal how the participation of these groups was rooted in a history of Luso-Brazilian engagements.

With regard to indigenous participation on the Paraguayan side, the situation is somewhat different and reflects the nature of state policy. The prevailing point of view among mid-nineteenth-century leaders of the republic was that "the indigenous peoples needed to be eradicated from the new socio-political order because they occupied lands illegitimately and blocked economic progress and the transition to modernity."[5] Even so, Francísco Solano López sought support from several ethnic groups for his bellicose goals, and a good part of his armed contingent was composed of indigenous people, principally the Guaraní. There are also references that other indigenous peoples, motivated by diverse reasons, were involved or allowed themselves to be involved in the conflict. The most famous example was the Evuevi-Payaguá, who lived close to Asunción. President López armed and recruited them as spear throwers, and they formed a "Payaguá regiment" that fought under the command of Paraguayan officials.[6] Indigenous groups in the Chaco, such as the Toba, also fought for Solano López, many motivated by the desire to obtain firearms.[7]

Other tribes, such as the Kaynguá, in the region of Concepción, tried to stay on the margins of the conflict. Nonetheless, according to *The Standard* newspaper of Buenos Aires, they entered into a strange alliance with Marshall López. To convince the Kaynguá to fight in his war, President López promised to give them Paraguayan women as wives at the end of the war.[8] It should be noted, however, that these Kaynguá "generally did not act in a cohesive group and mistrusted all white armed forces." In effect, the Kaynguá enjoyed trading and functioned as guides, serving both the Paraguayans and Brazilians at different times.[9] On their part, the Enlhit from the Chaco took advantage of the conflict to "assault warehouses of supplies in different settlements."[10] It is evident, then, that during the War of the Triple Alliance, these indigenous groups did not arrive at a cohesive position and fought for a variety of reasons reflecting their own individual group interests. This chapter will seek to explore these strategies, focusing on the participation of the indigenous groups of the Brazilian Pantanal. It will outline a general picture of their performance and emphasize the actions of the Mbayá-Guaikurú indigenous tribe. It argues that these native people fought in the war for their own goals, practicing what anthropologist M. C. da Cunha has called "indigenous politics,"[11] a political strategy that the Mbayá had been implementing since the middle of the eighteenth century, when they were forced to choose sides between the Portuguese and the Spanish.[12]

In Guaikurú consciousness, the Paraguayan War has acquired the reputation of a tribal watershed, a fact observed by Mônica Pechincha in 1992. During her research among the Kadiwéu—the remaining survivors of this great nation—Pechincha listened to the recounting of dozens of indigenous memories. She concluded that the Paraguayan War had been "the event that defined the relationship between the Kadiwéu and the Brazilian nation. The war constituted the fundamental framework within which they worked for the recovery of their territorial rights."[13]

Before the war, the Mbayá-Guaikurú peoples were composed of seven tribes—four Kadiwéu, one Beaquéo, one Atoquéo, and one Guatadéo—with a total of 1,500 people.[14] Nevertheless, documentation from the time reflects direct participation in the war by only the Guaikurú, Kadiwéu, and Beaquéo tribes. From the end of the eighteenth century, the Guaikurú had increased contacts with the Brazilians and had settled in the surroundings of Fort Coimbra and Villa de Albuquerque. These were settlements that the Portuguese government had ordered be established in the Pantanal, along the border with Spanish America. The other two tribes, the Atoquéo and the Guatadéo, had refused to be seduced by insistent proposals for permanent settlement made by Brazilian authorities. The Paraguayans, for their part, called all these groups the Mbayá.

This chapter will refer to these people collectively as the Mbayá-Guaikurú, or simply Guaikurú, except when the sources specifically mention a particular group. In this way I hope to honor a request made by Captain Guazú-Ãcã at the beginning of the twentieth century. When asked why "they were called the Caduvéus o Cadineos," the captain responded that "we were always Guaikurú, and wished to always be known only by that name."[15]

Historical Backdrop: Guaikurú-European Encounters and the Practice of Indigenous Politics

One of the central facts of Guaikurú history is their early acquisition of horses. There is debate as to exactly when the Guaikurú became equestrians, but the most reliable accounts trace this development to the end of the sixteenth century.[16] In any case, they already had horses when they attacked the Jesuit mission of Itatim and made that region between the Jejuí and Taquari rivers a "*terra mbaiânica*."[17] As conquerors, they gave their own names to geographic features: The rivers that the Spanish called Corrientes and Piray became the Apa and Aquidaban, respectively; they gave the areas formerly known as Pitun, Pray, and Itati the name of Aquidaban. Late eighteenth-century Spanish historian and naturalist Félix de Azara argued this renaming had "embroiled the geography and the demarcation of borders," but the names prove that the Guaikurú dominated the area.[18]

War had long been central to Guaikurú identity. The tribe recounts in its origin myths that after humans were created, a bird of prey—the caracara—was disappointed that in the world there were no Guaikurú; therefore, their tribe was also created and received as weapons the mace, spear, bows, and arrows. The Guaikurú used the weapons to war against other nations, from which they took captives and stole all they could.[19]

Anthropologist Darcy Ribeiro, who lived among the Kadiwéu in the 1940s, observed that their most distinctive philosophical trait was their minimal interest in elevating humble persons. On the contrary, "their heritage," affirmed Ribeiro, "reflects the mentality of a majestic and ethnocentric people with the belief they were predestined to rule the world."[20] While the wording of her statement reflects the romanticism of early Brazilian anthropology, the group's oral histories recount that they have conducted wars against all other peoples who crossed their path, whether indigenous or not. Perhaps the only exception was the Txané-Guaná tribe. The Kadiwéu had been allied with them since the Chaco and had established a complex intertribal relationship.

With such a strong self-identity, it is not surprising that when Iberian colonization was consolidated in the region, the Guaikurú came to view themselves as superior to the Europeans, whom they dismissed as small, weak, and ugly, nor is it surprising that war quickly followed.[21] When the Spanish settled at Concepción and Fort Borbón and the Portuguese at Coimbra, Albuquerque, and Miranda, a three-sided war broke out between the Portuguese, Spanish, and Guaikurú. The two Iberian powers fought against each other for control and the extension of their borders; the Mbayá struggled against both outsiders in defense of their lands. It became clear that the colonial victory would go only to the power that was able to successfully ally itself with the indigenous people. Aware of this, the Guaikurú shrewdly manipulated both enemies. Little by little, however, the Mbayá began to cooperate more closely with the Portuguese, with whom they felt less vulnerable. Finally, the tribe signed a peace and friendship treaty with

Portugal in 1791. For almost three decades there were no violent confrontations between the Luso-Brasilians and the Guaikurú. This contrasts with the relations between the Mbayá and the people of Asunción, where the Indians played a double-sided game, seeking an approximation but at the same time attacking the frontier. This intergroup violence intensified markedly after Paraguay's independence in 1811.

In 1791 chiefs Queima and Emavedie Chaúe, in the name of the Guaikurú groups that lived on the western side of the Paraguay and the Embotetéu (today called Miranda) rivers, signed a peace and friendship treaty with the Portuguese and became vassals of the Royal Portuguese Majesty. Five years later, in 1796, ranchers from Concepción killed eleven Guaikurú chiefs, among them Queima, as well as three hundred indigenous people. In revenge, the Mbayá systematically attacked Paraguayan ranches, stealing horses and cattle, which they traded with the Luso-Brazilians for weapons. In 1801 three Mbayá chiefs and one Guaná chief, longtime allies of the Portuguese, passed over to the Spanish side and the following year a Portuguese detachment led by Capt. Francisco Rodrigues do Prado, attacked a Paraguayan fort with the help of more than three hundred Guaikurú people.

Immediately after Paraguay's independence in 1811, the Mbayá took advantage of the young republic's political instability to attack Paraguayan farms in the Concepción Department, where they stole cattle, killed and decapitated men, and abducted women and children. In 1813 these native people besieged Colonel Gamarra, commander of Concepción, until they forced him to beg for clemency in order to not be completely destroyed.

In 1821 the Mbayá and Paraguayans negotiated a peace treaty, but the indigenous people refused to turn in their weapons, spoiling the accord. More and more, conversely, they cooperated with the Portuguese. Nevertheless, between 1826 and 1827, feeling doubly betrayed by the Paraguayans and principally by the Brazilians, the Guaikurú broke the Peace Treaty of 1791 and began to assault and loot Brazilian settlements near Coimbra y Albuquerque, even as they also attacked the Paraguayan territory.

It is evident that after signing the peace treaty with Portuguese authorities in 1791, the Guaikurú worked hard to keep their side of the accord. After the Portuguese colony became the Brazilan Empire following independence in 1822, the peace treaty fell apart. The Paraguayans apprehended and killed Guaikurú chief Cabála at Fort Borbón. Because a Portuguese settler in Albuquerque had taken the chief to the fort, the Guaikurú understood they had been betrayed. In retaliation, they attacked people and properties around Camapuã and Albuquerque, spreading fear throughout the region. Brazilians feared that the Guaikurú would reverse their alliances and go live "peacefully within Paraguayan borders."[22] But this did not occur.

By the end of the eighteenth century, the Guaikurú chose to oppose the government in Asunción and favor Brazil, a decision made most evident when the war broke out. Paraguayan president Francia decided to clear-cut a forest near the town of Concepción, where the Mbayá spent time every year harvesting palm fruit.[23] The deforestation only made the indigenous people's hatred worse and increased the violent attacks against Paraguayan ranches. At the same time, the Brazilians attracted the Mbayá by providing them with arms and ammunition as well as by purchasing the cattle and horses that the natives stole from Paraguayan ranches.

During the government of Paraguayan president Carlos Antonio López, Paraguayans constantly complained to Brazilian authorities about these events. The situation was extremely sensitive because Brazil was also trying to negotiate a treaty with Paraguay that would allow them free trade along the Paraguay River. Such an arrangement was of vital importance for Brazilian production in Mato Grosso.

In 1850 Brazilian captain Lapagate and his troop of native and Brazilian soldiers took Paraguayan Fort Olimpo at Fecho dos Morros. As events unfolded, authorities in Mato Grosso tried to discourage Guaikurú impetuousness. The provincial president, Augusto Leverger, confided in 1851: "these Indians have always threatened our good relations and understanding with Paraguay, as much because of their nature, as because they unfortunately find among us those who provide them with weapons and gunpowder, and who purchase the products of their thefts, which has at times been tolerated, agreed to and even encouraged by those who should suppress it."[24]

In 1856, after signing a treaty of free navigation with the neighboring republic, Brazil redoubled its efforts to keep the order. Authorities began a serious attempt to settle frontier indigenous people in permanent locations, a process known as *aldeamiento*.

Settlement goals were not new, but the Missions Statute of 1845 had accelerated the process of "converting and civilizing" the indigenous people. The agricultural Guaná in the Pantanal responded most readily to the state initiative. Mato Grosso fervently sought to permanently settle the Kadiwéu and made several failed attempts to those effects. According to provincial president Leverger, from time to time the Kadiwéu visited Brazilian frontier towns and even at times the provincial capital, "requesting protection from the province, announcing their intention of settling down and giving up their wandering way of life." At these brief encounters they obtained "work tools and other trinkets" and then disappeared again.[25]

Despite provincial efforts to cultivate good relations, however, the conflicts continued, enveloping even the indigenous groups on either sides of the border. According to a missive from the commander at Fort Coimbra, three Chamacoco (Yïshïro) indigenous men who claimed to come on behalf of their chief arrived on February 8, 1862, and requested transportation to move their community to the fort. The messengers stated their reason was "because they were constantly harassed by natives of other nations[tribes]."[26] In August of the same year, according to the director general of Indians of Mato Grosso, the Guaikurú from Nabilek attacked the Indians of Paraguay on their own accord, with permission from the local police agent, and captured two Cayúa (Guaraní) women, whom they carried away as prisoners.[27] The following year missionary Mariano de Bagnaia reported that "a Paraguayan by the name of João Estevão, who had lived in the place known as Chatoloto since 1860, was assassinated by the Guaikurú Labotto."[28] In addition, indigenous people from the Paraguayan border known as the Inima, who had tried to settle permanently at Miranda, were "attacked by the Guaycurús, who captured and took their children after beating and killing the adults." The terrified survivors hid in the jungle.[29]

It is evident, then, that the Mbayá-Guaikurú continued to confront the Paraguayans. These attacks, according to the director general, might "jeopardize the Empire's international politics, when Indians settled within our borders invaded neighboring territories.[30]

Despite this concern, it was not the indigenous people who unleashed the war. The conflict was latent, and some of its roots originated in the Colonial Period. In effect, the border between Paraguay and Brazil was still disputed, an unsettled issue that dated to the treaties of Madrid (1750) and San Ildefonso (1777). Paraguay believed its territory extended into the region north of the Apa River, the actual Brazilian State of Mato Grosso do Sul, an attractive area for the extension of ranching and farms. For the empire, however, Brazil's borders extended all the way to the Apa River. With that understanding, Brazil encouraged colonization, founding towns such as Miranda and Dourados and establishing missions to indigenous people, specifically among the Txané-Guaná people.

It was in this context of disputes that, in December 1864, Francísco

Solano López ordered Paraguay's army into Mato Grosso. In their own way and according to their own community-based goals and concerns, indigenous people participated actively on the battlefield.

Indigenous People in the War

Once the Paraguayans had entered Mato Grosso, the indigenous people of the Pantanal helped the Brazilians defend the territory. Already in the 1850s, imperial authorities had been aware of the possibility that Paraguayan forces might pass the Apa River to end Brazil's navigation on the Paraguay River. This move would have isolated the Mato Grosso province. Still, Brazil had done little to defend the border. The settlements of Dourados and Miranda were incapable of resisting, so the Paraguayans found almost no resistance when they arrived. Lopez' forces quickly took control of the port city of Corumbá, Fort Coimbra, and all the border region with Brazil in the province of Mato Grosso.

Brazil tried to defend Fort Coimbra with the help of Captain Lapagate and ten additional Guaikurú. Similarly, according to Lt. Afonso d'Escragnolle Taunay—who became a well-known historian—it was the Guaná and the Guaikurú who took the initiative to ambush and harass Paraguayan soldiers.[31] The indigenous people of the Pantanal, with their knowledge of the area, guided Brazilian fugitives through neighboring hills—a region that came to be known as "Morros"—where natives made it possible for them to survive during the years of the war.

Meanwhile, when asked "about the frontier Indians," the president of Mato Grosso, far from the battlefield, responded: "The benefit we might take from them is problematic. Cooperation with the Guaicurus, on which we had counted, has already failed when Fort Coimbra was invaded. We have received vague news about some good service from the Indians settled at Miranda, but I still cannot say anything positive to the effect."[32] Despite official statements to the contrary, it was nevertheless the Guaná and the Guaikurú who defended Brazil during the first moments of the war. To a certain degree, the indigenous people had been prepared for this role at the missions of Bom Conselho and Miranda. According to the mission statutes, the director's job included preparing the indigenous people to lend military service with the goal of in time creating indigenous companies.[33] It should therefore be no surprise, then, that Lieutenant Taunay included the Guaná when he listed national guards who had joined the Brazilian army.[34]

Within the Pantanal, the Txané-Guaná also carried on guerrilla warfare against the Paraguayans, although in a more isolated fashion. In September 1865, a Terana group defeated Paraguayan soldiers, killing three indigenous fighters and eleven of Francísco Solano's soldiers, whom they stripped of ponchos and munitions.[35] The following month, these indigenous people again confronted Paraguayan forces. Under a fierce crossfire, they forced the besieged enemy to flee the field, taking many of their animals. After running out of ammunition, the Guaná addressed imperial forces and requested to be resupplied. One Brazilian official suggested that their request be honored "because in part they have done so much."[36] On their side, the Paraguayans took the offensive against the Guaná. At the port of Joaquim Souza Moreira, for instance, "when the indigenous people disembarked, they were assaulted by [the Paraguayans] who captured an indigenous woman, killed her and then cut her up into pieces."[37]

In addition, the Guaná were valuable informants. Their reports allowed the government of Mato Grosso to monitor enemy troop movements. On July 24, 1865, for instance, some indigenous people from the frontier of the lower Paraguay River informed on the number of enemy forces and detailed the ships docked at Corumbá and Dourados.[38]

The existing documentation also registers the presence of the Guató, but only at the beginning of the conflict and as allies with the Paraguayans. During the decade of the 1860s, the Guató lived along the banks of the São Lourenço and Cuiabá rivers, and maintained friendly relations with the Brazilians. These riverine indigenous people, who traveled in canoes, had ruled the area until the decade of 1720, when the Payaguá defeated and subdued them. The Paraguayan War, though, also saw Guató lands invaded and their people scattered throughout the Pantanal. In that swampy area they attacked farmer Manoel Francisco Pereira and his family, killing some people and taking other prisoners.[39] Reports by a Brazilian fugitive from Corumbá document that at the settlement called Passa Vinte, the Guató were part of the Paraguayan detachment.[40] All indications, however, show a only brief alliance motivated by private affairs.[41] Shortly after, in fact, the Guató reported to the headquarters of the Brazilian Artillery Battalion of Infantry No. 2, that his group had "withdrawn from the Paraguayan company and now were close to the Paraguay River, near Uberaba. They intended to enter through the bays to the River São Lourenço, as soon as the river waters began to rise."[42]

And the Guaikurú . . .

The Guaikurú, as we have seen, had for some time carried on their own war against the Paraguayans. For their part, Mato Grosso authorities mistrusted Mbayá support in the case of armed conflict. In 1851 the provincial president Leverger argued that "there are those who think . . . that, in the case of war we would have these Indians as valuable helpers; I don't see it that way; they could help with espionage,[43] or in the case of ambushes, since the Guaikurú carry out only surprise attacks and do not enter into regular combat until after the conflict is already won, and then it is difficult to curb their excesses killing and pillaging the losers."[44] Lieutenant Taunay had the same opinion, expressed in the "General Account" he gave in 1867: "The Cadiuéos, bitter enemies of the Paraguayans, should not be trusted and at times have damaged the Brazilians as much as the enemies. These Indians have attacked Paraguayans on the Apa line, just as they have assassinated entire Brazilian families, as occurred with the unfortunate Bronzique family, in Bonito."[45]

In fact, documentation from the period by the police delegate from the Miranda District describes Guaikurú attacks against Brazilian persons and properties. The police delegate reported that when the Paraguayans invaded the Mato Grosso, the Guaikurú, led by captain Joaquim, attacked the Bonito farm where the family of Maria Clementina had taken refuge. The Guaikurú stole cattle and sheep and then assassinated the woman and all her family, leaving alive only the youngest boy, Miguel. In 1870 he was still living among the Mbayá as a captive.[46] Such events, however, were isolated and reflected private vendettas and individual incidents rather than widespread movements.

Despite such isolated attacks, throughout the entire war the Guaikurú remained allies of the Brazilian Empire. Early in the war they helped defend Fort Coimbra and the Villa de Miranda, and later on steadily served essential roles as advanced detachments. Their practical knowledge of the region allowed Brazil's army to move securely through areas that had never before been carefully mapped. Their acceptance as scouts and soldiers shows how much confidence Brazil had in these indigenous people's loyalties.

In addition, the Guaikurú carried out their own attacks. According to Czech traveler V. Fritch, mentioned in Baldus, in 1865 the Kadiwéu, commanded by Captain Nauvilla and armed with *espingards*, attacked the town of San Salvador.[47] The indigenous people looted and left the town in flames. The Kadiwéu carried off food, arms, and ammunition—among them many "*terciados*," wide-bladed swords about 70 centimeters long—weapons they still displayed on their waistbands in 1879. The attackers also retreated with many Guaraní and black women as captives.[48]

Lieutenant Taunay also mentioned that Captain Nadô, with all his tribe, was among those who volunteered to join the expeditionary Brazilian force that invaded Paraguay along the Apa River all the way to Hacienda Laguna.[49] The lieutenant later recounted this episode in his book *Retirada da Laguna*. The Mbayá appear throughout this book as scouts, fighting in battles and looting the victims. The author even commented: "The Guaikurú and Terena assistants were not among the last to pillage; in battle, on the contrary, they showed little enthusiasm, to the point that in our race we shouted to them as we ran past: 'Forward, brave comrades!' Their indolence, though, was balanced by a limitless ardor for plunder. They spread out through the fields of manioc and cane, quickly returning bowed over under the weight of heavy loads, but without slowing their step."[50] When the interim commander of the infantry battalion, José Tomás Gonçalvez, referred to the performance of the thirty indigenous soldiers who belonged to the light cavalry corp (*Caçadores a Cavalo*), he argued, "the Guaicurú and Terena Indians, contradicting the common opinion about them, displayed outstanding courage, and should be recognized for their behavior, which elevates the view of aboriginal people from the District of Miranda. Advancing bare-breasted, they dislodged the enemy from a grove, suffering a high death rate, following the example of my battalion's first company."[51]

Along with other members of the wretched expedition that entered Paraguay in 1867, the Guaikurú suffered hunger and illnesses. The worst plague was cholera, which indiscriminately wiped out blacks, whites, and indigenous people, women and men.

One of the first victims of cholera was a Terena, followed shortly by his tribal chief. The picture is terrifying. Commanders ordered the ill to be abandoned to their own fate. The indigenous people seemed to the soldiers to be unable to understand anything. According to Lieutenant Taunay, "these wretched savages were completely terrorized, but could no longer leave the column because the entire field was occupied by the enemy [the Paraguayans], who, if they captured the Guaikurú, would beyond a doubt kill them with the most terrible tortures."[52] For the Guaikurú, however, the world was ordered differently. Refusing to be trapped and condemned to such a destiny, the Mbayá left the column. Still according to Taunay, "not even fear of what might befall them if captured by the Paraguayans kept the Mbaya from deserting."[53] There is no account of what happened to these Indians, but surely many of them perished, and those who managed to survive took the cholera back to their communities.

Despite the epidemic, however, the Guaikurú did not abandon the war. They stayed with the Brazilians until the end of the conflict. Throughout the desperate flight of Paraguay's dictator, "The Supreme," in 1870, the Kadiwéu were armed with first-rate weapons and ordered to camp at the mouth of the River Branco.[54] The Gaston of Orleans, Count d'Eu, the emperor's son-in-law and commander-in-chief of the Brazilian army, instructed the Kadiwéu to guard the banks of the Paraguay River and Villa de Miranda to keep an eye on enemy troop movements.[55] Soon after, the war ended with a victory for the Triple Alliance nations.

The following question emerges: What might have changed the authorities' opinion regarding the Guaikurú's loyalty? Or put in a different way, what made these indigenous people, who had previously always been rebellious, submit to other leaders and remain under their authority for almost six years?

Many scholars have argued that Brazil's emperor, Don Pedro II, had promised indigenous people their land in exchange for helping the allied troops. Nevertheless, no document of this negotiation has been found. Such an absence, of course, does not mean that such a document does not exist or never existed; it may have been lost or destroyed, or it may have been a verbal pledge. Independently of the material remains, however, this act is firmly rooted in Kadiwéu tradition. According to the indigenous people themselves, as they told anthropologist Mônica Pechincha in 1992, the Brazilians owed them a debt for the victory the indigenous people had helped to achieve, and the prize was to be legalization of their lands. Furthermore, "they fought not only for Brazil, and the Brazilians would have lost territory to the Paraguayans had it not been for the Kadiwéu intervention in the war."[56] Gen. Raul Silveira de Mello, in fact, argued this very point in a chapter titled "Brazil owes Southern Mato Grosso to the Guaikurú," in the book *History do Forte de Coimbra*.[57]

After more than a century, it is impossible to overlook the fact that a very strong bond kept the Guaikurú fighting in the conflict. For them there had been a war within the larger war, a war in which victory would have given them the security of owning their lands.

One must also remember that even in this colonial period, these indigenous people put in practice their own political goals. Reflecting on the peace treaty that Guaikurú chiefs signed with Mato Grosso authorities in 1791, historian Chiara Vangelista has observed that when they formally subjected themselves to the Portuguese queen, "the pledges of faithfulness to the Portuguese Crown were for the Guaikurú a response to the new organization of their territory, a response Guaikurú chiefs created within the dynamic of interethnic and intertribal relations."[58] With that perspective in mind, then, it is not surprising that when Brazil and Paraguay went to war to define their borders, the Mbayá-Guaikurú opted to side with the empire.

After the War

The end of the war, however, did not mean the end of problems for indigenous people in the Pantanal. They faced a devastating smallpox epidemic, which had begun to kill people in 1867 and grew worse following the war. From the port of Corumbá, this terrible disease spread throughout the province and caused many indigenous deaths. A report in 1872 described the situation:

> The remains of the great Guaicurú nation still exist in nomadic state on the left margin of the Paraguay [River], from Fort Coimbra and below; the remains of the Chamacoco [Yïshïro] are wandering along the right margins of the same river. We say remains, because both nations were cruelly decimated by the smallpox epidemic. On the shores of the Gaiva lagoon and the Mandioré . . . on the S. Lourenço River, live the small remains of the Guató nation, which the smallpox epidemic almost completely wiped out.[59]

These indigenous survivors also had to live with the mass of unemployed ex-combatants, men who decided to stay in the area after arriving for the war. Many of them occupied indigenous land.[60] Furthermore, the opening of the Paraguay River and the resulting flow of "progress" into Mato Grosso changed the daily lives of the Pantaneros. Urban reforms, the growth of commerce, port life, and the construction of a railway as well as the creation of new ranches for cattle-raising and the planting of *yerba mate* all changed the lives of the indigenous people.[61] During that time, the Guaikurú defended themselves many times against police forces, even from soldiers sent by the government.[62] The indigenous people became cheap laborers, they lost most of their land, and their cultures changed as well. The Guaikurú faced the additional work of building the new railroad and loading freight at the port of Corumbá. They also worked as ranch hands on the cattle ranches that spread into the Pantanal.

Throughout the countryside, an epizootic disease known as the "hip pestilence" continued to claim victims. Since the beginning of the war, this disease decimated horses that were not used to the climate and mainly attacked animals that had arrived with the Brazilian troops. The disease rapidly also attacked horses in the Pantanal. It is easy to imagine what the loss of their horses meant for the equestrian indigenous tribes.

In 1889, ten years after the Brazilian Republic was proclaimed, the Kadiwéu's reservation boundaries were finally demarcated. The government of the Mato Grosso officially recognized the boundaries in 1903. The process, though, did not end there. Indigenous people still today live among those who have always tried to take their lands.

Notes

1. This article is based on the paper "Los Guaikuru y la Guerra de la Triple Alianza," which was presented at the colloquium "Le Paraguay á l'ombre de ses guerres," Paris, MAL-EHESS-IEP, in November 2005. A version of it was originally printed in the proceedings of that conference.

2. von Versen, *Historia da guerra do Paraguai*, 92.

3. Ibid., 92.

4. The tribal name Guaikurú is the Portuguese spelling for the same tribe that in Spanish is called Guaicurú and lives in the Chaco region of Paraguay and Argentina.

5. Areces, "Los Mbayás en la frontera," 20.

6. Súsnik, *Los aborígenes del Paraguay*, 140. I am grateful to Adelina Pusinere, director of the Ethnographic Museum, and Dr. Andrés Barbero, Asunción, for bibliographic references about indigenous people in Paraguay during this war.

7. Súsnik, *Los Aborígenes del Paraguay*, 46–47.

8. Susnik and Chase-Sardi, *Los índios del Paraguay*, 229.

9. Ibid.

10. Areces, "Los Mbayás *en la frontera*,"

11. Cunha, *"Introdução a uma história* indígena," 18.

12. Chiara Vangelista explored this issue in her article "Confines políticos y relaciones interétnicas."

13. Pechincha, *"Historias de Admirar,"* 135.

14. "Mappa da População Indígena da Província de Mato Grosso," in *Relatório do presidente da província de Mato Grosso Joaquim José Oliveira, em 3 de maio de 1849*, Rio de Janeiro, Villenueve e Comp., 1850: 32.

15. Rivasseau, *A vida dos índios Guaycurus*, 188.

16. Schindler, *Die Reiterstämme des Gran Chaco*, 48.

17. Uacury Ribeiro de Bastos defines *"terra mbaiânica"* as "the territory bounded approximately by the polygon formed [by] the Maracajú Range, the Paraguay, [and the] Jejuí and Mboteteu Rivers," in other words, the actual Miranda River in Mato Grosso do Sul, Brazil; Bastos, *Expansão do Brasil*, 126.

18. Azara, *Viajes por la América Meridional*, 219.

19. Prado, "História dos índios cavalleiros," n.p.

20. Ribeiro, *Kadiwéu*, 42.

21. Azara, *Viajes por la América Meridional*, 220.

22. D'Alincourt, *Reflexões Acerca*, 364–65.

23. Nidia R. Areces, "Paisaje fronterizo e historia," 70.

24. *Registro dos Ofícios da presidência da Província a vários Ministérios 1851–1853.* Livro 117, 55. Manuscript, Arquivo Público de Mato Grosso (hereafter, Mss., APMG).

25. "Para a legação Imperial no Paraguai. Reservado." In Livro 117, APMG, 13v.

26. *Registro da Correspondência Oficial da Diretoria Geral dos Índios com a Presidência da Província 1860–1873.* Livro 191, 22. Mss. APMG.

27. Ibid., 29.

28. Ibid., 34v.

29. Ibid., 44v.

30. Ibid., 29.

31. Taunay, *Memórias do Visconde de Taunay*, 187.

32. "Confidencial. Cuiabá 22 de abril de 1865." In *Ofícios Expedidos ao Império ano 1858–1866.* Livro 180, 97v. Mss. APMG.

33. Cunha, "Introdução a uma história indígena," 196.

34. Taunay, *Scenas de Viagem*, 205.

35. "Notícias dadas por Manuel de Gomes e Silva no Acampamento do Batalhão de Caçadores da Província de Goiás, no porto Colonial de Coxim, em 6 de setembro de 1865." Box [Caixa] 1865, Mss., APMG.

36. "Informações dadas por José Antonio Dias, Tenente-Coronel a Augusto Leverger, Campamento Volante na Fazenda de Água Fria, 8 de outubro de 1865." Box [Caixa] 1865, Mss., APMG.

37. Ibid.

38. "Ofício do Secretário de Polícia de Cuiabá ao Presidente da Província de Mato Grosso, 24 de julho de 1865." Box [Caixa] 1865, Mss., APMG.

39. "Relatório do Diretor Geral dos Índios, João Gualberto de Mattos ao Presidente da Província de Mato Grosso. Cuiabá 3 de maio de 1865." Box [Caixa] 1865, Mss. APMG.

40. "Cópia. Oficio do Capitão do Porto de Cuiabá, Antonio Cláudio Souto, em 19 de junho de 1865." Box [Caixa] 1865, Mss., APMG.

41. *Relatório do vice-presidente da província de Matto-Grosso, Augusto Leverger, em 17 de outubro de 1865*, Cuiabá, Typ. de Souza Neves, 1865, 21.

42. "Oficio do Quartel do Batalhão de Artilharia a pé no. 2, Poconé, 4 de dezembro de 1865." Box [Caixa] 1865, Mss., APMG.

43. The document uses the word "*bombeiros*," meaning spies.

44. "Para a legação Imperial no Paraguay, Reservado." Book 117, APMG, 13v.

45. Taunay, A. "Relatório Geral da Comissão," 320.

46. "Oficio do sub-delegado de Polícia do Distrito de Miranda, Luiz Generoso da Silva Albuquerque, ao Chefe de Polícia da Província de Mato Grosso, em 17 de setembro de 1870." Box [Lata] 1870 C, Mss., APMG.

47. *Espingards* are a long handgun or musket of North African origin.

48. Baldus, "Introdução," 37; and Colini, "Noticia histórica," 267.

49. Taunay, *Relatório Geral da Comissão*, 319.

50. Taunay, *A retirada da Laguna*, 94.

51. "Cópia de ofício de José Thomaz Gonçalvez, Major de Comissão interino, ao Coronel Carlos Moraes Camisão, Comandante das Forças em Operação. Acampamento do Batalhão 21 de Infantaria, no riacho Invernada, na República do Paraguay, 6 de maio de 1867." In *Revista Arquivo*, 3, 1993, 195–96.

52. Taunay, *A retirada da Laguna*, 191.

53. Ibid., 198.

54. "Carta de Fillipe Orlando Short," s/l, s/d. Box [Caixa] 1870 B, Mss., APMG.

55. "Comandante em Chefe de todas as forças brasileiras em operação na República do Paraguay, Quartel General de Vila do Rosário, 12 de fevereiro de 1870." Box [Lata] 1870 B, Mss., APMG.

56. Pechincha, *Historias de Admirar*, 146.

57. Silveira de Mello, *Historia do Forte*, 232.

58. Vangelista, "Los Guaikuru," 75.

59. Cited by Correa, *Historia e Fronteira*, 112.

60. Ibid.

61. *Yerba mate* is a plant used to brew tea.

62. Rivasseau, *A vida dos índios Guaycurus*, 54.

8

Illustrating Race and Nation in the Paraguayan War Era

Exploring the Decline of the Tupi Guarani Warrior as the Embodiment of Brazil

PETER M. BEATTIE

Brazil is not a serious country.
—Attributed to French premier Gen. Charles de Gaulle

For nationalists across the globe in the nineteenth century, war invited competitive assessments of national honor, virility, "race," and "serious-ness."[1] In this sense, the War of the Triple Alliance (better known as the Paraguayan War in Brazil, 1864–70) is not unique, but Brazil's racial hetero-geneity presented paradoxes for its nationalists. While serious attempts to square Brazil's national and racial myths of origin and destiny have inspired scholarly interest, less attention has been paid to humorists who exploited anxieties over them. This chapter examines this conundrum through heroic and humoristic representations of "race" and nation.[2] Many of these depic-tions are offensive, and I in no way promote racist humor under the cover of scholarship; rather, I assert that humor and the heroic are interconnected battlefields in which the memory of traumatic events are shaped, chal-lenged, and recast. The classic political theorist Thomas Hobbes postulated that humor was one's realization of their innate superiority over another. Others have stressed humor's subversive nature. In Brazil, scholars have focused on the parodies of Carnival, portraying them as a form of popu-lar criticism or resistance to powerful actors and forces in society.[3] Humor traced a reversed outline of what was heroic. Indeed, Thomas Carlyle con-ceives the "heroic" as an idealized form of manhood defined mostly by a vir-tuous seriousness or "sincerity."[4] I take the perspective that humor and the heroic are malleable, and they can serve a variety of purposes, intended and unintended. Humor and the heroic are dynamic phenomenon whose nature defies easy categorization, but to be effective, they must use and mold a language of signs and symbols recognizable to their intended audience.

Humorous depictions of blacks and Indians in the Americas often marked the distance between mostly "white" elites and subordinate nonwhite inhabitants, and they shaped the elite's changing "visions of liberty."[5] I argue that the Paraguayan War experience contributed to the decline of the Tupi Guarani Indian's popularity as a way of representing Brazil in certain political circles (although Indianist nationalism would see subsequent revivals).[6] I also contend that racial humor diminished the patriotic sacrifices of veteran Brazilian enlisted men of all races. The conflicts over these humorous images had serious implications for the Brazilian Empire's policies and legitimacy.

The Dilemmas of Distilling a National Racial Identity in Brazil

Many Brazilian nationalists spoke of their population as a branch of the Latin race although most conceded that France was the "flower" of this "race." Nationalists such as Sílvio Romero lamented that Brazil had the misfortune of being founded by the Portuguese: "We are descended from the most degenerate and corrupt branch of the old Latin race, to which were added two of the most degraded races in the world—the coastal Negroes and the American redskins." Despite Romero's passion for Brazilian folklore, which he recognized had been positively influenced by Africans, Indians, and their descendents, he expressed pessimism about Brazil's racial heterogeneity: "The senility of the Negro, the laziness of the Indian, the authoritarian and miserly talent of the Portuguese had produced a shapeless nation with no original or creative qualities."[7] As Thomas E. Skidmore shows, this sense of a shapeless national character haunted the literary ruminations of Romero's generation, which came of age during the Paraguayan War.[8]

If Brazilians were a Latin race, then what distinguished them from other nations colonized by Romance language empires? This question was mostly left unanswered, but referring to Brazilians as "Latin" diverted attention from African and Indigenous heritage without specifying the Portuguese. Brazilians remain unique in the Americas in that popular jokes about their imperial mother country's people stress their lack of culture and intelligence. Nationalists' pessimistic depictions of the Portuguese derived from the most powerful unifying force among Brazilians before and after

Independence: Lusophobia (fear of the Portuguese). Resentment toward the Portuguese could unite the Brazilian-born across racial and class divisions. Portuguese merchants and retailers continued to be a prominent force in postindependence Brazilian commerce, a fact that many Brazilian-born citizens resented. Nationalists also feared British and Vatican influence, but resentment toward the much more ubiquitous Portuguese fueled a more virulent animus that could boil over into *mata-marinheiro* (kill the Portuguese) riots.[9]

A counterpart of Lusophobia was Indianism, a movement that peaked, according to David Miller Driver, between 1854 and 1864, but no one, to my knowledge, has explored how or why the Paraguayan War chilled "Indianist mania."[10] During this craze, followers of Indianism legally adopted indigenous names and proudly claimed descent from aboriginal forebears as badges of nobility. An Indianist boom produced Brazil's great foundational novels by Conservative senator José Martiniano de Alencar, *O Guarany* (1857) and *Iracema* (1865), and inspired the epic poetry of Gonçalves Dias and Victor Meirelles's painting. As with any major artistic trend, critiques of Indianism existed since its emergence, but the tenor and political stakes of these critiques became more strident after the Paraguayan War. Emperor Pedro II, with the bluest of European blood (Braganza, Hapsburg, and Bourbon), patronized the work of Indianist artists as a young monarch. Imperial symbols and artwork replete with Indianist motifs creolized this Euro-American monarch whose heroic bearded image also stood as a patriarchal icon of Brazilian identity.[11] Similarly, the beardless Tupi Guarani warrior became the way that cartoonists such as the Italian-born Angelo Agostini and his fellow illustrators represented the Brazilian nation, just as Thomas Nast made Uncle Sam the personification of the United States. The Indianist craze was a way for Brazilians to assert nationalism and distance themselves from their Portuguese forebears. Who could be more Brazilian than the nation's original inhabitants? Or so nationalists in coastal urban centers reasoned.[12]

As Afonso Arinos de Melo Franco showed, the American Indian and, in particular, depictions of the Brazilian Tupi Guarani Indian were crucial to the development of the European idea of the noble savage. In turn, the noble savage was a key concept in the political theories of Jean Jacques Rousseau, Montesquieu, and John Locke, theories that criticized Thomas Hobbes and inspired liberation struggles across the Americas.[13]

While highbrow nineteenth-century myths of Brazil's national origin incorporated the Indian, they do not feature Africans and their descendents, despite their predominant share of the population.[14] Whereas white women and men form romantic unions with Indian men and women in Alencar's foundational novels, similar symbolic unions between Africans and whites were unpalatable to the author (a fierce defender of slavery) and most of his readers. Africans did not awaken the same fantasies of natural man and noble savagery in Brazilian literature.[15] As in much of the Americas, the black slave usually served a different symbolic purpose. While the Indian often represented freedom, bravery, and natural goodness, nationalists associated the black slave with submission, captivity, degradation, and cowardice. André Augusto de Padua Fleury voiced this stereotype in 1882 when he griped that Rio's police chief sent street urchins to work on plantations as this would expose the boys to "pernicious contact with slavery, that is to men without family, without religion, without morals, brutalized by ignorance, violence, and the stupor (embriaguez) of vices."[16] Similarly, many who fought for independence in the Americas asserted their righteous outrage that their metropolitan brothers condescended to them and treated them as if they were "slaves" to justify their wars of liberation. Mostly white patriots in many American nations masqueraded as Indians; to masquerade as a black slave would have been at cross-purposes in symbolic, economic, and political terms given the extent of slavery in the independence-era Americas.[17]

In this way, conceptions of black slaves and Indians served as symbolic touchstones to measure the rights, liberties, and imagined communities that free citizens should enjoy. These were not fixed measures, and some disagreed about how to interpret them. Nonetheless, most Brazilians shared an understanding of the symbolic significance of these racialized figures as part of a metanarrative of national community. Brazil's mobilization for the Paraguayan War, however, would challenge the deployment of these iconic symbols in unanticipated ways.

The Paraguayan War (1864–1870)

After local opposition factions supported by Brazil and Argentina forced Paraguay's political allies in Uruguay from power, Paraguay's president Francísco Solano López launched raids on Brazil in retaliation and violated Argentina's territory in 1864. The Triple Alliance (Brazil, Argentina, and Uruguay) joined forces against tiny Paraguay. The Brazilian army bore the brunt of the campaign because turmoil in Uruguay and Argentina limited their ability to deploy men.[18] Brazil mobilized more than four times as many men than it had in any previous campaign, deploying some 110,000 to 140,000 men. This represented less than 2 percent of Brazil's 9 million inhabitants, but because of crude recruitment methods, it strained the nation's social and political fabric.

While most commissioned officers came from middle-class backgrounds, Brazil's army and navy depended heavily on impressment to fill the enlisted ranks. In peacetime, officials used summary recruitment as a punishment for many nonhomicidal criminals, troublemakers, and vagabonds. Vulnerability to impressment marked an important line of stratification between the "protected" and the "unprotected" or patronless poor. Many enlisted volunteers who formed a minority of the ranks signed up to escape unemployment, homelessness, and sometimes even slavery. Soldiering's status was so low that attempts to use a color bar to exclude black and brown men had been abandoned by the mid-1800s. Black, brown, Indian, and white men served side by side in army ranks, but most soldiers were men of mixed race. Men of color were overrepresented in the enlisted ranks, but "whiteness" did not protect less fortunate Brazilian men from impressment. Most citizens and even some slaves perceived enlisted service as dishonorable, suitable for orphans, seducers, ex-slaves, men who abandoned their wives, "sodomites," common criminals, and vagabonds, but not the "sons and fathers of families." Marriage had long been an exemption from military service, and military impressment was a punishment for "men who disrespect families." In brief, the army enlisted ranks had a serious public image problem because most Brazilians, rich and poor, associated them with dishonor, criminality, captivity, and depravity.[19]

In 1865 Emperor Pedro II called on Brazil's free citizenry to volunteer to defend national honor and civilization against Paraguayan aggression. Many willingly volunteered in fits of patriotic fervor. Among them, black volunteers formed the Zuavo regiments in Bahia and Pernambuco. These units called upon colonial traditions in which militia regiments had been organized based on race.[20]

While many men of all races patriotically volunteered, their numbers were too few. The government soon began to call up national guardsmen (men who were legally protected from regular enlisted service in peacetime). It also created a force separate from army regulars known as the "volunteers of the fatherland." As opposed to army regulars, guardsmen and volunteers of the fatherland won higher enlistment bonuses and better contract terms with promises of land grants upon discharge. Still, many designated guards-men did not report for duty, and many volunteers of the fatherland did not volunteer to fight for national honor but were dragooned.[21]

In 1866, when mobilization efforts lagged, the state decided to buy and accept donations of slaves. Hundreds of slave "volunteers" were given let-ters of liberty conditioned upon their completion of a nine-year military contract. While homicide convicts were not welcome in the army in peace-time, during the war, the state liberated scores of inmates with pardons in exchange for military service. Press gangs hunted down most recruits, targeting the rural and urban poor. In many cases, authorities ignored traditional exemptions from military service, and indiscriminately threw together members of the "honorable" free poor (Guardsmen, "fathers of families," skilled laborers, etc.) with the "unprotectected" poor (convicts, ex-slaves, vagabonds, orphans, and the dissolute). Brazil's inability to mo-bilize effectively helped to turn what had been anticipated to be a brief war into a five-year ordeal. Despite Brazil's much larger population and economy, its military lacked the railroads, munitions works, capital, and manpower to respond quickly to the aggressions of tiny Paraguay.[22]

Securing cooperation for military mobilization in any nation requires fear of social stigma, credible legal action for noncompliance, and social acceptance and recognition for service. A perusal of wartime cartoons and editorials indicate that much more space was dedicated to ridiculing soldiers and recruitment profiteers than vilifying those who evaded press gangs, which indicates widespread sympathy for impressment dodging.[23] An 1867 illustration from Recife, for example, depicts the Tupi Guarani warrior chained like a slave to a series of platforms supporting the Brazilian throne. On each platform a threat to Brazil's freedom is listed: "barbarous [coercive military] recruitment, foreign subjugation, the Paraguayan War, venalities, and [foreign] loans." At the top of a canopy over the throne is written "corruption comes from above," which implies that Pedro II was the source of the civilized chains that fetter the noble savage.[24]

In contrast, there were also attempts in illustrated newspapers to make heroes out of Brazilians who did their part. Figure 8.1 depicts patriotic masters donating slaves for the war effort. At the war's outset, a fusionist Parliament of Liberals and a number of Conservatives who crossed the aisle formed the Emperor's influential Council of Ministers. This fusion cabinet was known as the Progressive League, which controlled Parliament during the war's outset.[25] The league's supporters sought to win public support for policies that manumitted slaves for the war to hasten slavery's demise.

Figure 8.1. The comendador Mathias Rôxo and his sons, Augusto and Frederic, make their slaves citizens, and of these citizens, soldiers. Reproduced in Magalhães, *O império em chinelos*, 29. Courtesy of the Biblioteca Nacional, Rare Works Division. Photo by Xavier.

Especially in Rio, merchants and politicians sought to please Pedro II by donating slaves. Many of them no doubt donated men to curry imperial favor for lucrative contracts and government patronage. Significantly, the illustration highlights the patriotism of the donors and not that of the "slave citizens," now "citizen soldiers." A similar illustration depicted without irony a master freeing a slave from chains and handing him a rifle; his liberty (symbolized by the white French republican female figure of Marianne) is granted to him by a white philanthropist, abolitionist, patriot, and "man of honor." Illustrators portrayed these master patriots as possessing lofty sentiments of public service and self-sacrifice while the slaves are mere grateful recipients of their noblesse oblige. The illustration's caption reads:

The Great Conde [d'Eu] [Pedro II's son-in-law] said that to end the war in the briefest space of time, two things were necessary: men and money: Mr. José Luiz Alves, a wealthy and respected business man in Rio, comprehended perfectly the Conde's axiom: he bought and manumitted a slave, and sent him to the theatre of war, paying him in advance one year's worth of uniforms, pay, and meals. Thus, he practiced an act of patriotism, diminishing the number of slaves and increasing the number of soldiers. Congratulations to the honorable Fluminense. Honor him and all who follow his example.[26]

Critics of this patriotism humorously pointed out the palpable ironies. The Rio magazine *Arlequim* lampooned this type of patriotism by depicting a master donating two slaves. The master sarcastically addressed an Afro-Brazilian veteran seated near the recruitment center who had lost an arm in the war: "You want to be decorated only because you lost an arm? Then what can I say who will lose no less than four."[27] Here metaphors of dismemberment and slave labor (commonly referred to as *braços* or arms) marked the distance between the sacrifices of a black veteran and the master in which the latter measures heroism as a kind of macabre commodity exchange of limbs.

Humorists also poked fun at the corruption that typified recruitment. In one illustration, a master presents to a recruiter a rail-thin slave with a tufted afro. The slave's slim frame indicates that he was either poorly nourished, suffered from illness, or both. In any case, the image suggests that the slave was not physically apt for military service, and the recruiting officer quips that he was only "fit to serve as a rod for cleaning cannons." This and other cartoons suggest that masters took advantage of the state's willingness to purchase slaves for the war to unload unhealthy and intractable slaves onto taxpayers. The policy opened the door to partisan collusion between recruiters (appointed by incumbent politicians) and their slave-owning allies.

One way that called-up guardsmen or dragooned "volunteers" could free themselves from recruitment was to present substitutes. To profit from this, some entrepreneurs contracted poor men whom they sold at auction as substitutes. Figure 8.2 shows guardsmen bidding on a substitute. The similarity of this scene to a slave auction was not lost on a Brazilian audience. The illustrator highlights that leaders (in this case a priest) treated these poor free men (in this case a white man with a decent coat and shoes) like slaves.

Another abuse depicted by illustrators was the use of recruitment to punish poor free men who defied political bosses. In a cartoon from *O Recife Illustrado* published in 1866, a hillbilly (*matuto*) is depicted asking his patron, a local doctor, to restore his liberty. In reply to the doctor's question "who imprisoned you?" the rustic replies: "The police subdelegate of my hometown recruited me as a *volunteer* [author's emphasis] because I said that I did not vote for the Liga Party's candidates." In truth, whether

Figure 8.2. Sign above states, "Substitute Auction (guaranteed)." Auctioneer, "One Conto de réis! One Conto de réis! One Conto de réis! No more bidders? One conto de réis! Last chance. One conto de réis! Going once, going twice, going three times. . . . Bam!" *Cabrião,* São Paulo, Dec. 2, 1866.

Conservatives or Liberals had dominated Parliament, they both used impressment to win elections. To emphasize the injustice, the illustrator depicted a woman and three children alongside the unfortunate hillbilly. Marriage legally exempted men from impressment, but wartime expediency led authorities to ignore these laws. This was an honorable "father of family" who upheld his patriarchal duties of protecting and providing for his wife and children. Notably, the victims appeared to be white, which made them more sympathetic to the mostly privileged reading public. The cartoon also shows the way that authorities abused the term "volunteer" as a euphemism for impressments; in it, the *matuto's* hands are bound and the police officer has his saber drawn. In making their point, however, the opposition downplayed the patriotism of poor men dragooned to serve the fatherland.[28]

Conservatives and Liberals used humor as part of their rhetorical arsenal to attack the Progressive League government during the first three years of the war, but the tables turned in 1868, when Pedro II used his constitutional moderating power to dissolve the Progressive League's cabinet (the Council of Ministers). In an unpopular move, he called on the Conservatives to form a new cabinet and hold parliamentary elections that predictably

Figure 8.3. Observe the latest defenders of the fatherland that were nabbed, put in uniform, and sent to the theater of war to defend there our national honor!!! We are elegant!!! *Cabrião*, São Paulo, May 26, 1866, 64–65. Courtesy of the Biblioteca Nacional, Rare Works Division.

brought their party to power in the capital and in provinces across Brazil. Now Liberals railed against the emperor and the Conservatives' abuse of impressment. In postwar parliamentary debates, politicians from both parties laid bare the hypocrisy of the exploitation of recruitment for partisan ends.[29]

While some cartoons pointed out how authorities abused their recruitment powers, others derided the enlisted soldiers. Figure 8.3 depicted Brazil's soldiers as awkward ragamuffins to point out the irony of sending men with little or no honor to defend Brazil's national honor. Many poor free men went about their daily routines unshod, for reason of preference or poverty, but the depiction is significant because in Brazil slaves were forbidden to wear shoes. On the one hand, the soldiers' lack of "elegance" and physical preparedness for war could be read as an attempt to shame those Brazilians who used their influence to avoid service, but on the other, it belittled the sacrifices that these enlisted men made. The illustration acknowledges the multiracial composition of Brazil's soldiery, but it also indicates that the whites, blacks, and others who served came from the lowest strata of the free poor. Their comic appearance made them more of an embarrassment than symbols of heroic national pride.

Ironically, these unflattering Brazilian caricatures of their enlisted men resembled those produced by Paraguayan illustrators who wielded racial caricature as a weapon. The Paraguayan newspaper *Cabichui* stereotyped all Brazilian soldiers and officers as black. They typecast Brazilians as feckless victims of a decadent slave regime ruled by a dissolute monarch and his servile cronies. They condemned slavery and mocked the purchase of slaves to fight at the front as a manifestation of Brazilian pusillanimity. Paraguayan propagandists claimed that the lack of Brazilian patriotism stemmed from its slave regime, its multiracial population, and the heterogeneous interests of the Triple Alliance's member nations. This heterogeneity is contrasted to the homogeneity of Paraguay's mostly mestizo population (European and Guarani Indian). While they presented Afro-Brazilians as victims of the avarice and cruelty of Brazil's elites, they also used racist stereotypes of blacks to insult their enemy and to mark the difference between them and freedom-loving Paraguayan mestizos. *Cabuchui* portrays black Brazilians as cowardly, ignorant, awkward, and lazy, as in one illustration where a group of black Brazilian soldiers flee before the advance of a single Paraguayan trooper.[30]

The Paraguayans delighted in leaving copies of *Cabichui* behind to incense Alliance troops. Humor here was a tactical weapon used to provoke dissension among the enemy, which was often rife. Its illustrators portrayed the marshal Marques de Caxias, who assumed command of Brazilian forces in 1866, as a rotund black man. Caxias, Brazil's most famous army officer, was also a prominent senator for the Conservative Party. Caxias reorganized allied forces and adopted a slow-moving siege campaign that was heavily criticized on the home front. *Cabichui* often showed Caxias riding a tortoise to mock his cautious strategy.

For different ends, Paraguayan and Brazilian illustrators made use of racial stereotypes to belittle Brazilian enlisted men. Many black Brazilians and former slaves served valiantly on the Paraguayan front alongside brown, white, and Indian men. Recently, historians have lavished merited attention on the contributions of women and African-descended troops to the war effort. The next section makes a small contribution to the still little-studied participation of Brazil's Indian allies.[31]

Not so Noble Savages?

Officials recruited Indian troops from across Brazil, but most of them who fought for the allies lived near Paraguay's border. Some signed on to settle their own scores with Paraguayans and others were dragooned. Many Indian soldiers were acculturated members of frontier Brazilian society, but others

Figure 8.4. "News from Paraguay. Long live the Brazilian nation!" *Mosquito*, Rio, Mar. 27, 1870.

maintained their cultural distance from "Brazilian" authorities even while cooperating in the war effort.[32] As with Ladino versus *boçal* (acculturated versus unacculturated African-born slaves), Indians who demonstrated less distance from Brazilian culture seemed more sympathetic. Still, Brazil's war against "mestizo" Paraguayans and the experience of fighting alongside the "original" Brazilians would lead some officers to question the concept of the noble savage so dear to nationalists who promoted Indianism.

The war gave Brazilian propagandists a new rival against which their national race could be reflected upon. Paraguay's Guarani heritage permeated its mestizo population. Unlike most of Latin America, its political leaders had encouraged miscegenation after independence to foment racial homogenization. For their part, Brazilians portrayed Paraguay's dictatorial political system, centrally directed economy, and indigenous racial composition as inferior to Brazil's constitutional monarchy, capitalist agro-export economy, and demographic base, which included more European descendants. In figure 8.4, Paraguay is embodied as an Indian savage that uniformed Euro-Brazilian leaders humiliated as the war drew to a close in 1870. The Indian wears garb typical of seminomadic Indians except for the clerical cap, which symbolized another stereotype of Paraguayan difference. While both Brazil and Paraguay were predominantly Catholic, in colonial times, Paraguay had been colonized by Jesuit missionaries. Since the mid-eighteenth century when the Jesuit order was expelled from Portuguese and later Spanish America, a negative image of the Company of Jesus became rooted in Latin America. Many postcolonial, anticlerical intellectuals, politicians, and military officers blamed Jesuit influence for a multitude of national problems. Paraguay's foundational relationship with the Jesuits made them more suspect and backward in the eyes of Brazil's anticlerical nationalists.

While many jingoistic Brazilian images of Paraguayans emphasized their Indian savagery, some tried to create heroic images of Brazil's Indian allies. These heroic images tended to privilege Indians who used European-style dress and who had adopted at least the outward forms of Western civilization, sedentary agriculture, and the Portuguese language. Celebrations of the heroic contributions of Brazil's Indian allies to the victory of the Triple Alliance, however, were few.[33]

In at least one case, an illustrator for a Liberal newspaper used the image of barbarous Indian allies to shame citizens who pulled strings to avoid military service. In it, a chief of the notoriously fierce Botucudo people, whose use of large lip plugs made them seem particularly exotic and savage, volunteers to march against the army of Paraguay. Here the journalist uses irony to challenge the patriotism and bravery of those who speak in the name of the fatherland yet who did not volunteer to fight.[34] In other illustrations, Francísco Solano López is depicted as Brazil's real enemy, not the Paraguayan people. For Brazilian illustrators, López represented the *caudillo* tradition that had led to decades of instability and warfare in the Platine republics. Propaganda depicted Brazilians as peaceful victims of López and as liberators of the Paraguayan people. Thus, not all portrayals of Paraguayans characterized them as savages. One Brazilian officer drew an illustration published in a Rio newspaper of elite Paraguayan women who sport elegant European attire (certainly too costly for most Paraguayans), while the men combine elements of traditional Indian garb with European dress to culturally locate them. Moreover, one man is busy tilling the earth with a hoe and the other wears cowboy gear. These are men who work at civilized, sedentary agriculture, not seminomadic savages like the one depicted in figure 8.4.[35]

While some depictions sought to ennoble Paraguayans, much of Brazil's propaganda centered on unflattering indigenous stereotypes. For Paraguayans, conversely, racial homogeneity accounted for their national unity and dogged resistance. One article praised the contributions to the war of Paraguayan women and expressed racial fears in sexual terms. "Comrades! This is how we sustain our mothers, wives, daughters, and sisters! And will they become captives of the voracious and ravenous wolves [Allied soldiers] who come to destroy our homes? No! One thousand times no! Blood and fire to the *black* [emphasis added] Alliance! Honor and glory to the Paraguayan Woman."[36] By referring to the alliance as "black," the editor intended not only to demarcate the Alliance as evil but also to stress fears that black soldiers might rape honorable Paraguayan women.

Paraguayan propaganda highlighted the racial heterogeneity of Triple Alliance armies and contrasted them to a leveled, homogeneous, and patriotic Paraguayan citizenry. Some differences among the Alliance forces were obvious: Spanish versus Portuguese language, constitutional monarchy versus republican governments, slavery versus free labor, and of course the fact that the percentage of Brazilians of African heritage was much higher than in the armies of Uruguay and Argentina.[37] Paraguayan propagandists ridiculed Argentine president Bartolomé Mitre, the titular commander of Allied forces until 1868, as a traitor to his nation and his race by becoming a pawn of the Brazilian emperor "Macacuna" (Big Monkey): "Yesterday you were Argentine, today you are Brazilian. Yesterday you were white, now you are black. Once you seemed great, but now you are lost among the insignificant."[38] In some instances, Uruguayans and Argentines became "black" through their alliance with Brazil, but in other instances, distinctions were emphasized. *Cabichui*'s editors conventionalized the differences between the allies by using totemic animal images: Brazilians were monkeys; Argentines, dogs; and Uruguayans, burros. The choice of the monkey as the totemic symbol of Brazil had blatant racist and Darwinian overtones. The use of different species to represent the soldiers of different nations could be read as a metaphor of the different national races that composed Allied forces. Even allied officers described the armies of the Alliance as constituted by different races. Brazilian officer Benjamin Constant wrote that the alliance had done nothing to soothe "the racial hatreds that existed between Brazil and these miserable Republics [Argentina and Uruguay]" although he expressed the wish that "before we return to Brazil, we erase [this hatred] here on the battlefields."[39]

For their part, the Paraguayans refused to follow Brazilian conventions and use the Tupi Guarani Indian as the symbolic embodiment of their enemy. This is likely because depicting Brazilians as Tupi Guarani would have symbolically made their enemies into distant ethnic kin instead of a racially distinct enemy. As if the differences between Allied forces were not enough, *Cabichui* reported with ironic delight that Marshal Caxias was negotiating a pact with the seminomadic Chaco Indians to form a "quadruple alliance."

An illustration depicts Caxias as a black man negotiating with two Indian chiefs: "Caxias—I need 2,000 Indians: The Emperor, my master, authorized me to pay four mares or stallions for each. What is more, my master offers to marry with two of the most beautiful noble women in your court."[40] *Cabichui* commentary specified that "There has formed an alliance with no more homogeneity than the consonance between the Argentine dog, the Uruguayan burro, and the Brazilian monkey. . .[as a result of the negotiations] to make Chaco Indians into allies and auxiliaries of the Alliance's forces. This is not the first time that Brazil in its impotence and desperation has turned its eyes toward the savages and found in them their hope." *Cabichui* added that "the allied army had lost its self respect to the point that, neither among their own populations, nor among foreigners, can the chiefs of the monkeys find anyone who wants to pick up a rifle to fight for the Alliance."[41] As with slaves manumitted to fight, *Cabichui* implies that the Alliance army purchased its Indian allies; its soldiers did not serve out of a sense of patriotism. *Cabichui* chided President Mitre by suggesting that he commanded the equivalent of a slave army, "you have 60,000 blacks valued at one conto de réis each."[42]

Some months later, *Cabichui* described the breakdown of negotiations: "The [Chaco] Indians, despite the promises and gifts made and distributed in the name of the Emperor of monkeys, by natural instinct, and a plausible love of liberty, that they enjoy—although licentiously in the nomadic life they lead—have comprehended at last that the plans of their allies was to extend the chains of black slavery, without any justification other than blind ambition and unchecked greed."[43] Once again, *Cabichui* argued, it was ultimately the desire to enslave Paraguayans and seminomadic Chaco Indians that drove Brazilian imperialism. By implication, Brazil's erstwhile allies would one day realize that they too would be enslaved by the South American giant's imperialistic designs. In this depiction the Chaco Indians are more perceptive and freedom-loving than are the Uruguayans and Argentines. While praising the independent stereotype commonly attributed to noble savages, *Cabichui* leaves no doubt that nomadic Chaco Indians, unlike mestizo Paraguayans, were not part of the brotherhood of civilized nations. By implying that Chaco Indians would become an equal partner in a "Quadruple Alliance," *Cabichui* scorned Brazilian claims of superior civilization and stereotypes of Paraguayans as Indian savages who blindly followed a caudillo chief. After all, the Brazilians courted "barbarous" Indian as their allies.

While Brazil's Indian allies represented numerically only a small part of its overall forces, they made the Paraguayan War even more of a multinational conflict than conventionally portrayed. Officers not only had to deal with communicating orders to Brazilians from every province, whose accents and slang were divergent, but also with Spanish-speaking troops and diverse Indian languages. Not surprisingly, misunderstandings and conflicts were common among allied forces, and *Cabichui* delighted in highlighting these divisions and tensions.

Race and Brazilian Memories of War

If propaganda won wars, Paraguay might not have succumbed to Allied forces. Even so, the victorious Brazilian army's homecoming was more ambivalent than triumphant.[44] Rio's English- and French-language newspapers described the Te Deum mass and military parade that celebrated victory on July 10, 1870, as an "unmitigated failure because the people of Rio were determined to manifest their opinion toward it by contemptuously abstaining from it." By the "people," these journalists referred to eight thousand dignified citizens honored with invitations to the event. Only some two hundred showed up, and most of those who did were state officials or foreign consuls who were obligated to appear. In the end, the emperor ordered guards who held back the city's uninvited "rabble" to let them enter the "utter solitude" of the stands bringing a "simulacrum of popular life" to them. Foreign observers found the spectacle laughable, noting the dark skin of most troops and the parade's rowdy spectators. Rio's cheeky French-language newspaper clucked that Pedro II was a poor organizer of solemn patriotic events but an excellent director of Carnival: a holiday when the poor took to the streets for raucous, drunken merriment.[45] For these foreign observers, the spectacle lacked the decorum or "seriousness" that should typify such an important nationalistic solemnity. The French language *Ba Ta Clan* depicted the Conservative president of the emperor's Council of Ministers, the Marquês de São Vicente (José Antonio Pimenta Bueno) directing the victory celebration. The marquês presides with a crown (many Carnival revelers dressed as kings or nobility) and a *palmatório* (an instrument used to castigate slaves and underlings) as a scepter. The *palmatório* scepter suggests that this was the legitimate instrument used to rule the "rabble" who attended the parade.

Why did so many prominent Brazilians fail to attend the victory celebration? Resentment toward the war, its veterans, and Pedro II sprang from many sources. Some complained of the debt Brazil mounted in foreign banks to fund the campaign. Others pointed to the corruption and the windfall profits made by unscrupulous entrepreneurs who produced shoddy war goods. Still others complained of the emperor's abuse of his power to wage a long and unpopular war instead of seeking an earlier negotiated settlement. Many prominent Conservatives and Liberals emerged from the war disillusioned with their monarch, and although some referred to veterans as the "Saviors of Brazil," most privileged Brazilians likely found distasteful the idea of honoring the services of enlisted men with such lowly social origins as their national heroes.[46]

The Paraguayan War had been a period of national self-encounter, an experience that could have laid the basis for a broader sentiment of nationalism as it brought together Brazilians from different provinces, races, and classes on an unprecedented scale in a common struggle, but in many respects, Brazilians seemed more divided than ever. Anger and controversy over the 1868 elections and wartime recruitment abuses by both parties set the stage for bitter partisan politics. A faction of the Liberal party became so upset with the emperor that they formed the Republican Party in 1870, which, among other things, they hoped would eventually do away with monarchy.

Postwar reformism did not reconcile contradictions that plagued the imperial political and economic order. In 1871 Parliament passed the Free Womb Law, which declared that no one could be born into slavery in Brazil thereafter. In 1873 a new controversy between Church and state led to the arrest and trial of two ultramontanist bishops who refused to cooperate with the crown's directives. In 1874 a new recruitment law sought to replace impressment with a conscription lottery. To the dismay of army officers, efforts to implement the law proved futile because most Brazilians refused to cooperate with authorities who were required to draw up enrollment lists. The political abuses of wartime recruitment and the erosion of significant thresholds of status among free poor men made the larger public suspicious of recruitment reform. Figure 8.5 shows how the memory of the war undermined support for recruitment reform.

Postwar partisanship also fueled culture wars over how Brazil should represent itself. Brazilian backlanders had played an important role in the war, supplying men, material, and wilderness guides. Paraguayan War veterans such as the Alfredo d'Escragnolle Taunay (later the Visconde de Taunay) promoted instead the cult of the *sertanejo* (backlands frontiersman) as a substitute for the Tupi Guarani warrior. But this symbolic alternative emerged from the serious realm of a new literary nationalistic movement

Figure 8.5. "Notice for all Brazilians over age 19" is a series of illustrations about the military draft. The illustration shows a young man drawing a black ball from a draft lottery cylinder. He then has his health inspection, active exercises (marching), passive exercises (taking care of a crying baby), then his baptism of fire in battle where a cannon ball dismembers him. He is then shown begging under a sign that reads disabled in the service of his fatherland at age 23. To the right, Senator Caxias measures the height of a resigned Brazilian Indian who holds a scrolled piece of paper that reads, "Brazil prepares itself for peace." *Mephistopheles*, Rio, July 31, 1875.

known as regionalism, not humoristic illustrated magazines where the Indian caricature continued to predominate until after the promulgation of a republic in 1889.

Indianism versus Sertanism in Postwar Politics

The mobilization of Brazilians from every corner of its territory awoke new curiosity and awareness about regional cultural differences, especially the thinly populated hinterlands or *sertão*. This was so much the case that literary critic and historian Nelson Werneck Sodré prefers the term "sertanism" to "regionalism." According to him, "sertanismo arose when Indianismo declined," and he identified three major exponents: Bernardo Guimarães, João Franklin de Silveira Távora, and Taunay. Of these, Sodré argued that "it is in the Visconde de Taunay that we encounter a novelist capable of saving sertanism from complete perdition."[47]

A junior army officer in the war, Taunay authored its most popular narrative, *A retirada da Laguna* (Retreat from Laguna, 1871). He realistically narrated his experiences as part of the disastrous Mato Grosso Expedition where troops marched from São Paulo to the northeastern corner of Paraguay before being forced to retreat. En route, this force was augmented by Indian allies and backland frontiersmen. More than a third of the expedition's members perished and hundreds more deserted before they even reached the Paraguayan border after a harrowing two-year march. Of 1,680 troops that entered Paraguayan territory only some 700 returned. *A retirada* became the official history of the war. Originally published in French, Pedro II funded its translation into Portuguese in 1874 and distributed two volumes of the book to the public libraries of each province. As he had with Indianism, Pedro also became a patron of sertanism, but his public image remained fused with Indianist romanticism.

Taunay's nationalistic narrative engaged the ideas of Rousseau, but rather than depict Brazil's Indian allies as noble savages, this Brazilian of French descent described them as barbarians who despite the threats of officers, persisted in reprehensible savage acts such as mutilating enemy corpses. He even suggested that Indians corrupted Brazilian frontiersman: "Those who have lived for a long time in the *sertão* are, more than other men, dominated by egotism; they learn this sentiment from the savages [Indians] . . . [and it] is intensified by the unshakable firmness with which the cruelest tortures are inflicted by a victorious enemy upon the vanquished."[48] Taunay's disparaging attitude toward Indian allies had been influenced by his horrific experience at the front and by the fact that Brazilians stereotyped Paraguayans as Indians, and Paraguayans stereotyped Brazilians as black. Racial and national identification were touchy issues on the front.

The "true" Brazilian hero in *A retirada* is the expedition's wilderness guide, the *sertanejo* José Francisco Lopes whom Taunay describes as a *caboclo*, a term usually signifying a mixture of European and indigenous heritage, but it can also refer to an acculturated Indian. According to one critic, "Of his [Taunay's] extensive work, in which repetitions succeed one another, only *Inocência* and *A retirada* are memorable, in which a character type, the guide Lopes, represents the role of the sertanejo . . . and is projected over all others."[49] Combining explicit romantic concepts from Rousseau with elements of Jacob Grimm, Taunay portrays the guide Lopes as a kind of "noble folk savage." This humble illiterate *caboclo* overcame his flaws to lead the expedition's survivors back to safety before both he and his son died. Lopes's

Figure 8.6. Quasimodo of Literature. O Guarany. *Mephistopheles*, Rio de Janeiro, Aug. 15, 1874.

ultimate patriotic sacrifice is contrasted to the Parliament's miserly support of the army and the many members of Brazil's coastal elite who used their influence to avoid military service.[50]

Taunay parlayed his literary fame and wartime service into a successful political career. He became a Conservative Party senator known for his progressive stance on issues such as slavery's abolition, but he spent most of his political energy supporting subsidized European immigration to Brazil. He was a major architect of Brazilian policies to "whiten" the national population, even though most of his ideas had to await the republic's advent to be implemented. Europeans would replace the dwindling number of slaves working on Brazil's plantations and would establish "civilized" colonies where Brazilians would learn from their industrious examples.

The controversy over the Indian as a national symbol became a political weapon used against Taunay's fellow Conservative senator and author José de Alencar. As noted earlier, Alencar authored the two most important In-dianist novels; in figure 8.6, *Mephistopheles* (the cartoon incarnation of the illustrated Republican Party newspaper) berates Alencar in 1874. Alencar's literature and the symbol of the Indian became a surrogate field of politi-cal struggle in rancorous postwar politics. In figure 8.6, Alencar is nailed to what appears to be a whipping post, reminiscent of a crucifix, above his head hangs the sign "Quasimodo of Literature," and below his feet his novel *O Guarany*.

Another republican newspaper, *Brazil Americano*, piled on the criticism of Alencar and Indianism:

> "coboclo literature" . . .is ineptly said to be the true Brazilian litera-ture. Literature is the expression and the character of a society. . . . Those who follow this doctrine are led by José de Alencar, and they ap-pear to ignore that commonly recognized truth. . . . The elements that exercise influence on the Brazilian are: the Portuguese, the Indian, and the African or mestizo. The fusion of these races with all their customs, traits, and other characteristics . . . is what can nationalize Brazilian literature, and deliver us from the judgement of the literary colony against which the obsessed defenders of Indianist literature pine for every day. In my opinion, a novelist should try to photograph everything that exists in a society. And we should turn away from those who follow the routine of English novelist.[51]

This Republican editorialist favored the realism of naturalist novelists over the more romantic literary traditions of Indianism and sertanism.

Another illustration in *Mephistopheles* portrays Alencar as Tantalus, who seeks to satiate his hunger for political power with a roast chicken labeled "Presidency of the Council of Ministers." However, a barefoot black man and a priest hold him back with chains. The symbolism suggests that Alen-car's staunch defense of slavery and ultramontantist clerics made him too extreme to assume the most important political post in the land. Not only had Alencar's political stances become passé in postwar Brazil but so had his literary production. Sensing that his novels had fallen out of fashion, Alencar jumped on the sertanist bandwagon with *O sertanejo* (1875), but this novel met with much less critical success, and his oeuvre continued to be identified with Indianism.

Those sympathetic to Republicanism seemed the most disturbed by the depiction of Brazil as a Tupi Guarani warrior. In 1875, *Brazil Americano* criticized the use of a "naked [Tupi] Indian" wearing feathers and armed with a bow and arrows to symbolize Brazil: "A savage in his primitive state represents Brazil, a nation that adopted the tribunals of civilization . . . having already raised arms—that is swords, firearms, and cannons—to civilize Paraguay, whose leader then was called chief and his people—a horde of barbarians."[52] Here, Republicans use the memories of the war to justify a change in symbolic guard. Although he and others did not specifically adopt the *sertanejo* as a substitute, it was one of the few well-developed patriotic archetypes available. The editorial reasoned that in Brazil, a nation of many races, the Indian was not the predominant type.[53] Even so, Republican newspapers like *Mephistopheles* continued to use the illustrations of Angelo Agostini who depicted Brazil as a tortured Tupi Guarani warrior. The Indian's demise as a national symbol was slow and never complete, and while the *sertanejo* emerged as an alternative in literature, he only later gained ground in visual representation. According to Elias Thomé Saliba, the Indian was only displaced as the national caricature by Monteiro Lobato's country bumpkin Zeca Tatu in the 1910s.[54]

Conclusions

Brazil's victorious military, particularly its enlisted personnel, could not shake their poor public image after the war. As Taunay himself put it, "The army at that time [early 1860s] was disrespected, this disrespect was suspended to a limited extent during the war, but it was greatly aggravated after the war."[55] Recife's *Diabo a Quatro* derided army discipline in the 1875 article "Facts that Prove the Discipline of our Army." Soldiers are shown beating up a policeman, two others thrash a woman, another robs a civilian, and yet another flees a rock-throwing crowd. A tombstone represents the outgoing year, and the illustrator predicts that the lack of security in Recife will make wandering about town armed to the teeth the new year's fashion trend, which the *flanuer* figure on the right models. Soldiers are portrayed as black brutes who abuse their authority to perpetrate crimes. Memories of the war had undermined government attempts to reform army recruitment, so the barracks continued to be a protopenal institution that harbored many common criminals and vagabonds alongside a minority of volunteers.

Just as in the 1870 victory parade, most privileged Brazilians ignored the services of Paraguayan War veterans. As Eduardo Silva notes, the privileged emphasized the legacy of the "club and rope recruit" to refute the patriotism of many genuine volunteers of humble origins and dusky complexions.

Paraguayan War monuments and new street names mostly celebrated white officers and battles, not enlisted men. This disregard did not go unnoticed. An English-language newspaper published in Rio, for example, ran a story "A Country Worth Fighting For," which reported that the navy minister refused to pay for the freedom of a slave who had run away and joined the navy where he won a wartime commendation for bravery. Instead of being treated like a patriot, the veteran languished in a jail while the dispute over his former owner's compensation dragged on for months.[56]

Low public esteem for enlisted men not only undermined postwar re-cruitment reform, it also contributed to a climate that made it easy to rebuff enlisted men who claimed contractual benefits. Most wartime enlistment contracts promised land grants, preferential hiring for government jobs, and pensions for the families of fallen patriots.[57] Few would ever collect on these promises. The case of the veteran musician Raymundo Alves da Silva was typical. On presenting his paperwork, officials informed the veteran that the provincial legislature had not yet allocated money to survey lands designated for veterans in Rio de Janeiro.[58] Most veterans who bothered to file paperwork never received a deed, and the few that did often sold them for a fraction of their worth to speculators because they were located in unfavorable, isolated sites. In a 1907 congressional debate, former army officer Lauro Sodré criticized legislation that would guarantee a pension to Paraguayan War veterans thirty-seven years after the conflict because it did not include funds for families who lost their main breadwinner. He observed that the legislation had been debated for decades and reminded Congress that the Republic had to honor obligations long ignored by the Empire.[59] His appeals fell on deaf ears. In 1914 Brazil's war minister re-ported that only 3,648 men collected a modest army pension. Of these, 1,332 were privates; 1,477, NCOs; and 839, commissioned officers.[60] This is a small number given that some 69,000 men's mobilization status quali-fied them for benefits, and it is a stark contrast with the Grand Ole Army of the U.S. Civil War. Sociologist Theda Skocpol argues that Civil War veteran benefits for soldiers and their families constituted the United States' first experiment with large-scale social welfare.[61]

The legacy surrounding Brazilian enlisted soldiers remained one that tended to satirize rather than lionize. One prominent Paraguayan War veteran who became a victim of elite ridicule in postwar Rio was Candido da Fonseca Galvão. Galvão claimed an honorable discharged with a junior officer's rank, having risen from the NCO ranks. He was assigned to an Invalid of the Fatherland Company in his home province, Bahia, and was subsequently expelled from it for insubordination and intemperance. Migrating to Rio, Galvão became a man about town who styled himself after Dom Obá II, an African king in exile. In Rio's Little Africa borough, black and brown Brazilians paid obeisance and tribute to Dom Obá II on the street, indicating that they supported his views, which he regularly published in newspapers. A loyal supporter of the Conservative Party and the monarchy, Dom Obá dressed elegantly and regularly attended *beija mão* audiences with Pedro II. He proudly wrote of his military service in editorials where he presciently warned that the monarchy was in grave danger in the 1880s. He argued against the "whitening" policies of Taunay, and advocated "blackening" Brazil by subsidizing free African immigration instead. He promoted efforts to improve enlisted military men's conditions and treatment, and, like many in Little Africa, he was suspicious of Republicans because many of their leaders were slow to embrace abolition and expressed disdain for African culture. Many elite Brazilians and foreign dignitaries believed Dom Obá to be an embarrassing eccentric because he bedecked his Brazilian army uniform with an African turban and a large plume and was rumored to be a sot. Some wondered why Pedro was so patient with this outlandish character. For many, Pedro's association with Dom Obá II indicated that he was a well-intentioned anachronism, out of step in an age of social Darwinian bigotry, unabashed European imperialism, and Republicanism.[62]

Not only had the war brought out the irony of portraying Brazil as a Tupi Guarani warrior, but more and more nationalists across the globe came to view martial capacity through a lens of bastardized Darwinian theory. In 1882 a Brazilian army periodical asserted that "[natural] laws are the same for individuals, races, and the vegetable and animal kingdom, the fundamental scientific formula of organic existence in the world [is] the struggle for life!"[63] Implicit to this analysis was a strengthening association of science, race, and the nation in arms (the armed forces). The same army periodical cited with envy the Prussians' "admirable unity of race," to which it credited their martial prowess, something Brazilian officers found lacking in their own population and soldiery. These theories perplexed even fervent Brazilian nationalists because to take strong hold over a population, nationalism requires a certain imagined homogenization and leveling of citizens that the nation's racial heterogeneity appeared to thwart.[64] Some patriots influenced feared that Brazil's racial, ethnic, and climatic heterogeneity could prevent it from becoming a united, modern, prosperous, and ultimately "white" nation. In the postwar period, white nationalists advocated whitening Brazil's population with European immigration. None

Figure 8.7. Pedro II in Noble Savage Drag. *Revista Illustrada,* Pernambuco.

other than the Paraguayan War veteran Taunay became a major advocate of European immigration to "whiten" and "modernize" Brazil. Here the sertanist supported giving advantages to foreigners that were not offered to most Brazilians, even those who had fought valiantly to defend national honor in Paraguay.

Brazil's veterans were not the only ones to emerge from the war with image problems. Lilia Schwartcz offers an interesting reflection on caricatures of Pedro II: "Official photography presented an image of security and stability of a 'civilized, citizen monarch.' But caricatures 'stole' or 'corrupted' these traits . . . highlighting the contradictions that surrounded the imperial state and its imperial representative."[65] She credits caricature with creating an image problem for Pedro II and the imperial order itself. Comic portrayals of "Pedro Banana" made his rule and the very imperial institutions whose buildings were festooned with Indianist imagery seem old fashioned (see figure 8.7).

The Tupi Guarani Indian as a national symbol was strongly associated with Pedro II's rule, and as Lilia Schwarcz observes, both became the target of increasing satirical attacks in the 1880s.[66] I argue that the deep roots of these more frequent attacks lay in the Paraguayan War experience. The emperor's conduct of the war had disillusioned Conservatives and Liberals alike and had given rise to the Republican Party.[67] The emperor, as an iconic embodiment of the nation, had become indistinguishable from Indianist symbolism. In figure 8.7, Pedro II is humorously dressed in Tupi Guarani noble savage drag; his incongruous appearance draws a chuckle from an incredulous young indigene. Humorous parodies and serious commentaries on the use of the Indian as a national symbol had become a surrogate means of attacking the emperor and the imperial order. It is telling that Republicans were among the most vocal critics of Indianism, and they would rapidly develop substitutes for these imperial symbols once in power.[68] The bloodless Republican army coup that brought regime change to Brazil on November 15, 1889, had literally been prefaced by symbolic humorous attacks on the Tupi Guarani warrior and Indianism's chief patron, Dom Pedro II.

Notes

1. See, e.g., Loveman, *For la Patria*, 78, 86.

2. Skidmore, *White into Black*; Schwarcz, *O espectaculo das raças*; and Sommer, *Foundational Fictions*, ch. 5. Miguel Angel Centeno explores war-making, state building, and the region's racial heterogeneity in *Blood and Debt*. Significant exceptions in the study of humor are Saliba, *Raízes do Riso*; and Lustosa, *Histórias de Presidentes*.

3. See, e.g., Roberto da Matta's *Carnavals, Rogues and Heroes*; Soihet, *Subversão pelo riso*; Pereira Cunha, *Ecos da folia*; and Saliba, *Raízes do Riso*, Introduction.

4. Carlyle, *On Heroes*.

5. Here I invoke Chalhoub's *Visões da liberdade*. On enlisted service and tropes of slavery, gender, age, and honor, see Beattie, "Measures of Manhood," 233–55; and Beattie, "National Identity and the Brazilian Folk," 7–43.

6. This is the same tribe described in chapter 13, which in Spanish is called Tupí-Guaraní.

7. Romero, "A poesia popular no Brasil," 30.

8. Skidmore, *Black into White*, 32–38.

9. de Carvalho, *Liberdade*, chap. 9; Mosher, *Political Struggle*, 192–97; and Ribeiro, *A liberdade em construção*.

10. Driver, *Indian in Brazilian Literature*; and Treece, *Exiles, Allies, Rebels*, 147–241.

11. Schwarcz, *As Barbas do imperador*, 132–50; and Barman, *Citizen Emperor*.

12. Angelo Agostini was Brazil's most influential nineteenth-century illustrator, famous for his renderings of the Tupi Guaraní Indian. He founded or collaborated with numerous periodicals analyzed here: *Cabrião, Arlequim, Vida Fluminense,* and *Revista Il-*

lustrada. Agostini's sympathies first aligned with the Liberal Party but later he supported Republicanism. He advocated abolition and criticized the Catholic Church.

13. Arinos de Melo Franco, *O Índio brasileiro.*

14. See, for example, da Costa, *Da senzala à colônia,* 323–56. In countries with strong abolitionist movements such as Britain, Africans were more often portrayed as noble savages; Davis, *The Problem of Slavery,* chap. 15.

15. Sommer, *Foundational Fictions,* intro. and chap. 5. Even in the naturalist novels of the 1880s and 1890s that featured sympathetic black and brown protagonists, the romantic unions between whites and Afro-Brazilians are infertile. In Azevedo's *O mulatto* (1881) the romantic coupling of a wealthy, university-educated mulatto (son of a slave and her white owner) and the white daughter of a Portuguese merchant ends in miscarriage and the mulatto's death. In Adolpho Caminha's *Bom Crioulo* (1897), the author's title (translated with its fullest linguistic force as "Good Nigger") played on the idea of the noble savage, rendered in Portuguese as *bom selvagem.* The novel narrates a romance set in the Brazilian Empire that further challenges the nationalist, heterosexual, and erotic narrative of Alencar by depicting a romance between a black sailor and a blond cabin boy. The gothic novel ends with the black sailor murdering the cabin boy in a jealous rage; Beattie, "Conflicting Penile Codes," 65–85.

16. Conselheiro Fleury cited in de Morais, *Prisões e instituições penitenciárias,* 79–80. On vices and slavery, see Beattie, "Slave Silvestre's Disputed Sale."

17. For an insightful analysis of indigenous masquerade and national identity in Puerto Rico in comparative perspective, see Scarano, " Jíbaro Masquerade"; and Earle, *Return of the Native.* Also see the Geertzean analysis of slave stereotypes and white masterhood in Greenberg, *Honor and Slavery.* On "white" working-class identity, Indians, and black-face humor, see Roediger, *Wages of Whiteness,* 19–42, 95–132.

18. For a concise breakdown of Paraguayan War historiography, see Reber, " Demographics of Paraguay,"289–90. Two more recent interpretations are Doratioto, *Maldita Guerra*; and Whigham, *Paraguayan War.*

19. Beattie, *Tribute of Blood,* chap. 1.

20. See, e.g., Silva, "O Príncipe Obá, um voluntário da pátria," 67–75. In a short story, Paraguayan War veteran Visconde de Taunay tells the tale of a muleteer pressed into army service who refuses to desert after promising to serve his country not so much out of a sense of duty but as a question of his honorable word. It is a bitter tale of a poor Brazilian man who finds that the love of his life has married another after a long tour at the front; Taunay, "Juca, o tropeiro," 257–301. On the Zuavos, see Kraay, "Patriotic Mobilization in Brazil," 61–80.

21. Beattie, *Tribute of Blood,* chap. 2.

22. Abente, " War of Triple Alliance"; and Beattie, *Tribute of Blood,* chap. 2.

23. This observation is based on illustrated newspapers consulted in the Obras Raras and Microfilm sections of the Biblioteca Nacional, Rio de Janeiro: *Cabrião, Mosquito, Semana Illustrada, Vida Fluminense, Mephistopholes,* and *Arlequim.* For a different view on illustration and patriotism, Silveira, *A batalha de papel.*

24. *O Recife Illustrada,* Recife, January 4, 1867, consulted in the Arquivo do Instituto Arqueológico, Histórico, e Geográfico, Pernambucano (AIA).

25. Needell, *Party of Order*, chaps. 5 and 6.

26. Illustration reproduced in Magalhães, *O império em chinelos*, 29.

27. *O Arlequim*, Rio, no. 5, May 1867, 5.

28. Cartoon in *O Recife Illustrado*, Recife, December 16, 1866. For a similar example see, *Mosquito*, October 24, 1869, 5.

29. Beattie, *Tribute of Blood*, chaps. 2 and 3.

30. *Cabichui*, Paraguay, October, 10, 1867.

31. See, e.g., Andrews, *Afro-Argentines of Buenos Aires*; Salles, *Guerra do Paraguai*; Kraay, " Slavery, Citizenship, and Military Service," 228–56; Prata de Souza, *Escravidão ou morte*; Ganson, "Following Their Children into Battle"; Potthast, "Protagonists, Victims, and Heroes"; and Ipsen, "Delicate Citizenship."

32. Indians had been recruited for previous campaigns; de Carvalho, "Os Índios de Pernambuco," 51–69. A couple of studies do consider Indian participation in the Paraguayan War; Wilcox, "Cattle Ranching on the Brazilian Frontier"; Siqueira, "Esse campo custou o sangue."

33. See, e.g., "Two Indians. Lieutenant Amaro. Captain Gabriel. Volunteers of the Fatherland." *A Semana Illustrada*, Rio, August 6, 1866.

34. *Cabrião*, São Paulo, December 16, 1866.

35. Col. José Joaquim Rodrigues Lopes, "Typos Paraguayos," *A Vida Fulminense*, Rio, October 17, 1868.

36. *Cabichui*, Paso Pucu, Paraguay, December 19, 1867.

37. As George Reid Andrews has shown, there were many black Argentine and Uruguayan soldiers and some officers in the Allied camps, but the historical memory of their participation faded rapidly. Andrews, *Afro-Argentines of Buenos Aires*, chap. 5.

38. *Cabichui*, Paso Pucu, Paraguay, January 9, 1968.

39. Cited in Lemos, "Benjamin Constant and the 'Truth' Behind the Paraguayan War."

40. *Cabichui*, Paraguay, July 11, 1867.

41. Ibid., November 25, 1867.

42. Ibid.

43. Ibid.

44. The authors of the two most important military histories of their generations, Alfredo d'Escragnolle Taunay and Euclydes da Cunha, both depicted Brazilian enlisted men in an ambivalent fashion. The latter described the Brazilian soldier as "a terrible but heroic blackgaurd." Taunay, *A retirada da Laguna*; and Beattie, *Tribute of Blood*, ch. 7.

45. "The Official Rejoicing," *The Anglo-Brazilian Times*, July 23, 1870, 2; and "La Fête du 10 Juillet," *Ba-Ta-Clan*, July 16, 1870, 1–2.

46. Lima, *O movimento da Independência*, 420–25.

47. Sodré, *A história da literatura brasileira*, 323–25.

48. Taunay, *A retirada da Laguna*; and Beattie, "National Identity and the Brazilian Folk," 7–43.

49. Sodré, *A história da literature brasileira*, 326.

50. Beattie, "National Identity and the Brazilian Folk," 7–43.

51. "Sciencias e Letras," *Brazil Americano*, Rio, July 28, 1875, 4.

52. "O Symbolo do Brazil," *Brazil Americano*, July 7 1875, 2.

53. Ponzio Sobrino, "O sertanejo patriotica."

54. Saliba, *Raízes do riso*, 128.

55. Taunay, *Memórias do Visconde de Taunay* (1946), 94.

56. "A Country Worth Fighting For," *Anglo-Brazilian Times* August 22, 1870, 3; and Silva, "O Príncipe Obá," 69–70.

57. To gain benefits, soldiers made numerous applications to the war ministry, but many did not have the time or the funds to do so. Silva, *Prince of the People*, 37–50.

58. Letter from the Finance Minister of Rio de Janeiro to War Minister Barão de Muritiba, August 12, 1870, Niteroi, Arquivo Público do Estado do Rio de Janeiro, fundo PP, coleção 8, pasta 12, maço 15, no folha nos. For a similar plea from a veteran impoverished by drought in Ceará, see Requerimento de José Caetano de Oliveira, April 1, 1877, Fortaleza, Arquivo Nacional, Rio de Janeiro, IG1585, doc. 28; For biting criticisms of the handling of veteran benefits, see *Annais do Senado Brasileiro* (Rio: Imprensa Nacional, 1871), *sessão* June 2, 1870, vol. April–June: 78; and Ibid., *sessão* July 15, 1871, 108–10.

59. *Annais do Senado Brasileiro* (Rio: Imprensa Nacional, 1908), June 28, 1907, II: 286–87.

60. See novelist Lima Barreto's short story about veterans and petitions, "A matematica não falha," in *Bagatelas* (Sao Paulo: Brasiliense, 1956), 177–84; and *Relatório apresentado ao Presidente dos Estados Unidos do Brasil pelo Ministro de Estado de Guerra General de Divisão José Caetano de Faria em Maio de 1915* (Rio: Imprensa Militar, 1915), 110.

61. Skocpol, *Protecting Soldiers and Mothers*.

62. Silva, *Prince of the People*, 107–27.

63. *Revista do Exército Brasileiro*, Rio de Janeiro, 1882, 1, in Arquivo Histórico do Exército. For similar assertions by Brazilian politicians, see "Assemblea," *O Globo*, Rio de Janeiro, August 21, 1874, 2; "O recrutamento e o Sr. Deputado Buarque de Macedo," *Imprensa Academica*, São Paulo, July 28, 1868, 1.

64. Anderson, *Imagined Communities*, 47–66.

65. Schwarcz, *As barbas do imperador*, 424–25.

66. Ibid., 149. Hendrik Kraay demonstrates that Indian symbols remained a central part of Bahia's unique July 2nd celebrations of Brazil's independence, but he notes that they became the objects of elite criticism in the 1870s and 1880s; Kraay, "'Cold as the Stone of Which It Must be Made.'"

67. Needell, *Party of Order*, 248–71.

68. On early Republican imagery, see de Carvalho, *A formação das almas*.

9

The Conquest of the Desert
and the Free Indigenous Communities
of the Argentine Plains

CARLOS MARTÍNEZ SARASOLA

Toward of the end of the nineteenth century, the Argentine state intensified a policy of military expansion that would ultimately destroy the autonomous socioeconomic systems of the indigenous peoples of the Pampas—
the central plains and its surrounding areas. The origins of the war lay in
the movement of settlers west and south from the capital city of Buenos
Aires to populate the plains. This frontier settlement brought nationals
into greater contact with the indigenous peoples who lived on the central
prairies and led to conflicts throughout the nineteenth century. As in the
United States during roughly the same time, the national occupation of the
plains was a contested venture, fought not only by pioneers and indigenous
inhabitants but also by politicians and the soldiers sent to eliminate the native peoples. This chapter argues that politicians in Argentina did not share
a common plan to exterminate native populations on their frontier. Rather,
the genocidal war that emerged late in the century resulted from a difficult
and contested negotiation at the heart of the nation's political leadership.

The Indigenous World of the Plains

Central Argentina extends from the central Pampa prairies to the steppes
and western mountains, from the sandy deserts of western La Pampa province, northwest to the hilly province of Neuquén (see map 1 at the front of
the book). By the early nineteenth century, the plains were the site of a great
political gathering that led to the climax of indigenous power, through the
unification of several ethnic groups. These tribes included the Tehuelches,
the original human population of the area; the Ranquels or *rankül-che*, of

mixed background of Tehuelches and Mapuches; and the various groups of Araucanos or Mapuches who had migrated from west of the Andes since pre-Hispanic times. All these groups were autonomous, but in exceptional circumstances they joined forces to form strong alliances. One example was the planning and fulfillment of large attacks on white settlements, called *malones*, such as the one that struck the towns of 25 de Mayo and 9 de Julio 1872 in the district of Alvear, involving almost six thousand Mapuches, Ranquels, and *gunün a küna* or Tehuelches warriors.

Indigenous leaders during this time extended their power widely over the plains. Most notable among this group was Chief Calfucurá, who had arrived in 1834 from his native Chile and came to control territory south all the way to Patagonia. This leader was charismatic and diplomatic; an accomplished strategist with a gift for words. Calfucurá's power was exceptional; not only was he a religious leader but as chief he also presided over the famous Confederation of Salinas Grandes, which grouped tribes, chiefs, and leaders under his command. At this time the Chaco region in the north of Argentina was occupied by the Guaikurús and the Mataco-Mataguayos. Almost half of the territory of Argentina at this time was thus under indigenous control.[1]

The indigenous world of the Pampas was an ethnic and cultural conglomeration where integration and mixtures were the rule. The natives often included in their communities the "other," even captives, who in many cases changed their identities to become part of indigenous society.[2] Native groups thus included an important number of people from the other side of the frontier: whites, blacks—descendants of the slaves who had arrived in the Americas since the sixteenth century—and gauchos, frontier settlers of mixed background. All of them lived together in the indigenous communities for such reasons as exile, captivity, trade, or simply for the desire to undertake a new life.

The *tolderías*, groups of *toldos*, mobile homes made of animal skins and branches, were led by chiefs who in some cases were of mixed race, such as Baigorrita or Pincén. There were also even cases of whites who became chiefs of the natives, such as Colonel Baigorria, who lived for years among the Ranquels. These indigenous leaders of mixed heritage resemble native leaders in early southeastern United States. Historian Theda Perdue has recently shown that biracial native leaders played important roles at a critical time of national expansion, white racism, and Native American cultural survival.[3]

Official documents and letters from indigenous leaders at the time commonly used the word "*tribus*," or tribes, to indicate groups under the leadership of a *cacique*. These chiefs assumed maximum power based on hereditary rights, although at certain times the position could be filled throughout an election process based on attributes of valor and leadership. Below them in tribal hierarchy came the *capitanejos*, or minor chiefs; the warriors; and finally those responsible for the spiritual life of the community, such as the *machi*, or shamans, who guided the rituals and ceremonies. Very often, the chief fulfilled all these characteristics. For important decisions, they resorted to the institution known as a parliament, a large gathering of chiefs, elders, *capitanejos*, and spiritual guides from one or many tribes.

In this respect it is important to consider that the sociopolitical organization of the communities, particularly their *caciques* and *capitanejos*, depended on an important structure based on lineage. "Marriages" were planned and formalized between men and women from different lineages and even from different ethnic groups to produce renewals of relationships and mobility between social scales. This phenomenon was not exclusive to the indigenous population but also occurred between the natives and white captives of both genders.

Paradoxically, these examples of integration show that pursued indigenous people were more willing to integrate people of different backgrounds than were the "whites," among whom the opposite was the case. This model of integration took place amidst rising conflicts with Buenos Aires, which carried out a nearly constant succession of military campaigns against the natives' territories. The native people sustained their communities not only by selling the cattle they rustled on the frontier but also by exchanging agricultural products in the towns and by hunting and gathering.[4] The indigenous people extended this way of life right up to the limits of white territory, leaving their imprint on the destiny of that sort of no-man's land that extended on either side of both contending groups.

Frontier Metaphor and the Politics of Extermination

The political consolidation project of the capital city of Buenos Aires attempted to separate national society from the indigenous world, a division it accomplished with the idea of "the frontier." This boundary had existed since the arrival of the Spanish conquerors; it was consolidated in the colony and in the emerging state during the seventeenth, eighteenth, and nineteenth centuries.

The frontier was an imaginary line that divided Buenos Aires and its outskirts, known as the *"campaña,"* from the indigenous territories. Early on, the Salado River had been the first natural geographic divider, but later the *fortines* (small forts) created an increasingly evident separation. The frontier divided both worlds and symbolized the creation of Argentina as a country. This frontier was a cultural boundary more than a political, military, and economic one and thus serves as a metaphor for one of Argentina's principal dilemmas: from its inception, the nation was already divided.

Ever since initial settlement, Europeans had shown little tolerance for an indigenous presence. The colonial viceroys had devised the first effective military plans against the indigenous people. Authorities viewed natives more and more as a nuisance to be eliminated because growing commercial traffic made expeditious communication necessary. After national independence was declared in 1816, the extermination model prevailed: Martín Rodríguez, brigadier general of the army and governor of Buenos Aires (1821–24), was obsessed with advancing the frontier and undertook several expeditions to push the inner limits to the Negro River.

During the most important campaign in 1823, Governor Rodríguez kept a diary titled *Diary of the Expedition to the Desert* in which he formally proposed the ideology of genocide that was gaining strength:

> The experience from all the events teaches us how to behave with these men: it guides us towards the conviction that war against them must be carried out until their extermination. We have heard many times from more philanthropic intellects that their civilization and industry are susceptible, and how easily they are enticed towards friendship. It would be an error to continue in this belief, and perhaps detrimental. It was necessary to be in contact with their customs, to see their needs, their characters and the progress to which their disposition is susceptible to convince us that that is impossible. . . . The only remedy is war, within the principle of discarding all ideas of civility and considering them as enemies whom it is necessary to destroy and exterminate.[5]

Rodríguez' last campaign, in 1824, ended in a disaster for national troops. Indigenous warriors and a hostile geography forced them into an embarrassing retreat and indicated that the mobilization of numerous contingents with heavy military hardware was destined to fail against lightly armed indigenous people who practically "flew" on horseback.[6]

Meanwhile, between 1826 and 1829, a Prussian military officer, Frederick Rauch, replaced Martín Rodríguez in the attempt to exterminate indigenous people. The first Argentine president, Bernardino Rivadavia, appointed Rauch to "eliminate the Ranguels," according to a decree from the time. Rauch had arrived in 1819 after serving in the Napoleonic armies, and he bragged about the peculiar method he used to annihilate his indigenous enemies: "to save bullets, today we have slit the throats of twenty-seven Ranquels."[7]

During the few but violent years in which this foreign military officer pursued and killed indigenous people on the plains, a series of confrontations made human losses on both sides number in the hundreds. Finally, in February 1829, Rauch was defeated and fled the battlefield. Caught by a group of natives, he was decapitated in the same manner that he had used to eliminate his own indigenous enemies.

Contact with national military campaigns altered the indigenous peoples. At this time, the use of "friendly Indians" by national military campaigns began to divide native communities and increased the contradictions within the different ethnic groups. Ever since the Revolution of 1810, when Buenos Aires severed colonial ties with Spain, and especially since having achieved independence in 1816, the native communities of the plains sent emissaries to contact the Argentine State. Natives employed frontier commanders, governors, special messengers, and even *caudillos* from the interior of the country to counter the growing political power of Buenos Aires. Since independence, Argentina had suffered civil wars between the Unitarist and Federalist parties that divided national politics for many years. Indigenous communities tried to benefit from their interactions with a three-pronged goal: to maintain their territories, to continue with their commercial activities, and, of course, to protect their cultures from rapid changes.

Juan Manuel de Rosas, governor of Buenos Aires from 1829–32 and from 1835–52, marked another milestone in Argentine policy regarding indigenous people. It is difficult to argue that Rosas was a proponent of extermination because his posture toward the native peoples was in many ways more one of engagement. Rosas had always been attracted to the indigenous world and had studied their customs. His father, León Ortiz de Rosas, had been a captive among natives for many years.[8] On his ranches, Rosas had employed indigenous laborers and at the beginning of his public career affirmed this was the proper way to integrate natives into the new society. As a rancher who fostered the trade in hides with England, Rosas also needed field hands and the friendly Indians proved an attractive labor force.

Nevertheless, Rosas' campaign of 1833 against the Ranquels is an outstanding example of military campaigns for extermination. Julio A. Roca, who led the later war against indigenous people in the 1880s, commented that Rosas' earlier campaign had served him as a model: "In my judgement, the best way to finish with the Indians, either by extinguishing them or by banishing them to the other side of the Negro River, is the offensive war followed by Rosas, which almost finished them off."[9]

Rosas was a controversial figure who played a central role in national politics. It is likely that beyond his many contradictions, Rosas actually conceived of an Argentine future "with" the Indians, as some of his documents testify:

> The tegüelches would remain south of the Negro river patrolling the Patagones command and united to the people of this settlement would be content in their commerce and lives. . . . The Ranquels would live where they are. The Boroganos, where they are and would contribute to the defense, support and advancement of Fuerte Argentino, whose people they should help take care so that they and their sons may be happily engaged in commerce. The Pampas would go to Tapalquén and Arroyo Azul and live there as they have lived. All these nations as seen would live in complete peace, would make their houses, especially the chiefs, would plant and be prosperous in their lands and settlements.[10]

Rosas' campaign in 1833 killed thirty-two hundred indigenous people, imprisoned twelve hundred more, and rescued almost one thousand captives. The army killed several of the main chiefs; others fled or were taken prisoner. As a result of Rosas' offensive, native communities of the prairie foresaw, as never before, their future territorial loss and the looming destruction of their cultures.

Within this contradictory policy, it is also true that Rosas maintained a sort of unspoken nonaggression agreement with the communities located in Salinas Grandes, led by Calfucurá; this unofficial pact lasted until Rosas fell in 1852. From then on, indigenous attacks on frontier settlements worsened and Buenos Aires and the provincial governors resumed their offensive program against the native communities because of the renewal of indigenous invasions.

Malones, Treaties, Battles, and the Great Trench

During the presidencies of Justo José de Urquiza (1854–60), Santiago Derquí (1860–61) and Bartolomé Mitre (1862–68), efforts to contain indigenous advances against frontier settlements continued. Likewise, the military continued to push native communities toward the farthest corners of the prairies. Tension mounted, but the free indigenous groups of the plains remained standing, facing off against a national government that could not find a way to defeat them. The indigenous raids, or *malones,* increased, and while the national government alternated warfare with treaty signing, the growing need to make those regions economically productive was increasingly evident.[11]

The Argentines certainly felt indigenous power: one notable example of actions for the period was the massive Indian raid of more than three thousand men led by Chief Calfucurá against the town of Azul in February 1855. Following the attack, Calfucurá retreated toward *tierra adentro,* the inland territories beyond the frontier, with sixty thousand captured head of cattle and one hundred captive families, leaving behind approximately three hundred dead settlers.[12]

Because of such attacks, minister of war and future president Col. Bartolomé Mitre decided to move against indigenous communities in the Buenos Aires province and halt the Ranquels' advances, which gave no respite to frontier settlements. Following a few successful battles, followers of Calfucurá defeated Mitre at Sierra Chica of Tapalqué, where they inflicted serious losses of lives—250 men dead and injured—and of supplies, because they killed the entire herd of horses.[13]

Then, in September of 1855, the Ranquels massacred a squadron led by Cdr. Nicolás Otamendi near the ranch of San Antonio de Iraola, with the loss of 126 men, including Otamendi himself. Only two soldiers survived the attack.[14] One week later, the same indigenous army, numbering an estimated three thousand warriors, attacked the town of Tandil.

Minister Mitre, faced with the seriousness of these frontier battles, took the offensive and organized the Ejército de Operaciones del Sur (Army of Southern Operations) under the command of Gen. Manuel Hornos. Three thousand men and their twelve artillery pieces advanced deep into indigenous territory. Chief Calfucurá drew the army into a gigantic swamp, a *guadal,* where, at the Battle of San Jacinto, his native warriors killed nearly three hundred soldiers and officers, injuring as many more troops. Cal fucurá thus turned Mitre and Hornos' attempts into a veritable disaster for national forces.[15]

Indigenous attacks continued: in 1859 Calfucurá attacked the town of 25 de Mayo and then, in 1859, invaded the city of Bahía Blanca. In 1864 indigenous troops led by Calfucurá struck the towns of Tapalqué and Tres Arroyos, and one year later stormed Claromecó and again Tapalqué.

In 1872, shortly after the signing of a treaty in which both sides promised to keep the peace along the frontier and at the height of Domingo Faustino Sarmiento's presidency, a great battle between national forces and the most important prairie communities led by Calfucurá took place in San Carlos, the present town of Bolivar in the province of Buenos Aires. The legendary indigenous chief was returning from one of the most impressive indigenous attacks in recorded history. Calfucurá had struck several frontier settlements to avenge the aggression that the commander of the southern frontier, Col. Francisco de Elías, had committed against his fellow chiefs Manuel Grande, Gervasio Cipitruz, and Calfuguir. State aggression had thus violated once more the treaties upon which both sides had earlier agreed. Chief Calfucurá, with six thousand warriors under the leadership of chiefs Catricurá, Reuque Curá, and Namuncurá, along with their allies Pincén and Epumer, were returning with nearly four thousand of his men, five hundred captives, and two hundred thousand head of cattle driven toward the inland territories by the other two thousand warriors.

Colonel Rivas and his indigenous allies, chiefs Cipriano Catriel and Ignacio Coliqueo and their five hundred native troops, surprised Calfucurá and his warriors at the height of their retreat. The element of surprise was critical to the battle; while at first Calfucurá's troops had the advantage, as the hours passed Rivas and his allies gained the upper hand. The presence of indigenous people fighting alongside whites and against other natives demoralized Calfucurá and his warriors. This battle is remembered both as a symbol of indigenous strength and as evidence of the contradictions at its very heart. That day Chief Cipriano Catriel had ordered the execution of those men who had refused to fight against their brothers. A short time afterward the executed had their revenge, so to speak, when Cipriano found death at his own brother's hands.

Enveloped once more in the internal politics of Buenos Aires, as allied indigenous groups particularly were, Cipriano Catriel had supported Gen. Bartolomé Mitre's 1874 uprising against President-elect Nicolás Avellaneda. Mitre had accused Avellaneda of winning the executive position in fraudulent elections. The revolt failed and, as a result, Juan José Catriel, brother to Cipriano, accused him of betraying his lineage and had him arrested. Juan José himself killed Cipriano by point of lance, according to indigenous custom. There were multiple reasons for such internal conflicts, but the memory of Cipriano and his men fighting against their brothers in the decisive battle of San Carlos was beyond doubt the most important.[16]

One year after the battle of San Carlos, Calfucurá died in his *tolderia*, presumably at the age of one hundred years, putting an end to a forty-year-long indigenous hegemony of the plains. On his deathbed the chief declared his famous phrase: "Do not abandon Carhué to the *huincas* [whites]."[17] For this strategist of the plains, control of the triangle of land between Choele Choel, Carhué, and Salinas Grandes was critical to continue the traffic in cattle that natives stole on the frontier and sold in Chile. The fall of Carhué to the *huincas* would mean the beginning of the end for indigenous communities of the Pampas.

However, before the final conquest of indigenous lands, a unique and emblematic event was yet to take place. The perceived need to divide the indigenous world from the white world required the physical separation of the "barbarous" from the "civilized." The frontier that for centuries had divided both worlds as a cultural boundary morphed into a physical barrier with the plans for the so-called trench of Alsina, a gigantic ditch designed by Minister of War Adolfo Alsina in 1875. Alsina intended this deep trench to run for nearly one thousand kilometers across the Buenos Aires Province, from Bahía Blanca to southern Córdoba, to halt the torrent of native people that invaded the populated centers and stole goods, animals, and people.

Foreign engineers helped design and build this great trench. One of them, Alfred Ebelot, left memorable pages about the indigenous world of the Pampas.[18] The planned trench led Domingo Faustino Sarmiento, formerly Argentine president from 1868–74, to declare that the idea of halting indigenous people with a great ditch was like trying to trap the wind.

Only 374 kilometers of the trench were ever constructed, between Carhué and Laguna del Monte. More important than the physical reality of the trench, though, was the conception and ideology that had nourished the plan. Remains of the great trench are still visible on the outskirts of important cities such as Trenque Lauquen in the province of Buenos Aires. Even today, as a living testimony to the ideology of denial, exclusion, and contempt, a highway sign along the road alerts travelers: "Here crossed the Trench of Alsina, Frontier of Civilization, year 1878."

Yet even as politicians tried to carry out these separation projects amid the violence of the day, the frontier continued to operate as a space of great fluidity and mobility, a world of coexistence. That other "frontier" showed that it might have been possible to create another type of society.[19]

Recent historical work has focused on the "myth" of the frontier. While scholars have traditionally described it as an impassable line of separation, these new approaches unravel a very different world where cultural exchange was the norm.[20] That the racist ideologies engraved onto the Argentine social consciousness would come to outweigh all others, leading to the extermination of both the frontier and the plains indigenous communities, was by no means inevitable. Yet following three hundred years of resistance, this world would all but disappear.

The Causes for the Annihilation of the Indigenous World of *"Tierra Adentro"*

Beyond any doubt, the primary motivations for the Conquest of the Desert were economic in nature. Argentine leaders hoped to establish an agro-export model based on meat, cereal, and hides that would open their economy to the world and especially to England.

These economic imperatives had their political counterparts, since leaders believed that to establish the country they idealized, it was essential to occupy the indigenous lands and eliminate them from the frontier and the wider prairies. In other words, the nation sought to consolidate a unified nation-state free from Indians. The idea of exterminating the indigenous groups had always been present, and it gained strength as the national project advanced. The ideologues of such ethnic cleansing believed in a true Western crusade that portrayed the native people as "irreconcilable enemies of civilization" and as inferior cultures and races whose inevitable destiny was to be extinguished in the face of Western superiority.[21]

Many Argentine policymakers of the day, such as Estanislao Zeballos and Domingo F. Sarmiento, admired the North American wars against native peoples. Following the Civil War, "Winning the West" had become a national goal for U.S. leaders, who hoped to reunite the country and open land for the white settlers moving west across Indian homelands on the Great Plains. Military campaigns were waged on the northern and southern plains, and the mindset behind them is best summed up by General Sherman's 1868 declaration that "these Indians require to be soundly whipped, and the ringleaders in the present trouble hung, their ponies killed, and such destruction of their property as will make them very poor."[22]

As in Argentina, however, the process of clearing the Great Plains was contested and controversial. Some tribes sided with the U.S. Army and used them as allies in struggles of their own against old enemies. The Crows, Pawnees, Arikaras, and Shoshonis all fought at times with the United States against the Lakota Sioux and their allies. Such differences between tribes complicated their responses to white expansion.

Frontier wars in the United States interested Argentine leaders, who looked north for possible solutions to their Indian problems. General Roca himself instructed his military attaché at the Argentine embassy in Washington D.C., Sublieutenant Miguel Malarín, to study U.S. policy regarding its indigenous peoples, especially the reservation system. Roca eventually discarded the U.S. policy of removal and confinement to small reservations, and instead Argentina adopted a program of extermination. The government carried out this plan not only through battles and as the injured retreated back to the *tolderías* but also through the death of uncountable native prisoners kept in detention camps, such as those at Retiro or Martín García Island in the River Plate. The forced removals to these camps, hundreds of kilometers away from the natives' original settlements, also caused many deaths.

Rather than examples from the United States, it was other models closer at hand that influenced Argentine policies. One example was the virtual genocide of the Charrúa indigenous people by the Uruguayan army before the Conquest of the Desert, or the almost contemporary war of extermination against the Mapuche in Chile. These models provided an encouraging regional context for Argentine state policies.[23] This context also conformed to the prevailing ideology that proposed the physical elimination of the natives as a quick and necessary solution when confronted with peoples who refused to exchange their "barbarism" for the progress of "civilization." These policies culminated in an official plan to actually substitute the native population with millions of European immigrants, in the unprecedented human surge that later took place early in the twentieth century.

Another reason for the genocidal policies was the expansion of military power made necessary by ranching interests and political forces. The military sought power by occupying the land that would finally establish clear boundaries for Argentina. Most important among these divisions was the border with Chile, traditionally fragile and always disputed.

But these military designs were not the only reasons for such policies.

Within a nation-building project that intended white skin color, homogenous thought, and uniformity in lifestyle to be the rule, the way of life on the inland Pampas provoked at the very least rejection, not to mention sheer terror, among national leaders. The fears that close proximity to the indigenous world on the frontier awakened in the enlisted soldiers are well known, for there were many desertions. Officers creatively tried to counteract these feelings: one of the forts in the area of 9 de Julio was specifically named "Men without fear."

Such fears had many causes, but beyond a doubt the near presence of the "other," and in this case the "savage other," was one of the strongest reasons. The indigenous communities, the *tolderías*, were in fact the very core of the difference. Their world was the opposite of ethnocentrism, exclusion, and racism. The "other" or the "different" certainly did not belong within the model advocated from Buenos Aires: the Indians of the plains—represented in the elite imagination as exotic beings with their hair blowing in the wind, mounted on horses that seemed bewitched, galloping over the infinite freedom of the prairies to assault settlements and take cattle and captives—created an intolerable image for the centers of power. That "other," which in their view belonged to a savage world, could not coexist with a conception of the world that idealized civilization.[24]

The combination of rejection and terror caused by the native social and cultural models resulted initially because the "other"—everything that implied a change to the value scale and those principles opposed to "civilization"—was feared. A second reason was that, paradoxically, this other model in some way sought to coexist, to live together with the society that whites were trying to build.

At the heart of the plains was where the destiny of the peoples that had originally lived there was played out as well as that of the Argentine future and consequently the nation that never was: an inclusive Argentina "with the Indians" that many people at the time thought and dreamt about but that never became reality. A long list of important names of the time show that another type of country might have been possible: famous patriots such as José de San Martín, Manuel Belgrano, Mariano Moreno, Juan José Castelli, and even the controversial and contradictory Rosas, among others, thought and felt a different way. They envisioned a society where the different indigenous communities could coexist with the rest of the population. Almost all these famous statesmen ended up being forgotten, exiled, and even mysteriously and prematurely dead, such as Moreno.

Moreover, in the debates that took place in parliament before the approval of the Conquest of the Desert, more than a few legislators declared their opposition to Roca's plans. These opponents included Bernardo de Irigoyen, Zeballos, Quesada, Dardo Rocha, Luís Maria Drago, and Sarmiento, among many others. But the promise of free land distribution and the need for "civilization" to triumph finally won the day.[25]

Many of the great indigenous leaders had shown, in addition to the violence they used to defend their cultures and territories, a desire to join the white society in formation, as long as their rights as original inhabitants were respected. But on the other side, the political will that would have made this alternative society possible did not prevail; quite the contrary.

There was, according to some scholars, a "spirit of the times," that would have in any case led to the extermination of the plains' communities. In a recent work, renowned Argentine historian Félix Luna has argued that "Roca incarnated progress, placed Argentina in the world; I entered his skin to understand what it meant to exterminate a few hundred Indians in order to be able to govern. One must consider the context of that period, which occurred within a Darwinian atmosphere that upheld the survival of the fittest and superiority of the white race. . . . With errors, with abuses, with costs he made the Argentina we today enjoy."[26] This chapter resists such simplistic and superficial analysis. This so-called spirit of the times had actually been taking root in Argentina for many years and had culminated in the so-called Generation of the 80s. The most prominent authors in this literary movement, such as Juan Bautista Alberdi, Sarmiento, or Mitre, laid the foundation of positivist ideology for the crusade of "civilization" against "barbarism" that was most brutally expressed in Roca's military campaign as well as in the parliamentary debates that preceded that action.[27] Yet, at the time, many other voices and projects were being raised, proposing another model of society, one that fundamentally included the Indians.

Even after the Conquest of the Desert, many parliamentary debates reflected this controversy, including self-criticism at the actions performed, and many voices opposed the methods used by civilization. One example was Aristóbulo Del Valle, who in 1884, on the occasion of the approval of a similar campaign in Chaco, declared, "we have taken families of the savage Indians, we have brought them to the center of civilization and we have not respected any of the rights they are entitled to, not only the rights of civilized men but those of human beings: we have enslaved the men, prostituted the women, torn the children away from their mothers' breast."[28]

Pages could be filled with examples of what was occurring with this singular model that some sought to install and that rejected everything coming from the indigenous world. I will not make such list because it would extend beyond the limits of this essay. Suffice it to mention some examples: The white captive women rescued from indigenous communities and who voluntarily returned to urban life became virtually "publicly dead," rejected by society; conscious of this sad reality, many of them preferred to remain with their children in the indigenous communities. When not directly executed, many people who returned were punished, accused of "having passed over to the side of the Indians." This was the case of rancher Francisco Ramos Mejía, on whose properties indigenous people gathered to enact treaties or simply to celebrate and congregate. Ramos Mejía finished his days in prison, suspected of being allied with the indigenous people.[29] Additionally, there were the so-called friendly Indians, who rejected their traditional customs but showed the desire to join the new society by sign-ing treaties, even though at times they suffered severe punishments as a result.

One important stream of Argentine historiography insists that the con-flict was inevitable.[30] These works emphasize the fallacious notion of "des-ert," or wilderness, with the justifying argument that the military conquest of the indigenous territories was correct because it was carried out against groups of Chilean natives who had arrived in the Argentine plains at the height of the nineteenth century. These views highlight the common ig-norance about the issue and uphold a line of thought central in Argentina, a concept that led to the idea of the frontier as a dividing line, later to the construction of a trench, and finally to a plan for ethnic "cleansing" to cre-ate a nation where "others" had no place. Furthermore, some important authors have recently shown a more condescending position toward those who promoted that project.[31] These positions indicate, at the very least, a deep ignorance of the original peoples.

The argument here is not to glorify indigenist positions that idealize the indigenous people. On the contrary, the point here refers to the possibil-ity that Argentina may yet reconceive of itself as a different country, one in which all of the different cultural expressions could live together, being conscious of and overcoming the chronic drama of having built a society that made exclusion its norm.

Even though Gen. Julio Roca is the most emblematic figure of the vio-lent resolution of the conflict with the plains' Indians, as is Gen. Benjamín Victorica for the Chaco, both of these conquests were final blows in a long process of wearing down, and were campaigns of physical repression that, as we have seen, had in other figures their most important antecedents.

In opposition to Alsina's trench, which he considered an exclusively defensive system, Roca proposed a fast, agile, and offensive war. After Alsina died in December 1877, Roca became minister of war and quickly presented his plan to President Avellaneda and the Congress. Roca's speeches, proclamations, and agendas are clear expressions of the dominant ideology and a true example of the "model of contempt" that had taken root in the dominant classes of Buenos Aires:[32] "Once and for all, we will seal with blood and forge with the sword this Argentine nationality that needs to be formed, like the pyramids of Egypt and the powers of empires, at the cost of the blood and sweat of many generations."[33]

Roca called the natives "bandits," "land pirates," "savages," and "barbarians." In the agenda that marked the beginning of the Conquest of the Desert, Roca rallied his troops, convincing them that the fight was not against brothers, but instead savages, whom he believed they were off to redeem:

> In this campaign you are not armed to injure compatriots and brothers estranged by political passions or to enslave and ruin peoples or conquer foreign territories. We arm for something greater and nobler, to fight for the security and enlargement of the Fatherland, for the life and fortune of millions of Argentineans and even for the redemption of these very savages who, so many years living by own instincts, have weighed like a scourge on the wealth and wellbeing of the Republic.[34]

Roca condemned the survivors of his massacres to submission to national laws and cultural dissolution, lost in the currents of the new Christian populations that would replace the original inhabitants.[35]

The Conquest of the Free Indigenous Territories and Its Consequences

Throughout all of 1878 and part of 1879, Roca arranged a preliminary offensive with small contingents of rapid deployment intended to wear down the natives and weaken their power while he prepared the final expedition. He imprisoned chiefs Juan José Catriel, Vicente Pincén, and Epumer. During this time at least four hundred indigenous people perished, another four thousand were taken prisoner, and nearly two hundred white captives were rescued.

The most well-known action of the Conquest of the Desert was the expedition that Roca conducted between April and May of 1879; however, this campaign was only the first stage. The second, the final action, took place between March of 1881 and January of 1885, when Sayhueque, the last of the great chiefs of the free territory of Patagonia, fell to federal troops. Earlier troops had imprisoned leaders Inacayal, Foyel, and Namuncurá. By this time Roca had become president of Argentina because of his successful war against the Indians.

The initial and thorough attack of 1879 was carried out by an expeditionary force of five divisions comprising six thousand soldiers. They were equipped with state-of-the-art armament, especially the famous rechargeable Remington rifle model 1871, which, with its innovative characteristics of fast, repetitive loading, devastated indigenous ranks.[36] To these effects an enthusiastic colonel Conrado Villegas, another known officer in the war against the indigenous people and responsible for the capture of Chief Pincén, wrote, "it is a shame. . . what is happening and what will occur while we do not take the offensive against the Indians. . . . Fight to death is what we should do. With the Remington we must convince them."[37]

The most important results of this first campaign include the occupation of the plains even beyond the Negro and Neuquén rivers, the construction of numerous fortifications, the liberation of some five hundred captives, the dismantlement of many indigenous communities, and the death of Ranquel chief Baigorrita. Between casualties and prisoners, the indigenous losses reached nearly fifteen thousand, according to the following details from the Department of War and the Marine:

5 principal chiefs taken prisoner,
1 principal chief killed (Baigorrita),
1,271 indigenous lancers imprisoned,
1,313 indigenous lancers killed
10,513 common indigenous persons imprisoned (elders, women, and children)
1,049 Indians subjugated [reducidos][38]

Throughout the second stage of the war, indigenous casualties also numbered in the thousands, though the last free communities offered exemplary resistance. Shortly after Chief Namuncurá surrendered to federal troops in March 1884, the most important chiefs, including Sayhueque, Foyel, and Inacayal, among others, gathered in one of the last native parliaments. Together they "arrived at the conclusion of not surrendering to government troops and to instead fight to [the] death."[39]

But shortly thereafter, although not before offering a strong and determined resistance, chiefs Foyel and Inacayal were also taken prisoner. Then on January 1, 1885, the same occurred to the great leader Sayhuenque. This chief, along with nearly seven hundred of his warriors, surrendered at Fort Junín de los Andes to avoid the inevitable massacre that loomed over them. To these last defeats several other consequences followed: the stripping of the land, the political division and economic transformation of the territories, and the replacement of the original population by settlers who hurtled themselves upon the new lands.

The immediate consequences of the Conquest of the Desert included the destruction of the indigenous world of the plains and the annihilation of the frontier culture; the political-administrative unification of the nation-state through the appropriation of the free indigenous territories; the establishment of an economic model long sought by the Argentine central authority based on the large estate or *latifundio* and the agroexportation model of meat, hides, and cereals; and the consolidation of national military power.[40]

Conclusion

The conquest of the free indigenous territories meant an immeasurable loss for the communities of the Pampas and a tremendous gain for the victors. As the classic work by Jacinto Oddone has shown, laws enacted following the conquest transferred more than 34 million hectares to ranchers, with the peculiarity that as few as twenty-four persons received tracts of land that extended from 200,000 to 650,000 hectares each.[41]

The indigenous people not only lost the land; they also entered fully into a deep process of cultural changes that resulted from a series of factors that destroyed their political, social, and economic structures. These factors included extermination, imprisonment, confinement into colonies, forced migrations to strange places far from their homelands, forced adoption of new ways of life, forced suppression of traditional customs and originary cosmovisions, dismemberment of their families, and disease epidemics.

In this way, added to the loss of the existential foundation that their lands had sheltered was a growing and cruel dismemberment that disappeared entire communities and dissolved others amid an actual system of human redistribution.[42] The incorporation into the educational system of some of them as well as their en masse conversion to Catholicism that resulted from missionary campaigns, especially by the Salesian Order, completed the sad outlook of human and cultural disintegration for the indigenous tribes.

Very similar plans were accomplished in the Chaco region, in the north of the country, which culminated around 1900 with the total dispersion of the indigenous communities.

The defeat of the Chaco bastion meant even more for native peoples in Argentina. It was the consummation of a policy of extermination begun in 1820. Between 1821 and 1899, an estimated 12,335 Mapuche, Ranquel, Tehuelche, Pehuenche, Mocoví, Abipón, and Toba people were killed in the free territories of the Pampas, Patagonia, and Chaco as a result of the annihilation campaigns designed by the state in its zeal to conquer those territories. These figures only include deaths in battle and therefore exclude the hundreds of injured who did not perish on the battlefield but far away, during retreats and in the days that followed. If to these numbers we were to add the four thousand Guaranies killed during the 1816–19 campaigns of Uruguayan general Artigas and his sublieutenant Andresito in the Argentine littoral, as well as a similar number of Yamanas and Onas who disappeared between 1880 and 1900, we could conclude that at least twenty thousand indigenous people perished as a result of violent military operations in the Pampas, Patagonia, and Chaco, and as a result of colonizing campaigns in the extreme south and expeditions by foreign powers (the Portuguese Empire in the northern littoral).[43] In the name of civilization, a new genocide had been consummated toward the end of the nineteenth century.

Acknowledgments

The author wishes to thank Graciana Dutto, Ana María Llamazares, and René D. Harder Horst for their assistance with translation and revision of this chapter.

Notes

1. Archive of the Estado Mayor del Ejército, cited in Martínez Sarasola, *Nuestros paisanos los indios*, 99.

2. Operé, *Historias de la Frontera*, 19.

3. See for example, Perdue, *"Mixed Blood" Indians*.

4. Mandrini and Ortelli, *Volver al país de los araucanos*, 77–78.

5. Rodríguez, *Diario de la expedición al desierto*, 67–68.

6. This particular native way of fighting had always fascinated the *criollos*. Military accounts are full of observations to this effect, emphasizing that when natives left their *toldos* for a *malón* (raid), they used very light saddle gear so as not to hurt the horse and

to double its resistance to that of the army horses. National fascination extended as well to the relationship between the warriors and horses, which for many soldiers implied a special communication between animals and natives. Testimonies abound as to the theft of army horses committed during the night by indigenous warriors, to whom the horses were said to show complete docility because they remained absolutely and inexplicably silent. See Ramayón, *Las caballadas en la guerra del indio.*

7. Bayer, *Rebeldía y esperanza*, 1993

8. Schoo Lastra, *El indio del desierto*, 111.

9. Julio A. Roca, Speech in October 1875, in Walther, *La conquista del desierto*, 238.

10. J. M. de Rosas, correspondance to Lieutenant Delgado, September 20, 1833, Archivo General de la Nación, Sala X.27.5.7. In Sulé, *Rosas y sus relaciones con los indios*, 259–60.

11. Levaggi, *Paz en la frontera*, 269.

12. Example No. 531 from *La Tribuna* newspaper, June 8, 1855, in the Mitre Museum.

13. Battle dispatch sent by Mitre to the governor of Buenos Aires, 2-6-55, in Hux, *Caciques Huilliches y Salineros*, 61.

14. General Mitre archive, XV, p. 130, in Walther, *La conquista del desierto*, 289.

15. Yunque, *Calfucura*, 242.

16. Sarramone, *Catriel y los indios pampas*, 266.

17. Cited in Viñas, *Indios, ejército y frontera*, 15; see also Martínez Sarasola, *Nuestros paisanos los indios*, 266.

18. Ebelot, *Recuerdos y relatos.*

19. Martínez Sarasola, "El sujeto en las fronteras," 242–45.

20. Operé, *Historias de la frontera*, 16.

21. Manuel Rubial to Pablo Belisle, Codihué, May 17, 1883, Archive of the Estado Mayor del Ejército, *Campaña contra los indios*, 1883, 104, in Delrio, *Memorias de expropiación*, 72. See also, Terzaga, *Historia de Roca*, II, 176–77.

22. Utley, *Frontier Regulars*, 144.

23. Pi Hugarte, *Los indios de Uruguay*, 140.

24. Martínez Sarasola, *Nuestros paisanos los indios*, 305.

25. Martínez Zuviría, "Concepto, desarrollo e importancia," 145.

26. Bayer "Sesenta fusilados."

27. Martínez Zuviría, "Concepto,desarrollo e importancia," 127–51.

28. Lenton, "Relaciones interétnicas," 33.

29. Ramos Mejía, *Los Ramos Mejía*, 99.

30. Durán, "Estudio Preliminar," 15.

31. Ibid., 119–20.

32. Martínez Sarasola, *Nuestros paisanos los indios*, 305.

33. Roca to Dardo Rocha, correspondence, April 23, 1880, in Viñas, *Indios, ejército y frontera*, 98.

34. Roca, Order of the Day, April 26, 1879, in Walther, *La conquista del desierto*, 450–52.

35. Ibid.

36. Bidondo et. al, *Epopeya del desierto en el sur argentino*, FX, 17

37. Conrado Villegas to Ataliva Roca, correspondence, Trenque Lauquén, September 26, 1877, published by the Roca Museum, Document V, *Documents prior to 1880, (1855–1880)*, Buenos Aires, 1966, 154.

38. Departamento de Guerra y Marina, *Memorias Anuales*, 1:6.

39. Ibid., 1884, Vol. 1, 78.

40. Pigna, *Mitos Argentinos*, 5.

41. Páez, *La conquista del desierto*, 111.

42. Mases, *Estado y cuestión indígena*, 50.

43. Martínez Sarasola, *Nuestros paisanos los indios*, 305.

10

"The Slayer of Victorio Bears His Honors Quietly"

Tarahumaras and the Apache Wars in Nineteenth-Century Mexico

JULIA O'HARA

On September 4, 1880, the *New York Times* published a brief notice titled "A Price for Victorio's Scalp." A single sentence in length, the piece announced that the governor of Chihuahua, Mexico, was offering "$2,000 for the scalp of Victorio, the Apache chief, and $250 for the scalp of any of his warriors."[1] The following month, the Mexican forces of Col. Joaquin Terrazas, in pursuit of Victorio and his men, arrived at a rough Sierra Madre outcropping known as Tres Castillos. Unexpectedly, they encountered a poorly armed band of Apache men, women, and children, and opened fire. In the ensuing battle, Terrazas's men killed dozens of Apaches and took nearly an equal number prisoner.

Military and political observers on both sides of the U.S.-Mexico border were slow to realize the significance of the events of that day, October 14, 1880. But once it was confirmed that Victorio himself had died at Tres Castillos, observers in Mexico and the United States quickly understood what this battle meant. Victorio's death finally brought an end to the "Apache wars," a lengthy and very bloody conflict that pitted the Apaches, Comanches, Navajos, and other Indians against the armies of two nations, countless militias and mercenaries, and civilian populations on both sides of the border. Throughout the nineteenth century, northern Mexico, especially the state of Chihuahua, had been a society geared for warfare against the Apache and other "stateless" Indians of the Greater Southwest. In the late eighteenth and early nineteenth centuries, peace had been maintained through an array of treaties between the Spanish crown and the "*indios bárbaros*" ("barbarous Indians") of the northern frontier. A system of presidios and military installations, combined with diplomacy in the form of elaborate gifts and lucrative aid, also helped the Spanish crown to "pacify" the region. Mexican independence in 1821, however, disrupted this era of relative peace; the leaders of the new nation were unwilling and unable to invest as many resources into frontier security. "Mexico was liberated from Spain," historian Enrique Krauze writes, "but Chihuahua was not liberated from the Apaches."[2]

In 1831 the era of treaties came to an end, and military and political officials in northern Mexico declared war on the Apaches. Major clashes took place between Apache bands, who had left their reservations in the southwestern United States, and the Mexican army and state militias of Sonora and Chihuahua. Over the next several decades, the realities of constant warfare with the Apaches shaped everyday life in northern Mexico, and shaped the relationship between the north and the rest of the nation. In his recent work on the Mexican-American War, historian Brian Delay writes that "when northern Mexicans spoke of the 'enemy' in 1846 and 1847, they as often meant *indios* as *norteamericanos*. The ruinous legacy of fifteen years of raiding and the ongoing threat of Indian violence left large segments of northern Mexico's population unable and probably unwilling to resist the U.S. Army."[3]

In the broadest sense, then, the Apache wars impeded the process of state formation by hindering the Mexican state's ability to establish control over its northern border and by limiting northerners' embrace of a unified national identity. Only after Victorio's death in 1880 and the 1886 surrender of his successor, Gerónimo, did residents of Chihuahua begin to transform their society from a tumultuous "Apache island" to an entity governed by civility and reason.[4] With the virtual extermination of the "barbarous" Apache behind them, intellectual and cultural elites in Chihuahua undertook the process of remembering—and finding meaning in—the Apache wars. On January 1, 1887, an editorial published in the newspaper *El Monitor Republicano* called for the repeal of the infamous Ley de Cabelleras ("Scalp Law") that, having been in effect since the mid-1830s, had come to symbolize the brutality of the Apache wars. Contemplating this legacy of extreme violence, the editorial raised a new "Indian question": what to do about the "tame" indigenous people—primarily the Tarahumara Indians— who continued to live within the borders of the state of Chihuahua. The anonymous authors wrote:

> It is notorious that, in this state, there are a great number of Indians who, although not Apaches, bear much resemblance to them, and,

like [the Apaches], wear their hair in an unkempt state. These Indians [are] entirely *mansos* [tame], honorable, and hard working, at least as much as possible given the backward condition in which they find themselves. . . . In our humble opinion, the grave causes that justified the law we decry have disappeared; yet, the law exists, and, because of it [we know of] an individual [who] recently indulged himself in the act of killing an Indian in the Cantón Degollado and bringing in his scalp. . . . The *indios mansos*, who constitute perhaps a third of the population of this state, live withdrawn in the remotest stretches of the great Sierra. . . . In these *rancherías* there are no authorities, the Indians have no civil organization whatsoever, they speak not a word of Spanish, and they live like genuine pariahs at the mercy of the whites.[5]

This short piece encapsulates many of the implicit assumptions that would come to characterize the way Mexicans have remembered the Apache war. In nineteenth-century public discourse, the category of *indios mansos*, or tame Indians, played a key role in distinguishing peaceful Indians, such as the Tarahumara, from rebellious Indians (such as the Yaqui of Sonora) and "barbarous" Indians, as the Apache were typically described. As anthropologist Ana María Alonso has written, *manso* was "a term used to refer to animals that had been castrated and domesticated. . . . *Indios mansos* had the status of children. Segregated in closed corporate communities, under the patrimonial tutelage of church and state, they were denied the prerogatives of a fully social being."[6] The editorial depicts the Tarahumara, or *indios mansos*, as essentially helpless victims of senseless violence carried out by self-serving whites. Yet, like many of the narratives about the Apache wars, this editorial is fascinating mostly for what it leaves out. The editorial neither discusses Tarahumara violence nor hints at Tarahumara agency in the events of the day. Absent, in other words, is any suggestion that the Tarahumara participated in the Apache wars and the "notorious" practice of scalp hunting.

This chapter, then, has dual purposes. It will explore the participation of Tarahumara Indians in the Mexican military during the Apache wars, and it will reflect on the meaning of the silence and ambiguity—pervasive not only in the immediate aftermath of the conflict but also in present-day narratives and commemorations—surrounding the collective memory of their participation. During the Apache wars, Tarahumara service on the battlefield frequently presented an exception to the racial ideologies of everyday life. Yet history and memory in northern Mexico have struggled to make sense of this unique field of interaction among non-Indians and Indians, whether Tarahumaras, Apaches, or others—a struggle that continues to shape debates over race, national identity, and the "Indian question" to the present day.

Blood Contracts: Civilization and Depravity on Mexico's Northern Frontier

That Tarahumaras would collaborate with state-sponsored military efforts to eradicate the Apaches was not inevitable, especially given their history of sharing customs, territory, peaceful trade relations, and resistance strategies with various Apache groups. In the late nineteenth and early twentieth centuries, natural scientists such as Carl Lumholtz and Campbell W. Pennington, who studied the Tarahumara, worked hard to uncover their cultural and historical links to the Apache. Lumholtz reported that the ancestors of the Tarahumara "had come from the country of the Apache."[7] Likewise, Pennington described "a tradition among the Tarahumar[a] [that held] that their ancestors came from [Apache territory in] the north and east."[8] Pennington also cited linguistic evidence that another indigenous group, the Pima Indians, referred to certain Apache bands as "Tarasoma," which Pennington points out "may be derived from the Tarahumar[a] words for foot (*rara*) and run (*júma*)."[9]

Speculations about the shared origins of Apaches and Tarahumaras aside, the two groups at times formed bonds of solidarity in resistance and opposition both to missionary activity and to encroaching settlements of nonindigenous people in the Sierra Madre region. During the late eighteenth century, the Tarahumara participated in large, multiethnic bands that raided throughout various parts of northern New Spain. Anthropologist William Merrill describes one such band, led by an indigenous man, likely an Apache, named Calaxtrin. Merrill paints an intriguing picture of a multiethnic band that included men, women, and children alike, and whose members "were extremely flexible and open in cultural matters, incorporating beliefs and practices from a variety of sources."[10] For the Tarahumara, perhaps the lasting legacy of their colonial-era resistance is that they became a focal point of suspicion for Spanish—and later Mexican—authorities. The Tarahumara could be found living in nonindigenous settlements as peaceful and "incorporated" members of society, yet they also frequently allied themselves with discontented and rebellious *castas*, Apache raiders, and others involved in violent resistance.

Tarahumaras and Apaches also shared a tradition of reciprocating violence that greatly shaped the relationship between the two groups. Warfare between the Tarahumara and the Apache is inscribed in popular memory, folklore, and even the landscape of the Sierra Madre, with place names such as Narárachi, which in the Tarahumara language means "in the place where they cried" and commemorates a Tarahumara victory over the Apaches.[11] And the written historical record—whether the documents of Jesuit and Franciscan missionaries, government-sponsored surveyors, or agrarian reform registers—provides a large body of evidence that Apache raids on Tarahumara settlements were as common, and as devastating, as similar raids on the settlements of nonindigenous Mexicans. As historian Paul Vanderwood writes, in the Papigochic River valley and throughout the Sierra Madre, "no one was safe: men, women, children, Tarahumaras, Hispanics—all, regardless of ethnicity or social standing, suffered depredations."[12]

Yet while Apache raids were common, an equal threat to the integrity of Tarahumara pueblos were the economic, demographic, and social changes that permanently redrew the map of the Sierra Madre during the nineteenth century. Industrialization and the discovery of new mining resources brought an influx of non-Indians into the Sierra Madre, and this, coupled with new liberal land-tenure legislation in the 1850s and 1860s, jeopardized the longstanding structure of Tarahumara lands and communities. While this occasionally provoked Tarahumara rebellions, as it did among the Yaqui Indians of Sonora, its main impact was that it pushed the Tarahumara off their lands in the fertile Papigochic River valley into ever-more inhospitable regions of the Sierra. By the end of the nineteenth century, some 60 percent of the Tarahumara population had been squeezed into the harshest, most remote regions of the Sierra, where the land is least appropriate for agriculture due to the lack of water, poor soils, and steep landscape.[13]

Additionally, new legal devices subordinated the Indians to the newly formed nonindigenous communities in the Sierra. During the presidency of Porfirio Díaz (1876–1911), the state of Chihuahua embarked on a campaign to systematically provide land titles to individuals, rather than communities. In the towns of Humariza and Nonoava, for instance, the state parceled out at least thirty-four individual plots of land. On the surface, this process appeared to favor the Tarahumara, who could be recognized as the legitimate property owners without showing title to the land in dispute while non-Indians were required to show this evidence before they could have disputed lands adjudicated to them.[14] However, the impact of liberal land-tenure legislation in the Sierra Madre mirrored the process elsewhere in Mexico during the nineteenth century. In an attempt to turn Indians into "productive" private-property owners, these laws emphasized individual, rather than communal, ownership of land. Land beyond that which was given in title to individual Tarahumaras either became the property of nonindigenous settlers or became national lands; either way, it became illegal for indigenous communities to use them.[15]

Thus, vengeance against their Apache enemies was not the only reward for Tarahumaras taking part in the "war for extermination" against the Apaches. In a context in which Tarahumara–white relations were typically characterized by patron–client ties, subordination, and abuse, collaborating with Mexican military objectives became an effective tool for claiming land and citizenship rights as well as the kind of equality and respect that were mostly absent in other spheres of daily life. As Alonso has noted, "distinction in warfare was one of the few sources of prestige open to 'pacified' Indians. Tarahumara Indians who fought the Apache alongside the gente de razón acquired a military honor that conflicted with and at times overrode their ethnic status as *mansos*."[16] Military encounters, then, provided a unique context in which Tarahumaras fought alongside the same "white" *serranos* who exploited them in other contexts.

Moreover, these encounters had meaning not only for the Tarahumaras who parlayed their distinction on the battlefield into social prestige and material rewards. They also shaped the way that nonindigenous Mexicans made sense of the apparent paradox of relying on indigenous allies in a protracted and costly war against an indigenous enemy. In his comparative work on nineteenth-century warfare in Latin America, Miguel Angel Centeno argues that "frontier wars," whether in Chile, Argentina, or Mexico, "served to unite white opinion" throughout centuries of history during which "the class and racial 'enemy within' has been much more important a target than any threat from outside."[17] Yet the military collaboration of a supposed class and racial "other" such as the Tarahumara complicates this argument. The presence of Tarahumara allies in Mexico's anti-Apache forces called into question what constituted whiteness and contributed to the debates over race, national identity, and the "Indian question" that emerged out of the revolution of 1910.

Beginning in the early 1830s, Mexican army commanders employed Tarahumara troops in their patrols and, as historian William Griffen points out, they "generally placed much reliance on Tarahumar[a]s when these Indians were available, as they were considered good and brave fighters."[18] Indeed, it seems that often military and political authorities played off racial animosity between Tarahumaras and white *serranos* as well as long-held racial stereotypes about the Indians in an effort to motivate their nonindigenous troops through shame-inducing comparisons to these "tame" Indians. Held up as models of skill, bravery, and the will to fight, Tarahumaras on the battlefield were sometimes portrayed as everything the nonindigenous soldiers were not. As weaponry, funding, and resources in general grew scarce, the Mexican army embraced indigenous weaponry, such as the bow and arrow; the Tarahumara were far more skilled in their use than white *serrano* combatants.

Additionally, Tarahumara prowess and endurance as long-distance runners, viewed as an effective battle tactic, became prized and, indeed, worthy of emulation. Griffen describes a series of reports from Chihuahua military and state officials that complained of "weak leadership and the lack of skill and bravery on the battlefield."[19] He points out that in 1834, "the Vice Governor of the state opined that part of the state's weakness stemmed from the 'cowardice and shameful and degrading feminization.'. . . of a great portion of the population. . . . Many men were said to have exhibited 'frightful disorder and cowardice,'" and the proffering of excuses "that they lacked both arms and the money with which to buy them; if they wanted to do so they could have used bows and arrow and other weapons like those of the Tarahumar[a] Indians."[20] The commanders and state officials, then, drew unflattering comparisons between brave, well-armed Tarahumaras and cowardly, poorly armed, and idle nonindigenous Chihuahuans, a comparison that simultaneously implied respect for the Tarahumaras and disrespect for "men of reason" who were not even as brave and industrious as the Indians.

Tarahumaras, like many white *serranos*, frequently chose to fight Apaches outside of the confines of the Mexican army by engaging in the collection of "evidentiary *piezas*." *Piezas*, which could be quite lucrative, included enemy prisoners or their remains (dead bodies or parts thereof, especially scalps and ears), as well as livestock and other goods that were presumed to have been stolen. It is scalp hunting, however, that is perhaps the most powerful symbol of the carnage produced by the Apache wars. Long a source of both fascination and revulsion for observers on both sides of the U.S.-Mexico border, it has served as shorthand for the dichotomy of civilization and barbarism—and for the brutal way that the excesses of the Apache wars had of plunging even the "civilized" into depravity.[21]

In 1835 the state of Sonora reinstituted a colonial-era law that created a bounty system for killing "barbarous" Indians and a monetary reward scale for those who presented evidentiary *piezas*. Two years later, officials in Chihuahua proposed Mexico's first-ever *proyecto* (program) to specifically offer compensation for Apache scalps: one hundred dollars for the forelock of an Apache warrior aged fourteen years and older; fifty for that of an Apache woman; and twenty-five dollars for Apache children under age fourteen. Historian Ralph Adam Smith points out, however, that "the national government of President General Antonio [*sic*] Bustamante canceled the *proyecto*, calling it unconstitutional, immoral, impractical, and repugnant to the civilization, pride, and religion of Mexico, an insult to the honor of its soldiers, and an attraction to armed 'foreigners or adventurers.'"[22] Still, Americans flooded into Mexico on "scalp-mining" expeditions. Among these brigades were those led by the infamous James Kirker, whose mercenary armies filled a void left by the absence of Mexican militias and the army, called away to fight off the French and Spanish invasions of their country. Always controversial, Kirker enjoyed an on-again/off-again partnership with Mexican state and local governments throughout the 1840s.

In 1849 the Chihuahua legislature passed the Ley de Cabelleras (Scalp Law), also known as the Ley Quinta (Fifth Law) or the Contratas de Sangre (Blood Contracts). This law reauthorized the purchase of Apache prisoners or their scalps via a system of contracts. This ushered in another heyday of scalp hunting that lasted nearly three decades. As Ricardo León García and Carlos González Herrera write, "the Law of 1849 rested on the notion that there was only one kind of *indio bárbaro*: the enemy, and that the war against him was the state's most urgent concern."[23]

Belying the characterization of Tarahumaras as "collateral damage" of the Scalp Law, many of them eagerly took part in "scalp hunting" in their own hunting parties and alongside nonindigenous Mexican Apache fighters and American mercenaries. Kirker was said to have employed many Tarahumaras in his mercenary army. In 1845,

> after meeting with leaders in Yepómera, Temósachic, Matachic, Villa de la Concepción (present-day Guerrero), and other Tarahumaran villages, he enlisted fifty-four men. His Tarahumarans wore bobbed hair, turbans, G-strings, and rawhide sandals. Traditionally, these Indians fought with bows, arrows, clubs, knives, lariats, slings, and spears, but [Kirker] supplied his recruits with guns, making them a formidable force. Their remarkable ability to run in hundred-mile foot

races enabled them to challenge the Apaches in the mountains and canyons. . . . With his 'international' army of Delawares, Shawnees, Tarahumarans, Americans, Mexicans, and others, [Kirker] followed the tracks of an Apache band northwestward to within fifteen miles of the border of Sonora.[24]

Starting in the 1860s, mercenary armies such as Kirker's were replaced by the northern state militias and the Mexican army, where Tarahumaras fought under Col. Joaquin Terrazas, alongside renowned Apache hunters Juan Mata Ortiz and Luis Zuloaga. Smith attributes Tarahumara skill at scalp hunting to "their prodigious feats as footmen. . . [who] disdain[ed] the effeminacy of riding." The Tarahumaras in Terrazas' contingent "made tough, productive companies, jumping swift, elusive game in the mountains during summer months and in the valleys during winter."[25]

A Man without a Flag, or Who Killed Victorio?

Throughout the 1860s and 1870s, Mauricio Corredor, a Tarahumara man from the pueblo of Arisiachic, sustained a fierce reputation as an Apache fighter and scalp hunter. It should not be surprising, then, that he played a key role in the Apache Wars and the Battle of Tres Castillos in 1880. Although the details of Victorio's death in this battle remain elusive, a majority of sources recognize Mauricio as Victorio's slayer. Indeed, the state of Chihuahua handsomely rewarded him for killing the great Apache chief. He reportedly claimed the governor's two thousand peso reward for Victorio's scalp, along with a fine suit of clothes and a nickel-plated revolver, among other things.[26] And he was greeted as a hero when Terrazas and his men rode into Chihuahua City to enjoy a spectacular victory parade through the streets of the city. Historian Dan Thrapp quotes at length one newspaper's description of the scene in Chihuahua:

The whole city turned out [for the parade]. . . . The housetops were covered, the balconies were alive, and banners were flying from all the masts. . . . First came an immense throng of people, men, women, and children, pushing each other to and fro, mad with excitement. Then came a band, whose music was drowned from time to time by the plaudits of the populace. Then came Colonel Terrassas [sic] and his staff officers, looking worn and travel-stained. Immediately after came the prisoners mounted upon ponies and mules. . . . After the prisoners came the scalp bearers and pack trains. . . . This campaign will cost the state not less than $50,000 cash outlay [for scalps]. The scalp of Victorio, tinged visibly with gray, was carried by the man who was given the credit of shooting him. . . . The slayer of Victoria [*sic*] has been presented with a suit that is neat and not gaudy, either. The short jacket is of crimson broadcloth; the vest and pants of black doeskin, trimmed with silver face; the hat a magnificent white fur broadbrim, and covered with spangles. He is a peaceful Tarahumare [*sic*] Indian, and bears his honors quietly.[27]

Thrapp goes on to point out that "an elaborate monument in recognition of [Terrazas'] conquest of Victorio was erected in the city of Chihuahua, a monument almost unique in all of Mexico, for Indian fighters, even successful ones, were not customarily so honored in that country."[28] Yet, although in 1880 Mauricio Corredor seemed destined to go down in history as a regional hero, a remarkable amount of ambiguity surrounds the memory of his contribution and that of his *compañeros* from Arisiachic and other Tarahumara pueblos. First off, there is the matter of how much respect Mauricio was afforded during his career; his title, rank, and social status are the subject of much disagreement. In a disparate variety of sources, he is alternately described as a captain, a major, a commander, and a scout. Some sources refer to him as "don Mauricio," others simply as a "runner" (the word "*corredor*" is Spanish for "runner").

Secondly, there is the matter of what really happened at Tres Castillos. Curiously, although Colonel Terrazas's official report noted Mauricio's "heroic conduct" in battle, it does not make a single mention of his having killed Victorio.[29] Moreover, in some versions of the story of Tres Castillos, Mauricio rushes ahead of the advancing Mexican battalion to "finish off" a gravely wounded Victorio.[30] In others, Mauricio and Victorio fight hand to hand to the death. Still other versions fail to mention Mauricio at all. Apache versions of the battle reveal yet another set of perspectives. Many Apaches refuse to accept the notion that Mauricio killed Victorio, remembering instead that Victorio and his men chose to commit suicide rather than suffer their fate at the hands of the Mexicans and their (subordinate) Tarahumara allies. Historian Eve Ball, who extensively recorded Apache oral histories, noted that "no Apache believes that Mauricio Corredo [*sic*] killed Victorio. . . . I know, of course, the recognition he got in Chihuahua, but they do not accept the account."[31] Indeed, when Apache informant James Kaywaykla described his childhood experience as an eyewitness to the battle of Tres Castillos, he emphatically denied that any Tarahumara had killed Victorio: "My grandmother was close to where Victorio and his men were. They were out of ammunition and he did not want to be taken prisoner . . . so they used their knives on themselves. . . . The story of the Indian who claimed to have killed him is not true. . . . The soldiers burned the bodies."[32]

Oral testimony compiled by anthropologist Sherry Robinson corroborates Ball's findings. Quoting one of her interviews, she writes that

Apaches always dismissed the claim of Maurício Corredo [sic] that he killed Victorio, but the two apparently did fight. "Victorio and the Tarahumara chief, Maurício, fought at Tres Castillos. . . . It was on a plain and Victorio chose the man who fought with him. Then he comes horseback with no escort—only the one man. Then Maurício is separated from the others and advances afoot. And a compadre, Roque. This challenge when they met, they start to fight at the same time. Victorio and Roque fell on his [unreadable]. Victorio fell from his horse. When the old Indians saw that Victorio had fallen, they cry and said, 'No fight more.' And they waited for night to escape, but they could not escape."[33]

Historian Dan Thrapp also writes that "an old Apache tale has it that Victorio was captured, then slain by boiling in oil, which, although preposterous, suggests the still-lingering hatred between the races."[34]

Multiple contradictory narratives about Mauricio and Victorio also permeate the folklore and popular literature of Chihuahua. The Apache Wars are fictionalized in the novel *Rencor Apache* (*Apache Rancor*) by Arturo Molina. The story's protagonist, Salvador, joins the ranks of Colonel Terrazas after his parents are brutally murdered by raiding Apaches. Despite being written from the perspective of a white Apache hunter, the book projects sympathy and respect for the Apache while depicting North Americans as greedy, Mexicans as desperate, and Tarahumaras as cowardly mercenaries. After being wounded, Salvador hallucinates an Apache, who tells him that "my brothers in blood are not as guilty as they seem; the white man of the north has forced them from their lands and pushed them south, where another not-so-white man forces them once more to flee."[35]

Real historical figures, including Mauricio and Victorio, appear in the book alongside the fictional characters. Molina disparages Mauricio's role at Tres Castillos, writing that he "allegedly bore the rank of captain and became famous for having killed the most valiant leader of the Chiricahua Apaches, the great Victorio."[36] For Molina, Victorio was double-crossed at

Tres Castillos by Mauricio, Roque Ramos, and the other "cowardly" Tarahumaras from Arisiachic. In order "to fill himself with undeserved glory," Mauricio assassinated Victorio in the act of negotiating a peace accord with Colonel Terrazas. Having committed this act of treachery, Molina concludes, Mauricio "shall pay for his crime when history judges him, as he is a man without a flag."[37]

In casting doubt on the worthiness of Tarahumara Apache fighters to be considered loyal Mexican citizens, Molina's narrative—obviously a work of fiction—is not subtle. Yet Tarahumara involvement in an international incident six years after the battle of Tres Castillos provides a concrete opportunity to explore the ambiguities of race and citizenship on the field of battle. On January 11, 1886, Mexican and U.S. troops, both combing the Sierra Madre for Gerónimo's Apaches, clashed accidentally, resulting in multiple casualties on both sides. The American troops, a detachment of Gen. George Crook's army, were commanded by Capt. Emmet Crawford. They entered Mexico with four officers, a Spanish interpreter named Tom Horn, and nearly one hundred Apache scouts. The Mexican troops, a force of irregulars led by Santa Ana Pérez, contained seasoned Tarahumara soldiers and officers, including Mauricio Corredor, who was listed as a captain in both nations' battle reports. Although existing treaties allowed American forces to enter Mexico in pursuit of "hostile" Indians, the entry of Apache scouts was expressly prohibited. Accounts of what took place when the two forces accidentally encountered each other vary widely. According to the American battle reports, once the Americans recognized the armed men they had encountered as their Mexican and Tarahumara allies, Captain Crawford attempted to communicate with them. These reports emphasized, however, that the Tarahumaras knowingly opened fire on the unsuspecting Americans, hitting Captain Crawford, who later died from his injuries.[38]

The Mexican reports, however, categorically deny that the Tarahumaras knowingly fired on members of the U.S. Army. Instead, the reports insist that they "maintained the firmest conviction that the forces of Captain Crawford were rebel Indians [Apaches] . . . because they bore no signs whatsoever that would distinguish them from the rebels."[39] These reports are fascinating, for they reveal not only the suspicion that the two nations, ostensibly allies in the war against the Apaches, had for each other but also how suspicious each nation was of its own Indian troops. One of the American officers involved in the incident, 2nd Lt. W. E. Shipp, had earlier expressed uncertainty about the comportment, discipline, and commitment of his own Apache scouts.[40] Similarly, the Mexican diplomat Matías Romero placed nearly all the blame on the Indians of both nationalities. In his report he explained that "as the volunteers of Chihuahua were not regular troops, they were, therefore, not under strictest discipline, and accordingly the order of their officers to stop firing when Captain Crawford proposed its cessation were not obeyed, as neither were those of [the American commander] obeyed by the Indian scouts of the United States Army in regard to the cessation of their firing."[41]

Mexicans and Americans argued over this incident for years to come, launching mutual accusations back and forth via the press and official diplomatic channels. Throughout the 1890s, anger over the "Crawford incident" was reignited whenever the two nations signed a new reciprocal border-crossing agreement.[42] Still, one fact upon which both the U.S. and Mexican reports agreed was that it was Mauricio Corredor who shot and killed Crawford. Indeed, this fact provided the Mexicans with additional evidence that their troops had mistaken the Americans' Apache scouts for "hostiles." According to the Mexican report, the shooting of Crawford occurred primarily because "when the Indians sent by the Americans learned that it was Mauricio Corredor whom they had encountered, they rapidly commenced to flee out of the fear that they had of him, for . . . it was well known [among the Apaches] that Mauricio had, years earlier, caused the death of the fearsome Victorio."[43] Significantly, both reports also acknowledged that Mauricio, too, was among the casualties on that day. Yet the Mexican report found irony in this fact, but the U.S. report did not: "The United States Government and its press were quite pleased with the success that the Mexican forces had at exterminating cruel Victorio. Who, then, could have predicted that, years later, because of a very regrettable chance encounter, the heroic Mauricio Corredor would be killed, precisely by an Indian force commanded by American officials! Just as Mexico and its Government deplored the loss of Captain Crawford, it is certain that the people of the United States will deplore the loss of Corredor."[44]

Remembering Tomochic: Rebellion and Revolution in the Tumultuous Sierra

In the 1890s, fears about Apache raiders turned to concern that other indigenous groups, especially the Tarahumara, would ultimately wage a violent "caste war" to eradicate nonindigenous northerners once and for all.[45] Yet persistent banditry and uprisings by nonindigenous *serranos* constituted a much more serious threat to the stability of the region.[46] In 1891–92, nonindigenous rebels in the pueblo of Tomóchic rose up against the government and the hierarchy of the Catholic Church, proclaiming loyalty to the regional folk saint Teresa Urrea, known as the "Santa de Cabora." The Sonora and Chihuahua state militias, together with federal troops, were dispatched to Tomóchic and, in a series of battles that cost thousands of lives, the entire pueblo was burned to the ground, leaving only a handful of women and children as survivors.

The rebellion and its tragic outcome immediately seized the nation's imagination, helping to fix the image of a tumultuous Sierra in the minds of Mexicans. Long regarded as a precursor to the revolution of 1910, Tomóchic has held a central place in the national narrative about the cruel and violent repression of the Mexican peasantry under President Porfiro Díaz. Indeed, in 1909, a Jesuit missionary named Pablo Louvet willfully ignored the anticlerical posture of the Tomóchic villagers. In a letter to his superior, he described the village as a *"pueblo de valientes,"* and lamented the deaths of the "intrepid" Tomochitecos who were burned to death inside the village church by the government's troops.[47] Very soon afterward, "'Remember Tomochic [*sic*]' became a battle cry in the Mexican revolution that overthrew Díaz."[48]

Yet, much like the battle of Tres Castillos and the Crawford incident, the process of "remembering Tomóchic" is complicated by significant disagreement on the question of what role Tarahumaras played in the rebellion and the government's efforts to subdue it. Although in the decades after Tomóchic, many continued to believe that the rebels had been Indians, rather than mestizo *serranos*, recent studies of Tomóchic show that the opposite was more likely true.[49] By the late nineteenth century, Tomóchic was a largely mestizo pueblo, with remaining Tarahumaras working as domestic labor or as field hands for non-Indians.[50] Historian Alan Knight writes that "the revolt was ethnically mestizo, and failed to attract significant (Tarahumara) support."[51] Rather, Knight points out, the label of "Indians" was applied to the Tomóchic rebels by authorities of the Porfirian state, as a way to "isolate and demonize the movement."[52] Moreover, it is fascinating to contemplate that the pueblo of Arisiachic and the memory of Mauricio Corredor once again contributed to the controversy surrounding these events. According to historian Paul Vanderwood, "the natives of Arisiachic openly disdained the mestizos of Tomochic."[53] In the early days of the Tomóchic disturbance, the Eleventh Infantry Battalion consisted of "ten to fifteen local volunteers spoiling for adventure and a little extra pay, and five Tarahumara Indians from the nearby village of Arisiachic, whose inhabitants had little fellow-feeling for the people of Tomóchic."[54]

Arturo Molina uses the relationship between Tomóchic and Arisiachic as another opportunity to paint the followers of Mauricio Corredor as cowards. A plot point in his novel turns on the moment in which, under cover of darkness, Roque Ramos, who had fought the Apaches at Mauricio Corredor's side, guides the Mexican army troops under General Rangel into Tomóchic, setting the stage for the final showdown.[55]

Furthermore, Vanderwood describes a scene that recalls the mercenary tendency of Tarahumara scalp hunters:

> The bitterly vengeful presidente of Tomochic, Juan Ignacio Chávez, had a suggestion for catching and punishing [the rebels]. He recommended that the Tarahumaras from Arisiachic, with their long-standing acrimony toward Tomochitecos—natives who not so long ago had been well paid to track down and scalp Apaches—now be turned loose on Cruz Chávez and his followers. He asserted that if offered a liberal price for the scalps of the faithful, the Tarahumaras would lift hair.[56]

Conclusion: Memory and Metaphor in the Mexican North

Today, civic and cultural groups in Chihuahua and throughout northern Mexico commemorate the Apache Wars in a multitude of ways. In 2003 authorities in Chihuahua City erected a statue to honor the hero of the Battle of Tres Castillos. Yet this time the hero being commemorated was Victorio. On October 14, 2007, the Proyecto Cultural Chihuahua Apache, A.C., celebrated the 127th anniversary of Tres Castillos. The interpretation offered at the ceremony emphasized that Terrazas' troops, using repeating rifles, had ambushed defenseless Apache men, women, and children who had been armed with little more than bows and arrows. One news story asserted that "today, Chihuahuans continue to remember Chief Victorio, who fought to the end for the freedom of his people, as one of the bravest men ever to live in these lands."[57] The ceremony made no mention of Mauricio Corredor. Indeed, coverage of the event by the news media reinforced a new version of the Tres Castillos story. In this version, although many Apache scalps were taken at Tres Castillos, the two-thousand peso reward for the scalp of Victorio was never collected. This version starkly contradicts nineteenth-century accounts of these events and seems almost intentionally to erase the memory of Mauricio's role in them.

What these accounts do reflect is the effort Chihuahuans have made in recent years, through official civic, political, and cultural activities, to reexamine their relationship to their Apache-fighting past, and to incorporate Apache ethnicity and identity within a more ample understanding of what it means to be Chihuahuan. Chihuahua sponsors an annual international culture festival that prominently features the cultures of multiple indigenous groups of the Greater Southwest, including Yaqui, Mayo, Hope, Seri, and Tepehuán as well as Tarahumara and Apache. Official publications advertising these festivals have urged the public to honor the memory of Victorio, Gerónimo, and other Apaches, who "were famous for their resilience in the struggle to recover the right of free transit through Chihuahuan territory."[58] And other media sources have explained that "today, attitudes toward the Apaches have arrived at a more honest consideration of their contribution to the development of Chihuahuan society, and the city of Chihuahua has granted them a special place for the courage they showed in their struggle . . . and public recognition with a magnificent statue that reminds us of the warrior who gave his life for the rights of his people."[59]

Missing from these commemorations, of course, is any mention of Mauricio Corredor. No monument to him exists anywhere in the state of Chihuahua or in Mexico. The celebration of Victorio, and the silence regarding Mauricio, serves as a metaphor for the contested meaning of the Apache Wars, their legacy, and the place of the Tarahumara in military history and national memory. Understanding the evolving memory of the Apache Wars and the Tarahumaras' roles in them helps to illuminate the complexity and their struggle for recognition, land, respect, and equality as citizens in the nineteenth, twentieth, and twenty-first centuries.

In comparison to other indigenous groups of the Greater Southwest, little has been written about the Tarahumara in the nineteenth century. When the historical literature mentions them, it is often to characterize them as the "docile" counterparts of the rebellious Yaquis, Mayos, or Apaches, and to point out that they have typically avoided, rather than resisted, the growing number of nonindigenous Mexicans in the Sierra Madre. Stressing the extent to which the Tarahumara have been silenced in the historical record, Rubén Osorio writes that "during the Porfiriato, the Tarahumara were born, lived, got sick, and died out in the mountains, apparently without anyone noticing."[60] And while those characterizations are not necessarily incorrect, they lack a full accounting of the diversity and variety of Tarahumara interactions with their nonindigenous neighbors and with the nation-state. By playing a part in the military engagements to close and pacify the frontier, the Tarahumara cannot be overlooked as playing a role in a process that was crucial to Mexico's process of consolidation as a nation-state. By doing so, they were vital to the public debates that were so central to the political life of the developing Mexican nation.

Although the Apache Wars ended in 1886, the culture of warfare and violence in northern Mexico did not, as evidenced by the Tomóchic and other rebellions in the 1890s and early 1900s. Most significantly, of course, popular protest in Chihuahua ignited the revolution of 1910, which quickly engulfed the entire country and produced a decade of violence that claimed at least 1.5 million Mexican lives. Tying the violence of the revolution directly to that of the Apache wars, Enrique Krauze asks "how can we explain the extremes of cruelty to which [Pancho] Villa and his Dorados were driven, without remembering the Apache wars? Aren't Villa's nomadic character, his ability to forever fly through the air on horseback . . . his marksmanship, and even the strains of his famous cavalry charges, in essence direct traces of that War?"[61]

Even more lasting than the violence associated with these conflicts are the lingering ambiguities about race and citizenship that neither the Apache Wars nor the 1910 revolution fully resolved. After 1917 Mexico's new leaders cultivated an image of the revolution as a *campesino* and Indian uprising. This thrust rural issues, and especially indigenous issues, to the forefront of the national agenda, and the debate over the "Indian question" acquired more urgency than ever. As historian Alexander S. Dawson has written, postrevolutionary leaders "hoped to transform the way all Mexicans understood their nation. For instance, they would constantly endeavor to empty the term 'Indian' of its racial content. They celebrated Indians as the national soul and the potential equals of all Mexicans."[62] But, at least in Chihuahua, the question of *which* Indians to celebrate threatens this inclusive vision. Memories of the Apache Wars, especially Tarahumara collaboration with the violent project for Apache extermination, are not easily reconciled with contemporary efforts to reimagine citizenship and national belonging in Mexico.

Notes

1. "A Price for Victorio's Scalp," *New York Times*, September 4, 1880.
2. Krauze, "Chihuahua, ida y vuelta," 33.
3. Delay, "Independent Indians and the U.S.-Mexican War," 61.
4. The phrase "Apache island" is from Krauze, "Chihuahua, ida y vuelta," 32.

5. For the full text of this editorial, see León García and González Herrera, *Civilizar o exterminar*.

6. Alonso, *Thread of Blood*, 64.

7. Lumholtz, "Among the Tarahumaris," 296.

8. Pennington, *Tarahumar of Mexico*, 12.

9. Ibid., 13.

10. Merrill, "Cultural Creativity and Raiding Bands," 144.

11. Pennington, *Tarahumar of Mexico*, 12.

12. Vanderwood, *Power of God*, 113.

13. León García and González Herrera, *Civilizar o exterminar*, 72.

14. Ibid., 77–78. The authors assert that "in general, the authorities demonstrated a noticeable intention to validate the rights of indigenous communities and to avoid illegal actions against them."

15. Ibid., 79–82.

16. Alonso, *Thread of Blood*, 102.

17. Centeno, "War in Modern Latin America," 160–61.

18. Griffen, *Utmost Good Faith*, 174.

19. Ibid, 173–74.

20. Ibid.

21. Novelist Cormac McCarthy's masterpiece *Blood Meridian* used scalp hunting as the central metaphor in a meditation on violence, inhumanity, and the nature of evil. Ralph A. Smith, a leading authority on scalp hunting, describes scalp hunters in extremely colorful language, referring to them alternately as "hair hunters," "barbers," "head peelers," and "artisans of the hair dresser's craft."

22. Smith, *Borderlander*, 71.

23. León García and González Herrera, *Civilizar o exterminar*, 175.

24. Smith, *Borderlander*, 154.

25. Smith, "Apache Plunder Trails Southward," 23–24.

26. Ralph A. Smith calls the Battle of Tres Castillos a "scalp harvest." It resulted in not only the 2,000–peso reward to Mauricio for Victorio's scalp but also "15,250 pesos for scalps of sixty-one warriors at 250 pesos each, and 10,200 pesos for sixty-eight adult and small captives of both sexes at 150 pesos each, for a grand total of 27,450 pesos. But the committee approved no payments for the sixteen scalps of women and boys, a denial that followed the Fifth Law." *Borderlander*, 234.

27. Thrapp, *Victorio and the Mimbres Apaches*, 311.

28. Ibid., 311.

29. Mexico, Secretaría de Relaciones Exteriores, *Correspondencia diplomática cambiada entre el gobierno de los Estados Unidos Mexicanos y los de Varias Potencias Extranjeras desde el 30 de junio de 1881 a 30 de junio de 1886. Edición Oficial. Tomo III* (Mexico City: Tipografía "La Luz," 1887), 673. Terrazas' report contained the following language of commendation: "The sons of the state fought valiantly, but worthy of special mention for their heroic conduct are Political Chief of Galeana and second in command Juan Mata Ortiz; Captain of Public Safety Rodrigo García, and Captain of the Arisiachic forces, Señor Mauricio Corredor."

30. Thrapp, *Conquest of Apachería*, 206.

31. Quoted in Robinson, *Apache Voices*, 25.

32. Quoted in ibid., 19.

33. Quoted in ibid., 21

34. Thrapp, *Conquest of Apachería*, 304.

35. Molina, *Rencor Apache*, 28.

36. Ibid., 6.

37. Ibid., 29.

38. United States Department of State, *The Executive Documents of the House of Representatives for the Second Session of the Forty-Ninth Congress, 1886–1887)*. See also Gatewood, *Lt. Charles Gatewood and his Apache Wars Memoir*, 205–35.

39. Mexico, Secretaría de Relaciones Exteriores, *Correspondencia diplomática*, 624.

40. Hatfield, *Chasing Shadows*, 92.

41. Ibid.

42. Ibid., 122.

43. Mexico, Secretaría de Relaciones Exteriores, *Correspondencia diplomática*, 670.

44. Ibid., 673–74.

45. During a series of Tarahumara uprisings in 1895 in the pueblos of Agua Amarilla and Chinatú, a group of Tarahumaras attacked and killed members of a government commission sent to measure the indigenous communities' land. On the fear of a new caste war, see León García and Gonzalez Herrera, *Civilizar o exterminar*, 100–102, 128. See also Almada, *Resumen de la historia del Estado de Chihuahua*.

46. Historian Alan Knight emphasizes that "protest and revolt were common in the region during the Porfiriato," and cites strikes and uprisings in Pinos Altos, the Papigóchic Valley, and throughout the Rio Grande Valley during the 1880s and 1890s. Knight, "Review: Rethinking the Tomóchic Rebellion," 378.

47. Archivo Histórico de la Provincia Mexicana, Mexico City. *Carta del P. Louvet al P. Socio, Chihuahua, February 14, 1909*.

48. Gordon, *Great Arizona Orphan Abduction*, 84.

49. Bertocchi, *Apuntes históricos*, 126.

50. See León García and González Herrera, *Civilizar o exterminar*, 100. See also Almada, *Apuntes históricos del Cantón Rayón*, 119; and Osorio, *Tomóchic en llamas*.

51. Knight, "Review: Rethinking the Tomóchic Rebellion," 379.

52. Ibid., 380.

53. Vanderwood, *Power of God*, 77.

54. Ibid., 5.

55. Molina, *Rencor Apache*, 108.

56. Vanderwood, *Power of God*, 155.

57. "Conmemoraron el 127 aniversario de la Batalla de Tres Castillos," *Tiempo*, October 15, 2007.

58. "Segundo Festival Internacional Chihuahua," *Boletines de Prensa*, n.d.

59. "127 aniv. de la Batalla de Tres Castillos," *El Agora de Chihuahua*, October 14, 2007.

60. Osorio, *Tomóchic en llamas*, 39.

61. Krauze, "Chihuahua, ida y vuelta," 35.

62. Dawson, *Indian and Nation in Revolutionary Mexico*, xix.

11

Embattled Identities in Postcolonial Chile

Race, Region, and Nation during the War of the Pacific, 1879–1884

JOANNA CROW

This chapter examines the participation of Araucanía and indigenous Mapuche people in the War of the Pacific, a bloody conflict fought between Chile and its northern neighbors Peru and Bolivia in the late nineteenth century (1879–84).[1] The conflict was probably the most significant "national" experience for Chile since independence (1810–18). The story of Araucanía is fascinating in this regard because in 1879 the region was not yet fully incorporated into the Chilean state; much of it was still independent Mapuche territory (see map 3 in the front of the book).[2] This state of affairs was to change, however, during the War of the Pacific: at the same time as the Chilean army was occupying large tracts of the nitrate-rich desert region in the north, it was pushing on with its "pacification" of Mapuche territory in the south. By 1883 it had crushed the remaining Mapuche resistance, and subjugated both the region and its indigenous population to the laws of the Chilean state.

In this chapter I draw on the existing historiography of the War of the Pacific, and on scholarship on nationalism and national identity in Latin America, together with a wide range of primary material including congress debates, ministerial reports, military records and local and national newspapers, to offer an analysis of the conflict from the perspective of Araucanía. How was the war experienced in the region, which was itself a contested territory? How did Mapuche people there respond to the war? What role did the region play in the war on a more discursive level? What place was ascribed to its indigenous inhabitants in discourses of nationhood at a time when the government and various mediating institutions such as the press were desperately trying to instill patriotic sentiments in the populace? The archival documents help to tease out the answers to these questions, and in doing so demonstrate the complexities of constructing and "imagining" a Chilean national identity.

In line with recent scholarship that highlights the significance of war in shaping national identities in nineteenth-century Latin America but that also shows that these identities remained very much in flux,[3] I argue that dominant discourses of *chilenidad* were neither static nor uncontested during the War of the Pacific. My focus is the place allocated to and assumed by the Mapuche (the most numerous of Chile's indigenous peoples) in such discourses. Traditionally, historians tended to envisage indigenous populations as peripheral actors in the wars of the nineteenth century and in the political developments of Latin America's emergent nation-states. They often noted how indigenous peoples were affected by military, political, or social changes but rarely acknowledged indigenous peoples as active agents in these processes. This is particularly the case in narratives of Chilean national history. This chapter challenges such narratives, building on the work of Florencia Mallon, which reassessed the role played by Peru's highland indigenous communities in the War of the Pacific, and that of Nancy Appelbaum, which explored indigenous communities' involvement in Colombia's partisan rivalries and civil wars.[4] It demonstrates the significance of the Mapuche in the process of constructing and imagining "Chile" during the War of the Pacific. That is, as objects in contested discourses of nationhood, as active agents in political developments in Araucanía, as enemies of the Chilean nation that sought to colonize their own land, and—contrarily—as participants in the War of the Pacific, fighting on Chile's side.

The War of the Pacific: A Brief Chronology

Governments first became aware that the Atacama Desert was rich in natural resources when guano and nitrates were discovered there in the 1860s. The land was officially Bolivian, but Chilean corporations were allowed to operate in the province, and they paid taxes for the privilege. It is widely accepted that the Bolivian government sparked the conflict by increasing these taxes, thereby contravening treaties signed with Chile in 1874. When the Chilean-owned Compañia de Salitres y Ferrocarril [Nitrate and Railway Company] refused to pay the surcharge, the Bolivian government confiscated its property and announced that it would be put up for auction. On February 14, 1879, the day of the proposed auction, Chilean troops occupied the provincial capital of Antofagasta. Two weeks later Bolivia declared war on Chile. By April 1879, Bolivia's longstanding ally, Peru (they had fought together against Chile in the 1830s), had also joined the conflict.

The first two years of the conflict (1879–81) are known as the "active war." In January 1881, after the battles of Chorrillos and Miraflores, Chilean troops occupied the Peruvian capital, Lima, and Chileans rejoiced because they believed that all that remained was to sign a peace treaty allowing their loved ones to come home.[5] Things turned out very differently, however. Because there was no central government in charge of Peru at the time (state authorities had fled Lima after the Chilean occupation, leaving the country in disarray), it was impossible to enforce a peace treaty. Hence, Chile continued to occupy the north, entangled in a dirty war of attrition that lasted another two years. In October 1883 Peru finally capitulated and Bolivia signed an armistice in April 1884.

The Definitive Occupation of Araucanía (1880–1883)

While the military campaign raged on in the north, the Chilean government continued its "pacification" campaign against the Mapuche in the south. Undoubtedly, the War of the Pacific—an international war against two neighbors with substantially larger armies over the nitrate-rich desert region—was prioritized over an internal war against supposedly inferior Indians, which had already been under way for two decades. Indeed, parliamentary records show that the government was criticized for becoming too absorbed in "los asuntos del norte" (events in the north). Yet they also testify to politicians' efforts to keep the "gran cuestión de Arauco" (the great question of Araucanía) on the political agenda and confirm that the government responded to such criticisms and concerns.[6]

In his annual report to congress in 1881, the Chilean minister of war was proud to claim that, despite the war against Peru and Bolivia, he had made the occupation of Araucanía a priority.[7] As if to prove the point, a military expedition was sent to the frontier region that same year to punish rebel Mapuche. Recounting the events of this expedition, the ministerial *Memoria* of 1882 asserted that "the Indians, who were caught unawares by the suddenness of the military advance, put up only a weak resistance." Yet it then contradicted itself by noting the number of people (on both sides) who had been killed in battle, the reinforcements that were brought in to secure the new advances, the need for increased funding, and the work being done by the civic brigades. Clearly, these last developments were a response to the continued resistance of Mapuche people. Nevertheless, by 1882, the government declared that the only part of Araucanía not yet occupied was that between the Cautín and Toltén rivers; apparently the Araucanians had been "materially and morally defeated by civilisation."[8]

Official Discourses of Race in Nineteenth-Century Chile

Many historians have emphasized the racist content of official discourses of Chilean nationhood during the nineteenth century.[9] They often quote Liberal parliamentarian and historian Benjamín Vicuña Mackenna (1831–86), a figure renowned for his vehement attacks against indigenous peoples.[10] In one congressional session on the "Pacification of Araucanía" in the late 1860s, he pronounced, "Enough of this shame of three-hundred years! Let us stop being the play toy of the whims and the lance of the barbarian. We must rip the poisonous arrow of their savage revenge out of the heart of the Republic. . . . [Let there be] no more frontiers, no more of the Araucanian question, no more barbarism!"[11] For Vicuña Mackenna the Mapuche, who had once been proclaimed the founding fathers of the Chilean nation (having heroically resisted Spanish colonialism for centuries), were now distinctly "other" to *chilenidad*: "The ravaged face, a sign of the barbarism and ferocity of the Araucanian, denounces the real capacity of a race that forms no part of the Chilean people."[12]

Fifteen years later, during debates about the construction of railroads in the south, congressman Novoa called for the eradication of "this stain on our nationality, known as the Araucanian frontier, a stain which no other nation in the world suffers. . . . We are talking about our territorial integrity which today is interrupted, broken by barbarism."[13] Once Chilean troops had definitively subdued Araucanía in 1883, President Domingo Santa María, subscribing to a slightly less violent version of the civilization versus barbarism narrative, declared that "the inhabitants of those territories . . . have given themselves up . . . trusting in the civilizing protection of our laws."[14] (In contrast to official depictions of Roca's conquest of the "desert" in Argentina, the Chilean state preferred to sideline its use of military force, underscoring the ways in which the conquered would benefit from their incorporation into national society).

The colonization of Mapuche territory was thus justified as a "civilizing" mission. The occupation of Peruvian and Bolivian territory was presented in a similar manner; as noted by Silke Stab and Kristen Hill Maher, state authorities liked to emphasize the discipline, virility, and whiteness of the

"Chilean race" in opposition to the disorderly and backward Indians of Peru and Bolivia.[15] This often meant denying the existence of Chile's Mapuche population altogether (claiming they had been assimilated or eliminated) or, like Vicuña Mackenna, neatly separating Mapuche and Chilean identities.

There is little doubt that state authorities promoted such a national self-image, but my research suggests that this was not the only definition of Chilean nationality to be developed during the War the Pacific. As will be shown below, some writers and newspaper editors actually asserted the Indian-ness of the Chilean "race" by drawing on the heroic legacy of sixteenth-century Mapuche warriors. Moreover, sometimes such pride in Chile's indigenous past led to their implicit recognition of the country's indigenous present, and—despite the conflict in the south—this allowed some space for Mapuche people to assert themselves as loyal citizens of the Chilean nation.

Explaining Chile's Victory

Many foreign observers at the time saw Chile as a superior military force to both Peru and Bolivia, and attributed such superiority to the country's distinctive racial ingredients. They highlighted the deep internal divides afflicting Bolivia and Peru, claiming that Indians made up the majority of the population and that, as disaffected, marginalized peasants, they showed no loyalty to their nation-states. Chile, in contrast, was understood to have a strong sense of national identity because it did not suffer such divides; its indigenous population had been successfully incorporated through a process of *mestizaje* that dated back to colonial times. Shortly after Chile had occupied Lima, British geographer Sir Clements Markham commented that "the Chilean lower orders are descendents of half-castes; all speak Spanish and they have lost all tradition of their Indian ancestry. They make good fighting machines."[16] Predicting Chilean victory in the early stages of the war, Parisian newspaper *XIX Siècle* stressed the lamentable ethnic diversity of Bolivia and Peru compared to Chilean society, which was "completely white," run by an "intelligent oligarchy," and had experienced a "normal and rapid development."[17] *La Nación* of Montevideo was equally confident of Chile's success, claiming it was "a homogenous people, without classes or castes."[18]

Until recently, scholarship on the war largely reinforced the significance of the racial factor.[19] Some studies acknowledged Chile's indigenous ancestry but even in doing so managed to set the country apart from Peru and

Bolivia. U.S. historian Herbert Millington pointed out "the marked difference in character between the Indians whom the Spanish colonists found in Peru and Bolivia and those whom their kinsfolk and other Europeans found in Chile." In the former, he said, "the Indians were quickly and completely conquered" while in Chile "the colonists encountered one of the most formidable tribes of the New World. They refused to be conquered and it was not until after the War of the Pacific that their territory was incorporated into Chile."[20]

Revisionist Historiographies

Since the 1980s several scholars have challenged the narrative of Chile's victorious military campaign. Renowned Chileanist William Sater has raised two key arguments against it. In *The Grand Illusion* (1999), co-authored with Holger Herwig, he claimed that Chile won the War of the Pacific not because its military was good but because its adversaries were not.[21] In his earlier work *Chile and the War of the Pacific* (1986) we read of an ill-prepared Chilean army that found it difficult to recruit the necessary troops, an inadequate national infrastructure (in terms of hospitals and medical teams), and exhausted fiscal resources.[22] Sater's second major contention was that nineteenth-century Chile was far from a unified country; the idea that its citizens had a highly developed sense of national identity was, he said, "simply without foundation."[23] Sater did not specifically engage with Chile's ethnic diversity but did emphasize that "most of its rural populace had little notion that they lived in a country called Chile."[24] Overall his point is both valid and important, yet in the case of Araucanía I argue that many people were in fact aware of this "country called Chile" because they had recently been or were in the process of being incorporated into it by military force.

The most significant revisionist work on Peru is that of Florencia Mallon (1987, 1995). According to her narrative, indigenous peasants made up the backbone of the resistance campaign in Junín, in the central highlands, while many landowners there collaborated with the Chilean troops in order to keep their property.[25] They were more afraid of the (mobilized and increasingly autonomous) peasants than they were of the invaders.[26] Peasants in Cajamarca, in the northern highlands, also took up arms against Chile but here they joined with the landowning elite "in defence of a common interest they termed Peruvian."[27]

As noted by Bonilla, it is unclear whether the national bonds that Mallon discussed extended to other fractions of the peasantry in other parts of

Peru.[28] Yet even if the emergent peasant nationalism was limited to specific regions with unique characteristics, Mallon's findings made an important contribution to a more nuanced understanding of nationalism and nation formation in Latin America. We can trace important parallels between the experience of indigenous peasants in Peru during the War of the Pacific, as told by Mallon, and that of Mapuche people in Araucanía. Appelbaum's work on Colombia also provides a useful way of thinking about the relationship between (racialized) regional and national identities, and indigenous participation in regional and national politics. To be sure, there are sharp discontinuities between the Chilean, Peruvian, and Colombian experiences, but the fact that we can also detect some similarities allows us to question the consensus that Chile is an exception to the history of ethnic conflict in Latin America.

War, Racialized Regional Identities, and Indigenous Agency

Despite "three centuries of colonial rule and fifty years of republican domination," Mallon claimed that peasants of the Mantaro and Yanamarca valleys "had developed a viable and relatively autonomous form of household economy, village culture and communal politics."[29] This did not mean to say that peasant communities were isolated from Peru's commercial economy; they actively participated in it but on their own terms. The same could be said of Mapuche communities of Araucanía: prior to state occupation (1860–83) they maintained control over their resources, developed their own cultural practices, and followed the rules established by their own political authorities. Yet they were also an important part of frontier society: they communicated and negotiated with creoles/Chileans, selling local produce to them and buying other products from them.[30]

Mallon underscored the significance of regional class conflict in nineteenth-century Peru. She contended that peasants of the central highlands developed "nationalist" sentiments not despite this conflict but rather as a result of it: by fighting for the Peruvian "nation," against the Chilean invaders, they were protecting their own lands and trying to improve their position vis-à-vis local elites. My research shows that many Mapuche people of Araucanía decided to fight on behalf of Chile in the War of the Pacific. Such actions could be understood as an illustration of their desire to be recognized as part of the Chilean national community, but it could also be that—like the indigenous population of the Peruvian highlands—they saw such collaboration as a way of defending their own (family's, community's) interests or as a way of raising their stakes in their own regional conflict (i.e., the state occupation of Araucanía).

Appelbaum's *Muddied Waters* (2003) revealed how strong regional identities helped to undermine the power of the central state in Colombia during the period 1846–1948. Peru had (and still has) similar problems. In contrast, government authorities in Santiago de Chile managed to establish effective control over the entire national territory relatively soon after independence—apart from Araucanía, of course, where state presence was far from strong, even in the areas officially incorporated into the Chilean nation.

Appelbaum's study also demonstrated that certain regions in Colombia were seen as less Indian or less black and therefore more progressive than other regions. It detailed the case of Cauca, where elites sought to encourage immigration from "whiter" Antioquia in a bid to improve the local population. In a similar fashion, Chilean governments sought to improve the southern regions by promoting European (particularly German) colonization of the land. In official discourse, the frontier region of Araucanía was coupled with "Indian-ness" and, hence, backwardness, savagery, and danger. But it was also associated with the noble Araucanian warrior of old, who so valiantly fought against Spanish colonialism. Furthermore, the frontier, with its dangers and conflicts, was associated with virility, and such images proved particularly useful during the War of the Pacific.

According to Appelbaum, indigenous people were always active participants in Colombian national and regional politics. They were able to make demands of the different political parties and regional governments because the latter often needed their electoral or military support. Her point was not to deny the reality of power relations but rather to look at how marginalized peoples sought to negotiate these. For example, she explained that some indigenous leaders supported the state's land privatization laws if they felt they could profit from them; they cast themselves as key players in the scheme "in order to promote their own collective and individual interests."[31] Again we see a clear link with the Mapuche people of Araucanía. Despite a strong sense of a common ethnic identity, which Appelbaum does not detect in Colombia,[32] some Mapuche leaders decided to collaborate with the Chilean state; like the *indígenas* of Colombia, they presented themselves as active participants in the state's "national" project if they felt it could serve their own purposes.

Living the War of the Pacific in Araucanía

Chilean scholar José Bengoa has claimed that, once local troops had been sent north in 1879, the frontier zone was left with only "a few lowly army officers" and "some artillery-men to protect the new forts," which had been established during military advances into Araucanía. According to Bengoa, the absence of troops meant the frontier was "exposed to colonists and all types of private interests eager to increase their booty, at the expense of *los indígenas*."[33] Yet one could reasonably argue that when army officers were present, they not only failed to protect the Mapuche but also gravely mistreated them. In May 1884, shortly after the War of the Pacific had finished, the governor of Toltén accused troops stationed in the region of committing unnecessary violent acts against local indigenous people.[34] A month later, the governor of Lebu appealed to the authorities in Santiago to keep local military commanders under control, insisting that they could not and should not administer their own justice. He complained that the "abuses committed by the [military] authorities" threatened the "tranquility of the province and the complete submission of the indigenous population" (intimating that if pushed much further, the Indians were likely to rebel again). By requesting that the government confirm civil, as opposed to military control of the occupied territory, the letter also testified to a certain amount of confusion over who was in charge in the region.[35]

Details about the abuse of Mapuche people (either by colonists or by military troops) do not tell the whole story, however. In 1881 the minister of war reported on government efforts to proceed with the occupation of Araucanía and pledged to increase the number of troops stationed along the southern frontier. Such developments were explained as a response to Mapuche "hostilities" in the area. "Towards the end of last year," the report said, "the Indians, knowing that there were few troops stationed along the frontier, began to commit acts of banditry against the towns; they were repressed by the military reinforcements that arrived shortly afterwards."[36] It also warned congressmen that communications between the Indians of Chile and their compatriots across the Andes in Argentina had greatly increased. To the minister's mind, such communications suggested possible joint rebel action and therefore had to be stopped.[37] The issue of Mapuche violence was often raised in congress, and newspapers in the south made claims that local populations were being terrorized by their Mapuche neighbors. As early as November 1879, *La Araucanía Civilizada* (Mulchen) printed a letter from a resident of Collipulli who declared that life was becoming unbearable "due to the fear of living next to the indomitable Araucanians."[38] The Mapuche were not mere victims, then; indeed, some groups exploited the situation (especially the lack of troops) to try to reclaim their ancestral territory.

There is also another version of events to consider. Several local newspapers openly rejected the fearful image of savage Mapuche Indians invading the towns that had already been "civilized." They told readers that reports of Indian uprisings and rebellions were mere rumor and gossip.[39] Indeed, they often portrayed the *indios* as upstanding citizens of frontier society who were peacefully getting on with their daily chores such as selling their produce in local markets.[40] Not only that, in the "pacified" towns some Mapuche people joined the newly created civic brigades, which, in the absence of the regular army contingent, did their best to defend the frontier line against rebel attacks.[41]

Thus, in contrast to traditional historiography, which allocates the Mapuche only one-dimensional historical agency (if it allocates them any at all) we see a far more complex picture emerge, with the indigenous inhabitants of Araucanía taking on a variety of different roles during this period.

The Press: Images of Araucanía's Legendary Warriors

Local Chilean newspapers often portrayed the Mapuche as an important part of contemporary frontier society; they also drew on this people's heroic military past (their successful resistance against the Spanish) to inspire a whole nation as it faced the realities of war. On July 24, 1879 *El Araucano* (Lebu) included a poem by Arturo Segundo Cariaga called "Glory to our Heroes": "Chile, if today they want/ those perfidious tyrants/ with rifles and canons/ to destroy us/ We will prove to these infamous Peruvians/ that there still boils in our veins/ the noble blood of brave Araucanians." National newspapers were also keen to extol Chile's indigenous roots. On April 2, 1879, the Valparaíso daily *El Mercurio* published a short piece titled "To War We Go!" Peru, it admitted, had "the advantage of pre-planning [this war], but we have that of valour, that of the irresistible force of our soldiers, in whose veins flows the fiery blood of the Spaniard mixed with the volcanic lava of Arauco." It persisted in its praise of Araucanian bravery: "Pizarro beheaded thousands of Atahualpa's Indians in Lima's main square as if they were sheep; Valdivia could not manage to kill a single Araucanian without being punished for it. The former were less than women, the latter much more than men, they were titanic patriots."[42] Far from promoting the "whiteness" of the Chilean army, *El Araucano* and *El Mercurio* drew on the nation's indigenous roots to assert its military strength. In glorifying Chile's indigenous past, they also defended it, keen to narrate a collective history shared by Chileans and Mapuche. Notably, political and military elites also appropriated the symbol of the indomitable Araucanian warrior: warships were named after the legendary heroes Caupolicán and Colo-Colo, and two of the battalions that were crucial to Chilean victory in the battles of Miraflores and Chorrillos were baptized Caupolicán and Lautaro. The commander of the latter once wrote to his superiors lauding the bravery of his troops, who had "honoured the memory of our Araucanian hero" on the battlefields of Peru.[43]

The press in Peru and Bolivia frequently noted the "Indian-ness" of the Chilean army, although the motive for doing so was very different. Two poems that were published in Peruvian newspapers in 1879 are particularly worthy of analysis. The first, "War on Chile!" by Emiliano Niño, read: "Peruvians, have you heard?/ War has been declared/ by the fatherland which gave birth to Caupolicán/ And, we, the glorious Inca race/ . . . have answered back."[44] Countering claims that the Peruvian army was "more Indian" and therefore less disciplined than the army of Chile, the poet presented the military conflict as one between two equally indigenous nations. Caupolicán also appeared in J. V. Camacho's poem "To Chile": "Where are you headed proud Araucanians?/ Where are you going to?/ Glory is not [found] on unprotected beaches/ March to Santa Cruz/ . . . / Imitate the courage and bravery/ of the great Caupolicán/ . . . You no longer search for honour/ Chilean Falange/ [you search for] guano, copper, nitrate/ for foreign riches."[45] Camacho makes Araucanian synonymous with Chilean, but there is little glory left: in fighting the war as it did, Chile had betrayed the memory of "the great Caupolicán" (a symbol of heroic resistance throughout Latin America).

During the first year of the conflict, Santiago's *El Ferrocarril* reproduced several articles from the Bolivian newspaper *El Comercio*, one of which was titled "Long Live Bolivia! Long Live Peru! Death to Chile!" (March 20, 1879). This began by denouncing "the Araucanian cowards" whose "daggers have ripped through our beautiful flag" and who committed "the most infamous crimes on the blessed soil of the fatherland." Two weeks later, on April 3, 1879, it printed another report that compared the honor and self-sacrifice of the Bolivian military officials to the barbaric Chileans, claiming that the former had agreed to forego their extra rations so the regular troops would be given more to eat. This was, the author proclaimed, "a noble example of the Bolivian soldier, who—in sacrificing his own necessities—knows how to do his duty." He then asked, "And the Araucanian army, that horde of savages, will it imitate the noble behaviour of our brave men?"[46] Again, Araucanian and Chilean were used interchangeably, but on both occasions the Araucanians were imaged as unscrupulous savages; Bolivians had become the noble warriors.

Mapuche Participation in the War of the Pacific

Given that the Chilean state was in the process of occupying their lands, one might presume that the only way Mapuche people would have fought on behalf of Chile against Peru and Bolivia would have been through forced conscription. It was certainly possible that a Mapuche person could end up in an army regiment against his will. The minister of war fervently denied that any such thing could possibly happen in Chile, reiterating time and again that it was illegal, but many congressmen complained that their constituents were being press-ganged into military service during the early 1880s.

This was not always the case, however. Many Mapuche signed up for duty voluntarily. In June 1879, *El Araucano* of Lebu communicated the news that the previous Sunday, "when we were least expecting it, chief Nanco came to visit us accompanied by most of his *mocetones*. He left the group camped out on the main thoroughfare and made off to the barracks . . . where an incredibly long meeting was held [with army officials]. It was not difficult to verify the reason behind such an unexpected visit: they came to offer their services to the government and to ask for arms in order to prepare for war."[47]

Later that year the same newspaper published a particularly revealing series of articles on the movements of the Arauco Battalion. On November 13, 1879, reporting on the large number of people who had turned out to bid farewell to the troops, it said: "What a beautiful spectacle! The chords of the national anthem were accompanied by loud shouts of 'hurrah!,' which revealed the immense and never doubted enthusiasm and patriotism of the sons of Lautaro." It then exclaimed: "Onwards sons of Lautaro!" This gushing pride in the troops' indigenous heritage was, however, questioned—or rather openly denied—on November 20:

> *El Correo de Quillota*, which was covering the [movements of the] Arauco Battalion, says that it is made up almost entirely of indigenous

people. It has made a great mistake. Special care was taken not to admit one single indigenous person into the battalion; at least we can be sure of this for the two sections that were formed in this town and we believe Cañete and Arauco followed the same procedure. This is not because indigenous people are bad soldiers or because they are unwilling to serve the Chilean government, but rather because there was no need to accept the indomitable and uncultured sons of Caupolicán. The civilized population of Arauco province has enough people to send not only one but two regiments of brave and selfless defenders of the fatherland to the battlefields.

Within two weeks the description of the battalion's soldiers had changed again. On December 4, 1879, the newspaper informed readers that the Arauco Battalion, with nine hundred men—"a beautiful group of young, robust, mighty men"—had just arrived in Santiago. It was undoubtedly true, it said, "that in the battalion are many truly American types, whose features reveal the indomitable arrogance of the pure race of this land." More praise of the troops was to come: "they were legitimate descendants of Caupolicán and Lautaro, who marched [northward] to support their native fatherland which they had so heroically defended in bygone times." *El Araucano* thereby presented contesting images of the local army contingent, depending on the (positive or negative) remarks made by others regarding the Indian-ness of the troops.

The indigenous identity of Chilean troops was not merely an image or an idea. Official military records—a list of the men who fought in the famous battles of Chorrillos (January 13, 1881) and Miraflores (January 15, 1881), and the registers for different regiments during the period 1879–81 (Chillán, Lautaro, Victoria, the Carabineros of Yungai, the "Third in Line," and the Zapadores)—include many Mapuche names: Huentupil, Catrihual, Pailapán, Paillamilla, Maripán, Calquin. Most of them were rank-and-file soldiers, but some, such as Horacio Huentupil, rose to the position of sergeant. Several Mapuche were awarded medals for their brave conduct in these two major battles.[48] The military authorities thus recognized and praised their efforts to defend the Chilean nation at the same time that congressmen denounced the barbarism of their compatriots in Araucanía.

Newspapers from the southern region, which reported on local people who had died or been injured in battle, provide more evidence about the Mapuche people who enrolled in Chile's army brigades. On June 12, 1880, *El Araucano* (Lebu) included sublieutenant Milleo, of the Second Artillery

Regiment, in the list of wounded officials. (The paper paid tribute to them all as heroes of the "patria.") Finally, we have the testimonies provided by Mapuche soldiers themselves. These are rare, but they are nevertheless invaluable sources of information. *Las últimas familias*, compiled by Tomás Guevara and Manuel Mañkelef (1912), includes the testimony of Lorenzo Kolümañ.[49] As son of a Mapuche cacique who had been an *indio amigo* (Indian friend) of the Chilean government, Kolümañ was sent under the care of Gen. Cornelio Saavedra to receive an education in Santiago. (Chilean authorities frequently demanded that Mapuche leaders send one of their children to a Chilean school as proof of their loyalty to the government.[50]) Kolümañ later recalled that, after three years in Santiago, he had become rather bored: "At the time, Chile was at war with Peru. I presented myself to the General and asked for his permission to go and fight in the north." He was put forward as sergeant of the Aconcagua regiment. He remembered having "fought in the mountains, where I met many Peruvian Indians. My superiors ordered me to speak with them, but I couldn't understand a single word." His Indian identity was deemed useful but completely misunderstood.

Even if they did not engage in active combat, Mapuche people—like Chileans—found other ways to contribute to the war effort. On August 23, 1879, *El Araucano* of Lebu published a list of those who had donated funds to help acquire another *Esmeralda* (the warship that was destroyed in the Battle of Iquique). Out of a list of fifteen people, two were Mapuche: Don Pedro Millaleo and Don Juan Quilamán; they both gave twenty pesos, which was a significant amount of money at the time. According to the newspaper, the people of Arauco thus offered proof of their "burning patriotism."

Overall, my research provides information on approximately sixty individually named Mapuche men who fought in the War of the Pacific. This is a modest number. However, it is reasonable to assume that the actual number was much larger than this, and that others could be identified through further archival research. First, only the first surname was printed on the official military lists; in many cases, a soldier's Mapuche identity may only have been detectable in the second surname. Second, Mapuche people were often illiterate, and the officials responsible for registering them tended spell their names as they sounded, so again their Mapuche identity might go unnoticed.[51] And third, as I have shown, several Chilean newspapers commented on the Indian-ness of the army recruits.

Explaining Mapuche Participation

Why would a Mapuche person choose to fight for a Chilean army that was simultaneously engaged in a campaign against his own people? Interestingly, it is precisely this campaign—the state occupation of Araucanía—that helps to answer the question. Chilean governments have traditionally depicted the invasion and conquest of Mapuche territory as a peaceful, unproblematic event. In his opening speech to Congress in 1883 (referenced earlier in this chapter), President Domingo Santa María asserted that it had been achieved "without resorting to armed conflict or inflicting any harm" on the Araucanians.[52] One of Chile's most prominent historians, Sergio Villalobos, has also promoted this version of events, claiming that there was more drinking and dancing than fighting to be seen in Araucanía.[53] Since the 1980s, however, many scholars have contested such narratives. In his landmark book *Historia del Pueblo Mapuche* (1985), José Bengoa described the campaigns as genocide, underscored the atrocities committed by the Chilean army, and detailed the "great insurrection" of 1881 against Chilean occupation in which, he said, "practically all Mapuche groups participated."[54]

A third story challenging and complicating these counterposed accounts can be found in the testimonies of Mapuche people who lived through the occupation campaigns. According to Pascual Coña, there was indeed much violence and Chileans did commit atrocities, but he also recalled some brutal acts committed by Mapuche people.[55] More important, he claimed that not all Mapuche had resisted Chilean occupation. Rather, he remembered how he and many others had sided with the Chilean army and thus fought against their own people.[56] Such collaboration is borne out in other firsthand accounts (collected by Guevara and Mañkelef) and in official correspondence documenting the number of Mapuche being paid for "services" rendered to the government during this period. These "services" included trying to prevent Mapuche communities from rebelling or informing the authorities of any forthcoming rebellion, should its prevention be impossible.[57]

While still proclaiming their Mapuche identity, some leaders favored incorporation into the "civilized" Chilean nation, if the government promised that this would be advantageous to them and their families. (In many cases they did not decide immediately but hedged their bets, waiting to see which side looked the most likely victor.[58]) In his memoirs, Coña recounted how a fellow Mapuche leader Pascual Painemilla went to Santiago after the occupation campaigns to meet with President Santa María and request compensation for his collaboration.[59] Painemilla came away empty-handed, but he thought it was worth going to Argentina, where President Julio Roca, who had recently "conquered" his own indigenous population, provided him and his family with land.[60] Another Mapuche leader, Domingo Paynefilu, was more fortunate: he visited Santa María to tell him of the impending rebellion against occupation in 1881 and was given some new horses in return.[61]

In Lorenzo Kolümañ's case, it seems he went to fight in Peru because he wanted some excitement. (He was proud to recount later that while he had not been very good at marching, he had proved his manliness by coping well with the hunger and thirst.[62]) Yet, his account also suggests that he felt a personal loyalty and duty to General Saavedra, who—it should be noted—arranged a posting for Kolümañ when he returned from the war. Kolümañ, like Paynefilu, benefited, or at least felt he was benefiting, from being an *indio amigo*. Congress debates, which provide evidence of the numerous petitions made by Mapuche people to the authorities in Santiago during the same period, add weight to this explanation for Mapuche collaboration: as a way of justifying their demands, the petitioners stressed how loyal they had been the government.[63] Finally, as we read in the testimonies put together by Guevara and Mañkelef, Mapuche *caciques* who sided with the government were often given arms and other military support to help them assert their own authority in the region (i.e., to eliminate or at least subdue their adversaries within the Mapuche community).[64] They could use their loyalty to at least try to secure titles to their lands (once these were under the jurisdiction of the Chilean state), or they could emphasize their allegiance to place themselves in a better position than that of their rivals. So there were both economic and political motives for siding with the Chilean state.

Conclusion

Mapuche participation in Chilean wars was by no means a new phenomenon in the 1880s. Juan Lorenzo Colipí (1818–39), son of the infamous Juan Colipí who fought with the *patriotas* against the Spanish during the wars of independence, has been officially hailed as one of Chile's war heroes.[65] He registered as a soldier in the Valdivia Battalion when he was only seventeen years old, rose quickly through the ranks, and was praised for his bravery during the war against the Peru-Bolivia Confederation in the 1830s. He was promoted to captain after fighting in the Battle of Yungay and died in Santiago in 1839 when he was only twenty-one years old. On an official trip to Concepción shortly after, General Bulnes presented Colipí senior with a medal in honor of his son's bravery; the Mapuche leader merely replied, "but why such a commotion, did you not know he was a son of mine?"[66]

This tale exemplifies a history of Mapuche collaboration and negotiation with Chilean governments. It coexists alongside a history of resistance and confrontation. Mapuche people responded in different ways to the independence wars, just as they did to the occupation campaigns and the War of the Pacific. One could argue that Mapuche willingness to fight on Chile's side against Peru and Bolivia illustrates their successful incorporation into a racially homogenous Chilean nation. Yet many Mapuche also took advantage of the chaos caused by the War of the Pacific to defend their independence and reclaim their ancestral lands. Moreover, even those who did fight on Chile's side did not necessarily reject their "Mapuche-ness": many proclaimed their distinctive ethnic identity and demanded recompense as a member of a community who was hiring out their services to the Chilean state rather than someone who had a duty to serve that state.

In conclusion, the evidence shows that the Mapuche people were not entirely subsumed or assimilated within the Chilean nation, and that there were multiple imaginings of this nation during the late nineteenth century. Mapuche people were often treated appallingly by the Chilean government and armed forces. Thousands of Mapuche were killed or robbed of their land during the nineteenth century. But because they had shown a willingness to fight on Chile's side, and because the state could make great use of their heroic military past, a space—albeit a very limited one—was opened up for the Mapuche within the Chilean nation. Their alternative plural vision of nation could be voiced, even if it was not always accepted. As noted by Appelbaum, "effective colonizing has historically involved the participation of the colonized, who have simultaneously resisted and adapted to colonization, thus shaping the different colonial systems that resulted."[67] This is not a new argument for scholars working on colonialism in Latin America, but it has rarely been applied to the republican state's colonization of the Mapuche. Once we do this, the notion of Chilean ethnic "exceptionalism" becomes highly questionable and we begin to understand the complex, multiple roles played by the Mapuche in both the physical and discursive construction of the Chilean nation.

Notes

1. Mapuche people are often referred to as Araucanians, a term invented by the Spanish. Historically, many Mapuche called themselves *araucanos*, but today this term has been largely rejected by those who self-identify as Mapuche because they see it as a colonialist, racist appellation, which relegates them to the past.

2. What are now the Chilean towns of Carahue, Chol Chol, Ercilla, Freire, Galvarino, Imperial, Lautaro, Nielol, Temuco, Victoria, and Villarica were still part of Mapuche territory in 1879.

3. See for example, Brown, "Not forging nations but foraging for them"; and Guerra, *Modernidad y independencia*.

4. Mallon, "Nationalist and Anti-State Coalitions," 232–79; and Mallon, *Peasant and Nation*; and Appelbaum, *Muddied Waters*.

5. Sater, *Chile and the War of the Pacific*, 198.

6. In one parliamentary session, congressman Señor Novoa proclaimed that "the question of Arauco is the most important problem facing the country. It is more important than Tarapacá [the province of Atacama]. For, what is the question of Tarapacá? [It means] nothing more than extending our northern territory by a few miles of desert, to protect us from future attacks by Peru, while the definitive incorporation of Araucanía into the Republic marks the end of the shameful offence of the Araucanians, who for centuries controlled our richest provinces in the south." He concluded, "how on earth can you not see that Araucanía is worth far more than Tarapacá?" Gobierno de Chile, *Archivo Sesiones del Congreso Nacional* (1882), 269. Unless otherwise stated, all translations are my own.

7. *Memoria del Ministro de Guerra*, 1881.

8. *Memoria del Ministro de Guerra*, 1882, xxx.

9. Pinto, *De la inclusión a la exclusión*; Herrera,"La cuestión de Arauco"; and Bengoa, *Historia del Pueblo Mapuche*.

10. Rebecca Earle makes several references to Vicuña Mackenna's writings in her excellent study *The Return of the Native*; she rightly notes that his attacks against the Mapuche, or at least the conquest-era Mapuche, became less vehement once Chile had completed its occupation of Araucanía.

11. Cited in Herrera "La cuestión de Arauco," 75.

12. Vicuña Mackenna, "Cuarto discurso sobre."

13. Gobierno de Chile, *Archivo Sesiones del Congreso Nacional* (1882), 269.

14. Domingo Santa María, Inaugural speech to Congress in 1883, 13.

15. Stab and Maher, "Dual Discourse," 87–116. See also Larraín, *La identidad chilena*, 265.

16. Markham, *War between Peru and Chile*, 97.

17. The article was reproduced in full in the *Boletín de la Guerra del Pacífico*, August 6, 1879.

18. Cited in the *Boletín de la Guerra del Pacífico*, September 30, 1879.

19. See Burr, *By Reason or Force*, 143; Nunn, *Military in Chilean History*; and Bonilla, " War of the Pacific," 92.

20. Millington, *American Diplomacy*, 10–11.

21. Sater and Herwig, *Grand Illusion*, 31.

22. Sater, *Chile and the War of the Pacific*, 3.

23. Ibid., 77.

24. In a more recent monograph, Sater acknowledged that the "whiteness" of Chilean society caused some debate during the nineteenth century, but he provided very little detail on this debate. See Sater, *Andean Tragedy*, 13. See also Sater, *Chile and the War of the Pacific*, 77.

25. Mallon, "Nationalist and Anti-State Coalitions," 233.

26. Ibid., 244.

27. Ibid., 234.

28. Bonilla, "The Indian Peasantry."

29. Mallon, "Nationalist and Anti-State Coalitions," 238.

30. Key works on frontier society in southern Chile include Villalobos et al., *Relaciones fronterizas en la Araucanía*; Villalobos, *Los pehuenches en la vida fronteriza*; and Pinto, *Misioneros en la Araucanía, 1600–1900*.

31. Appelbaum, *Muddied Waters*, 89.

32. She claimed that indigenous people negotiated and fought on behalf of "their parcialidad, their district, and their partisan political faction—rather than on behalf of any transcendent ethnic identity"; ibid., 103. That many people in Araucanía self-identified as Mapuche has been well documented by secondary sources and Mapuche testimonies. See for example, Bengoa, *Historia del pueblo Mapuche*; Coña, *Memorias de un cacique Mapuche*; and Guevara and Mañkelef, *Historias de familias*.

33. Bengoa, *Historia del pueblo Mapuche*, 271.

34. Archivo Nacional, *Correspondencia de Arauco, 1883–1887*, letter dated May 26, 1884.

35. Ibid., letter from Lebu dated June 9, 1884.

36. *Memoria del Ministro de Guerra* (1881), 78.

37. Ibid., 80.

38. *La Araucanía Civilizada* (Mulchen), November 2, 1879, quoting a letter from Collipulli dated October 29, 1879.

39. *El Araucano* (Lebu) January 31, 1880, and February 14, 1880.

40. *La Araucanía Civilizada* (Mulchen), March 25, 1879; and *El Nuble* (Chillán), April 5, 1879.

41. The name Lorenzo Paillao, for example, appeared several times in the registers for the Escuadrón de Caballería Cívica de Cañete. Comandancia General de Armas, *Correspondencia con Arauco* (1877–1879).

42. Cited in Ahumada, ed., *La Guerra del Pacífico*, 208–9.

43. Letter from Eulogio Robles to commander-in-chief of the 4th Division, dated May 30, 1880, printed in the *Boletín de la Guerra del Pacífico*, July 9, 1880.

44. Cited, with the date of April 6, 1879, in Ahumada, ed., *La Guerra del Pacífico*, 201.

45. Ibid., 285.

46. This was taken from *El Comercio* (La Paz), March 19, 1879.

47. Quoted in Aravena Carrasco, *Chilenos a la Guerra*, 40.

48. Archivo General del Ejército, *Lista de Revista* (1879–1881), and *Relación Nominal Batallones de Chorrillos y Miraflores* (1881).

49. This book has recently been republished as Guevara and Mañkelef, *Historias de familias* (2002). Kolümañ's memories of the war can be found on p. 45.

50. Bengoa, *Historia del pueblo Mapuche*, 386.

51. I am very grateful to the staff of the Department of Military History (Edificio de las Fuerzas Armadas, Santiago) for pointing this out to me.

52. Kew Public Records Office, "Señor Excelencia el Presidente de la República de Chile en la apertura del Congreso Nacional de 1883," FO 16/223 (1883).

53. Villalobos, *Historia del pueblo Chileno.*

54. Bengoa, *Historia del pueblo Mapuche*, 285.

55. Coña relayed the horrific tale, passed on to him from others, of cacique Marimán ripping out the hearts out of captured Chileans while they were still alive. See Coña, *Memorias de un cacique Mapuche*, 275.

56. Ibid.

57. In a letter dated August 12, 1882, the governor of Toltén complained to the central government that payments to Mapuche leaders Neculman, Coñoepán, Manquehuir, and Curihuentro had been delayed. He urged that this be rectified immediately, given the important role being played by these men in the "pacification" of Araucanía. Archivo Regional de la Araucanía, *Libro registro de comunicaciones enviados por el Gobernador de la zona entre el Imperial y el Toltén* (1882).

58. According to Coña's account, this was the case for Painén and Quilempán. See Coña, *Memorias*, 278.

59. Ibid., 290.

60. Ibid., 315.

61. See Guevara and Mañkelef, *Historias de familias*, 119.

62. Ibid., 45.

63. In the Chamber of Deputies on November 30, 1881, congressman Rodríguez don Zorobabel made a request on behalf of two Mapuche, Luis Marileo and Juan Colipí, who argued that the expropriation of indigenous lands should not be able to proceed without the approval of congress; they also asked that the lands expropriated not include theirs because they had always supported the government.

64. See especially the testimonies of Lorenzo Kolümañ and Juan Kallfukura.

65. Estado Mayor General del Ejército, *Galería de Hombres* and *www.ejercito.cl/historia/heroes.php.*

66. Estado Mayor General del Ejército, *Galería de Hombres de Armas de Chile.*

67. Appelbaum, *Muddied Waters*, 13.

12

Racial Conflict and Identity Crisis in Wartime Peru

Revisiting the Cañete Massacre of 1881

VINCENT C. PELOSO

This chapter subjects the historiography and evidence of the massacre of Chinese immigrants in the Cañete valley by Afro-Peruvian peasants, led by women during the War of the Pacific, to critical analysis in light of recent discussions of the nexus of race, culture, and nation. It validates the motives of the peasants who carried out the massacre by examining the event as an aspect of racial and cultural identity formation. The study highlights the self-serving character of contemporary evaluations, and it gives attention to the cultural tensions and ambiguous meanings present in the massacre, which illustrate the character of national identity projects in late nineteenth-century Peru.

Early in the War of the Pacific (1879–84), the calm imposed by the Chilean occupation of Peru was disrupted by a massacre. The massacre occurred in the Cañete valley south of Lima and was unusual in several respects: sparked by Ash Wednesday holiday festivities, it featured the slaughter of more than a thousand Chinese men by a mob led by women; it continued for several months without intervention and went unreported by witnesses; it was ignored after the war and went unregistered in Peruvian sources for a decade thereafter. The event was overlooked until the 1970s, when modern theories of nation formation stimulated further questions and debate. Together with the publication of Chilean wartime correspondence, fresh perspectives reshaped Peruvian historiography, offering clues that further advanced analysis of the "national question."[1] Without directly addressing the affair, the new historiography suggested further possibilities. This essay revisits the Cañete Massacre of 1881. It examines the variations in past explanations and offers a fresh interpretation of the event in light of recent discussion of questions of cultural and national identity in late nineteenth-century Peru.[2] Above all, it examines available evidence more closely than heretofore in a search for the weight of race and identity in nineteenth-century Peruvian culture as reflected in the actions of the women who led the attacks upon the Chinese men.

Some attention has been devoted to each of the participant populations in the massacre, but the social fabric that wove them together prior to the War of the Pacific is not well known and deserves summary at this point. At the outbreak of war, antagonisms between the Chinese and the Afro-Peruvians had increased considerably. In the Cañete valley, about fifty miles south of the capital where commercial sugar and cotton plantations were dominant, peasants of African descent—former slaves and descendants of slaves—made up the vast majority of the impoverished, landless coastal peasantry along with fellow peasant cholos.[3] The women and children harvested cotton for part-time pay, and men often worked as field security and enforcers, the first line of social contact with the Chinese field hands. The Chinese were the remnants of a large, indentured, heavily abused, all-male labor force imported (between 1849 and 1874) to work the guano islands and the cotton and sugar fields of the coastal valleys. Physical violence between the two populations became commonplace in the era of indenture, and when the indenture system ended in freedom for many of the Chinese, hostilities between them continued. The direct links between the intergroup violence and the massacre have not been closely examined.[4]

An invasion of Peru by the Chilean army provided the setting for the massacre. The invasion followed a conflict between Chile and Bolivia over unanswered claims of discrimination against Chileans in the coastal Bolivian Atacama desert. The Chile-Bolivia war astonished the Peruvians by calling into play a so-called secret treaty of mutual support signed by Bolivia and Peru in 1873 (and revealed to the Chileans almost immediately). When challenged, Peru's Prado regime refused to retract the treaty, and after Bolivia was easily swept aside in April 1879, Peru and Chile faced one another. The initial battles were fought at sea, where the two countries seemed evenly matched. But Peruvian heroics were overwhelmed by superior Chilean technical advances; within a few months, the Chileans commanded their mutual coastline. All of the remaining action took place on land in Peru. The Chilean military executed a two-pronged attack aimed at capturing Lima, dominating the peace settlement, and absorbing the Atacama mining deposits and other strategic portions of Peruvian coastal territory. Initial victories in the south propelled the Chileans northward through the coastal valleys where they easily overcame provincial garrisons. Another

Chilean force invaded by sea at the Bay of Paracas, just south of the port of Pisco. Thereafter they marched toward Lima where, at the battles of San Juan and Miraflores on January 13–15, they defeated the Peruvians and occupied the city.[5]

As they neared the city, Chilean army divisions under Patricio Lynch undertook a forced night march through the coastal desert provinces. The difficulties of the night march were multiplied by the distractions caused by Peruvian guerrillas. Although the coastal towns were poorly defended, the local guerrillas were supported by the Peruvian defense forces under Nicolás de Piérola, who was coordinating a defensive war of attrition in the Andean highlands.[6] It is not clear why the Chileans did not station a rearguard force in the important export town of Cerro Azul, where the massacre occurred, despite the repeated incursions of mounted armed guerrillas during the march northward as well as afterward. The Chileans further refused to send soldiers to Cerro Azul after the massacre, despite the pleas of the Cañete planters. That they dismissed those pleas until months afterward is a question that continues to haunt this case.[7]

The least well-understood elements of the massacre are the activities of the recently arrived Chinese field hands and those of the local peasants of African descent and *cholos* who had inhabited the coastal valleys and Lima for centuries. These were, relatively speaking, free people who worked as day laborers for brief periods at the plantations, and some privileged few held more prestigious jobs as field captains and guards. The Chileans encountered the formerly indentured Chinese when they invaded the plantations on their way north. They registered less surprise at finding them than they did at their condition. Indenture had ended formally in 1874, and they were startled to find the Chinese sickly, weak, and undernourished. Some were in plantation jails, some in chains, and a few reportedly had been in such conditions for five years. These men were freed, and the Chileans quickly incorporated the ablest and most willing of them into the invasion forces in a variety of nonmilitary capacities: nurses, undertakers, cooks, ambulance drivers, minesweepers, and the like. In effect, the Chinese were aiding the Chilean war effort against Peru, a conclusion that hostile local peasant nationals might easily draw. It would not be difficult for them to conclude that the flight of the despised Asians to the Chilean side constituted acts of disloyalty.[8] How many Chinese joined the Chileans is a question that deserves attention for its contribution to a comprehension of the magnitude and character of the massacre.

The war experience of peasant nationals contrasted sharply with the experience of the Chinese. Many men were dragooned into local militias, hastily trained, and thrown before the advancing Chileans, who defeated them with ease. Even the regular Peruvian units who finally opposed the Chileans in the fateful battles on the outskirts of Lima were composed largely of ill-trained indigenous and coastal peasant recruits.

Unquestionably demoralized by their poor treatment, many of the regulars abandoned the trenches before the advancing enemy and their Chinese allies on January 15 and fled in disarray into Lima. In the streets of the capital, armed and untrammeled by authorities, many sought vengeance for the insult of having to confront the Chinese twice, once in the battlefield and once again in the city. Given leave by the Chileans, the Chinese irregulars had sought out the local shops obviously in search of shelter and information about a return to China. Chinese merchants and shopkeepers who offered them temporary refuge suffered the consequences of their kindness. The Chinese quarter of Lima was fire damaged to a far greater extent than the rest of the city until a hastily formed urban guard and the Chilean army restored order.[9]

No doubt stunned by the distance and the cost of a return trip, needing sustenance and under attack in Lima, the Chinese veterans were faced with two unpleasant alternatives. They might try to return to Cañete where the prospect of plantation labor was possible, or they might remain in Lima in the hope of surviving the transition to an occupied peace and menial employment in a hostile environment. Which they chose and how many opted for each alternative are not clear. Although important details need to be addressed, it is not difficult to foresee the climax of the narrative. During the Ash Wednesday holiday market in Cañete, conflict between Chinese and Peruvian holiday revelers broke out in the town of Cerro Azul and quickly moved to the plantations of the surrounding countryside. Overwhelmed by the Afro-Peruvians and *cholos*, the Chinese fled to nearby partially abandoned structures, including plantation houses that they probably knew well. Plantations became killing fields. The Afro-Peruvians attacked them with stones, knives, and farm tools. The bodies of some of the men trapped in the patios of plantation houses were reportedly mutilated. The peasants' most effective weapon was to set afire the surrounding fields thick with cane where many Chinese hoped to hide, and where they now succumbed to the smoke or ran into the hands of the waiting peasants.

The death toll of five hundred to one thousand men murdered in a single day, as claimed in several sources, becomes plausible under such conditions. Only the delay by the Chileans, who refused to send a significant number of troops to Cañete until the following June, helps to explain the deaths of another five hundred to seven hundred Chinese men in the intervening months. When the Chileans finally returned in force, they apparently were met by a mixture of Peruvian guerrillas and armed peasants. Several skirmishes ensued before the Chileans regained control of the area. The return of relative calm (despite continued guerrilla activity) allowed the Chileans to then respond to a plea by Chinese merchants, escorting about two thousand of their fellow merchants and peddlers south from Cañete to Pisco, an act later inscribed in Chilean folklore.

The scenario recounted here revisits and highlights persistent questions about the massacre that have lingered for more than a century with little modification. Its foundation is flimsy: essays written long afterward and military reports based on information gathered months later, folklore, and latter-day studies that in turn rest upon the earlier claims and rumors. Several contested themes bind the sources together: the number of Chinese killed, the sources, the reasons for the delay in the Chilean response, and the motives for the attack. The sources, which sometimes vary sharply from one another, deserve closer scrutiny for what they can add to clarifying the motives of the peasant nationals. Viewed in the context of recent discussions of cultural and national identity in Peru, the seemingly outrageous killings take on a more understandable character.[10] A critique of the records is in order—first those provided by the Peruvians, then those given by the Chileans. Recent studies in turn will be linked to these sources, and together they will yield a final assessment.

The Peruvian Account

The dearth of detailed information is matched by a lack of contemporary studies of the massacre. The lone surviving account, the aforementioned essay by Juan de Arona, is flawed by self-interest and by being written in the heat of the moment. Juan de Arona (the pseudonym of Pedro Paz Solda'n y Unanue), a diplomat, writer-poet, planter, and owner of Hacienda Montalván, a large plantation in the Cañete valley whose house and fields were destroyed in the rioting, took his pen name from one of several neighboring haciendas that met a similar fate in the war. Arona was a patrician, the scion of a family with roots in colonial Peru and the grandson of Hipólito Unánue, an illustrious eighteenth-century intellectual.[11] The Ash Wednesday chaos had destroyed Arona's idyllic Cañete country home and shattered his paternalistic cultural illusions about the special bond of trust and responsibility thought to exist between planters and peasants, and his recollection of the events of Ash Wednesday is laden with bitterness and sarcasm.

In his famous essay, Arona joined numerous other authors of the era in pleading for renewal of the national immigration project despite its past failures. Like them, he linked the survival of the country's creole culture to a successful immigration campaign, but unlike them he sought to illustrate how badly the current population served the task of regenerating the national economic culture.[12] Arona argued that the presence of so many highland indigenous peasants, *cholos*, and coastal peasants of African descent ("manumisos y parásitos desde 1855") in the labor force would lead to cultural degeneration.[13] As substitutes for the locals, he liked the Asians who he said were—after the admittedly unattainable Europeans—the most desirable immigrants the creole elite might attract not to revive indentured servitude but rather to people the country with a middle sector of small merchants, shopkeepers, and restaurateurs. His observation that Asians had done well in commerce probably rested on his personal experience with the Chinese merchants who provided necessities, daily goods, and small loans near the coastal plantations. He also lauded the value of Chinese men as domestic servants, but overall his immigration ideal aimed at importing more merchants, not field hands.

Arona argued the need for people of an "ancient" civilization to replace the "uncivilized" and "brutal" blacks and *cholos* by featuring a description of the Cañete massacre in his immigration essay.[14] His account ignored the interracial rivalries (Afro-Peruvians and *cholos* versus the Chinese)—of which as a resident planter he would be acutely aware—that had emerged with the importation of the Chinese. Arona drove home the point that the lowly behavior to which the peasants sank when left to their own devices had obviated any consideration of their "race" as citizens in a broader, reinvigorated Peruvian culture.

Arona drew attention only to the Afro-Peruvians through his apocryphal declaration that the massacre was sparked by a chance confrontation in the Cerro Azul marketplace between a Chinese man and an Afro-Peruvian market woman, his observations that the Afro-Peruvian women eagerly mutilated their Chinese victims and that the Afro-Peruvian peasants attacked the Chinese primitively in "a thousand ways," and his claim that the Afro-Peruvians torched plantation houses and cane fields in pursuit of the Chinese. He mentioned in passing that at the end of that deadly day about one thousand Chinese field workers fortified themselves in the plantation buildings of Hacienda Casablanca and over the next few months held off repeated attacks, trading fire with the locals until the Chileans arrived. Arona's description was heavily weighted to crystallize his vision of a capricious, impetuous, unpredictable, even savage coastal peasantry in Peru, and he aimed his invective specifically at the motives of the women who led the attacks upon the Chinese men.[15] No one could hope, he implied, to build a national labor force with this peasantry. He claimed as well that when the Chileans finally entered the region more than three months later, the besieged Chinese, emaciated and ill, were taken to Lima where they promptly and graciously forgot the affair. He ends his account with patronizing praise of the Chinese for their forbearance, another clear sign of their "ancient" civilization.

Despite the often vague and scornful character of Arona's description, it remained for decades the source of conventional wisdom on the massacre. No other text provided so much detail or presented it with such conviction, almost a testimonial statement. A close reading of the relevant pages in the context of a quest for cultural and national identity, however, raises many questions. Arona clearly intended the massacre to represent all that the creole elite found objectionable in the African-descended peasants of Peru. In addition to horror he felt at the behavior of the Cañete peasants, he expressed an especially deep distaste for the local Afro-Peruvian women, whose ritual mutilation of the dead he found appalling. He shared his repugnance by testifying to the blood-driven cries of the women as they fell upon the mortally wounded men, one of whom he quotes as purportedly shouting, "leave that one for me."[16] The gender distinction is critical for understanding how Arona rested Peru's national identity on race.

Arona spread his invective around liberally and in some cases with justification. He accused *Orden*, the unofficial newspaper of occupied Lima, of ignoring the slaughter, and he blamed the Lima elite for failing to investigate this huge crime after the war. He bitterly chided the Chileans for failing to come to the rescue until the local landowners agreed to pay them ("mediante una fuerte remuneración consiguieron los hacendados que fuera a Cañete una fuerza chilena").[17] Another curious detail is the apparent inconsistency in his citation of some facts. Arona attributed the death of a thousand Chinese field hands to the initial one-day peasant assault, and the death of another five hundred men during the subsequent four-month siege of Hacienda Casablanca to the continued actions of the Peruvian peasants, but he makes no mention of the guerrillas operating around Cañete (p. 102). As a local resident, he would have known about—and feared—guerrilla operations.

A dissonance has arisen between the Arona description of the massacre and the partial accounts left by his contemporaries. Newspapers, diplomatic messages, and military reports indeed authenticated parts of Arona's narrative, yet they also affirm that his narrative contains some questionable assertions, as noted earlier. Arona lumped all the peasants together indiscriminately without regard to gender or status. He ignored the possibility that men were as important as women in the clash of ethnicities, and he disregarded more serious motives for the peasant action. Notably, his report of the numbers of Chinese dead later became a curious thread that wound its way throughout the discourse of massacre. Two other contemporary sources gave figures on the dead similar to those Arona would cite. Within weeks of the massacre, a Chilean newspaper reported that five hundred Chinese had died in a riot in Cañete. British ambassador Spencer St. John cited the same figure based on a rumor he had heard, but he also gave an estimated range, stretching the number to a possible seventeen hundred dead in the initial attack. While St. John's estimate and the figure claimed by Arona were similar, the figures five hundred and seventeen hundred later will serve as emblems for the enigmatic absence of a satisfactory explanation of the motives for massacre. To examine some of the discrepancies between the Arona narrative of the massacre and another, less well-known but equally fascinating account, it will be necessary to turn to the contemporary Chilean view of events.

The Chilean Military Perspective

The accuracy of the Chilean version of Ash Wednesday and its aftermath rests on the account of Patricio Lynch, the commander-in-chief of the Chilean occupation of Peru. Lynch, of Anglo-Peruvian parentage, rose slowly to prominence through a naval career. A dedicated professional who clashed occasionally with his peers, his performances as a field commander in the early battles against Bolivia and in Tacna and Arica impressed his superiors in Santiago, and by the time he undertook the important forced night march across the Cañete desert, Colonel Lynch had climbed several rungs up the career ladder.[18] The signal operations that clinched his promotion to rear admiral and generated a legendary reputation were the capture of Lima and the devastating north coast campaign, in which offshore bombardment of fields, towns, and infrastructure in several wealthy north coast sugar plantation areas of Peru crippled the government's ability to finance its own defense. Thereafter Lynch, by now dubbed the "Red Prince," had the nearly unanimous support of the Chilean military establishment, the rank of rear admiral and appointment as the commander-in-chief of the Chilean occupation.[19] Lynch's promotion outraged several powerful officers but it also made him virtually invulnerable, and he quite easily survived other wartime scandals that drew negative press and embarrassed the military establishment.

In contrast to Arona, Patricio Lynch provided the Chilean account of the massacre in a military memorandum. Not quite an eyewitness report, the assiduous integration into it of information sent from subordinates in Cañete gave the text a ring of authority.[20] Formal in style and in most respects precise, it did not directly challenge the Peruvian account. Read post facto, it cools the heated quality of the Arona narrative and places events in military perspective. This angle of vision reduced the attention the Chinese received to an afterthought. Above all, Lynch's officers aimed to define and defeat an enemy. If they mentioned the massacre and the Chinese only in passing, it may be they were preoccupied with regaining control of the area. It was never clear to the Chileans if their opponents for control of the towns and plantations of Cañete were peasants who mounted a spontaneous resistance, or guerrilla irregulars, or both.[21] For the purpose of understanding how the massacre occurred, then, the Chilean report suggests that the participants in the February massacre of Chinese may just as likely have been guerrillas as peasants.

The 1882 Lynch version of events in Cañete on Ash Wednesday and after antedated and foreshadowed that of Arona, but not in all respects. Lynch had a military agenda and he evidently was determined to hew closely to that line of argument no matter what he knew. His view of the proper agenda obviated mention of any influence on his decision to send troops to Cerro Azul, save for the disorders. He mentioned neither the pleas of the planters nor the diplomatic appeal of the Pisco merchants. Yet by referring to the massacre at all, indicating that the Chileans returned to Cañete more than three months afterward, he left room for the charge that only a bribe by the Cañete planters won the attention of the occupation army. Moreover, by implying that the Chileans were not present at the massacre, Lynch's report also helped to clarify the proper meaning of the folkloric Chilean claim to have "saved" the Chinese.[22]

Lynch had several opportunities to remove the Chinese from the area and thus to have avoided a massacre. When his troops first swept through the south coast in late 1880 and recruited Chinese into his army, Lynch had in effect carried out a partial rescue. It could be argued that he erred in leaving a decision to escape to the Chinese, yet such an argument would rest purely on hindsight. Another opportunity arose when Chilean troops escorted Chinese merchants from Cañete to Pisco in July 1881, months after the massacre. In fact, the escort operation provided the content of the Chilean legend. Lynch's only obvious failure occurred in the interim between those successes, when the Chinese suffered the unrelieved hostility of the Cañete peasants. In those months between late February and June 1881, when the pleas of the planters went unheeded and the condition of the Chinese fortified at Hacienda Casablanca slowly deteriorated, Lynch failed to act on their behalf. It was a glaring failure. The most noteworthy item of interest in this instance is that the bulk of the survivors at Hacienda Casablanca were field hands, not merchants.

The thinking of the Chilean military leaders regarding the Chinese is not hard to figure out. Chilean documents note that about two thousand former indentured Chinese participated in the Chilean victories in Lima. Arona further declared that some one thousand Chinese were returned to Lima by the Chileans following the lifting of the siege of Hacienda Casablanca. Lynch and Arona stated that a mere sixteen Chinese were returned to Cañete by ship. Lynch reported that three thousand Chinese were escorted to Pisco from Cañete by Chilean troops. These movements were carried out by the Chilean army and they raise questions about Chilean tactics: were only sixteen Chinese men escorted from Lima back to Cañete by ship before Ash Wednesday, or did others precede them? Who were the Chinese who later were escorted to Pisco by Chilean troops? Lynch cited the escort of Chinese to Pisco, but he ignored in his report the return of the Hacienda Casablanca massacre survivors to Lima, as noted by Arona. Why call attention to the one group of Chinese and dismiss the other? The Chilean record of heroism was marred by selectively shaded military and class interests.

Reviewing events in his 1882 report, Lynch made some interesting comments on the conduct of the June-July Cañete campaign. He pointed to "armed blacks" who "carried out repugnant acts of barbarity," taking pleasure (se complacían) in killing "asiáticos," making it necessary to send forces to "contain" and punish them.[23] His cryptic statement confirms that the massacre took place although it gives no clue as to when it happened, who the attackers were, or when Chilean forces were sent to stop them. Nor does it identify the "armed blacks." Because Arona had charged that the attack was carried out with stones and farm tools, did Lynch seek to raise the quality of the enemy by implying that guerrillas, not mere peasants, carried out the massacre? When did Lynch think the "acts of barbarity" occurred? Were those acts led by women, as Arona charged? Nor does his report mention the site of the massacre. The brevity and vagueness of his words on these subjects contrasted sharply with the remainder of Lynch's detailed description of the June 15–July 21 military campaign of reoccupation, where he named the officers, the size of the Chilean force, dates, distances, troop movements, weapons used by both sides, dead and wounded estimates for both, places where "the enemy" was engaged, and estimates of the size of the "enemy" force. On the last point, as suggested earlier in reference to civilians and guerrillas, the implied identity of "the enemy" was a military (guerrilla) force, not an unruly mob of peasants. Needless to say, it would embarrass an army to engage civilians in combat, particularly when the engagement proved to be so nettlesome.

Difficulties of two sorts arose when Lynch sent troops to Cañete. One involved the landing and actions to pacify the region, and the other occurred when the Chileans tried to leave. On June 15, Lynch sent a troop transport, the *Amazonas*, to Cerro Azul with a division of 476 infantry, 63 artillerymen, and 131 cavalry soldiers under the command of Col. Enrique Baeza. Baeza later reported "light" encounters with *montoneras*, whom the Chileans pursued into Cañete center and several other towns. Lynch lamented dryly that these encounters required the destruction of plantation houses where the enemy was barricaded. One of the houses was Hacienda Montalván, Arona's house, where artillery killed 57 Peruvians who had set "fire to the interior of the buildings." After heavy fighting, the nearby town of Imperial "was reduced to ashes." Another exchange of fire took place at Hacienda Casablanca.[24] These reports of military action strangely recall the version of events given by Arona, who claimed that the destruction of the very same plantation houses and the fires in the fields had all been undertaken by black and *cholo* peasants the previous February, not, as Lynch reported, in June. Hacienda Casablanca was the same plantation house where Arona later said a thousand Chinese nearly starved to death while holding out for months against the local peasants. The Lynch report devoted not a word to these embattled Chinese. Such reticence was also at odds with the earlier Chilean expressions of surprise and disgust at finding the Chinese enchained on the haciendas when they first marched through the region. At any rate, thereafter the air became extremely heavy with smoke from smoldering cane field fires set, said the Chilean reports, by "the bandits." Lynch's officers reported that breathing illnesses began to affect the Chilean troops. They returned to Cerro Azul, where by July 16, after a one-month campaign, they awaited embarkation for Lima. Colonel Baeza then sent the cavalry units overland south to the port of Pisco, and the remaining forces departed on July 21 for Callao, having "punished the bandits with full rigor."[25]

The Lynch report of 1882 lent further credibility to Arona's 1891 accusation by affirming that the Chileans did nothing to stem the Ash Wednesday massacre or to lift the siege of Hacienda Casablanca. If he wanted to talk about the February massacre at all, Lynch was forced to rely on his memory, his subordinates, and other reports. His military perspective contrasted quite sharply with that of Arona, the plantation owner. The Chilean's description emphasizes the June engagements in Cañete to the total exclusion of the February massacre. He suggests strongly that Peruvian guerrillas were as much opponents of the Chilean professionals as were civilian irregulars, regardless of gender. Further, the cryptic description of the lifting of the siege of Hacienda Casablanca seems strange. Why this major action—rescuing some one thousand Chinese men found "emaciated," as Arona noted—received no fanfare either in the reports sent to Lynch or in the commander's final essay is a matter for conjecture. Whether Arona exaggerated beyond reason, or Colonel Baeza dismissed the importance of the event (unlikely), or Lynch overlooked the heroic details cannot be ascertained.[26] What is clear, however, is that Lynch and his subordinates failed to report on the Hacienda Casablanca episode, which disappeared from view until Arona revived it a decade later. It is possible that the absence of outside attention to the emaciated Hacienda Casablanca survivors reflected their lack of political support. In contrast, the Cerro Azul escortees to Pisco were merchants with clout, succored by fellow merchants and the diplomatic community. The Chileans unquestionably were aware of the immense publicity value of the Chinese merchants.

In reporting the June arrival of the Chileans in Cañete, Lynch mentioned the embattled Chinese merchants only once, and he did not refer to their presence in the province at any time during the ensuing military operations. One wonders if they stood by watching the proceedings. He may have recalled the small tempest that the use of the Chinese as troops in the weeks leading up to the battles of San Juan and Miraflores had stirred in Santiago. Not wishing to further anger his superiors, Lynch wisely steered his images toward description of the positive Chilean gains in Cañete. But the question of numbers indirectly returned the Chinese to prominence in the Chilean records. Describing the battle for control of the town of Cañete, Lynch mentioned the number of people involved in it. This unusual encounter between professionals and irregulars—the latter supplied by Nicolás de Piérola from the highlands—lasted three and a half hours and involved "500 of our men and 1,700 adversaries" ("*500 de los nuestros i [y?] 1,700 adversarios*").[27]

These numbers are interesting for what they reveal about the confusing ties between the massacre and the rescue. First, the word "adversaries" avoids the peasants-or-guerrillas identity quandary, suggesting how troubling that subject was for the Chileans. More importantly, they eerily duplicate the range of estimates of the number of Chinese massacred in Cañete on Ash Wednesday 1881, cited earlier by British ambassador Spencer St. John and others. Rounded figures ordinarily would be part of a rumor, but a commanding officer who filed a military report would (as in citing the number of Chilean troops sent to Cerro Azul) presumably be more precise. The rounded imprecision of the numbers is less a cause for wonder than the way they are used in Lynch's report. Lynch cites them not to document the numbers of Chinese dead but rather to indicate the numbers of troops said to have fought on each side in a decisive battle—a coincidence, perhaps, but one so startling as to raise further questions. Is it possible that Lynch erroneously repeated in his official report the figures given in the rumor about the extent of the massacre of February 1881? Did Lynch have access to St. John's figures after the fact, decide to insert them into his report, and then perhaps in haste confuse the numbers of dead with the numbers of troops? Might he have consulted the British ambassador? The two men clearly were in contact.[28] Lynch also may have received those numbers from Arona, the owner of Hacienda Montalván, and the rear admiral, writing a year after the event, possibly confused an estimate of the numbers of those massacred given to him by Arona with his estimate of the numbers who fought on each side. In any case, the remarkable coincidence of numbers casts a shadow on the trustworthiness of Lynch's report.

A review of the numbers of Chinese claimed in this puzzling affair is in order. The Chinese escorted to Pisco undoubtedly were the remnants of the Chinese living in the Cañete region, the survivors of the massacre, most of whom had remained behind when others fled to the Chilean lines. But their numbers fluctuate from source to source. As noted above, Lynch stated that 3,000 men stood waiting for protection as the Chileans prepared to embark for Lima in mid-July. Given wartime conditions, this is another astounding figure. Having seen Lynch toss a few numbers around before, it might be helpful to recall that the number of Chinese men who lived in the Cañete region before the Chilean invasion (at least 958), the number who joined the Chileans as they marched through the wider south coast region toward Lima in late 1880 (about 2,000), the number who died on Ash Wednesday 1881 (between 500 and 1,000), and the number returned to Lima after the siege of Hacienda Casablanca (1,000) come to no more than two-thirds of that total in any other count.[29]

Lynch's dealings with the Cañete Chinese also require further examination. If the figure reported by Lynch is credible, the Chileans carried out a genuinely heroic operation, a sort of biblical transfer of a refugee population across a hostile region. The Chilean cavalry, Lynch reported, escorted the Chinese from Cerro Azul to Pisco, a trek of some forty miles, and underwent only one minor skirmish with Peruvians. That number of Chinese refugees (three thousand) could not be moved overland in one day and perhaps spent several days on the march.[30] No doubt the motive for this difficult march was the request transmitted to Lynch via Ambassador St. John from the Chinese merchants in Pisco. On March 7, 1881, St. John had received a plea for protection of the Cañete Chinese from the Chinese merchant community of Pisco because "a considerable number of Asians were recently victimized by a gang of bandits" in Cañete. The appeal for help provides a clue for solving the puzzling isolation of the Chilean cavalry on the wharf at Cerro Azul while the remaining forces returned safely to Lima. No doubt Chilean hesitation about committing a large cavalry force to escort Chinese refugees was overridden when the combined pleas of Chinese merchants and a British diplomat identified the victims as merchants rather than peasants.[31]

Race also was a major issue. While Lynch acted creditably, he was slow in reacting at all, a response no doubt motivated by a preoccupation with the larger military campaigns in the mountains as well as his lack of concern for the Chinese residents of Cañete. His belated response nevertheless takes something away from the Chilean action and makes it a bit difficult to endorse Chilean heroism. With regard to the Chinese at Hacienda Casablanca, Arona's last survivors of the ordeal of February to May 1881, Lynch never mentions them, leaving open the possibility that they were as much an embarrassment to him as would have been the death of so many the previous February. By reducing the importance of the Chinese in his report of the Cañete military operation, Lynch sought to divert attention from an issue that was a potential blemish on his military record, one that might detract from a rising career.

Peruvian refusal to confront the problems of interracial animosity in the shaping of a Peruvian national identity before the war had consequences beyond the curiosity of Lynch's inaction. How historians of Peru have analyzed that shortcoming of the Peruvian elite in a society riddled by a liminal obsession with race must be considered in judging the place of the Cañete massacre in the evolution of Peruvian identity. We turn now to the theories that have been offered to explain the massacre as an event as well as a mirror of Peruvian culture.

Racism and Consciousness

Several explanations have accounted for conflict and violence between two powerless sectors of Peruvian society in the nineteenth century, peasants of African descent and postindenture Chinese field workers. Among them are theories of colonial marginalization, sexual competition, ethnic rivalry, and national consciousness, and they have together generated useful debates on the motives for the attacks. One theory stressed the dynamics of ethnic rivalry and pay-rate differences exacerbated by the general crisis in capitalism.[32] Other theories stressed extraeconomic considerations. The entry of women and children into the plantation labor force complicated the pay issue and led to speculation about competition for sexual companionship. Chinese workers undoubtedly sought women during and after indenture, and the rivalry this spurred between men of different ethnic groups must have figured into the massacre. Yet to argue that sexual competition stimulated the incident is too unicausal.[33] The curtailment of indenture in 1874, which set loose large numbers of Chinese young men in the countryside, must have intensified fears everywhere on the coast and no doubt raised the specter of cultural and racial pollution among the families of Afro-Peruvian peasants. Those fears gained strength from plantation conflicts and the dissemination of rumors about drug-induced, depraved religious celebrations, and observations of barracks behavior. To the horror of local peasants, Chinese men successfully competed for jobs and female companions. Racial stereotyping had infected the entire social spectrum and relegated the Chinese to the bottom of the racial ladder. In the eyes of Afro-Peruvians, allowing the Chinese to couple with their daughters might signify a loss of status in the social order of Peru. Mothers especially had reason to fear that by joining Chinese men in consensual unions their daughters would lose the protection of the Church.

The links envisioned between capitalist commercial markets and the massacre raised the event from an isolated incident to a more general phenomenon. In the eyes of Heraclio Bonilla, for example, the massacre was best understood as a displacement response to postcolonial conditions. For Bonilla, colonial division and oppression had not merely impeded the articulation of collective interests of the oppressed as a group but also concealed the real enemy, displaced the conflict, and thus led the popular masses into mutual destruction.[34]

Later scholars, in agreement on the repressive tactics of the ruling elite, nonetheless rejected the victimization of the peasants seen in Bonilla's analysis. Studies of the highland peasantry in the decades leading up to the war suggest that peasant communities were in the midst of considerable ambivalence with respect to their associations with the larger polity. In many cases, the literature indicates that a serious rivalry—complicated by ethnic struggles between *mistis* (Andean ethnic middlemen) and communities—for control of precious Andean lands was already under way. Yet when the Chilean invasion reached into the highlands, many communities responded to the call for loyalty to the defending forces with a cohesion born of a collective sense that identified the "nation" with their community ties. For those communities that joined the campaign of defense against the invaders, a consciousness of community muted rising ethnic tensions over land and local power.[35]

In contrast, Chinese communities in the highlands and north coast regions of the country were divided. Although many workers on the coastal plantations in the north fled to the Chileans as had the Chinese on the south coast, urban Chinese in highland Cajamarca joined a local faction vying for national control.[36] These differences raise the possibility that class distinctions and local conditions held greater importance for understanding the Chinese response to the war than has thus far been recognized. Circumstances in Cajamarca elicited a response from northern highland Chinese that differed sharply from that of Chinese plantation workers but was strikingly similar to Chinese merchants in south coastal Ica. A further distinction among these groups is worth citing. While Chinese in the north gave their loyalty to a Peruvian faction, in Ica the merchant Quintín Quintana, whom the Chileans dubbed "a species of Rothschild of this yellow tribe," aided the Chileans, and in nearby Pisco, the isolated Chinese merchants sought help for their brother merchants through diplomatic channels.[37]

Viewing relations between the Chinese and Afro-Peruvians on the south coast in this light, the differences between the coastal and highland peasants comes down to the motives for the loyalties they displayed in a critical moment. In contrast to the idea that a colonial ethnic mentality prevailed among the peasants, it is more plausible to conclude that while the interests of the coastal peasants were complex, the land question was not paramount in their thinking. More seductive was the nation as represented by the elite's widely known hegemonic version of "Peru," a creole vision that Afro-Peruvians had been absorbing since the abolition of slavery some thirty years before and that was linked closely to a market discourse the two groups increasingly shared, albeit highly unevenly. Examining high Andean indigenous politics, Thurner sees this condition as "postcoloniality," a "subaltern . . . predicament" in which the subalterns are subjected to (the object of) the creole project of selective decolonization but still marginal to, indeed unimagined in, the new creole nation.[38]

In contrast to the Andeans, Afro-Peruvians were not protecting the power represented in tangibles like land and public office. Power relations between the two subaltern groups were unstable. Afro-Peruvians knew the Chinese as sometime merchants (small lenders), competitors (for income and sexual partners), and sometime subordinates, especially when Afro-Peruvians held positions as plantation security men and overseers. Those experiences inclined them toward hostility and—given their elite-framed knowledge of Chinese cultural practices—even loathing. Afro-Peruvians were Christians, and they harbored fears that Chinese Buddhism, atheism, worship of strange gods, and the use of opiates might pollute their own precariously situated ethnicity. The hostile feelings of the Afro-Peruvians had erupted in clashes with the Chinese on the plantations numerous times in the previous thirty years, a history that has gone unnoticed with few exceptions.[39]

Since the abolition of slavery, Afro-Peruvian peasants had been seeking opportunities for inclusion in the "nation" as full-fledged citizens, and their view of the indentured Chinese was formed by the sour history of their relations as ethnicities. Wartime linked the identity of individuals and groups in a seamless web of relations centered in the palpable demands of loyalty. The Peruvian state sought evidence of loyalty in the commitments it required of citizens and residents alike, and it rewarded such demonstrations with prizes, honors, and, in the case of residents, the promise of citizenship. The state often formulated the steps necessary to demonstrate loyalty and good citizenship, but particularly in wartime, it also rewarded spontaneous demonstrations of love and sacrifice for the state.[40]

In the late nineteenth century, the national project of the Peruvian creole elite aimed at cultural homogeneity. Elites sought to implant in the public discourse a desire for an agreement about a form of cultural unity whose most obvious failing was racial. The argument for unity was aimed at gaining widespread agreement that the Europe-driven, creole culture of the elite was in fact the definition of Peruvian culture. The rationale for such a desideratum was simple: the Andean majority cultures were unacceptable as representative of Peru for the simple reason that in the eyes of the creole elite, they did not match the models of modernity that the elite viewed as a standard of civilization. The Afro-Peruvians and *cholos* of the coast were judged through this same myopic lens: lightness of skin, urbaneness of social habits, a European phenotype ideal, and modern values. The project rested on the unspoken conviction that culture and nation were one, which required that the nation be represented by a single culture. In the modern creole elite-fabricated nation, two or more cultures could not be permitted to coexist.[41]

The creole elite also recognized that they lived with the fruit of a colonial heritage they accepted only with deep ambiguity. The majority, non-European population in a modern republic could not be done away with, but some means nevertheless had to be found to exclude it from the ranks of citizens or at least reduce its access to citizenship. It was left to the intellectuals, writers like Arona, to construct arguments for rejecting the unwanted populations from consideration as members of the national culture. Creole intellectuals framed descriptions of such groups in deprecatory terms that invoked images of group effeminacy, impetuosity, violence, and lack of capacity for self-control, all of which were thought to be marks of a group savagery that justified exclusion of the target population from citizenship. The Cañete massacre thus could be at once ignored and resurrected as a classic illustration of the illegitimacy of Afro-Peruvian claims to inclusion in the nation. The actions of the peasants obviated any possibility that such an ethnic group might be included among those designated as "creole," a coded word for "civilized." By pressing their claim through impetuous, illegitimate actions unguided by legitimate leaders (not to mention having followed the lead of women), the Afro-Peruvian peasants of Cañete had displayed a dangerous form of cultural inferiority and thereby, in the eyes of creole elite intellectuals, had delegitimized their claim to citizenship. It went unacknowledged that, by attacking the Chinese, the Afro-Peruvians were fighting for their group interests—a complex web of desires to control jobs, family, and religious attachments—and to gain recognition for their ethnicity that is best summarized in the concept of identity. By destroying the Chinese among them, the Cañete peasants could accomplish two critical goals, part of which they shared with the creole elite: they could affirm their loyalty to the nation, and they could rescue their cultural identity as Afro-creoles. The one factor in this network of concepts they sought to obliterate was race, the very concept upon which creole elite ideology most clearly rested.

The massacre occurred in Cañete and not elsewhere in the coastal valleys where the Afro-Peruvian and Chinese populations were similarly situated. Two conditions made Cañete unique. One was the absence of authorities. The Chileans did not leave a rearguard contingent in this important place, and for that Patricio Lynch was negligent. Another condition was the military situation. Nowhere else did the Chileans amass an army on the offensive, receive fleeing Chinese, and find it necessary to defend themselves against patriotic forces as well. Put otherwise, nowhere else did the Peruvian guerrilla campaign on the coast require as much attention and receive as little until it was too late. The combination of circumstances raised the ire of guerrillas who no doubt passed their convictions on to the willing peasants who, combining cultural vengeance with exculpatory patriotism, seized the moment.

Race, Culture, and National Identity: An Alternative View

It remains to ask what drove the Afro-Peruvian and *cholo* peasants to satisfy their needs by slaughtering their neighbors. The massacre was not carried out at the command or even at the direct urging of members of the elite. Cañete valley peasants—the men often employees of the plantations—for years heard managers and owners revile the Chinese for their cultural degeneracy, a condition that in the eyes of the powerful made for slow, incompetent, and unhealthy field workers. Their appearance, the violence in their daily lives, and general behaviors were the object of repeated casual speculation whose intention was to disparage, dehumanize, and justify the conditions of their indentured lives. An inevitable consequence of this discourse was the dehumanization of its practitioners, both owners and employers. One predictable result was the creation of conditions that encouraged the peasants to attack the Chinese "intruders" as "traitors." The sudden reversal of roles that emerged on Ash Wednesday 1881, in which the Chinese were free and the local peasants were in effect prisoners of war, triggered a violent, vengeful response. The racism that seems obvious in these circumstances was not simply one in which people of African and indigenous descent attacked Chinese men. Rather, the racism was composed by the Peruvian and Chilean elite reporters of the events, who failed to realize the distinctions that existed within the Chinese population in the Peruvian valleys. The Chinese peasants were not the objects of peasant vengeance; rather, the Chinese merchants were the objects of vengeance. When the peasants realized they had an opportunity to suddenly and quickly be rid of their debt burdens as well as their sexual competitors, feelings of patriotic vengeance merged easily with their cultural visions.

In contrast to the *serranos*, the blacks and *cholos* of Cañete had lost no land to look back on and root their expression of national sentiment. What then could be the basis of such heated feelings? To be sure, the memories of past repression under slavery were present in their minds. One contemporary French traveler put it this way: "Above them floats this bad memory, this nightmare, slavery . . . whose memory . . . seems ineradicable. It is often said that although they are free one sees in them a controlled rage against a past that has been reclaimed but can never be erased."[42]

Afro-Peruvians were the established population of the valley towns upon whose activities local commerce depended. The basis for their actions came more likely from a sense of pride in being creole Peruvians, a sentiment contextualized in recognition of their ethnic contribution to the identity of creole culture in Peru. The image of creole culture, like the national identity of Peru, was not clear in the broader community. It might signify a unique mixture of African and European traditions, to which the Afro-Peruvians had made significant contributions that had been kept alive through the era of slavery and abolition and that had been institutionalized in many public expressions.[43]

These institutions were endangered by the Chinese, who not only brought non–Roman Catholic practices to the Afro-Peruvian community and had begun to compete heavily for the women of the region but who also were associated with filth and danger. Although many were freed from indenture and numbers of them had converted to Roman Catholicism, they had not lost their reputation as opium users and as violence-prone men. Immolation and brutalization were handy instruments, accessible to peasant women, for purifying and redeeming a community whose creole identity was threatened by association with the Chinese on the plantations.

The events described at the outset of this analysis were part of a series of uprisings that took place in the coastal valleys of Peru and in Lima between 1875 and 1881. The uprisings were not straightforward peasant uprisings against the plantation owners, nor were they national movements in favor of the Peruvian regime against the Chilean invaders. On the contrary, they demonstrate the existence among the coastal Peruvian peasants of powerful and contradictory impulses: loyalty to the homeland (the *patria*) in wartime, loyalty to the culture in its creole and Afro-creole forms, convictions of sympathy and hopefulness toward liberals who had abolished slavery in 1855, and a general resentment against their economic conditions and against creole elite arrogance.[44] These were deeply held ambivalent sentiments brought dramatically to the surface by the war. The unspoken national creole heritage was composed of elements of the African background in combination with a Peruvian experience. In this context, the massacre was an expression of Afro-Peruvian loyalties by peasants who cleansed themselves of the Chinese and recovered their own culture as they identified it.

Notes

Editor's note: This chapter is an authorized reprint from *Social Identities: Journal for the Study of Race, Nation and Culture* 11, no. 5 (2005): 467–88, courtesy of Routledge.

1. Bonilla, "The War of the Pacific."

2. Méndez, "Incas sí, Indios no"; Thurner, "Historicizing 'the Postcolonial'"; Anderson, *Imagined Communities*; Hobsbawm and Ranger, *Invention of Tradition*; Bhabha, "Freedom's Basis in the Indeterminate"; Laclau, "Universalism, Particularism, and the Question of Identity"; Hall, "Cultural Identity and Diaspora"; Hall, "Introduction: Who Needs Identity?"; and Hall, "New Ethnicities."

3. The term *cholo* has been defined as "urbanized indigenous." See Manrique, *La piel y la pluma*, 17; Thurner, *From Two Republics to One Divided*, 8. De la Cadena, *Indigenous Mestizos*, 147–52, 215–17, discusses various racialized and gendered contexts in which the word has been used.

4. Cuche, *Poder blanco*; Pastor, *Herederos del dragon*; and Trazegnies Granda, *En el pais de las colinas de arena*.

5. Bulnes, *Guerra del Pacifico*; Dellepiane, *Historia militar del Peru*; Arana, *Historia de la Guerra del Pacifico*; Vicuña Mackenna, *Historia de la campaña de Lima*; and Castilla, "Impacto de la Guerra del Pacifico."

6. Moreno, *Guerra del Pacifico*, IV: 252–53, 275, 392–93.

7. Ibid., V: 93–118; VII: 427.

8. Manrique, *Campesinado y nacion*, 23; Stewart, *Chinese Bondage in Peru*; Segall, "Esclavitud y trafico de Culies en Chile," 117–33; and Moreno, *Guerra del Pacifico*, IV: 407–8.

9. Moreno, *Guerra del Pacifico*, IV: 255–60; Peri Fagerstrom, *Los batallones Bulnes y Valparaiso*; Wu Brading, *Testimonios Britanicos de la ocupacion chilena de Lima*; Martiniere, *La ocupacion de Lima*, 56–70.

10. Manrique, *Campesinado y nacion*, 105–10.

11. Larrabure y Unanue, *Manuscritos y publicaciones*, vol. I, 34; vol. II, 357.

12. For similar views expressed by other coastal planters, see Albert, *Essay on the Peruvian Sugar Industry*; and Swayne y Mendoza, *Mis antepasados*.

13. Arona, *La inmigracion en el Peru*, 100.

14. Ibid.

15. Ibid.

16. Ibid., 102.

17. Ibid., 103.

18. Congrains Martín, *La expedicion Lynch*; and Larenas Q., *Patricio Lynch*.

19. Bulnes, *Guerra del Pacifico*, vol. II, 280–87; Gonzales, "Chinese Plantation Workers," 331–34; Rodríguez Sepúlveda, *Patricio Lynch*; Sater, *Chile and the War of the Pacific*, 70–73; and Vicuña Mackenna, *Historia de la campaña de Lima*.

20. Lynch reported to the government in Santiago annually from 1882 on. His 1884 report (Lima, 1884) was a thin summary composed of broad generalities and vague dating in its descriptive sweeps through the various Chilean military campaigns in Peru. It contains no mention of the Cañete affair. In contrast, the 1882 version contains much detail on the Cañete episode. For the latter, see "Memoria que el Contra-Almirante don Patricio Lynch, Jeneral en Jefe del ejército de operaciones en el Norte del Peru, presente al Supremo Gobierno de Chile, Lima, 17 de mayo, 1882," reprinted in Moreno, *Guerra del Pacifico*, vol. VII, 111–45, of which about one double-columned page is dedicated to the Chilean return to Cañete; and in Larenas Q., 1981, appendix.

21. Lynch in Moreno, *Guerra del Pacifico*, vol. VII, 111–45.

22. The folk tune "Los chinos de Cerro Azul" misleadingly lauds the heroic Chilean action that saved the "Chinese of Cerro Azul." See Bonilla, "The War of the Pacific," 108. E. del Canto, the Chilean general who escorted the Chinese refugees, briefly mentions the postmassacre march in his memoirs (*Memorias militares*, 153). A search of the relevant records in the Archivo Nacional de Chile, Fondos Ministerio de Guerra, Tomos 184, 198, 486, 487, 608, 817–36, 889–94; Inválido, Tomos 895, 954, 964–1000; Archivo General de Guerra. Sumarios y Procesos, Tomos 47–55, 129; Ministerio de Interior, Tomos 945, 995–99, 1022, 1235, turned up not a single reference to the Cañete massacre of February 1881.

23. Moreno, *Guerra del Pacifico*, VII, 140–41; Manrique, *Campesinado y nacion*, 12–13; and Mallon, "Nationalist and Anti-State Coalitions," 241.

24. Moreno, *Guerra del Pacifico*, VII, 141; and Witt, *Diario y observaciones sobre el Peru*, 338.

25. Quoted in Moreno, *Guerra del Pacifico*, VII, 141.

26. Moreno, *Guerra del Pacifico*, V, 476–77.

27. Moreno, *Guerra del Pacifico*, V, 473; VII, 141.

28. Bonilla, "The War of the Pacific," 104.

29. Arona, *La inmigracion*, 99–102; St, John to Granville, Lima, May 3, 1881, reported a "rumor" that the number of Chinese massacred was 700–1500, FO/61/333. In the same 1882 report to the Chilean government (Moreno, *Guerra del Pacifico*, VII, 141), Patricio Lynch gave the number of Chinese massacred on Ash Wednesday as precisely 1,086, without further comment. The total population of Cañete district according to the local *gobernador eclesiástico* was 4,501, including 3,093 males and 1,408 females. No age, ethnic, racial, or national categories were used in this count. Razón del número de habitantes de ambos sexos comprendidos en todos los lugares anexos a esta doctrina, Cañete, 11 June 1880, Archivo Arzobispal de Lima, Expedientes Curatos, Legajo 10, Exp. XI, fols. 65, 65v.

30. Moreno, *Guerra del Pacifico*, V, 473–75.

31. Letter from Chinese merchants of Pisco to St. John, March 7, 1881, FO/177/168. A supporting statement (in English) by the Chinese merchants of Lima is in St. John to Granville confidential with enc., August 10, 1881, FO/61/334.

32. Bonacich, "The Past, Present, and Future of Split Labor Market Theory"; Bulnes, *Guerra del Pacifico*; and Bailey, *Immigrant and Native Workers*.

33. Cuche, *Poder blanco*, 105, 158–60.

34. Bonilla, "The War of the Pacific," 108–9.

35. Thurner, *From Two Republics*, 28–69.

36. Mallon, *Peasant and Nation*, 240; Lausent-Herrera, "Les Chinois du Perou," 169–83; and Lausent-Herrera, "L'emergence d'une elite," 127–53.

37. Moreno, *Guerra del Pacifico*, IV, 405–6.

38. Thurner,"Historicizing 'the Postcolonial,'" 5.

39. Roggero and de los Ríos, *Sublevacion de campesinos negros en Chincha 1879*; Cuche, *Poder blanco*, 95–106; Vicuña Mackenna, *Historia del campaña de Lima*, 718–21; and Gonzales, "Chinese Plantation Workers," 407, 415–18.

40. Sabato, *Many and the Few*; and Marx, "Contested Citizenship," 159–84.

41. Poole, "National Identity and Citizenship"; and Gould, *To Die in This Way*.

42. Quoted in Cuche, *Poder blanco*, 43–44; and Andrews, *Afro-Latin America*, 101

43. Fuentes, *Lima*; Romero, "Papel de los descendientes de africanos," 53–93; Romero, *El negro en el Peru*; Bowser, *African Slave in Colonial Peru*; Tardieu, *Los negros y la iglesia en el peru*; Flores Galindo, *Aristocracia y plebe*; Hünefeldt, *Paying the Price of Freedom*; Blanchard, *Slavery and Abolition*; Aguirre, *Lo africano en la cultura criolla*; del Busto Duthurburu, *Breve historia de los negros del Peru*; Stokes, "Etnicidad y clase social"; Godoy, *Etnicidad y discriminación racial*; and Chambers, "Little Middle Ground."

44. Kapsoli, "Lambayeque en la coyuntura."

13

Crossfire, Cactus, and Racial Constructions

The Chaco War and Indigenous People in Paraguay

RENÉ D. HARDER HORST

Between 1932 and 1935, Bolivia and Paraguay fought a brutal war for ownership of the sparsely populated Chaco territory. Having lost its outlet to
the Pacific in the earlier War of the Pacific, 1879–84, Bolivia sought fluvial
access to the Atlantic via the Paraguay River. Both nations debated the possibility of Chaco oil reserves, although Argentina at the time fueled the
rumors of black wealth under the dry soil to tarnish Bolivia as a competitor
to its own state oil company.[1] Yet although Bolivia used Indian troops and
the war took place largely on land occupied by indigenous people, until recently scholars have paid scant attention to the war's effects for the native
groups in the area of conflict.

This chapter argues that the Chaco War had important results for indigenous people in both of the involved countries. Natives helped to shape the
frontier and its exploration by both Bolivia and Paraguay. Fear of indigenous
uprisings, despite critical dependencies on native skills and knowledge of
the Chaco area, led the nations to carefully consider native people when
extending state hegemony. Although only Bolivia used Indian soldiers,
they were involved in some of the war's most critical battles. Both armies
relied on indigenous guides and native languages for communication and
used natives as spies. Soldiers took advantage of indigenous resources and
women for prostitution. When possible, both sides used massacres to clear
natives off the frontier. For indigenous people, the war produced epidemics
and demographic decline, gut-wrenching choices for women who protected
families, cultural changes, and forced removals that altered group identity
until the present. As I have explained elsewhere, the violent conflict also
brought nationals and many Chaco indigenous people into contact for the
first time and led to an *indigenista* movement in Paraguayan literature that
helped integrate natives into national economic structures. In Bolivia the

war led to peasant uprisings that culminated in the momentous Movimiento Nacionalista Revolucionario (MNR) revolution of 1952.[2]

Indigenous perspectives contribute new insights to histories on both sides of the Chaco War. René de la Pedraja's recent *Wars of Latin America, 1899–1941* does not mention indigenous roles.[3] It is vital to uncover in greater depth how indigenous people, the earlier users of the land, experienced the violence between the whites who occupied their territories. In her path-breaking *Peasant and Nation: The Making of Postcolonial Mexico and Peru*, Florencia Mallon has shown that peasant actions, ideas, and linguistic experiences in warfare are essential to explaining national politics and ideological debates in nineteenth century Peru and Mexico.[4] In *The Defense of Community in Peru's Central Highlands*, Mallon found that peasants, when faced with a prolonged Chilean occupation in the War of the Pacific, organized *montonero* militias to harass Chilean patrols and invade collaborator haciendas. Armed peasants threatened authorities even more than an occupying army and ultimately took control of the countryside.[5] In some wars, native people have played decisive roles in shaping outcomes. Perhaps even more significantly for the grassroots level, all wars decisively influence the lives of peasants and indigenous people for years to come. Anthropologist Gastón Gordillo has shown that memories of the Chaco War continue to shape indigenous experiences in the area to this day.[6]

One difficulty in research about native experiences is chronological documentation, because a lineal account of historical events does not fit within the hunter-gatherer mentality of cultures to which Chaco indigenous peoples belong. My own elderly informants were unable to attach dates to the events they described. Nivaclé families speak nostalgically of times when there were no *tucus* (Bolivians, literally meaning "ants" because they were so numerous) or *lhafcatas* (Argentines) in their lands, and even the *nuus* (Paraguayans) did not yet threaten their borders.[7] These oral memories, however, illuminate the war in a new way and shed light on different aspects of its history.

Indigenous Peoples of the Chaco before the War

Traditionally known as the Gran Chaco, the dry area of western Paraguay, northeastern Argentina, southeastern Bolivia, and southwestern Brazil was by 1930 sparsely populated by native peoples from four linguistic families. The Ayoreode and Yïshïro were members of the Zamuco linguistic group in the northern Chaco, the Ayoreode closer to Bolivia and the Yïshïro nearer the Paraguay River. The Enxet, Angaité, Sanapaná, Guan'a, and Enenl-hit belonged to the Lengua-Maskoy linguistic group and lived in central and eastern lower areas of the Chaco. The Enlhit (western relatives to the Enxet), Yofuaxa, Nivaclé and Mak'a shared a Mataco-Mataguayo linguistic ancestry and lived in central and southern areas closer to the Pilcomayo River. Finally, the Toba-Qom, a Guaicurúan people, resided in the south-eastern Chaco. In pre-Columbian times, some Tupí-Guaraní had migrated west across the Paraguay River and settled in the Chaco highlands.[8] The Western Guaraní and the Guaraní-Ñandeva, both Guaraní speakers, lived in the dry territory that became the western border with Bolivia.[9]

Paraguay had initially avoided contact with the tribes in the Chaco, who they regarded as fearsome and warlike. It was President Francisco Solano López who, after 1862, first pushed to occupy and develop the area. The president forced the Evueví tribe to oversee state lumber barges along the Paraguay River until the tribe eventually became extinct.[10] López' disastrous War of the Triple Alliance with Argentina and Brazil killed indigenous people in the Pantanal and later allowed foreigners to purchase much of the lower Chaco. The sale forced natives into the cash economy as cheap laborers for the Argentine and British ranchers, fragmented their societies, and opened the way for British missionaries to initiate proselytism to the Enxet.[11] Focused on trying to occupy and develop its Chaco frontier, Paraguay virtually ignored the native people until the 1920s, when Bolivia also expressed interest in claiming Chaco land.

Internal frontier expansion and the accompanying socioeconomic and cultural changes quickly altered the Chaco tribes in the 1920s. Native people experienced the most violence before the war, when exploration and settlement caused many conflicts. Here I use the term "frontier" to determine an area between two or more previously distinct societies.[12] Access to resources and intertribal warfare both contributed to the frontier struggles. By the 1920s natives crossed the Pilcomayo River yearly to work at sugar mills in Argentina, where they experienced disease and alcoholism.[13] Indigenous people recall conflicts with other tribes. The Enlhit fought with the Ayoreode to the north and, together with the Nivaclé, warred against the Toba, Pilagá, and Wichí across the Pilcomayo River in Argentina.[14] The native context for the war was thus already one of conflict.

The aggressive Nivaclé, in whose matrifocal and matriarchal society women are called Nivacché, posed the most serious obstacle to Bolivian advances. Bolivians saw their "civilizing" and permanent settlement to be an urgent matter. Further west, the Guaraní Ñandeva and Western Guaraní struggled against Bolivians as they extended forts into native lands. According to José Seelwische, a Salesian missionary in the Chaco, "the Chaco peoples maintain live memories of the times when there were not yet whites trespassing on their lands. . . . The invasion of the Bolivian, Argentine and Paraguayan armies challenged them to an uncompromising fight to defend their independence. There are stories about their brave struggles and the variety of strategies they used against the overwhelming fire arms; successful battles that overran entire military units, and on the other hand massacres of entire Nivaclé communities."[15] Indigenous people blamed the Bolivians for introducing coca and alcohol into the Chaco. "They would drink pure alcohol," one Nivaclé had heard from a parent.[16] Elders recall that in 1920, Bolivians offered to feed the Nivaclé if they would dig a large hole. Over the advice of their elders and in the presence of enticing barbecued meat, young men did the work and then got into line to receive the food. The Bolivians opened fire and killed more than one hundred natives, throwing them into the hole. The Nivaclé in retaliation overran and slaughtered the entire troop, escalating the frontier violence.[17]

Bolivians also employed natives to kill their own people. A Nivaclé named Lhancumeet guided a troop of 150 soldiers back from Bolivia to attack an indigenous village. At the last minute, however, he changed his mind and informed the chief. After accepting tobacco and clothing from the Bolivian soldiers, in a surprising turn the village men massacred them all.[18]

Paraguayans, however, were just as violent as the Argentines or Bolivians. At Fort Isla Poí, following a discussion of the effectiveness of Paraguayan weapons, an officer lined up two dozen Nivaclé men and women in front of a bag of bread. The official then shot into the chest of the first indigenous person, killing many of the people with one shot, allegedly to show his rifle's fine qualities.[19] The rapid exploration and creation of forts led to violence between native people and all groups of outsiders on the frontier.

Missionaries entered the fray in 1925, when Catholic Oblates of Mary Immaculate order arrived at the invitation of the Bolivian government. Superior Enrique Breuer and the commander at San José de los Esteros visited the feared and highest Nivaclé chief, Tofaai, who for the first time allowed white persons to leave his presence alive. Tofaai believed the missionaries might be useful, for he told a Nivaclé assembly, "it is good that they [the Oblates] have arrived; perhaps they will rescue [salvar] us."[20] Missionaries settled in Laguna Escalante and Esteros and pressured troops to stop the extermination. Bolivians in turn accused the priests of being Paraguayan spies.[21]

Missionary accounts reveal that throughout the 1920s, Bolivia tried to exterminate indigenous people as it settled the Chaco. Bolivia moved forts eastward but was unable to convince its' highland Indians to migrate down into the area.[22] Both countries relied on indigenous guides. In August 1925 Bolivians at Fortín Sorpresa captured a Paraguayan scouting team that included 2nd Lt. Adolfo Rojas Silva, three soldiers and their indigenous guide.[23] A rise in Bolivian assassinations of anyone who spoke Guaraní followed, Paraguayans reported.[24] Indigenous people in retaliation pillaged white travelers along such roads as between Santa Crúz and Puerto Suárez, where attacks and thefts by Tobas reportedly provoked a Bolivian military response.[25] Travelers at the time reported that Indian people from Bolivia had spread all along the Pilcomayo River.[26] To block Bolivian penetration, Paraguayans later built Fort General Aquino near that waterway.

The conflicts escalated as both sides struck back out of vengeance; Nivaclé warriors overran entire military units in the face of overwhelming white firepower, and Bolivians massacred complete Nivaclé towns.[27] According to missionaries, "There is no theme that is repeated more in the accounts of the elderly Nivaclé than this one: the Bolivians were about to exterminate the Nivaclé people, it was a true war. The Bolivians were aggressive, the Bolivians made us suffer."[28] As one Nivacché recalled,

> Our fear was tremendous. There was still fear, fear of the Bolivians; they were still at war with the Nivaclé. Ay! They arrived at Esteros; that way the Nivaclé came together. . . . It was the Bolivians, only they were mean [malos]. They warred against the Nivaclé. Ay . . . I was as old as my granddaughter [is now]. They killed the Nivaclé. The people left their flocks of sheep, my grandmother left many sheep. That's where the sun was when my people ran. They heard the Bolivians attacking.[29]

As war loomed, the arrival of the Paraguayan army at first seemed to offer the Nivaclé an alliance against the Bolivians. Cross-cultural clashes, though, prevented such an arrangement. What followed for indigenous people was an all-out fight on three fronts against whites until the end of the war. On July 5, 1927, "savage Indians," according to a Paraguayan commander at Fort Toledo, surprised and killed two guards on patrol.[30] The Bolivian colonel in charge of Fort Esteros, recalled the Nivaclé, lured them to the fort with promises of free clothing and food. Surrounded by an electric fence, soldiers ordered the Nivaclé to dig a deep hole. Later soldiers barbecued cows; when the men were eating, the soldiers shut the gate and opened fire, killing all of the Nivaclé. Soldiers threw the men's bodies in the hole and then raped the women before releasing them.[31] Such massacres may not be so surprising when viewed within fears generated by recent Indian uprisings in southern Bolivia; in the Chayanta Rebellion of 1927, natives actually ate a rancher in a cannibalistic ritual out of revenge for unpaid labor.[32] The extermination of Chaco natives continued until the war claimed precedence.[33]

As Bolivians pushed eastward, Paraguay allowed Mennonite settlers from Russia and Canada to migrate to the Chaco as a way to populate and extend Paraguayan hegemony over the territory.[34] In 1927 and 1930, settlers purchased land from the state in the central Chaco where the Northern Enlhit lived and began to clear it for farming. Early encounters between settlers and indigenous people were amicable, and native people guided Mennonites through the dry, thorny thickets.[35]

Native scouts led explorers, troops, and settlers through hostile territory, but bloody encounters followed.[36] As in the colonization of the Americas, the promise of goods and food was a powerful incentive for indigenous workers, even when it meant growing white intrusions.[37] Bolivian general Ovidio Quiroga Ochoa, sent to map the Chaco, used Enlhit guides and fed them with scraps from the fort. By this time many indigenous people had also fled from their homes into the forests because hunting had declined due to white intrusions.[38] Settler accounts resemble reports by the first Europeans who found the American frontier depopulated, unaware that their own diseases had caused a demographic collapse.[39]

The dry, hostile climate posed problems for both armies, who struggled to maintain supply lines to the front. The Nivaclé recall that soldiers were so desperate for water and food that they traded weapons for either. "From then on," an elder recalled, "the Nivaclé had rifles, because the Paraguayan soldiers traded them for watermelons. Then soldiers would not return to the front because they had lost their weapons."[40] Paraguayan soldiers frequently referred to the depressed "collas," as they called the Indians who were conscripted by Bolivia to the front and executed if caught trying to escape.[41] Military requests to Argentines across the Pilcomayo included gunpowder, cloth, and necklaces to trade with the Indians for food.

While hostilities increased, four indigenous people died in the fighting when the Bolivian 8th Infantry overran Paraguayan Fort Boquerón on

December 14, 1927.[42] A year later, in December 1928, Paraguayan major Rafael Franco destroyed a Bolivian fort in a surprise attack. As the confrontations and retaliations escalated, Czarist general Juan Belaieff, a Russian soldier that Paraguay contracted in October 1924 to explore the Chaco and direct its war strategy, used Mak'a and Yïshïro indigenous people as guides and porters.[43] As the Mak'a later recounted, "When we met [the whites], it was not their way of speaking or dressing that surprised us, but rather how they treated each other. We lived in what is called Boquerón, and we saw how they began to mistreat each other. It was very sad to see people kill each other and kill us. Thanks to the will of a Russian named Juan Belaieff we were not exterminated."[44] The nomadic Mak'a had long struggled against the Bolivians, and in 1928 four Mak'a men, led by their chief, Cikinokou, also called Captain Francisco, perished as they helped to defend Paraguayan Fort Mariscal López against a Bolivian attack.[45] Paraguayan colonel Arturo Bray reported friendly relations with the Mak'a who begged at his fort for food. Still, Bray complained about the natives' terrible smell.[46] Cultural differences complicated potential military alliances.

Given that the lands in conflict had until then been tribal territories, though, why do military accounts during the war so often overlook native people? Does this absence perhaps reflect racism or preoccupation with the military escalation, or were native people hiding and staying out of sight during the war?[47]

Escape into the brush appears to have been the best survival strategy, as explained in this Nivaclé account:

In those days, the Bolivians arrived where we were and built forts. Their chiefs talked with ours and, since then, they accepted those who voluntarily offered to fight on their side. They armed and equipped our warriors and gave them good food. When they had learned to use the new weapons and felt satisfied, one day they went to the woods. Our mothers took their children, along with the most valuable things, and met the warriors. They traveled through the most secret and thorny paths in the Chaco. All of them, even the elderly, went from the village to that secret place. One day we passed close to a Bolivian patrol. Our chief passed along the word to be absolutely quiet. It is possible that they had already started to persecute us for what we had done. An infant began to cry. Its mother nursed it but it continued to cry. There was not way to quiet it. Its own father smothered it with his hand. That's how we, the Nivaclé, are; ready to make any sacrifice for the good of our people. I think our parents made a mistake, because from that moment the Bolivians chased us day and night and hurt us very much.[48]

This passage suggests that, as Adams has shown in Guatemala, "retreat, avoidance and humility were strategies of survival" as well as a form of resistance during the war.[49]

Some indigenous people saw their role as guides for the armies as active defense of their territories. Toba Qom leader Francisco Ramírez explained to me the role his uncle and chief, Francisco Acazará, had played as a guide during the Chaco War, as well as his resentment that the native contributions have so often been overlooked.

> The only point I want to make is that . . . we are not mentioned in the histories, but we know that our people helped in the war. . . . Our role as guides is not recognized . . . by any Paraguayan historians, they take us out . . .[and write] that only they did everything. Our warriors . . . our Chief Larroza, helped in the war [as a guide] but nobody recognized him; the indigenous people were never paid for their help in the war. . . . During the war . . . we worked together to defend the land; [the whites] did not do this alone, but also with indigenous participation. . . . We still believe that we are owners of the land . . . because our people defended it; we were not going to watch with folded arms while they fought over the land. We have read the histories many times and indigenous people do not appear.[50]

Native people saw the war as a threat by both nations that sought to occupy their homelands. Ramírez' testimony suggests that, beyond the annoyance of being ignored by historians, native people saw their participation and resistance as an active defense of their lands from both expanding states.

By 1930 encounters with natives had increased along with rising war tensions. Paraguayan major Melgarejo, regiment commander at Puerto Pinasco, reported that "daring and irresponsible Tobas were rustling cattle and openly threatening ranchers and troops in the area." In response, the Ministry of War instructed him to "protect the ranchers but under no conditions fight or provoke the Indians so they do not rise up."[51] The last thing authorities wanted as conflict with Bolivia loomed was an Indian war on their hands. Paraguayan soldiers at this time captured an Enlhit woman and forced her to show them the way to Fort Nanawa, so they continued using native guides.[52] Yet when soldiers shot indigenous people near forts, ranchers begged Asunción to stop them out of nervousness that natives would lose all fear of outsiders and hamper further frontier settlement.[53] Once outsiders had settled and no longer desired guides, natives were superfluous and needed to be removed as obstacles to frontier civilization.

In March 1931, with indigenous guides, Belaieff became the first white person to reach Pitiantuta, a five kilometer by two kilometer lake in a desert region, where Paraguay promptly built Fort Carlos Antonio López on the eastern shore.[54] Beholden to native guides, in his final report Belaieff recommended the creation of a troop of indigenous people on horseback to protect Chaco borders.[55] Paraguay, though, was far from ready to arm its native people, even those who did cooperate with national goals. His advice ignored, Belaieff abandoned his odyssey without even reporting to superiors, apparently a broken man.[56]

Bolivians forcefully occupied Fort Carlos Antonio López in May 1932, to link the forts under their Fourth Division in the south with those at Roboré and Puerto Suárez in the north. With poor supply lines, a common complaint by soldiers on both sides as the war developed was constant thirst. Native guides were instrumental; not only did they know secret paths but their knowledge of water sources and even how to extract moisture from cacti was critical to soldiers in the desert climate.[57]

The Chaco War

Growing nationalist sentiment and further exploration by both nations as well as the failure of international mediation finally led to war in 1932. The odds at first seemed to favor Bolivia because German general Hans Kundt had modernized its forces with obligatory military service and foreign supplies, and had based his forces in the Western Chaco at Arce. Strapped for cash, Paraguay, conversely, could at first hardly even arm its troops. President Ayala had commissioned Belaieff to explore the Chaco but was unable to post even more than a few hundred soldiers to defend the territory.[58]

Elsewhere in the Americas, those difficult depression years of the mid-1930s also saw conflicts between states and indigenous communities. In Sutiaba, Nicaragua, natives armed with machetes, shovels, picks, and stones defended their cultural and religious traditions. In Jinotega, Nicaragua, natives rose up in 1934 and 1935 to oppose the construction of a chapel because it would coerce their labor and threaten autonomous use of land.[59]

Bolivia also saw significant indigenous uprisings in the years immediately before and during the war, spreading out from La Paz into surrounding highlands.[60]

In the Chaco, meanwhile, on September 17, 1932, Paraguayan forces overran and reclaimed the long-besieged Fort Boquerón, filled with Indian troops from all parts of Bolivia who had even eaten their mules to survive the long siege. As Zook recounted, "When all the mules were gone, the bones were scraped and eaten, the hides soaked and chewed."[61] Paraguayans reported that the Bolivian troops, or "collas," as they pejoratively called them in reference to an Indian ancestry, were poor, wretched and in a depressed spirit. Despite poor conditions, soldiers on both sides were shot for fleeing the battlefields.[62] Later, on July 4, 1933, Bolivia used Indian troops to charge the Paraguayan fort of Nanawa in the largest mass frontal attack of the war. More than two thousand soldiers from the Altiplano lost their lives in the attack, fragments of their bodies scattered and, according to Marshall Estigarribia, left in a "huge, rotting, putrefying mound of human flesh and bones."[63] Zook has attributed Bolivian losses to the "subordinate position of the Andean Indian, [not] integrated into the life of his country . . . incapable of the personal initiative which made the Paraguayan a brilliant and aggressive soldier."[64]

As the war escalated, Bolivia relied even more heavily on Indian soldiers. When the war first broke out, the Andean nation had initially exempted highland peasants from military service. A count of Indian farm workers, though, found them to be numerous enough to be expendable for the war effort. What is more, a series of peasant uprisings during the first years of the war unnerved authorities concerned about the public support. In April 1934 Bolivia imposed a quota system that mobilized 30 percent of its Indian peasant workers to the front and allowed the remainder to stay on farms to grow food for the troops in the Chaco.[65]

By September Paraguayans reported that Bolivian soldiers were deserting in large numbers and that their morale was low due to the lack of food and water and because of poor treatment. When fleeing the forts, Bolivians stopped at indigenous communities and traded their clothing and blankets for fish. Native workers also dug pits to bury the dead, such as 180 Bolivian casualties at Platanillos in August of 1932.[66]

By January 1933, following six months of warfare, indigenous Chaco people had retreated into the brush to escape the violence. Both armies were left hard-pressed for guides. Paraguay's Southern Command requested that superiors send trackers to direct the transport of ammunition boxes. Even

Figure 13.1. Paraguayan scouts (front row) and indigenous guides (second row) employed by Paraguay during the Chaco War. Instituto de Historia y Museo Militar del Ministerio de Defensa Nacional, Ascuncion, Paraguay. Used by permission.

as native people dropped out of official communiqués as the war escalated, forts depended more on their survival skills.[67]

Both sides continued to use native guides. Bolivia also employed Indians to carry contraband supplies for its soldiers back across the Pilcomayo River from Argentina.[68] When one indigenous tracker showed Bolivian mayor Ayala a hidden Paraguayan trail, he refused to believe him, calling him "a liar who only wants to get food which is needed by our troops." The guide, though, may have enjoyed the last laugh. Ninth Infantry regiments under Paraguayan colonel Eugenio Garay later slipped around the Bolivian flank along that very trail in September, 1933. The same Paraguayans surrounded the Bolivian Second Cavalry and Fourth Infantry and their victory ended the myth of Bolivian general Kundt's invincibility.[69] During the resulting siege of Fort Campo Grande in November, Paraguayans used Bolivian prisoners to plead with comrades in Quichua and Aymara to surrender, a strategy used throughout the war. Likewise, Bolivian turncoats translated their side's intercepted messages and radio broadcasts, often in Aymara or Quichua, for Paraguayan intelligence. The Paraguayans also employed Guaraní for radio transmissions during the war, a strategy akin to the famous Navaho code talkers of World War II.[70] Native tongues thus became useful tools to best opposing forces. General Franco of Paraguay also used the Guaraní language to unite and encourage his troops. As Paraguayan soldiers pushed into Bolivia during the second stage of the war, in late 1934 to early 1935, local indigenous people of Guaraní ancestry guided them through forests and advised them on Bolivian troop dispositions. Caught in the crossfire, native peoples between the forces functioned as "nocturnal eyes" that monitored changing troop positions. Soldiers from both sides, though, also executed many Indian people so their opponents would not use them as informers and spies.[71]

Demographic Results of Greater Contact

The Chaco War and new contact with outsiders gave many native peoples their first exposure to Western diseases. As early as 1930, when a typhoid fever epidemic broke out in the Mennonite colonies, authorities feared that natives who begged for food there would spread the disease. The director of military health ordered assistance for the settlers and put an end to all indigenous visits to quarantined Mennonite towns.[72]

More than 35 percent of the Northern Enlhit in the forests perished from a chickenpox epidemic that swept through their communities during the war.[73] Tajingvoy, an elder of mixed Nivaclé and Enlhit ancestry, attributed a rise in disease among his people to the conflict: "Following the war an epidemic of mumps attacked our groups. It was a terrible time! There were settlements where most of the people perished. My wife also contracted the disease and died. In the terror of the situation I picked up my small son and fled to live alone."[74]

Anthropologist Walter Regeher has found that wartime dietary changes also contributed to illnesses. As fighting limited mobility and the range of hunting and gathering declined, the war led to monotonous nutrition for indigenous groups that had previously gathered and hunted for diets rich in protein. The resulting weakness and epidemics were long-range results of the war and military occupation of tribal territories.[75] But if deadly for natives, life in the Chaco also proved fatal for the soldiers, as evidenced by frequent and urgent requests from commanders in the field for medical personnel and quinine to treat malaria.[76]

In addition to disease, the use of natives as unofficial troops contributed to indigenous mortality. An elderly Nivacché named Tii'i recalled that the Paraguayans had paid her people for each Bolivian head they presented, as well as troop cattle, and even provided them with rifles to kill enemy soldiers. The Bolivians also paid for Paraguayan heads, so the Nivaclé served both sides, killing any troops they could ambush in the woods and then turning in the scalps for a prize—often pieces of bread—to the appropriate authorities. A girl at the time, Tii'i emphasized her memories of native deaths, such as occurred when a group of Argentines crossed the river, prepared a barbecue for the Nivaclé, and then massacred them all. Her father, one of the ill-fated group, was spared from death because he was collecting wood for the fire at the time.[77] Impressions of chaos and death suggest the seriousness of the traumas.

Military forces terrorized the people they captured, including this Nivaclé:

> When the combats between Bolivians and Paraguayans began our groups escaped to the woods. . . . One day . . . suddenly we fell into an ambush placed by a contingent of Bolivian soldiers. . . . The soldiers closed in a circle around us, all armed with rifles. In the middle was a table. There sat the leader. He was cleaning his pistol. He accused us of being Paraguayans. Finally he asked: How do you prefer to die, with a machete or with a pistol?[78]

Testimonies show that while there had previously been conflicts between native peoples, because non-Indians brought firearms and new diseases, the Chaco War proved a devastating experience.

Gendered Aspects of the War

Soldiers on both sides took advantage of the conflict to abuse indigenous women; violence against women is a well-documented result of wars.[79] Even before the Chaco War, Argentine soldiers would cross the Pilcomayo and capture Nivacché to take home to use as forced servants. Félix Ramírez, a Nivaclé, lost his older sister in such a raid and has had no contact with her since she was stolen. "She must be 70 or 80 years of age now," he painfully recalled.[80] In some of the most tearful memories, women recall actually beating their infants to death when they would not stop crying because of their hunger, out of fear that the Paraguayan soldiers would hear them.[81] The Nivacché also remember sexual abuse from both sides:

> If it had not been for two or three cases we knew and for that bad custom the Paraguayans had with women, we would have joined their side.

. . . The Paraguayans could not stand to see our women. They would go crazy. Like dogs in heat they would fall on them. Poor women! For this reason we called them *palavái nuu*, [Paraguayan dogs]. I don't know how they could do that by force of paying with provisions. I could not [have had sex] in that way.[82]

Cultural misunderstandings and sexual abuse also must have complicated the conduct of the war. In Homero Guglielmini's novel *Death in the Chaco*, soldiers threaten each other for misbehavior with being cast out of the fort to the neighboring Mak'a people, whom they feared as cannibals. The main character finally escaped boredom at his fort for a night of pleasure in the Mak'a village.[83] Toyedo paid four precious bullets to the Mak'a chief for sex with his daughter, and then, as he was about to leave, the chief offered the soldier news about Bolivian positions in exchange for his gold tooth. As Toyedo spit blood after a painful extraction, the chief explained exactly how many and where the Bolivians were situated.[84] With this information the fort repelled three Bolivian attacks that night, while the delirious Toyedo writhed on his cot in horrible pain and fever. Although a fictitious account, this book suggests that soldiers took advantage of native information for strategy and native women for diversion.

By the close of 1934 Paraguay had managed to turn the tide of the war to its advantage. As the Bolivian army retreated into the highlands, it left the debris of its collapsed forces along the way. Marshall Estigarribia, Commander in Chief of Paraguay's army, reported, "Those prisoners declared that a great number of their companions have perished, principally from thirst . . . the road covered by the enemy in his retreat is strewn with corpses, and some of them were burned—killed by their officers because they refused to continue the march."[85] Paraguay believed the end was in sight. Still, their own supply lines were stretched, finances were very low, and Bolivia had reorganized its army with more capable officers.[86] Paraguay could not claim an overwhelming victory, but it finally defeated Bolivian forces.

Postwar Political Developments and Indigenismo

After their victory in June 1935, as Paraguayan troops retreated from Bolivia into the Chaco, thousands of Western Guaraní and Guaraní-Ñandeva returned with them to Paraguay. The Guaraní Indians feared that Bolivians would take revenge on them for having collaborated with Paraguayans, whom they had seen as countrymen. What is more, troops had promised to replace the native cattle they had slaughtered for food along the way.[87] Paraguayans brought these people back in vehicles to Guachaia, later renamed Pedro de la Peña, which was traditional Nivaclé territory. Paraguayans transported others to the area of Fort Toledo, fifty kilometers west of Mariscal Estigarribia, and abandoned them without water or food, but General Andino later rescued and took them by truck to Mariscal.[88] Oblate missionaries settled more than one thousand of these returning Western Guaraní, who became known as Guarayos and finally received formal Paraguayan citizenship in 1955.[89]

The Guaraní-Ñandeva, unlike the Western Guaraní, had fought for the Bolivian side. Paraguay therefore imprisoned them as traitors at forts Camacho and Toledo. After being released following the armistice of June 1935, most of the Guaraní-Ñandeva migrated back home, although they suffered heavy losses. Out of 3,000 people in the tribe before the conflict, only half are said to have safely reached Bolivia.[90] As many as 650 of the Ñandeva also stayed behind in the Paraguayan Chaco.

After the war had ended, Nivaclé chief Tofaai ordered an end to hostilities and symbolically gave up weapons and ammunition to Paraguayan forces, but there was still more work to do.[91] The Nivaclé recall that after the war,

> the Paraguayans . . . ordered them to collect the lost rifles and load them in trucks. Day to day they carried loads of weapons, because the war had finished. Twenty Nivaclé worked to collect rifles, hatchets, and machetes. Then the Paraguayan commander gave rifles and machetes to the Nivaclé, and that way the Nivaclé remained very friendly with that commander, he also gave them a *guampa* [gourd] with his *bombilla* [straw for drinking mate] and yerba [mate tea].[92]

In Bolivia, the war and the high mortality it produced led to a national crisis, economic depression, and peasant uprisings that shaped politics for years to come. The unexpected defeat produced a deep sense of loss over territorial dreams, a feeling of Bolivian inferiority, and anger at the old oligarchic liberal state that veterans and citizens blamed for having misled the nation throughout the war.[93] More than during the conflict, peasant uprisings in the years that followed racked Bolivia due to poor living and working conditions. The middle classes withdrew their support from the military government. In 1945, after futile labor stoppages, tens of thousands of Indians marched on La Paz in an attempt to end the *colonato* labor peonage system. The resulting First National Indigenous Congress energized the peasantry and led to the Canchas uprising and later the Ayopaya Rebellion of February of 1947, when angry peasants attacked the Yayani hacienda with dynamite.[94] The civil unrest ultimately contributed to the 1952 revolution, in which the National Revolutionary Movement led by Paz Estenssoro took power and finally enacted limited agrarian land reform and approved universal suffrage in Bolivia.[95]

In Paraguay, likewise, the war experience and contact with indigenous people in the Chaco shaped national politics. In 1936 General Franco led conservatives to power and promised a national revolution marked by a new era of social justice. For recently contacted indigenous peoples, the president created a National Indigenous Patronage that made them wards of the armed forces.[96] Wartime nationalism had led to a resurgence of the Guaraní language, and Franco officially made the tongue a second national language. Paraguay became the first and only nation in Latin America with a bilingual policy, a unifying political strategy.[97]

Contact with native people also influenced cultural developments. Paraguayan literature during Franco's rule mirrored state *indigenismo* and glorified what writers saw as the indigenous heritage and foundation of national society.[98] At the same time, however, the authors' "prejudice and denigration of native people also left its mark."[99] These indigenist writers influenced the first politicians to display an interest in the indigenous population. Out of gratitude for their service and fearful of their future prospects, in April of 1938 Belaieff brought seventy Mak'a dancers and musicians to perform an "Indian Fantasy" at the National Theater in Asunción. The drama's climax was the heroic death of the Mak'a chief Cikinokou at Fort Mariscal López in 1928.[100] In 1939 the Mak'a even traveled to Buenos Aires and presented their "Indian Fantasy" at the world-famous Colon Theater.[101] The trip earned enough for the new Paraguayan Indigenista Association to resettle the Mak'a tribe behind the botanical gardens in the capital, from where they could wander the city to sell artwork and present dances. The Mak'a people still live near the capital today.[102]

Memories of the war have remained alive in the consciousness of the Chaco indigenous people. Talking with the Toba, anthropologist Gastón Gordillo discovered that bones and material remains have seemingly "impregnated the Paraguayan bush with living echoes of the Chaco War." One informant, Tomás, explained that his friends often came across human bones and rusty weapons in the Paraguayan forest, in places haunted by souls. "In Paraguay, there [are] plenty of bullets, skulls, bones of the Bolivians. At night, you hear screams, people screaming over there. . . . All the *campo* is full of arms, some in good shape: rifles, carbines, everything. Trucks, plenty of trucks, left out there in the bush." Other men also relayed the way in which bones and material remains still "impregnate the Paraguayan bush with living echoes of the Chaco War." Informants reported that while hunting iguanas they heard the noise of trucks, screams of men, shots, airplanes. "And the noise stopped. It wasn't there anymore. Then, we heard the screams of men, shots. But it wasn't true [real]. We only heard them. In those places, memory seems to be eternally inscribed in space, erasing historical time and making old battles linger indefinitely."[103]

The Chaco War changed the lives of indigenous Chaco peoples and the governments of Paraguay and Bolivia as it redrew national boundaries, brought nationals and natives into contact with each other for the first time, and influenced the states' treatment of the native peoples. Including indigenous perspectives on military conflicts helps uncover the history of the people that the war affected and displaced. This chapter has shown that both Paraguay and Bolivia tried to clear indigenous tribes out of the Chaco. Natives at first fought to defend their land as internal frontiers expanded. Later, indigenous people served both armies as guides, porters, and informants. Military forces used their languages and knowledge to communicate and survive in the harsh desert environment. The war displaced entire tribes and led to greater contact with indigenous people and groups within both Bolivia and Paraguay.

Notes

1. Mora and Cooney, *Paraguay and the U.S.*, 78.

2. Horst, *Stroessner Regime*, 19. See also Albó, "From MNRistas to Kataristas to Katari," 382.

3. Pedraja, *Wars of Latin America*, 325–92.

4. Mallon, *Peasant and Nation*, 322 and 329.

5. Mallon, *Defense of Community*, 87, 88, 98.

6. Gordillo, *Landscapes of Devils*, 241–42.

7. Seelwische, "Las Misiones Nivacle," 1.

8. The Guaicurú in this chapter are the same indigenous tribe designated as Guaikurú in Portuguese in chapter 8. The same difference applies to the spelling of Tupi Guarani (Portuguese) in chapter 8 and Tupí-Guaraní (Spanish) in this chapter.

9. Horst, *Stroessner Regime*, 10–11.

10. Ganson, "The Evueví of Paraguay," 486.

11. Horst, *Stroessner Regime*, 14–15.

12. I use the term "frontier" as defined by Lamar and Thompson, "not as a boundary or line, but as a territory or zone of interpenetration between two previously distinct societies." Lamar and Thompson, *The Frontier in History*, 7–8. See also Colloway, *New Worlds for All*; Cayton and Teute, eds., *Contact Points*; and Otto, *Dutch-Munsee Encounter in America*, 6–14.

13. Felipe Ramírez, Nivaclé, interview with author, May 18, 2005.

14. Nordenskiöld, E., *La vie des Indiens*, 18. See Lt. Ramón Pandos, Pilcomayo Military Outpost General Delgado, to Eliseo Da Rosa, Minister of War and Marine, December 6, 1927, in file "Reserved Notes on Troop Movements, 1926–1928," Ministry of National Defense Archive (hereafter AMD), Asunción.

15. Seelwische, "Los Misioneros," 1.

16. Félix Ramírez, Nivaclé, interview in Mariscal Estigarribia, May 18, 2005.

17. Miguel Fritz, interview with author in Mariscal Estigarribia, May 19, 2005.

18. Seelwische, *Sui papi catsinôvot p'alhaa na lhcootsjat*, 99, 101, 103, 105.

19. Chase Sardi, *¡Palavai Nuu!*, 1, 180.

20. Fritz, *Los Nivaclé*, 43. See also Renshaw, *Los indígenas*, 52.

21. Ministry of Foreign Relations to Eliseo DaRosa, Minister of War and Marine, November 28, 1927, in file "Reserved Notes on Troop Movements, 1926–1928," AMD, Asunción.

22. Farcau, *Chaco War*, 10.

23. Horst, "Indigenous People," 15; Zook, *Conduct of the Chaco War*, 43; Farcau, *Chaco War*, 11; and Bray, *Armas y letras memorias*, 179.

24. Col. Melgarejo Ledesma, Paraguayan spy, to Chief of Army, Embarcación, June 14, 1928, in file "Reserved Notes on Troop Movements, 1926–1928," AMD, Asunción.

25. Casabianca, *Una guerra desconocida*, 41.

26. Ibid., 41–42.

27. Seelwische, "Los Misioneros," 1.

28. Miguel Fritz, interview with author, May 19, 2005.

29. Quoted in Fritz, *Nos han salvado*, 97.

30. José Campos, Commander of Fort Toledo to Ministry of War and Navy, Asunción, July 31, 1927, in file "Reserved Notes on Troop Movements, 1926–1928," AMD, Asunción.

31. Seelwische, *Sui papi catsinôvot p'alhaa na lhcootsjat*, 107, 109, 111.

32. Langer, "Andean Rituals of Revolt," 238.

33. Seelwische, "Los Misioneros," 2.

34. Paraguayans reported constant arrival of Bolivian troops to the Chaco, half of them Guarayo Indians, in 1928. Juan Camerón to Ministry of War, Corumbá, March 8, 1928, in file "Reserved Notes on Troop Movements, 1926–1928," AMD, Asunción. See also Klassen, *Mennonites in Paraguay*, 65.

35. Klassen, *Mennonites in Paraguay*, 66.

36. Bray, *Armas y letras memorias*, 179.

37. In the Military Museum in Asunción, I found a picture (figure 13.1) of indigenous guides used as trackers by Paraguay. They stand in tattered rags behind a line of armed Paraguayan scouts; AMD, Asunción.

38. Casabianca, *Una guerra desconocida*, 44.

39. See, for instance, Jennings, *Invasion of America*.

40. Seelwische, *Sui papi catsinôvot p'alhaa na lhcootsjat*, 159.

41. Col. Melgarejo Ledesma to Chief of the Armed Forces, Embarcación, June 14, 1928; Horacio Yosna to José Guggieri, President of Paraguay, Jujuy, June 5, 1929, in file "Reserved Notes on Troop Movements, 1926–1928," AMD, Asunción.

42. Zook, *Conduct of the Chaco War*, 50.

43. Galiano and Serna, "Los Maká," 37.

44. Ibid., 38.

45. Ibid., 37, 40.

46. Bray, *Armas y letras memorias*, 184.

47. James Scott lists concealment as one of the arts of resistance; I would argue that in the Chaco case the strategy could include staying hidden in the forest during the fighting. See Scott, *Domination and the Arts of Resistance*, 50–52.

48. Chase Sardi, *Pequeño decamerón Nivaclé*, 205.

49. Adams, "Ethnic Images and Strategies in 1944," 157.

50. Francisco Ramírez, Toba Qom leader, interview with author, Asunción, May 29, 2005.

51. Major A. Melgarejo, Regiment Valois Rivarola, to Ministry of War, Asunción, January 16, 1930, in file "Reserved Notes on Troop Movements, 1926–1928," AMD, Asunción.

52. Casabianca, *Una guerra desconocida*, 41–42.

53. José Casado to Manlio Schenoni, Minister of War, Asunción, January 29, 1931, in file "Reserved Notes on Troop Movements, 1926–1928," AMD, Asunción.

54. Zook, *Conduct of the Chaco War*, 69.

55. Juán Belaieff, Final Belaieff Report, in file "Reserved Notes on Troop Movements," Archives of Ministry of Defense, Asunción, September 10, 1928, 461–62.

56. C.I.F. 231/28/0, August 31, 1932, File "Telegrams February 1931–June, 1932," AMD, Asunción.

57. Seelwische, *Sui papi catsinôvot p'alhaa na lhcootsjat*, 159.

58. Zook, *La conducción de la Guerra del Chaco*, 83.

59. Gould, *To Die in this Way*, 182–83.

60. Aguirre, *Guerra y conflictos sociales*, 88.

61. See Zook, *Conduct of the Chaco War*, 99; and Sarmiento, *Memorias de un soldado*, 131.

62. Col. Melgarejo Ledesma, Paraguayan spy, to Chief of Army, Embarcación, June 14, 1928, in file "Reserved Notes on Troop Movements, 1926–1928," AMD, Asunción.

63. Zook, *Conduct of the Chaco War*, 146–47.

64. Ibid., 148.

65. Aguirre, *Guerra y conflictos sociales*, 41.

66. Julio Fiore, Chief of Ministerial Section, to Ministry of War, September 3, 1932,

Notes Received from Puerto Guaraní, Founded Forts, Fort Olimpo, 1921–1936, AMD, Asunción.

67. Telegram from the Southern Command No. 844/39 to Ministry of War, January 23, 1933, File "Telegrams" February–November, 1933, AMD, Asunción.

68. Caledonio Melgarejo Ledesma, Minister of Foreign Relations, to Justo Pastor Benítez, Paraguayan Consulate in Corumbá, Office Note #287, May 22, 1934, AMD, Asunción.

69. Farcau, *Chaco War*, 143, 168.

70. Melgarejo, *Transmisiones en la Guerra del Chaco*, 407.

71. Klassen, *Mennonites in Paraguay*, 301.

72. Col. León Díaz, Dirección Superior de Sanidad Militar, to Ministry of War and Marine, No. 604, Asunción, November 18, 1930, AMD, Notes Sent and Received, 1928–1930.

73. Wilmar Stahl, interview with author, Filadelfia, ASCIM, May 20, 2005.

74. Stahl, Escenario indígena chaqueño, 27.

75. Quoted in Klassen, *Mennonites in Paraguay*, 156.

76. Telegram from Villa Militar, Chaco, to Ministry of War, No. 1538/49, May 4, 1933, File Telegrams February 1931–June 1932, AMD.

77. Tii'í, Nivacché, interview with author, May 19, 2005.

78. Quoted in Stahl, *Escenario indígena chaqueño*, 65.

79. See Copelon, "Surfacing Gender."

80. Félix Ramírez, interview with author, Mariscal Estigarribia, May 18, 2005.

81. Anonymous Enlhet testimony recorded by Hannes Kalisch, cited in his chap. 38, unpublished manuscript held by Kalisch at Yalve Sanga. Translated from German by Gerhard Reimer. Courtesy of Kalisch. Infanticide was also documented by Klassen, *Mennonites in Paraguay*, 149.

82. Tii'í, Nivacché, interview with author, May 19, 2005; See also the Nivacché testimony in Chase Sardi, *Pequeño decamerón Nivaclé*, 205.

83. Guglielmini, *Muerte en el Chaco*, 21.

84. Ibid., 29.

85. Estigarribia, *Epic of the Chaco*, 126.

86. Mora and Cooney, *Paraguay and the U.S.*, 81.

87. Klassen, *Mennonites in Paraguay*, 76.

88. Miguel Fritz, interview with author, Mariscal Estigarribia, May 18, 2005.

89. Prieto and Rolón, *Estudio legislación indígena*, 14.

90. Klassen, *Mennonites in Paraguay*, 76.

91. Seelwische, "Los Misioneros," 2.

92. Seelwische, *Sui papi catsinôvot p'alhaa na lhcootsjat*, 163.

93. Mercado, *La Formación de la Concienca Nacional*, 49.

94. Ergueta, *Las grandes masacres*, 96; see also Dandler and Torrico, "From the National Congress," 364.

95. Albó, "From MNRistas to Kataristas to Katari," 382.

96. Prieto and Rolón, *Estudio legislación indígena*, 15.

97. Turner and Turner, "The Role of Mestizaje," 146.

98. See for an analogous example in Mexico, Knight, "Racism, Revolution, and Indigenismo," 98–101.

99. Wayne Robins, *Etnicidad, Tierra y Poder*, 78.

100. Galiano and Serna, "Los Maká," 39.

101. Ibid., 40.

102. Ibid., 44. See also AIP "Annals," 1945, No. 1, (October, 1945), AIP Archives, Asunción (AMD), pp. 4–5.

103. Gordillo, *Landscapes of Devils*, 241–42.

Bibliography

Newspapers and Periodicals

Alcance del Registro Oficial, San Fernando
The Anglo-Brazilian Times, Rio de Janeiro
O Arlequim, Rio de Janeiro
Ba-Ta-Clan, Rio de Janeiro
Boletín de la Guerra del Pacifico, Santiago, Chile
Boletín Democrático, Cali
Boletín Político i Militar, Pasto
Boletín Oficial, Bogotá
Boletín Oficial, León
Boletín Oficial, Managua
Brazil Americano, Rio de Janeiro
Cabichui, Paso Pucu, Paraguay
O Cabrião, São Paulo
Comalapan, Guatemala
El Comercio, Quito
Diario de Centro América, Guatemala
Diario de Zayas, Cuba
El Defensor del Orden, Granada
El Democrática: Órgano del Partido Liberal Independiente, Palmira
El Ecuatoriano, Quito
El Espectador, Pasto
Gaceta del Cauca, Popayán
Gaceta de Nicaragua, Managua
O Globo, Rio de Janeiro
El Guante, Guayaquil
La Igualdad, Havana
El Imparcial, Guatemala
Imprensa Academica, Sao Paulo
El Liberal Progresista, Guatemala
Las Máscaras, Pasto
Mephistopheles, Rio de Janeiro
Mosquito, Rio de Janeiro

New York Times, New York
Nuestro Diario, Guatemala
O Recife Illustrado, Pernambuco
Registro Oficial, León
Registro Oficial, Popayán
Registro Oficial, San Fernando
Revista do Exército Brasileiro, Rio de Janeiro
Revista Militar Ilustrada, Guatemala
A Semana Illustrada, Rio de Janeiro
El Telégrafo, Quito
The Times, London
La Tribuna, Buenos Aries
A Vida Fluminense, Rio de Janeiro
La Voz de la Juventud, Popayán

Archives

Archivo Arzobispal de Lima
Archivo Biblioteca de la Función Legislativa, Quito (ABFL)
Archivo Central del Cauca, Popayán (ACC)
Archivo del Congreso, Bogotá (AC)
Archivo del Instituto Colombiano de la Reforma Agraria, Bogotá
Archivo General de Centro América (AGCA)
Archivo General de la Nación, Bogotá (AGN)
Archivo General de la Nación, Buenos Aries
Archivo Historico Arquidiocesano, Guatemala City
Archivo Histórico del Banco Central
Archivo Histórico Municipal de Cali
Archivo Histórico do Exército, Rio de Janeiro.
Archivo Municipal de Patzicía (AMP)
Archivo Municipal de San Juan Comalapa, Guatemala (AMC)
Archivo Municipal de Sololá, Guatemala
Archivo Nacional de Chile, Santiago
Archivo Nacional de Cuba, Havana
Arquivo do Instituto Arqueológico, Histórico, e Geográfico, Pernambucano (AIA)
Arquivo Nacional, Rio de Janeiro
Arquivo Público de Mato Grosso (APMG)
Biblioteca Luis Angel Arango, Bogota (BLAA)
Biblioteca Nacional, Bogotá (BN)
Biblioteca Nacional, Rio de Janerio
Biblioteca Nacional de Música, Rio de Janeiro
Joaquin Zavala Solís Collection, Tulane University, Latin American Library (JZS)
Ministry of National Defence Archive, Asunción
Public Record Office, London
United States National Archives, Washington D.C.

Books and Journals

Abente, Diego. "The War of the Triple Alliance: Three Explanatory Models." *Latin American Research Review* 22 (1987): 47–67.

Academia Nacional de la Historia. *Juan Manuel de Rosas y la redención de cautivos en su campaña al desierto (1833–1834)*. Buenos Aires, ANH, 1979.

Adams, Richard N. *Crucifixion by Power: Essays on Guatemalan National Social Structure, 1944–1966*. Austin: University of Texas Press, 1970.

———. "The Development of the Guatemala Military," *Comparative Sociology Monographs*, St. Louis: Washington University, 1969.

———. "Ethnic Images and Strategies in 1944." In *Guatemalan Indians and the State: 1540–1988*, edited by Carol Smith, 163–82. Austin: University of Texas Press, 1990.

———. "Etnicidad en el ejército de la Guatemala liberal (1870–1915)." FLACSO Guatemala, *Debate*, 30 (1995).

Aguilar Piedra, Raúl. "La guerra Centroamericana contra los filibusteros en 1856–1857: Una aproximación a las fuentes bibliográficas y documentales." *Boletín AFEHC*, no. 36 (June 4, 2008). http://afehc-historia-centroamericana.org/index.php?action=fi_aff&id=1947.

Aguirre, Carlos. *Agentes de su propia libertad: Los esclavos de Lima y la desintegración de la esclavitud, 1821–1854*. Lima: Pontificia Universidad Católica del Perú, 1993.

———. *Lo africano en la cultura criolla*. Lima: Fondo Editorial del Congreso del Perú, 2000.

Aguirre, René Danilo Arze. *Guerra y conflictos sociales, el caso rural boliviano durante la campaña del chaco*. La Paz: Centro de Estudios de la Realidad Económica y Social, 1987.

Ahumada, Pascual, ed. *La Guerra del Pacífico. Documentos oficiales, correspondencias y demás publicaciones referentes a la guerra, que ha dado luz la prensa de Chile, Peru y Bolivia. Tomo I y II*. Santiago: Andrés Bello, 1982.

Alaix, M. M. *No sin desconfianza en mis propios fuerzas me propongo refutar la carta que el señor Julio Arboleda ha publicado en el número 9.0 de "El Misóforo."* [No title listed, this is first line of text]. Popayán: n.p., 1850.

Albert, William. *An Essay on the Peruvian Sugar Industry, 1880–1920, and the Letters of Ronald Gordon, Administrator of the British Sugar Company in Cañete, 1914–1920*. Norwich, U.K.: University of East Anglia, 1976.

Albó, Xavier. "From MNRistas to Kataristas to Katari." In *Resistance, Rebellion and Consciousness in the Andean World, 18th to 20th Centuries*, edited by Steve Stern, 379–419. Madison: University of Wisconsin Press, 1987.

Almada, Francisco R. *Apuntes históricos del Cantón Rayón*. Chihuahua: Ediciones del Gobierno del Estado de Chihuahua, 1988.

———. *Resumen de la historia del Estado de Chihuahua*. Mexico City: Libros Mexicanos, 1955.

Alonso, Ana María. *Thread of Blood: Colonialism, Revolution, and Gender on Mexico's Northern Frontier*. Tucson: University of Arizona Press, 1995.

Al Público: Una cuestión grave y de la mayor importancia para el estado se exajita actualmente con la Asamblea Constituyente (Managua: n.p., 1848).

Alvarenga, Ana Patricia. *Cultura y ética de la violencia: El Salvador 1880–1932*. San Salvador: EDUCA, 1994.

Alvarez Montalván, Emilio. *Las fuerzas armadas en Nicaragua: sinopsis histórica, 1821–1994*. Managua, 1994.

Annais do Senado Brasileiro. Rio de Janeiro: Imprenta Nacional, 1870; 1871; 1907.

Anderson, Benedict. *Imagined Communities: Reflections on the Origins and Spread of Nationalism*. London: Verso, 1991.

Andrews, George Reid. *The Afro-Argentines of Buenos Aries 1800–1900*. Madison: University of Wisconsin Press, 1991.

———. *Afro-Latin America, 1800–2000*. Oxford: Oxford University Press, 2004.

Anonymous. *El amigo del soldado*. Guatemala: Tipografía Nacional, 1904.

Anthias, Floya, and Nira Yuval-Davis. *Woman-Nation-State*. New York: St. Martin's Press, 1989.

Appelbaum, Nancy. *Muddied Waters: Race, Region and Local History in Colombia, 1846–1948*. Durham, N.C.: Duke University Press, 2003.

Appelbaum, Nancy P., Anne S. Macpherson, and Karin Alejandra Rosemblatt, eds. *Race and Nation in Modern Latin America*. Chapel Hill: University of North Carolina Press, 2003.

Arana, A. Barros. *Historia de la Guerra del Pacifico, 1878–1881*. Santiago: Editorial Andrés Bello, 1979.

Aravena Carrasco, Lisandro Bernardo. *Chilenos a la guerra: la movilización en el conflicto*. Universidad de Santiago de Chile: Tesis de Licenciatura, 2002.

Arbelo, Manuel. *Recuerdos de la última guerra por la independencia de Cuba, 1896 à 1898*. Havana: Imprenta Tipografía Moderna, 1918.

Arboleda, Julio. "El Misóforo, Número noveno—Popayán 27 de noviembre de 1850." In *Prosa de Julio Arboleda: Jurídica, política, heterodoxa y literaria*, 307–59. Bogotá: Banco de la República, 1984.

Archer, Christian I. "'La Causa Buena': The Counterinsurgency Army of New Spain and the Ten Years War." In *Rank and Privilege: The Military and Society in Latin America*, edited by Linda A. Rodriguez, 11–36. Wilmington, Del.: Scholarly Resources, 1997.

Areces, Nidia R. "Los Mbayás en la frontera norte paraguaya. Guerra e intercâmbio em Concepción, 1773–1840." *Suplemento Antropológico* 33, no. 1–2 (December 1998): 77–113.

———. "Paisaje fronterizo e historia en el Paraguay de los López." Text presented at the *XI Jornadas Interescuelas/Departamentos de Historia*. Tucumán, Argentina, 2007 (Edition on CD-Rom).

Arevalo Martinez, Rafael. *Ecce pericles*. San José: EDUCA, 1983.

Arinos de Melo Franco, Afonso. *O índio brasileiro e a revolução francesca: As origens brasileiras da teoria da bondade natural*. Rio de Janeiro: J. Olympio, 1937.

Arona, Juan de. *La inmigración en el Perú*. Lima: Enrique R. Lulli, 1971. (Originally published in 1891)

Asturias, Miguel Angel. *Sociología Guatemalteca: El problema social del indio*. Translated by Maureen Ahern. Tempe: Arizona State University, 1977. (Originally published in 1923)

Atkins, Edwin A. *Sixty Years in Cuba*. Cambridge, Mass.: Riverside Press, 1926.

Ayala, Enrique. "De la revolución alfarista al régimen oligárquico liberal," in *Nuevo historia del Ecuador*, Vol. 9, *Época Republicana II*, edited by Enrique Ayala, 117–65. Quito: Corporación Editora Nacional, 1990.

Ayón, Tomás. "Apuntes sobre algunos de los acontecimientos políticos de Nicaragua en los años de 1811 á 1824." In *Historia de Nicaragua: Desde los tiempos más remotos hasta el año de 1852*, Vol. 3., 405–32. Managua: Fondo de Promoción Cultural-BANIC, 1993.

———. *Historia de Nicaragua: Desde los tiempos más remotos hasta el año de 1852*. Managua: Fondo de Promoción Cultural-BANIC, 1993.

Azara, Félix de. *Viajes por la América Meridional*. Traducción. Madrid: Espasa Calpe, 1969. Originially published as *Voyages dans l'Amérique Méridionale: Depuis 1781 jusqu'en 1801*. París: Dentu, 1809.

Azcuy Ameghino, Eduardo. *Artigas y los indios*. Montevideo: Ediciones Andresito, 1991.

Azevedo, Aluízio. *O Mulatto*. São Paulo: Martin Claret, 2002. (Originally published in 1881)

Bailey, T. R. *Immigrant and Native Workers: Contrasts and Competition*. Boulder, CO: Lynne Reinner, 1987.

Baldus, Herbert. "Introdução." In *Os Caduveos*, edited by Guido Boggiani. São Paulo: EDUSP—Belo Horizonte: Itatiaia, 1975.

Bancroft, Hubert Howe. *History of Central America, 1801–1887*. Vol. 8 of *The Works of Hubert Howe Bancroft*. San Francisco: History Company, 1887.

Barman, Roderick. *Citizen Emperor: Pedro II and the Making of Brazil, 1825–91*. Stanford, Calif.: Stanford University Press, 1999.

Barnet, Miguel. *Biografía de un cimarrón*. Havana: Editorial de Ciencias Sociales, 1986.

Barr-Melej, Patrick. *Reforming Chile: Cultural Politics, Nationalism and the Rise of the Middle Classes*. Chapel Hill: University of North Carolina Press, 2001.

Barros, A. D. *Historia de la Guerra del Pacifico, 1878–1881*. Santiago: Editorial Andrés Bello, 1979.

Bastos, Santiago. *Etnicidad y fuerzas armadas en Guatemala: Algunas ideas para el debate*. Guatemala: FLACSO, 2004.

Bastos, Uacury Ribiero de. *Expansão do Brasil colonial no vale do Paraguay 1767–1801*. São Paulo: EDUSP, 1972.

Batrell, Ricardo. *Para la historia: Apuntes autobiográficos de la vida de Ricardo Batrell Oviedo*. Havana: Seoane y Alvares Impresores, 1912.

Baud, Michiel. "Campesinos indígenas contra el estado: La huelga de los indígenas de Azuay, 1920–21." *Procesos: Revista Ecuatoriana de Historia* 4, no. 1 (1993): 41–72.

Bayer, Osvaldo. *Rebeldía y esperanza*. Buenos Aires: Group Editorial Zeta, 1993.

———. "Sesenta fusilados." In *Contratapa*, Buenos Aires, Sabado, October 22, 2005, 12.

Bean, Richard. "War and the Birth of the Nation-State." *Journal of Economic History* 33, no. 1 (1973): 203–21.

Beattie, Peter. "Conflicting Penile Codes: Modern Masculinity and Sodomy in the Brazilian Military, 1860–1916." In *Sex and Sexuality in Latin America*, edited by Donna Guy and Daniel Bouldersten, 65–85. New York: New York University Press, 1997.

———. "Measures of Manhood: Poor Free Men, Honor, and Slavery's Decline in Brazil, 1850–1889." In *Changing Men and Masculinities in Latin America*, edited by Matthew C. Guttman, 233–55. Durham, N.C.: Duke University Press, 2003.

———. "National Identity and the Brazilian Folk: The Image of the *Sertanejo* in Taunay's *A Retirada da Laguna*." *Review of Latin American Studies* 4, no. 1–2 (1991): 7–43.

———. "The Slave Silvestre's Disputed Sale: Mental Health, Sexuality, Corporal Punishment, and 'Vices' in Recife, Brazil, 1869–1878." *Estudios Interdisciplinarios de America Latina y El Caribe* 16, no. 1 (2005): 41–65.

———. *Tribute of Blood: Army, Honor, Race and Nation in Brazil, 1864–1945.* Durham, N.C.: Duke University Press, 2001.

Becker, Marc. *Indians and Leftists in the Making of Ecuador's Modern Indigenous Movements.* Durham, N.C.: Duke University Press, 2008.

Belli, Humberto. "Un ensayo de interpretación sobre las luchas políticas nicaragüenses: De la independencia hasta la revolución cubana." *Revista del Pensamiento Centroamericano* 32, no. 157 (1977): 50–59.

Bengoa, José. *Historia del pueblo Mapuche, Siglos XIX y XX.* Santiago: Ediciones Sur, 1985.

Berlin, Ira, Joseph P. Reidy, and Leslie S. Rowland, eds. *Freedom's Soldiers: The Black Military Experience in the Civil War.* Cambridge, Mass.: Harvard University Press, 1998.

Bernal, Irma. *Rosas y los indios.* Concepción del Uruguay: Ediciones Búsqueda de Ayllu, 1997.

Bertocchi, Cayetano. *Apuntes históricos y episodios de la vida del R. P. José Alzola de la Compañía de Jesús.* Guadalajara: El Regional, 1913.

Bhabha, Homni. "Freedom's Basis in the Indeterminate." In *The Identity in Question*, edited by John Rajchman, 46–57. New York: Routledge, 1995.

Bidondo, Emilio Angel, et al., eds. *Epopeya del desierto en el sur argentino.* Buenos Aires: Circulo Militar, 1979.

Black, Jeremy. *Rethinking Military History.* London: Routledge, 2004.

———. *War in the Modern World Since 1815.* London: Routledge, 2003.

Blanchard, Peter. *Slavery and Abolition in Early Republican Peru.* Wilmington, Del.: Scholarly Resources, 1992.

Boggiani, Guido. *Os Caduveos.* Traducción. São Paulo: EDUSP–Belo Horizonte: Itatiaia, 1975. Originally published as *Viaggi di un artista in America meridionale.* Roma: Ermanno Loescher & C., 1895.

Bonacich, Edna. "The Past, Present, and Future of Split Labor Market Theory." *Research in Race and Ethnic Relations* 1 (1979): 17–64.

Bonilla, Heraclio, "The Indian Peasantry and Peru during the War with Chile," in *Resistance, Rebellion and Consciousness in the Andean Peasant World, 18th–20th Centuries*, ed. Steve Stern, 219–31. Madison: University of Wisconsin Press, 1987.

———. "The War of the Pacific and the National and Colonial Problem in Peru." *Past and Present* 81 (November 1978), 92–118.

Bowser, Frederick. *The African Slave in Colonial Peru, 1524–1650.* Stanford, Calif.: Stanford University Press, 1974.

Boza, Bernabe. *Mi diario de la guerra desde Baire hasta la intervención Americana.* Havana: Imprenta La Propagandista, 1900.

Bray, Arturo. *Armas y letras memorias*, Vol. 1. Asunción: Ediciones NAPA, 1981.

Brewster, Keith. *Military, Ethnicity and Politics in the Sierra Norte de Puebla, 1917–1930.* Tucson: University of Arizona Press, 2003.

Brown, Matthew. *Adventuring through Spanish Colonies: Simon Bolivar, Foreign Mercenaries and the Birth of New Nations*. Liverpool: Liverpool University Press, 2007.

———. "Not Forging Nations but Foraging for Them: Uncertain Collective Identities in Gran Colombia." *Nations and Nationalism* 12, no. 2 (2006): 223–40.

Buitrago Matus, Nicolás. *León: La Sombra de Pedrarias*, 2 vols. León: Fundación Ortíz Gurdián, 1998.

Bulnes, G. *Guerra del Pacifico*. 4th ed. 3 vols. Santiago: Editorial del Pacifico, 1979.

Burguete, Ricardo. *¡La guerra! Cuba. (Diario de un Testigo)*. Barcelona: Maucci, 1902.

Burns, E. Bradford. *Patriarch and Folk: The Emergence of Nicaragua, 1798–1858*. Cambridge, Mass.: Harvard University Press, 1991.

Burr, Robert. *By Reason or Force: Chile and the Balancing of Power in South America, 1830–1905*. Berkeley and Los Angeles: University of California Press, 1965.

Bushnell, David. *The Making of Modern Colombia: A Nation in Spite of Itself*. Berkeley and Los Angeles: University of California Press, 1993.

del Busto Duthurburu, J. A. *Breve historia de los negros del Perú*. Lima: Fondo Editorial del Congreso del Perú, 2001.

Cabal, Miguel. *Contestación al inmundo pasquín titulado "La revolución del Cauca."* Cali: Imprenta de Hurtado, 1866.

Cabello de Balboa, Miguel. *Descripción de la Provincia de Esmeraldas*. Edición, introducción y notas de José Alcina Franch. Madrid: Consejo Superior de Investigaciones Científicas, Instituto de Historia, Departamento de Historia de América, 2001.

Cabero, Alberto. *Chile y los Chilenos*. Santiago: Editorial Lyceum, 1948.

Cabrera, Primo. *¡A Sitio Herrera! Narración de un viaje a la sierra de los órganos, intercalada con las aventuras revolucionarias del coronel don Nicolás de Cárdenas y Benítez y con algunas otras referencias que no deben olvidarse. Año 1921*. Havana: Imprenta y Papelería Rambla, Bouza y Cía., 1922.

de la Cadena, Marisol. *Indigenous Mestizos: The Politics of Race and Culture in Cuzco, Peru*. Durham, N.C.: Duke University Press, 2000.

Caminha, Adolpho. *Bom Crioulo*. São Paulo: Martin Claret, 2002. (Originally published in 1897)

Campbell, Leon G. "The Army of Peru and the Tupac Amaru Revolt." *Hispanic American Historical Review* 56, no. 1 (1976): 31–57.

del Canto, Estanislao. *Memorias militares del Jeneral D. Estanislao del Canto con un prólogo de D. Carlos Silva Vildósola. Tomo I: Desde enero de 1856 hasta agosto de 1891*. Santiago: Imprenta la "Tracción," 1927.

Carey, David, Jr. "A Democracy Born in Violence: Mayan Perceptions of the 1944 Patzicía Massacre and the 1954 Coup." In *After the Coup: An Ethnographic Reframing of Guatemala, 1954*, ed. Timothy J. Smith and Abigail Adams. Urbana: University of Illinois, 2010.

———. *Engendering Mayan History: Kaqchikel Women as Agents and Conduits of the Past, 1875–1970*. New York: Routledge, 2006.

———. *Our Elders Teach Us: Maya-Kaqchikel Historical Perspectives. Xkib'ij kan qate' qatata.'* Tuscaloosa: University of Alabama Press, 2001.

Carlyle, Thomas. *On Heroes, Hero Worship and the Heroic in History*. East Sussex, U.K.: Gardners Books, 2007.

Carmack, Robert M. *Historia Social de los Quiches*. Guatemala: Editorial "José de Pineda Ibarra," Ministerio de Educación, 1979.

———. "Spanish-Indian Relations in Highland Guatemala, 1800–1944." In *Spaniards and Indians in Southeastern Mesoamerica: Essays on the History of Ethnic Relations*, edited by Murdo J. MacLeod and Robert Wasserstrom, 215–52. Lincoln: University of Nebraska Press, 1983.

———. "State and Community in Nineteenth-Century Guatemala: The Momostenango Case," in *Guatemalan Indians and the State: 1540 to 1988*, edited by Carol S. Smith, 116–40. Austin: University of Texas Press, 1990.

de Carvalho, José Murilo. *A formaçao das almas, O imaginario da Republica no Brasil*. Sao Paulo: Companhia das Letras, 1990.

de Carvalho, Marcus J. M. "Os Índios de Pernambuco no ciclo das insurreicões liberais, 1817/1848: Ideologias e resistência," *Revista da SBPH* 1, no. 11 (1996): 51–69.

———. *Liberdade: Rotinas e ruptures do escravismo, Recife, 1822–1850*. Recife, Brazil: Ed. Universitária UFPE, 1998.

de Carvalho Neto, Paulo. *Estudios afro: Brasil, Paraguay, Uruguay, Ecuador*. Caracas: Universidad Central de Venezuela, 1971.

Casabianca, Ange-Grancois. *Una guerra desconocida: La campaña del Chaco Boreal*, Vol. 1. Asunción: Editorial El Lector, 1999.

Casanova Fuertes, Rafael. "Orden o Anarquía: Los intentos de regulación proto-estatal en Nicaragua. Década de 1840." In *Nicaragua en busca de su identidad*, edited by Frances Kinloch Tijerino, 277–94. Managua: IHN-UCA, 1995.

Casaús Arzú, Marta Elena. *La metamorfosis del racismo en Guatemala*. Guatemala: Cholsamaj, 1998.

Castañeda, Pedro C. *Trabajo técnico militar, escrito para el Ejército Guatemalteco, por el capitán de infantería*. Guatemala: Tipografía Nacional, 1903.

Castilla, R. Pachas. "Impacto de la Guerra del Pacifíco en las haciendas de Ica, Chincha, Pisco y Cañete." In *La guerra del Pacifíco*, vol. 1, edited by Wilson Reategui Chávez et al., 197–220. Lima: UNMSM, 1979.

Castro, M. M. *Informe que el Secretario de Gobierno en el Estado del Cauca presenta al Gobernador*. Popayán: Imprenta del Colejio Mayor, 1859.

Castro Chiriboga, Alfonso. "La Revolución de Concha." In *El negro en al historia de Ecuador y del sur de Colombia*, edited by P. Rafael Savoia. Cayambe: Centro Cultural Afro-Ecuatoriano, Talleres Abya-Yala, 1988.

Cayton, Andrew, and Fredrika Teute, eds. *Contact Points: American Frontiers from the Mohawk Valley to the Mississippi, 1750–1830*. Chapel Hill: University of North Carolina Press, 1998.

Centeno, Miguel Angel. *Blood and Debt: War and the Nation State in Latin America*. University Park: Penn State University Press, 2002.

———. "War in Modern Latin America," in *War in the Modern World since 1815*, edited by Jeremy Black, 142–68. New York: Routledge, 2003.

———, ed. *Warfare in Latin America*, 2 vol. London: Ashgate Publishers, 2007.

Cerutti, Franco. "Documentos para la historia de la literature Nicaragüense II: Panfelots anónimos sobre la Guerra Civil de 1854." *Revista Conservadora de Pensamiento Centroamericano* 26, no. 126 (March 1971).

Céspeces, Augusto. *Sangre de Mestizos*. La Paz: Urquizo, S.A., 1979.

Chalhoub, Sydney. *Visões da liberdade: Uma história das ultimas décadas de esravidão na Corte*. Sao Paulo: Companhia das Letras, 1990.

Chambers, Sarah. *From Subjects to Citizens: Honor, Gender, and Politics in Arequipa, Peru, 1750–1854*. University Park: Penn State University Press, 1999.

———. "Little Middle Ground: The Instability of a Mestizo Identity in the Andes, Eighteenth and Nineteenth Centuries." In *Race and Nation in Modern Latin America*, edited by Nancy P. Appelbaum, Anne S. Macpherson, and Karin Alejandra Rosemblatt, 32–55. Chapel Hill: University of North Carolina Press, 2003.

Chamorro, Fruto. "Mensaje de S. E. el general director supremo don Fruto Chamorro a la Asamblea Constituyente del Estado de Nicaragua, instalada el 24 de enero del año de 1854," in *Las constituciones de Nicaragua*, ed. Emilio Alvarez Lejarza (Madrid: Ediciones Cultural Hispánica, 1958).

Chamorro Zelaya, Pedro Joaquín. *Fruto Chamorro*. Managua: Editorial La Unión, 1960.

———. "¿Fué Bernarndo Méndez coactor en el asesinato del Jefe del Estado Coronel José Zepeda?" *Revista de la Academia de Geografía e Historia* 11, no. 2 (January–March 1952): 173–78.

Chance, John K. "The Urban Indian in Colonial Oaxaca." *American Ethnologist* 3, no. 4 (November 1976): 603–32.

Chase Sardi, Miguel. *¡Palavai Nuu! Etnografía Nivaclé*. Asunción: Biblioteca Paraguaya de Antropología, 2005.

———. *Pequeño decamerón Nivaclé*. Asunción: Ediciones NAPA, 1981.

Chiavenato, Júlio José. *Genocidio Americano: A guerra do Paraguai*. 2nd ed. Rio: Ed. Brasiliense, 1978.

———. *O negro no Brasil: Da senzala à guerra do Paraguai*. 14th ed. São Paulo: Ed. Brasiliense, 1982.

———. *Os voluntários da pátria e outros mitos*. São Paulo: Global Ed., 1983.

Chiriboga, Leonardo. *El problema del Indio desde el punto de vista militar*. Quito: Imprenta Ministerio de Previsión Social, 1939. Reprinted in *Indianistas, Indianofilos, Indigenistas. Entre el enigma y la fascinación: una antología de textos sobre el "problema" indígena*, edited by Jorge Trujillo, 583–638. Quito: ILDIS/ Abya-Yala, 1993.

Chiriboga, Leonardo. "Revolución de Concha." *El Negro en la historia del Ecuador y del sur de Colombia*. Quito: Ediciones Abya-Yala, 1988.

Chomsky, Aviva. *West Indian Workers and the United Fruit Company in Costa Rica, c.1870–1940*. Baton Rouge: Louisiana State University Press, 1996.

Citino, Robert M. "Military Histories Old and New: A Reintroduction." *American Historical Review* 12, no. 4 (2007): 1070–90.

Clark, A. Kim, and Marc Becker, eds. *Highland Indians and the State in Modern Ecuador*. Pittsburgh: Pittsburgh University Press, 2007.

Clayton, Andrew R. L., and Frederika Teute, eds. *Contact Points: American Frontiers from the Mohawk Valley to the Mississippi, 1750–1830*. Chapel Hill: University of North Carolina Press, 1998.

Collier, Simon. *Chile: The Making of a Republic, 1830–1865.* Cambridge: Cambridge University Press, 2003.

Colloway, Colin. *New Worlds for All: Indians, Europeans, and the Remaking of Early America.* Baltimore: Johns Hopkins University Press, 1997.

Colini, G. A. "Noticia Histórica e Etnográfica sobre os Guaicuru e os Mbayá." In *Os Caduveos,* edited by Guido Boggiani. São Paulo: EDUSP—Livraria Itatiaia Editoras, 1975.

Comando General de Ejercito. Dirección de Estudios Históricos. *Política seguida con el aborigen.* 5 vols. Buenos Aires: Circulo Militar, 1973–76.

Coña, Pascual. *Memorias de un cacique Mapuche: Copia fascimilar de "Vida y Costumbres de los indígenas araucanos en la segunda mitad del siglo XIX."* Santiago: ICIRA, 1973.

Congrains Martín, Eduardo. *La expedición Lynch.* Lima: Editorial Ecoma, 1973.

Conrad, Joseph. *Nostromo: A Tale of the Seaboard.* New York: Penguin Books, 1990. (Originally published in 1904)

Cope, R. Douglas. *The Limits of Racial Domination: Plebeian Society in Colonial Mexico City, 1660–1720.* Madison: University of Wisconsin Press, 1994.

Copelon, Rhonda. "Surfacing Gender, Reengraving Crimes against Women in Humanitarian Law." In *Women and War in the Twentieth Century,* edited by Nicole Ann Dombrowski, 332–60. New York: Routledge, 2004.

Coronel Urtecho, José. "Introducción a la época de anarquía en Nicaragua, 1821–1857." *Revista conservadora de pensamiento Centroamericano* 134 (1971): 39–49.

Corral, Manuel. *¡El Desastre! Memorias de un voluntario en la campaña de Cuba.* Barcelona: A. Martinez, 1899.

Correa, Ángela. *A los negros argentinos salud!* Buenos Aires: Nuestra América, 2006.

Correa, Lúcia Salsa. *Historia e Fronteira: O sul de Mato Grosso 1870–1920.* Campo Grande: UCDB, 1999.

Cortéz, Rosalío. *Opiniones de Rosalío Cortez en contestación al juicio particular del Señor Licenciado Don José María Estrada.* Masaya, Nicaragua: Imprenta de la Fraternidad, 1848.

da Costa, Emilia Viotti. *Da senzala à colônia.* São Paulo: Ed. Ciências Humanas, 1982.

Costales, Piedad Penaherra de, and Alfredo Costales Sanmiego. *Historia social del Ecuador,* Vol. II. Quito: Editorial Casa de la Cultura, 1964.

Cruz, Arturo J. *Nicaragua's Conservative Republic, 1858–93.* New York: Palgrave, 2002.

Cruz Salazar, José Luis. "El ejercito como una fuerza politica." *Estudios Sociales: Revista de Ciencias Sociales* 7 (April 1972): 74–98.

———. *Escritos de José Luis Cruz Salazar.* Guatemala City: ASIAS, 1980.

Cuadra Cea, Luis. "Conferencia del honorable profesor Don Luis Cuadra Cea, en el Teatro Municipal de León, Nicaragua, la Noche del 6 de Febrero de 1936 al Conmemorarse el XX Aniversario de la Muerte de Rubén Darío." *Revista de la Academia de Geografía e Historia de Nicaragua* 32 (1967): 6–22.

Cuadra Pasos, Carlos. "Don Anselmo H. Rivas: Apuntes biográficas." In *Nicaragua. Su Pasado. Ojeada Retrospectiva,* edited by Anselmo Hilario Rivas, i–xxv. Managua: Ediciones de La Prensa, 1936.

Cuche, Denys. *Poder blanco y resistencia negra en el Perú.* Lima: Instituto Nacional de Cultura, 1975.

Cunha, Manuela Carneiro da. "Introdução a uma história indígena." In *História dos Índios no Brasil*, edited by M. C. da Cunha, 9–24. São Paulo: FAPESP/Companhia das Letras, 1992.

———, ed. *Legislação Indígena no século XIX*. São Paulo: EDUSP/Comissão Pró Indio, 1992.

Curry, Glenn. "The Disappearance of the Resguardos Indígenas of Cundinamarca, Colombia, 1800–1863." Unpublished Ph.D. dissertation, Vanderbilt University, 1981.

Cusicanqui, Silvia Rivera. *"Oppressed but Not Defeated": Peasant Struggles among the Aymara and Quechua in Bolivia, 1900–1980*. Geneva: United Nations Research Institute for Social Development, 1987.

D'Alincourt, Louis. *Reflexões Acerca da Província de Mato Grosso*.

Dandler, Jorge, and Juan Torrico A. "From the National Indigenous Congress to the Ayopaya Rebellion: Bolivia, 1945–1947." In *Resistance, Rebellion, and Consciousness in the Andean Peasant World, Eighteenth to Twentieth Centuries*, edited by Steve J. Stern, 334–78. Madison: University of Wisconsin Press, 1987.

Davis, David Brion. *The Problem of Slavery in Western Culture*. Ithaca, N.Y.: Cornell University Press, 1969.

Dawson, Alexander S. *Indian and Nation in Revolutionary Mexico*. Tucson: University of Arizona Press, 2004.

Deas, Malcolm. "The Man on Foot: Conscription and the Nation State in Nineteenth Century Latin America." In *Studies in the Formation of the Nation-State in Latin America*, edited by James Dunkerley, 77–93. London: Institute of Latin American Studies, 2002.

———. "Poverty, Civil War and Politics: Ricardo Gaitán Obeso and His Magdalena River Campaign in Colombia, 1885." *Nova Americana* 2 (1979): 263–303.

Delay, Brian. "Independent Indians and the U.S.-Mexican War," *American Historical Review* 112, no. 1 (February, 2007): 35–68.

Dellepiane, Carlos. *Historia militar del Perú*. 3rd ed. 2 vols. Buenos Aires: L. Bernard, 1941.

Delrio, Walter M. *Memorias de expropiación: Sometimiento e incorporación indígena en la Patagonia*. Bernal: Editorial Universidad Nacional de Quilmas, 2005.

Departamento de Guerra y Marina, *Memorias Anuales*, vol. 1, *Memories of the Department of War and the Marine*, Buenos Aires: Ed. oficial, 1879, 1884.

Díaz Lacayo, Aldo. *Gobernantes de Nicaragua (1821–1956): Guía para el Estudio de Sus Biografías Políticas*. Managua: Aldilá Editor, 1996.

———. *Nicaragua, acuerdos políticos: 1. Aucerdos Jerez/Martínez (1856–1857)*. Managua: Aldilá Editor, 1999.

Dirección Política de las F.A.R., ed., *Historia de Cuba*. 1967; reprint, Havana: Instituto Cubano del Libro, 1971.

Dominguez, Jorge. *Insurrection or Loyalty: The Breakdown of the Spanish Empire*. Cambridge, Mass.: Harvard University Press, 1980.

Doratioto, Francisco. *Maldita Guerra: Nova História da Guerra do Paraguai*. São Paulo: Companhia das Letras, 2002.

Dore, Elizabeth. *Myths of Modernity: Peonage and Patriarchy in Nicaragua*. Durham, N.C.: Duke University Press, 2006.

Dore, Elizabeth, and Maxine Molyneux, eds. *Hidden Histories of Gender and the State in Latin America*. Durham, N.C.: Duke University Press, 2000.

Doubleday, C. W. *Reminiscences of the "Filibuster" War in Nicaragua*. New York: G. P. Putnam's Sons, 1886.

Driver, David Miller. *The Indian in Brazilian Literature*. New York: Hispanic Institute in the United States, 1942.

Duthurburu, del Busto. *Breve historia de los negros del Perú*. Lima: Fondo Editorial del Congreso del Perú, 2001.

Durán, Juan Guillermo. "Estudio Preliminar." In *Episodios en los territorios del Sur (1879)*, edited by Estanislao S. Zeballos, 15–148. Buenos Aries: El Elefante Blanco, 2004.

———. *Frontera, indios, soldados y cautivos: Historias guardadas en el Archivo del Cacique Manuel Namuncurá (1870–1880)*. Buenos Aires: Universidad Católica Argentina y Bouquet Editores, 2006.

Earle, Rebecca. *The Return of the Native: Indians and Myth-Making in Spanish America*. Durham, N.C.: Duke University Press, 2007.

———, ed. *Rumours of War: Civil Conflict in Nineteenth Century Latin America*. London: Institute of Latin American Studies, 2000.

Ebelot, Alfredo. "Estudio preliminar." In *Episodios en los territorios del sur (1879)*, edited by Estanislao S. Zeballos, 15–148. Buenos Aires: El Elefante Blanco, 2004.

———. *Recuerdos y relatos de la guerra de fronteras*. Buenos Aires: Plus Ultra, 1968.

Ecuador, Dirección Nacional de Estadística. *Ecuador en cifras, 1938–1942*. Quito: Imprenta Estadística, 1944.

Ergueta, Luis Antezana. *Las grandes masacres y levantamientos indígenas en la historia de Bolivia, 1850–1975*. La Paz: Liberia Editorial Juventud, 1994.

Escorcia, José. *Sociedad y economía en el Valle del Cauca. Tomo III: Desarrollo político, social y económico, 1800–1854*. Bogotá: Biblioteca Banco Popular, 1983.

Esgueva Gómez, Antonio, ed. and comp. *Documentos de la historia de Nicaragua, 1523–1857*. Managua: Universidad Centroamericano, 1993.

———. *Las constituciones políticas y sus reformas en la historia de Nicaragua*. 2 vols. Managua: IHNCA-UCA, 2000.

———. *Las leyes electorales en la historia de Nicaragua*. With an introduction by Rosa Marina Zelaya Velásquez. Managua: Editorial El Amanecer, 1995.

Espinosa y Ramos, Serafín. *Al trote y sin estribos (Recuerdos de la guerra de independencia)*. Havana: Jesús Montero Editor, 1946.

Estado Mayor General del Ejército. *Galería de Hombres de Armas de Chile, 1826–1885*. Tomo II. Santiago: Empresa Industrial Grafica Barcelona.

Estevez, Juan José. *Pincén: Vida y leyenda*. Buenos Aires: Dirección de Impresiones del Estado y Boletín Oficial de la Provincia de Buenos Aires, n.d.

Estigarribia, José Félix. *The Epic of the Chaco: Marshal Estigarribia's Memoirs of the Chaco War: 1932–1935*. New York: Greenwood Press, 1969.

Estupiñán Bass, Nelson."Artistas Negras." *Cultura: Revista del Banco Central del Ecuador* 4, no. 10 (1981): 51–80.

———. *Cuando los Guayacanes Florecían*. Quito: Editorial Casa de la Cultura, 1954.

Estupiñán Tello, Julio. *Esmeraldas de ayer: Crónicas y anecdotario del pasado esmeraldeño*. Esmeraldas: REDIGRAF, 1996.

Fagerstrom, R. Peri. *Los batallones Bulnes y Valparaiso en la Guerra del Pacifico*. Santiago: Imprenta de Carabineros, 1981.

Farcau, Bruce W. *The Chaco War: Bolivia and Paraguay, 1932–1935*. Westport, Conn.: Praeger, 1996.

Federal Bureau of Investigation. *Guatemala Today*. (July 1944).

Fergusson, Erna. *Guatemala*. New York: Alfred A. Knopf, 1938.

Fernández Mascaró, Guillermo. *Ecos de la manigua (El Maceo que yo conocí)*. Havana: Imprenta de P. Fernández y Cía., 1950.

Ferrer, Ada. *Insurgent Cuba: Race, Nation, and Revolution, 1868–1898*. Chapel Hill: University of North Carolina Press, 1999.

Findji, María Teresa, and José María Rojas. *Territorio, economía y sociedad Páez*. Cali: Universidad del Valle, 1985.

Flint, Grover. *Marching with Gómez: A War Correspondent's Field Note-Book Kept during Four Months with the Cuban Army*. Boston: Lamson, Wolffe, and Company, 1898.

Flores Galindo, Alberto. *Aristocracia y plebe: Lima 1760–1830*. Lima: Mosca Azul Editores, 1984.

———. *Buscando un Inca: Identitidad y Utopia en los Andes*. 5th ed. Lima: Casa de Estudios de Socialismo, 2005.

Foner, Eric. *Reconstruction: America's Unfinished Revolution, 1863–1877*. New York: Harper and Row, 1988.

Foner, Philip S. *Antonio Maceo: The "Bronze Titan" of Cuba's Struggle for Independence*. New York: Monthly Review Press, 1977.

Foote, Nicola. "Race, State and Nation in Early Twentieth Century Ecuador." *Nations and Nationalism* 12, no. 2 (2006): 261–78.

———. "Race, Gender and Nation in Ecuador: A Comparative Study of Black and Indigenous Populations, c. 1895–1944." Unpublished Ph.D. dissertation, University of London, 2005.

Fowler, Will. "Civil Conflict in Independent Mexico, 1821–1857: An Overview." In *Rumours of War: Civil Conflict in Nineteenth Century Latin America*, edited by Rebecca Earle, 49–86. London: Institute of Latin American Studies, 2000.

Fowler, Will, and Peter Lambert, eds. *Political Violence and the Construction of National Identity in Latin America*. New York: Palgrave Macmillan, 2006.

Franco, José L. *Antonio Maceo: Apuntes para una historia de su vida*. 3 vols. Havana: Editorial de Ciencias Sociales, 1975.

Fritz, Miguel. *Los Nivaclé: Rasgos de una Cultura Paraguaya*. Quito: Abya-Yala, 1994.

———. *Nos Han Salvado*. Quito: Abya Yala, 1994.

de la Fuente, Alejandro. *A Nation for All: Race, Inequality, and Politics in Twentieth-Century Cuba*. Chapel Hill: University of North Carolina Press, 2001.

Fuentes, M. A. *Lima, or, Sketches of the Capital of Peru, Historical, Statistical, Administrative, Commercial and Moral*. London: Trubner and Co, 1866.

Gabbert, Wolfgang. "Of Friends and Foes: The Caste War and Ethnicity in Yucatan." *Journal of Latin American Anthropology* 9 (2004): 90–118.

Gaitán, Luis, Julio Roberto Herrera, Carlos Martínez Durán, and Hernán Martínez Sobral, "Contribución al estudio del tifus exantemático en Guatemala," *Boletín Sanitario de*

Guatemala, órgano de la Dirección General de Sanidad Pública de Guatemala XI, no. 48 (December–January 1940): 34.

Galiano, Eva Herrero, and David Berná Serna. "Los Maká." *Suplemento Antropológico* 39, no. 2 (December 2004): 13–122.

Gámez, José Dolores. *Historia de Nicaragua desde los tiempos prehistóricos hasta 1860: En sus relaciones con España, México y Centro-América*. Managua: Tipografía de "El Pais," 1889.

Ganson, Barbara. "The Evueví of Paraguay: Adaptive Strategies and Responses to Colonialism, 1528–1811." *The Americas* 45, no. 4 (April 1989): 461–88.

———."Following Their Children into Battle: Women at War in Paraguay 1864–1870," *Americas* 66, no. 3 (1990): 335–71.

Garcia-Barrio, Constance. "Blacks in Ecuadorian Literature," in *Cultural Transformations and Ethnicity in Modern Ecuador*, edited by Norman Whitten Jr., 535–62. Chicago: University of Illinois Press, 1981.

García Granados, Jorge. *Evolución sociológica de Guatemala: Ensayo sobre el gobierno del Dr. Mariano Gálvez*. Guatemala: Sánchez & De Guise, 1927.

Garfield, Seth. *Indigenous Struggle at the Heart of Brazil: State Policy, Frontier Expansion and the Brazilian Indians*. Durham, N.C.: Duke University Press, 2001.

Gatewood, Charles B. *Lt. Charles Gatewood and his Apache Wars Memoir*. Edited and with additional text by Louis Kraft. Lincoln: University of Nebraska Press, 2005.

Geggus, David P. *Haitian Revolutionary Studies*. Bloomington: Indiana University Press, 2002.

Gleijeses, Piero. "La aldea de Ubico: Guatemala, 1931–1944." *Mesoamérica* 17 (June 1989): 25–59.

Gobat, Michel. *Confronting the American Dream: Nicaragua under U.S. Imperial Rule*. Durham, N.C.: Duke University Press, 2005.

Godoy, S. O'Phelan. *Etnicidad y discriminación racial en la historia del Perú*. Lima: PUCP, Instituto Riva Aguero, 2002.

Gómez, Máximo. *Diario de campaña, 1868–1899*. Havana: Instituto del Libro, 1968.

Gomez, Michael A. *Exchanging Our Country Marks: The Transformation of African Identities in the Colonial and Antebellum Period*. Chapel Hill: University of North Carolina Press, 1998.

Goncharovo, Valeria. "Los indígenas en la revolución liberal de Eloy Alfaro," in *Los Pueblos autóctonos de América Latina: Pasado y presente*. Moscow: Ciencias Sociales Contemporáneos, Academia de Ciencias de USSR, 1984.

Gonzales, Michael J. "Chinese Plantation Workers and Social Conflict in Peru in the Late Nineteenth Century." *Journal of Latin American Studies* 21 (1989): 331–34.

Gordillo, Gastón R. *Landscapes of Devils, Tensions of Place and Memory in the Argentinean Chaco*. Durham, N.C.: Duke University Press, 2004.

Gordon, Linda. *The Great Arizona Orphan Abduction*. Cambridge, Mass.: Harvard University Press, 1999.

Gould, Jeffrey. *To Die in This Way: Nicaraguan Indians and the Myth of Mestizaje, 1880–1965*. Durham, N.C.: Duke University Press, 1998.

Graham, Richard, ed. *The Idea of Race in Latin America, 1870–1940*. Austin: University of Texas Press, 1990.

Gramajo, José Ramón. *Las revoluciones exteriores contra el ex-residente Estrada Cabrera*. 2 vols. Guatemala: Tipografía Torres, 1937–1943.

Grandin, Greg. *The Blood of Guatemala: A History of Race and Nation*. Durham, N.C.: Duke University Press, 2000.

Granizo Romero, Rodrigo. "Lideres de pies des calzos." *Kipu: El mundo indigena en la prensa ecuatoriana* 1, 1985.

Greenberg, Amy S. *Manifest Manhood and the Antebellum American Empire*. Cambridge, Mass.: Cambridge University Press, 2005.

Greenberg, Kenneth S. *Honor and Slavery: Lies, Duels, Noses, Masks, Dressing as a Woman, Gifts, Strangers, Humanitarianism, Death, Slave Rebellions, the Proslavery Argument, Baseball, Hunting, and Gambling in the Old South*. Princeton, N.J.: University of Princeton Press, 1996.

Grieb, Kenneth J. *Guatemalan Caudillo: The Regime of Jorge Ubico, Guatemala 1931–1944*. Athens: Ohio University Press, 1979.

Griffen, William B. *Utmost Good Faith: Patterns of Apache-Mexican Hostilities in Northern California Border Warfare, 1821–1848*. Albuquerque: University of New Mexico Press, 1988.

Guardino, Peter. *Peasants, Politics, and the Formation of Mexico's National State: Guerrero, 1800–1857*. Stanford, Calif.: Stanford University Press, 1996.

———. *The Time of Liberty: Popular Political Culture in Oaxaca, 1750–1850*. Durham, N.C.: Duke University Press, 2005.

Gudmundson, Lowell. "Firewater, Desire, and the Militiamen's Xmas Eve in San Gerónimo, Baja Verapaz." *Hispanic American Historical Review* 84, no. 2 (2004): 239–76.

Guerra, François-Xavier. *Modernidad y independencia*. Madrid: Editorial MAPFRE, 1992.

Guerra Martinière, Margarita. *La ocupación de Lima (1881–1883): El Gobierno de García Calderón*. Lima: PUCP Fondo Editorial, 1991.

———. *La ocupación de Lima (1881–1883): Aspectos económicos*. Lima: PUCP Fondo Editorial, 1996.

Guevara, Tomás, and Manuel Mañkelef. *Historias de familias, Siglo XIX*. Temuco and Santiago: Liwen/Colibris, 2002.

Guglielmini, Homero M. *Muerte en el Chaco*. Buenos Aires: Editorial Ayacucho, 1947.

Guzmán, Hans Heiman. *Los inmigrantes en el Ecuador: Un estudio histórico*. Quito: Casa Editora Leibmann, 1942.

Haefkens, Jacobo. "Viaje a Guatemala y Centroamérica (1827, 1832)." In *Nicaragua en el Siglo XIX*, translated by Theodora J. M. van Lottum, compiled by Jorge Eduardo Arellano, 44–62. Managua: Fundación Uno, 2005.

Hale, Charles A. *The Transformation of Liberalism in Late Nineteenth Century Mexico*. Princeton, N.J.: Princeton University Press, 1989.

Hall, Stuart. "Cultural Identity and Diaspora." In *Identity, Community, Culture, Difference*, edited by Jonathan Rutherford. London: Lawrence & Wishart, 1990.

———. "Introduction: Who Needs Identity?" In *Questions of Cultural Identity*, edited by Stuart Hall and Paul Du Gay, 1–17. London: Sage, 1996.

———. "New Ethnicities." In *Identities: Race, Class, Gender, and Nationality*, edited by Linda Martin Alcoff & Eduardo Mendieta, 90–95. Oxford: Blackwell Publishing, 2003.

Hall, Stuart, and Paul De Gay eds. *Questions of Cultural Identity*. London: Sage, 1996.

Hamill, Hugh M., ed. *Caudillos: Dictators in Spanish America*. Norman: University of Oklahoma Press, 1992.

Handy, Jim. *Gift of the Devil: A History of Guatemala*. Boston: South End Press, 1984.

———. "Resurgent Democracy and the Guatemalan Military." *Journal of Latin American Studies* 18 (November 1986): 383–408.

Hatfield, Shelley Bowen. *Chasing Shadows: Indians along the United States–Mexico Border, 1876–1911*. Albuquerque: University of New Mexico Press, 1998.

Helg, Aline. "La Mejorana Revisited: The Unresolved Debate between Antonio Maceo and José Martí." *Colonial Latin American Historical Review* 10, no. 1 (Winter 2001): 61–89.

———. *Liberty and Equality in Caribbean Colombia, 1770–1835*. Chapel Hill: University of North Carolina Press, 2004.

———. *Our Rightful Share: The Afro-Cuban Struggle for Equality, 1886–1912*. Chapel Hill: University of North Carolina Press, 1995.

Hernández de León, Federíco. *Viajes presidenciales: Breves relatos de algunas expediciones administrativos del General D. Jorge Ubico, presidente de la República*. Guatemala: Tipografía Nacional, 1940.

Herrera, José Isabel. *Impresiones de la guerra de la independencia (Narrado por el soldado del Ejército Libertador)*. Havana: Editorial "Nuevos Rumbos," 1948.

Herrera, Patricio. "La cuestión de Arauco: Un problema de dignidad nacional durante el siglo XIX." In *Los proyectos nacionales en el pensamiento político y social chileno del siglo XIX*, edited by Manuel Loyola and Sergio Grez, 75–88. Santiago: Ediciones UCSH, 2002.

Hobsbawm, Eric, and Terence Ranger, eds. *The Invention of Tradition*. Cambridge: Cambridge University Press, 1992.

Houdaille, Jacques. "Negros franceses en América Central a finés del siglo XVIII." *Revista de Antropología e Historia de Guatemala* 6, no. 1 (1954): 65–67.

Holden, Robert H. *Armies without Nations: Public Violence and State Formation in Central America, 1821–1960*. New York: Oxford University Press, 2004.

Horsman, Reginald. *Race and Manifest Destiny: Origins of American Racial Anglo-Saxonism*. Cambridge, Mass.: Harvard University Press, 1986.

Horst, René D. Harder. "Indigenous People, the Chaco War, and State Formation in a World History Context." *World History Bulletin* 22, no. 2 (Fall 2006): 14–17.

———. *The Stroessner Regime and Indigenous Resistance in Paraguay*. Gainesville: University Press of Florida, 2007.

Hünefeldt, Christine. *Paying the Price of Freedom: Family and Labor among Lima's Slaves, 1800–1854*. Berkeley and Los Angeles: University of California Press, 1994.

Hux, Meinrado. *Caciques huilliches y salineros*. Buenos Aires: Marymar, 1991.

Huxley, Aldous. *Beyond the Mexique Bay*. New York: Harper & Brothers Publishers, 1934.

Ipsen, Wiebke. "Delicate Citizenship: Gender and Nation-Building in Brazil, 1865–1891." Unpublished Ph.D. dissertation, University of California–Irvine, 2005.

Jaramillo Castillo, Carlos Eduardo. "Guerras civiles y vida cotidiana." In *Historia de la vida cotidiana en Colombia*, edited by Beatriz Castro Carvajal, 291–309. Bogotá: Grupo Editorial Norma, 1996.

Jaramillo Uribe, Jaime. *El pensamiento Colombiano en el siglo XIX*. Bogotá: Editorial Temis, 1964.

Jennings, Francis. *The Invasion of America: Indians, Colonialism and the Cant of Conquest.* New York: Norton, 1976.

Kapsoli, E. W. "Lambayeque en la coyuntura de la Guerra del Pacifico." In *La Guerra del Pacifico*, Vol. 2, edited by Wilson Reátegui Chávez et al., 75–102. Lima: UNMSM, 1984.

Kennedy, John G. *Tarahumara of the Sierra Tarahumara: Survivors on the Canyon's Edge.* Pacific Grove, Calif.: Asilomar Press, 1996.

Kerr-Ritchie, Jeffrey R. "Rehearsal for War: Black Militias in the Atlantic World," *Slavery and Abolition* 26, no. 2 (2005): 1–34.

King, James F. "The Colored Castes and American Representation in the Cortes of Cádiz." *Hispanic American Historical Review* 33, no. 1 (February 1953): 33–64.

Kinloch Tijerino, Frances. *Nicaragua: identidad y cultura política (1821–1858).* Managua: Banco Central de Nicaragua, 1999.

Klassen, Peter, P. *The Mennonites in Paraguay.* Vol. 2. Kitchener: Pandora Press, 2002.

Knight, Alan. "Racism, Revolution, and Indigenismo: Mexico, 1910–1940." In *The Idea of Race in Latin America, 1870–1940*, edited by Richard Graham. Austin: University of Texas Press, 1990.

———. "Review: Rethinking the Tomóchic Rebellion," *Mexican Studies/Estudios Mexicanos* 15, no. 2 (Summer, 1999): 373–93.

Konetzke, Richard, ed. *Colección de documentos para la historia de la formación social de Hispanoamérica, 1493–1810.* Madrid: Consejo Superior de Investigaciones Científicas, 1953–62.

Kraay, Hendrik. "'Cold as the Stone of Which It Must Be Made': Caboclos, Monuments and the Memory of Independence in Bahia, Brazil, 1870s–1900." In *Images of Power: Iconography, Culture and the State in Latin America*, edited by Jens Anderman and William Rowe, 165–94. London: Berghahn Books, 2005.

———. "Patriotic Mobilization in Brazil: The Zuavos and Other Black Companies." In *I Die with My Country: Perspectives on the Paraguayan War, 1864–1870*, edited by Hendrick Kraay and Thomas L. Whigham, 61–80. Lincoln: University of Nebraska Press, 2004.

———. *Race, State, and Armed Forces in Independence-Era Brazil: Bahia, 1790s–1840s.* Stanford, Calif.: Stanford University Press, 2001.

———. "Slavery, Citizenship, and Military Service in Brazil's Moblization for the Paraguyan War." *Slavery and Abolition* 18, no. 3 (1997): 228–56.

Kraay, Hendrick, and Thomas L. Whigham, eds. *I Die with My Country: Perspectives on the Paraguayan War, 1864–1870.* Lincoln: University of Nebraska Press, 2004.

Krauze, Enrique. 115 *Vuelta*, "Chihuahua, ida y vuelta," (June 1986): 32–43.

Kuhsiek A., Guillermo. "La importancia del indio para el Ejército de Guatemala," *Revista Militar Ilustrada; Órgano de la academia militar y del ejército de la república. Publicación mensual* Año I, núms. 2 y 3. Guatemala, diciembre de 1915 y enero de 1916.

Laclau, Ernesto. "Universalism, Particularism, and the Question of Identity." In *The Identity in Question*, edited by John Rajchman, 93–110. New York: Routledge, 1995.

Lamar, Howard, and Leonard Thompson. *The Frontier in History: North America and Southern Africa Compared.* New Haven, Conn.: Yale University Press, 1981.

Langer, Erick. "Andean Rituals of Revolt." *Ethnohistory* 37, no. 3, (Summer 1990): 227–53.

Larenas, Q. *Patricio Lynch: Almirante, general, gobernador y diplomático*. Santiago: Editorial Universitaria, 1981.

Larrabure y Unanue. *Manuscritos y publicaciones: Literatura y critica literaria*, 3 vols. Lima: Editorial Americana. 1934–36.

Larraín, Jorge. *La identidad chilena*. Santiago: Ediciones Lom, 2001.

Larson, Brooke. *Trials of Nation Making: Liberalism, Race, and Ethnicity in the Andes, 1810–1910*. Cambridge: Cambridge University Press, 2004.

Lasso, Marixa. *Myths of Harmony: Race and Republicanism during the Age of Revolution, Colombia, 1795–1831*. Pittsburgh: University of Pittsburgh Press, 2007.

———. "Race War and Nation in Caribbean Gran Colombia, Cartagena, 1810–1832." *American Historical Review* 111, no. 2 (2006): 336–61.

———. "Revisiting Independence Day: Afro-Colombian Politics and Patriot Narratives, Cartagena, 1809–1815," in *After Spanish Rule: Postcolonial Predicaments of the Americas*, edited by Mark Thurner and Andres Guerrero, 223–47. Durham, N.C.: Duke University Press, 2003.

Las Sombras, *Documento para la historia del estado de Nicaragua* (Masaya, Nicaragua: Imprenta de la Fraternidad, 1846), 5, Latin American Library, Tulane University.

Lausent-Herrera, Isabelle. "Les Chinois du Perou: Un Identité Reconstruite." *Journal de la Société des Américanistes* 80 (1994): 169–83.

———. "L'émergence d'une élite d'origine asiatique en Pérou," *Caravelle* 67 (1997): 127–53.

———. "Los caucheros y comerciantes chinos en Iquitos a fines del siglo XIX (1800–1900)," in *Los raíces de memoria: América Latina, ayer y hoy. Quinto encuentro*, edited by Pilar García Jordan et al., 467–82. Barcelona: Universitat de Barcelona, 1996.

Lemos, Renato. "Benjamin Constant and the 'Truth' behind the Paraguyan War." In *I Die with My Country: Perspectives on the Paraguyan War*, edited by Hendrik Kraay and Thomas L. Whigham, 81–104. Lincoln: University of Nebraska Press, 2004.

Lenton, Diana. "Relaciones interétnicas: Derechos humanos y autocrítca en la generación del '80." In *La problemática indígena: Estudios antropológicos sobre pueblos indígenas de la Argentina*, edited by Juan Carlos Radovich and Alejandro O. Balazote, 27–65. Buenos Aires: Centro Editor de América Latina, 1992.

León García, Ricardo, and Carlos González Herrera. *Civilizar o exterminar: Tarahumaras y Apaches en Chihuahua, Siglo XIX*. Mexico City: Centro de Investigaciones y Estudios Superiores en Antropología Social, 2000.

Lesser, Jeffrey. *Negotiating National Identity: Immigrants, Minorities and the Struggle for Ethnicity in Brazil*. Durham, N.C.: Duke University Press, 1999.

Levaggi, Abelardo. *Paz en la frontera: Historia de las relaciones diplomáticas con las comunidades indígenas en la Argentina (Siglos XVI–XIX)*. Buenos Aires: Universidad del Museo Social Argentino, 2000.

Lévy, Pablo. *Notas geográficas y económicas de la República de Nicaragua*. Paris: Librería Española de E. Denné Schmitz, 1873.

Lhevinne, Isador. *The Enchanted Jungle*. New York: Coward-McCann, 1933.

Lima, Oliveira. *O movimento da Independência: O Império Brasileiro, 1821–1889*. 2nd ed. São Paulo: Melhoramentos, n.d.

Lima Barreto, Afronso Henriques de. "A matematica não falha," in *Bagatelas*, 177–84. Sao Paulo: Brasiliense, 1956.

Little, Walter E. *Mayas in the Marketplace: Tourism, Globalization, and Cultural Identity*. Austin: University of Texas Press, 2004.

———. "A Visual Political Economy of Maya Representation in Guatemala, 1930–1944." Paper presented at New England Council of Latin American Studies conference, Bowdoin College, Brunswick, Maine, October 1, 2005.

Llaverías, Joaquín, and Emeterio S. Santovenia, eds. *Actas de las asambleas de representantes y del consejo de gobierno durante la guerra de independencia*. 6 vols. Havana: Imprenta y Papelería de Rambla, Bouza y Cía., 1928–1933.

López-Alves, Fernando. "Wars and the Formation of Political Parties in Uruguay, 1810–1851." In *Wars, Parties and Nationalism: Essays on the Politics and Society of Nineteenth Century Latin America*, edited by Eduardo Posada-Carbó. London: Institute of Latin American Studies, 1995.

Los criminales, al presidio. Cali: Imprenta de Nicolás Pontón i Compañía, n.d.

Los Editores. *Documentos curiosos, escojidos de entre otros muchos que se interceptaron últimamente, en el Cauca, a los rebeldes Canal, Arboleda, Enao i compañeros*. Bogotá: Imprenta del E. de Cundinamarca, 1862.

Loveman, Brian. *For la Patria: Politics and the Armed Forces*. Wilmington, Del.: SR Books, 1999.

Lumholtz, Carl. "Among the Tarahumaris: The American Cave-Dwellers," *Scribner's Magazine*, 16 no.,1 (July 1894): 31–49.

Lustosa, Isabel, *Histórias de Presidentes: A república na Catete*. Petropolis, Rio de Janeiro: Vozes, 1989.

Lynch, John. *Caudillos in Spanish America, 1800–1850*. New York: Oxford University Press, 1992.

Maceo, Antonio. *Ideología política. Cartas y otros documentos*. 2 vols. Havana: Sociedad Cubana de Estudios Históricos e Internacionales, 1950.

Magalhães, Raimundo, Jr. *O impeìrio em chinelos*. Rio de Janeiro: Editóra Civilização Brasileira, 1957.

Mallon, Florencia. "Constructing Mestizaje in Latin America: Authenticity, Marginality, and Gender in the Claiming of Ethnic Identities." *Journal of Latin American Anthropology* 2, no. 1 (1996): 170–81.

———. *Courage Tastes of Blood: The Mapuche Community of Nicolás Ailío and the Chilean State, 1906–2001*. Durham, N.C.: Duke University Press, 2005.

———. *The Defense of Community in Peru's Central Highlands: Peasant Struggle and Capitalist Transition*. Princeton, N.J.: Princeton University Press, 1983.

———. "Nationalist and Anti-State Coalitions in the War of the Pacific: Junín and Cajamarca, 1879–1902." In *Resistance, Rebellion and Consciousness in the Andean Peasant World*, edited by Steve J. Stern, 232–79. Madison: Wisconsin University Press, 1987.

———. *Peasant and Nation: The Making of Postcolonial Mexico and Peru*. Berkeley and Los Angeles: University of California Press, 1995.

Maloney, Gerado. "El Negro y la cuestión nacional," in *Nueva Historia del Ecuador*, Vol. 13, *Ensayos Generales*, edited by Enrique Ayala Mora, 59–98. Quito: Corporación Editora Nacional, 1993.

Mandrini, Raúl, and Sara Ortelli. *Volver al país de los araucanos*. Buenos Aires: Sudamericana, 1992.

Manrique, Nelson. *Campesinado y nación: Las guerrillas indígenas en la Guerra con Chile*. Lima: CIC, Editora Ital Peru, S.A. 1981.

———. *La piel y la pluma: Escritos sobre literatura, etnicidad y racismo*. Lima: Sur. Casa de Estudios del Socialismo, 1999.

Markham, Clements. *The War between Peru and Chile, 1879–1882*. London: S. Low, Marston, Searle and Rivington, 1882.

Martí, José. *Obras completas*. 27 vols. Havana: Editorial de Ciencias Sociales, 1975.

Martin, Congrains. *La expedición Lynch*. Lima: Editorial Ecoma, 1973.

Martínez Sarasola, Carlos. "De la mano de las piedras sagradas: Los grandes cacicazgos de las llanuras (1830–1880)." In *Hijos del Viento. Arte de los pueblos del sur Siglo XIX*. Exposición de la Colección Eduardo P. Pereda, 17–22. Buenos Aires: Fundación Proa, 2002.

———. "El mayo indígena." In *¡Libertad, muera el tirano! El camino a la independencia en América: Ensayos*, edited by Norberto Galasso et al., 51–69. Buenos Aires: Ediciones Madres de Plaza de Mayo, 2006.

———. "El sujeto en las fronteras: Pasajes, diversidad y encuentro." In *Identidad y lazo social: Fronteras, pasajes, diversidad*, edited by Claudia Roqueta and Claudio Steckler, 242–45. Buenos Aires: Grama Ediciones, 2004.

———. "Ferocidades de la Argentina," In *Violencias en la Administración Pública*, edited by Diana Scialpi, 200–201. Buenos Aires: Catálogos, 1999.

———. *Los hijos de la Tierra: Historia de los indígenas argentinos*. Buenos Aires: Emecé Editores, 1998.

———. *Nuestros paisanos los indios: Vida, historia y destino de las comunidades indígenas en la Argentina*. Buenos Aires: Emecé Editores, 1992.

Martínez Zuviría, Gustavo. "Concepto, desarrollo e importancia de la conquista del desierto: Antecedentes, oposición y lucha para llevarla a cabo." In *Epopeya del desierto en el sur argentino*, edited by Emilio Ángel Bidondo y Otros. Buenos Aires: Circulo Militar, 1979.

Martiniere, Guerra. *La ocupación de Lima (1881–1883): El gobierno de García Calderón*. Lima: PUCP Fondo Editorial, 1991.

Marx, Anthony. "Contested Citizenship: The Dynamics of Racial Identity and Social Movements." In *International Review of Social History* 40, Supplement 3 (1995): 159–84.

Mases, Enrique Hugo. *Estado y cuestión indígena: El destino final de los indios sometidos en el sur del territorio (1878–1919)*. Buenos Aires: Prometeo Libros/Entrepasados, 2002.

Mato Grosso. *Relatório do vice-presidente da província de Matto-Grosso, Augusto Leverger, em 17 de Outubro de 1865*. Cuiabá: Typ. de Souza Neves, 1865.

Matta, Roberto da. *Carnivals, Rogues and Heroes: An Interpretation of the Brazilian Dilemma*. Notre Dame, Ind.: University of Notre Dame Press, 1991.

Maxwell, Judith. "The Path Back to Literacy: Maya Education through War and Beyond." Paper presented at the conference From a Springtime of Democracy to a Winter of Cold War: The 1954 Guatemalan Coup and Its Lasting Impact on U.S./Latin American Relations, University of Illinois Urbana-Champaign, April 11, 2005.

McCarthy, Cormac. *Blood Meridian: Or, the Evening Redness in the West*. New York: Random House, Inc., 1985.

McCreery, David. *Rural Guatemala 1760–1940*. Stanford, Calif.: Stanford University Press, 1994.

McGuinness, Aims. *Path of Empire: Panama and the California Gold Rush*. Ithaca, N.Y.: Cornell University Press, 2007.

Meléndez Obando, Mauricio. "Presencia africana en familias nicaragüenses." In *Rutas de la esclavitud en América Latina*, edited by Rina Cáceres, 341–60. San Jose: Editorial de la Universidad de Costa Rica, 2001.

Melgarejo, Juán E. *Transmisiones en la Guerra del Chaco*, vol. 1. Asunción: Editorial El Gráfico, 1969.

Memoria del Ministro de Guerra. Santiago: Imprenta de la Epoca, 1881.

Memoria del Ministro de Guerra. Santiago: Imprenta de la Epoca, 1882.

Méndez, Cecilia. "Incas sí, Indios no: Notes on Peruvian creole nationalism and its contemporary crisis." *Journal of Latin American Studies* 28 (1996): 197–225.

———. *The Plebeian Republic: The Huanta Rebellion and the Making of the Peruvian State, 1820–1850*. Durham, N.C.: Duke University Press, 2005.

———, ed. "Populismo militar y etnicidad en los Andes," *ICONOS: Revista de Ciencias Sociales* 26 (2006). Special edition.

Mercado, Ramón. *Memorias sobre los acontecimientos del sur, especialmente en la provincia de Buenaventura, durante la administración del 7 de Marzo de 1849*. Cali: Centro de Estudios Históricos y Sociales "Santiago de Cali," 1996. (Originally published in 1855)

Mercado, René Zavaleta. *La Formación de la Concienca Nacional*. Cochabamba: Los Amigos del Libro, 1990.

Merrill, William L. "Cultural Creativity and Raiding Bands in Eighteenth-Century Northern New Spain," in *Violence, Resistance, and Survival in the Americas: Native Americans and the Legacy of Conquest*, edited by William B. Taylor and Franklin G. Y. Pease, 125–51. Washington, D.C.: Smithsonian Institution, 1994.

Metalli, A. "A civilizar la cayapa." *El Bien Social*, Esmeraldas, December 1901–November 1902.

Metz, Brent. *Ch'orti'-Maya Survival in Eastern Guatemala: Indigeneity in Transition*. Albuquerque: University of New Mexico Press, 2006.

———. "Without Nation, Without Community: The Growth of Maya Nationalism among Ch'orti's of Eastern Guatemala." *Journal of Anthropological Research* 54, no. 3 (fall 1998): 325–49.

Mexico, Secretaría de Relaciones Exteriores. *Correspondencia diplomática cambiada entre el gobierno de los Estados Unidos Mexicanos y los de Varias Potencias Extranjeras desde el 30 de Junio de 1881 a 30 de Junio de 1886. Edición Oficial*. Tomo III. Mexico City: Tipografía "La Luz," 1887.

Millington, Herbert. *American Diplomacy and the War of the Pacific*. New York: Columbia University Press, 1948.

Miró Argenter, José. *Cuba: Crónicas de la guerra*. Havana: Editorial de Ciencias Sociales, 1970.

Molina, Arturo E. *Rencor Apache: Sangre Chiricahua*, 3rd ed., Mexico, D.F.: El Autor, 1997. (Originally published in 1991)

Molina Argüello, Carlos. "Poblaciones fundadas en Nicaragua durante el siglo XVII." *Revista Conservadora del Pensamiento Centroamericano*, no. 27 (December 1962): 31–44.

Monteforte Toledo, Mario. *Guatemala: Monografía sociológica*. México, D.F.: Instituto de Investigaciones Sociales, Universidad Nacional Autónoma de México, 1965.

Montes, Arturo Humberto. *Morazán y la Federación Centroamericana*. México, D.F.: Libro México, 1958.

Montúfar, Lorenzo. *Walker en Centro-América*. Guatemala: Tipogafía "La Unión," 1887.

Mora, Frank O., and Jerry W. Cooney, eds. *Paraguay and the United States: Distant Allies*. Athens: University of Georgia Press, 2007.

de Morais, Evaristo. *Prisões e instituicões penitenciarias no Brazil*. Rio de Janeiro: Candido de Oliveira, 1923.

Moreno, Ahumada. *Guerra del Pacifico: Documentos oficiales, correspondencias y demás publicaciones referentes a la guerra, que ha dado a luz la prensa de Chile, Perú y Bolivia*. 8 Vols. Santiago: Editorial Andrés Bello, 1982.

Moreno, Segundo Luis. *La campaña de Esmeraldas de 1913–1916, encabezada por el Coronel Graduado Don Carlos Concha Torres*. Cuenca: Tipográfico Universidad, 1939.

Mörner, Magnus. "La política de segregación y el mestizaje en la Audiencia de Guatemala." *Revista de Indias* 24, no. 95–96 (1964): 137–52.

Mörner, Magnus, and Charles Gibson. "Diego Muñoz Camargo and the Segregation Policy of the Spanish Crown." *Hispanic American Historical Review* 42, no. 4 (November 1962): 558–68.

Mosher, Jeffrey Carl. *Political Struggle, Political Ideology and State-Building: Pernambuco and the Construction of Brazil 1817–1850*. Lincoln: University of Nebraska Press, 2008.

de Mosquera, T. C. *Memoria sobre la geografía, física y política de la Nueva Granada*. New York: Imprenta de S. W. Benedict, 1852.

———. *T. C. de Mosquera, gobernador del Estado Soberano del Cauca, i presidente de los Estados Unidos de Colombia, as sus conciudadanos*. Bogotá: Imprenta de la Nación, 1861.

Muñoz, José Trinidad. "El Acta de Limay (23 de Marzo de 1846)," *Revista de la Academia de Geografía e Historia de Nicaragua* 7, no. 3 (1945): 51.

Muñoz Vicuña, Elias. *Primero entre iguales: General Carlos Concha Torres*. Guayaquil: Universidad de Guayaquil, 1984.

Musgrave, George Clarke. *Under Three Flags in Cuba: A Personal Account of the Cuban Insurrection and Spanish-American War*. Boston: Little, Brown, and Company, 1899.

Nacuzzi, Lidia R., ed. *Funcionarios, diplomáticos, guerreros: Miradas hacia el otro en las fronteras de pampa y Patagonia (Siglos XVIII y XIX)*. Buenos Aires: Sociedad Argentina de Antropología, 2002.

Nagy, Mariano. *Conquista del desierto: exterminio, incorporación o disolución tribal: Aproximación desde un estado de la cuestión*. www.filo.uba.ar/contenidos/secretarias/seube/catedras/ddhh/textos/genocidio/conquista-del-desierto.htm.

Naro, Nancy Priscilla, ed. *Blacks, Coloreds, and National Identity in Nineteenth-Century Latin America*. London : Institute of Latin American Studies, 2003.

Needell, Jeffrey D. *The Party of Order: The Conservatives, the State and Slavery in the Brazilian Monarchy, 1831–1871*. Stanford, Calif.: Stanford University Press, 2006.

Nelson, Diane. *A Finger in the Wound: Body Politics in Quincentennial Guatemala*. Berkeley and Los Angeles: University of California Press, 1999.

Nordenskiöld, E. "La vie des Indiens dans le Chaco (Amérique du Sud)." *Revue de Géographie* 6, no. 3 (1912): 4–130.

Nunn, Frederick. *The Military in Chilean History: Essays on Civil-Military Relations, 1810–1973.* Albuquerque: New Mexico Press, 1976.

———. *The Time of the Generals: Latin American Military Professionalism in World Perspective.* Lincoln: University of Nebraska Press, 1992.

———. *Yesterday's Soldiers: European Military Professionalism in South America, 1890–1940.* Lincoln: University of Nebraska Press, 1983.

O'Connor, Erin. *Gender, Indian, Nation: The Contradictions of Making Ecuador, 1830–1925.* Tucson: University of Arizona Press, 2007.

O'Phelan Godoy, Scarlett, ed. *Etnicidad y discriminación racial en la historia del Perú.* Lima: PUCP, Instituto Riva Agüero, 2002.

Operé, Fernando. *Historias de la frontera: El cautiverio en la América Hispánica.* Buenos Aires: FCE, 2001.

Ortega Arancibia, Francisco. *Cuarenta años (1838–1878) de historia de Nicaragua.* 4th ed. Managua: Fondo de Promoción Cultural-BANIC, 1993.

Ortiz, Adalberto. *Camino y puerto de la angustia: poemas.* Guayaquil: Isla: 1945.

———. "Captura de un caudillo." Available on *http://www.ecuadorprofundo.com*, accessed January 25, 2008.

———. *Cuentos.* Guayaquil: Ediciones Populares, 1966.

———. *Juyungo, historia de un negro, una isla y otros negros.* Buenos Aries: Editorial Amerilee, 1943.

———. *Los contrabandistas.* México, 1945.

———. *Tierra, son y tambor: cantares negros y mulatos.* México, D.F.: Ediciones La Cigarra, 1945.

Ortiz, Cecilia. *Indios, militares e imaginarios de nación en el Ecuador del Siglo XX.* Quito: Abya-Yala, 2006.

Osorio, Rubén. *Tomóchic en llamas.* Mexico City: Consejo Nacional para la Cultura y las Artes, 1995.

Otto, Paul. *The Dutch-Munsee Encounter in America.* New York: Bergmann Books, 2006.

Pachas Castilla, Rolando. "Impacto de la Guerra del Pacifico en las haciendas de Ica, Chica, Pisco y Cañete." In *La guerra del Pacífico*, edited by Wilson Reátegui Chavez et al. 2 vols. Lima: UNMSM, 1979.

Padrón Valdés, Abelardo. *El general José: Apuntes biográficos.* Havana: Instituto Cubano del Libro, 1973.

Páez, Jorge. *La conquista del desierto.* Buenos Aires: Centro Editor de America Latina, 1971.

Pagden, Anthony. *The Fall of Natural Man: The American Indian and the Origins of Contemporary Ethnology.* Cambridge: Cambridge University Press, 1982.

Palacios, Marcos. *El café en Colombia, 1850–1970: Una historia económica, social y política.* Mexico City: El Colegio de México, 1983.

Palacios, Nicolás. *Raza chilena.* Santiago: Colchagua, 1988.

Pastor, H. Rodríguez. *Herederos del dragón: Historia de la comunidad china en el Perú.* Lima: Fondo Editorial del Congreso del Perú, 2000.

Paz, Ricardo, Mercedes Bullrich, and Carlos Martínez Sarasola, eds. *Mapuches del Neuquén: Arte y cultura en la Patagonia argentina*. Buenos Aires: Luz Editora, 2001.

Pechincha, Mônica. "Historias de Admirar: Mito, rito e história Kadiwéu." Unpublished master's thesis, Universidade de Brasília, 1994.

de la Pedraja, René. *Wars of Latin America, 1899–1941*. Jefferson, N.C.: McFarland & Co., 2006.

Pennington, Campbell W. *The Tarahumar of Mexico: Their Environment and Material Culture*. Guadalajara, Jalisco, Mexico: Editorial Agata, 1996. (Originally published by the University of Utah Press, 1963)

Perdue, Theda. *"Mixed Blood" Indians: Racial Construction in the Early South*. Athens: University of Georgia Press, 2003.

Pereira Cunha, Maria Clementina. *Ecos da folia: Uma história social do Carnaval Carioca*. Sao Paulo: Companhia das Letras, 2001.

Pérez, Jerónimo. *Obras históricas completas*. 2nd ed. Edited by Pedro Joaquín Chamorro Zelaya. Managua: Fondo de Promoción Cultural-BANIC, 1993.

Pérez, Louis A., Jr. *Cuba between Empires, 1878–1902*. Pittsburgh: University of Pittsburgh Press, 1983.

Pérez Concha, Jorge. *Carlos Concha Torres: Biografía de un luchador incorruptible*. Quito: Editorial "El Conejo," 1987.

Peri Fagerstrom, René. *Los batallones Bulnes y Valparaíso en la Guerra del Pacifico*. Santiago: Imprenta de Carabineros, 1981.

Pi Hugarte, Renzo. *Los indios del Uruguay*. Montevideo: Ediciones de La Banda Oriental, 1998.

Pigna, Felipe. *Mitos Argentinos*. Buenos Aires: Colección Clarín, 2007.

Pinto, Jorge. *De la inclusión a la exclusión: La formación del estado y la nación, y el pueblo mapuche*. Santiago: Instituto de Estudios Avanzados, Universidad de Santiago de Chile, 2000.

———. *Misioneros en la Araucanía, 1600–1900: Un capítulo de la historia fronteriza*. Bogotá: Consejo Episcopal Latinoamericano, 1990.

Pion-Berlin, David, ed. *Civil-Military Relations in Latin America: New Analytical Perspectives*. Chapel Hill: University of North Carolina Press, 2001.

Ponzio Sobrino, Francisco. *O sertanejo patriotica*, n.p. 1870. Archive copy in the Biblioteca Nacional de Música, Rio de Janeiro.

Poole, Ross. "National Identity and Citizenship." In *Identities: Race, Class, Gender, and Nationality*, edited by Linda M. Alcoff and Eduardo Mendieta, 271–80. Oxford: Blackwell Publishing, 2003.

Popkin, Samuel L. *The Rational Peasant: The Political Economy of Rural Society in Vietnam*. Berkeley and Los Angeles: University of California Press, 1969.

Porter, Bruce. *War and the Rise of the State: The Military Foundations of Modern Politics*. New York: Free Press, 1994.

Potthast, Barbara. "Protaganists, Victims, and Heroes: Paraguayan Women during the 'Great War.'" In *I Die with My Country*, edited by Hendrick Kraay and Thomas Whigham, 44–60. Lincoln: University of Nebraska Press, 2004.

del Pozo, José Yanez. *Yo declaro con franqueza/Chashnami causaschcanchic: memoria oral de Pesillo-Cayambe*. Quito: Ediciones Abya Yala, 1986.

Prado, Francisco Ribeiro do. "História dos índios cavalleiros ou da nação Guaycuru." *Journal O Patriota*. Rio de Janeiro, 1814.

Prata de Souza, Jorge. *Escravidão ou morte: Os escravos brasileiros na Guerra do Paraguai*. Rio: ADUESA, 1996.

Prieto, Esther, and Guillermo Rolón. *Estudio legislación indígena: Legislación ambiental*. Asunción: CEDHU, 1991.

Primelles, León, ed. *La revolución del 95 según la correspondencia de la delegación cubana en Nueva York*. 5 vols. Havana: Editorial Habanera, 1932–1937.

Radcliffe, Sarah, and Sallie Westwood. *Remaking the Nation: Place, Identity and Politics in Latin America*. London: Routledge, 1996.

Ramayón, Eduardo. *Las caballadas en la guerra del indio*. Buenos Aires: Eudeba, 1975.

Ramos Mejía, Enrique. *Los Ramos Mejía. Apuntes históricos*. Buenos Aires: Emecé Editores, 1988.

Rappaport, Joanne. *Cumbe Reborn: An Andean Ethnography of History*. Chicago: University of Chicago Press, 1994.

Rasler, Karen A., and William R. Thompson. *War and State Making*. Boston: Unwin Hyman, 1989.

Reber, Vera Blinn. "The Demographics of Paraguay: A Reinterpretation of the Great War, 1864–70," *Hispanic American Historical Review* 68, no.2 (1988): 289–319.

Reed, Nelson. *The Caste War of Yucatan*. Stanford, Calif.: Stanford University Press, 1964.

Reeves, René. *Ladinos with Ladinos, Indians with Indians: Land, Labor, and Regional Ethnic Conflict in the Making of Guatemala*. Stanford, Calif.: Stanford University Press, 2006.

Relatório apresentado ao presidente dos estados unidos do Brasil pelo Ministro de Estado de Guerra General de Divisão José Caetano de Faria em Maio de 1915. Rio de Janeiro: Imprensa Militar, 1915.

Renshaw, John. *Los indígenas del Chaco Paraguayo: Economía y sociedad*. Asunción: Intercontinental Editora, 1996.

Revista Arquivo. Año 1. Volumen IV: *Colección facsimilar completa 1904–1906*. Várzea Grande: Fundação Júlio Campos. Coleção Memórias Históricas, vol. 3, 1993.

Reyes, Oscar Efrén. *Breve historia general del Ecuador*. 5th ed. Quito: Editorial Fray Jodoco Ricke, 1955.

Ribeiro, Darcy. *Kadiwéu: Ensaios etnoloìgicos sobre o saber, o azar e a beleza*. Petrópolis, Rio de Janeiro: Vozes, 1980.

Ribeiro, Gladys Sabina. *A liberdade em construção: Identidad nacional e conflictos antilusitanos no primeiro reinado*. Rio de Janeiro: Relume Dumará, 2002.

Rivas, Patricio. "El presidente provisorio de la República de Nicaragua á sus habitantes," *Boletín Oficial* (León), September 20, 1856.

Rivasseau, Emilio. *A vida dos índios Guaycurus: Quinze dias nas suas aldeias*. São Paulo: Companhia Editora Nacional, 1936.

Rivera Cusicanqui, Silvia. *Oppressed but Not Defeated: Peasant Struggles among the Aymara and Quechua in Bolivia, 1900–1980*. Geneva: United Nations Research Institute for Social Development, 1987.

Robins, Wayne. *Etnicidad, Tierra y Poder*. Asunción: Editora Litocolor S.R.L., 2000.

Robinson, Sherry. *Apache Voices: Their Stories of Survival as Told to Eve Ball*. Albuquerque: University of New Mexico Press, 2000.

de la Rocha, Jesús, ed. *Código de la legislación de la República de Nicaragua en Centro América*. (Managua: Imprenta de "El Centro-Americano," 1873–74).

de la Rocha, Pedro Francisco. *Revista Política sobre la historia de la Revolución de Nicaragua en defensa de la Administración del Ex-Director Don José Leon Sandoval* Granada: Imprenta de la Concepción, 1847.

Rodas, Isabel, and Edgar Esquit. *Élite Ladina-vanguardia indígena: De tolerancia a la violencia, Patzicía 1944.* Guatemala City: CAUDAL, 1997.

Rodriguez, Linda Alexander. *The Search for Public Policy: Regional Politics and Government Finances in Ecuador, 1830–1940.* Berkeley and Los Angeles: University of California Press, 1985.

Rodríguez, Mario. *The Cádiz Experiment in Central America, 1808–1826.* Berkeley and Los Angeles: University of California Press, 1978.

Rodríguez, Martín. *Diario de la expedición al desierto.* Buenos Aires, Editorial Sudestada, 1969.

Rodríguez Pastor, Humberto. *Herederos del dragón: Historia de la comunidad china en el Perú.* Lima: Fondo Editorial del Congreso del Perú, 2000.

Rodríguez Sepúlveda, Juan Agustín. *Patricio Lynch, vicealmirante y general en jefe.* Santiago: Editorial Nascimiento, 1967.

Roediger, David R. *The Wages of Whiteness: Race and the Making of the American Working Class.* New York: Verso, 1991.

Roggero, Sotomayor, and Aranda de los Ríos. *Sublevación de campesinos negros en Chincha 1879.* Lima: Universidad Nacional Mayor de San Marcos, 1979.

Romero, Fernando."El mestizaje negroid en la demografía del Peru," *Revista Historica*, 28 (1965): 231–52.

———. *El negro en el Perú y su transculturación lingüística.* Lima: Editorial Milla Batres, 1987.

———. "Papel de los descendientes de africanos en el desarrollo económico-social del Perú." *Historica* 4, no. 1 (1980): 53–93.

Romero, Silvio. "A poesia popular no Brasil," *Revista Brasileira* 7 (1881): 30.

Romero Vargas, Germán. *Las estructuras sociales de Nicaragua en el siglo XVIII.* Managua: Vanguardia, 1988.

Roquie, Alaine. *The Military and the State in Latin America.* Berkeley and Los Angeles: University of California Press, 1987.

Rosada Granados, Hector. *Soldados en el poder: Proyecto militar en Guatemala.* San José, Costa Rica: FUNDAPEM/ Universidad de Utrecht, 1990.

Roseberry, William. "Hegemony and the Language of Contention." In *Everyday Forms of State Formation: Revolution and Integration of Rule in Modern Mexico*, edited by Gilbert M. Joseph and Daniel Nugent, 355–66. Durham, NC: Duke University Press, 1994.

Rosell y Malpica, Eduardo. *Diario del teniente coronel Eduardo Rosell y Malpica (1895–1897).* 2 vols. Havana: Imprenta "El Siglo XX," 1949–50.

Rueda Novoa, Rocío. *Zambaje y Autonomía: Historia de la gente negra de la provincia de Esmeraldas, siglos XVI–XVII.* Quito: Abya-Yala, 2001.

Sabato, Hilda. *The Many and the Few: Political Participation in Republican Buenos Aires.* Stanford, Calif.: Stanford University Press, 2001.

Safford, Frank. "Reflections on the Internal Wars of Nineteenth Century Latin America." In *Rumours of War: Civil Conflict in Nineteenth Century Latin America*, edited by Rebecca Earle, 6–28. London: Institute of Latin American Studies, 2000.

Safford, Frank, and Marco Palacios. *Colombia: Fragmented Land, Divided Society*. New York: Oxford University Press, 2002.

Saliba, Elias Thomé, *Raízes do Riso: A representação humorística na história brasileira: Da Belle Époque aos primeiros tempos do rádio*. São Paulo: Companhia Das Letras, 2002.

Salinas, Sebastián (León), to Máximo Jerez, June 15, 1857, in "Documentos relativos a la Guerra Nacional," *Revista de la Academia de Geografía e Historia de Nicaragua* 2, no. 1 (1937): 89-102.

Salles, Ricardo. *Guerra do Paraguai: Escravidão e cidadania na formação do exército*. Rio: Paz e Terra, 1991.

Sanders, James E. "'Citizens of a Free People': Popular Liberalism and Race in Nineteenth-Century Southwestern Colombia." *Hispanic American Historical Review* 84, no. 2, (2004): 277–314.

———. *Contentious Republicans: Popular Politics, Race, and Class in Nineteenth-Century Colombia*. Durham, N.C.: Duke University Press, 2004.

Sandoval, José León. "Discurso pronunciado por el Sr. Director Supremo José Leon Sandoval al presentarle á la A. L. del Estado en la sesión del 22 del presente mes de Marzo de 847," *Registro Oficial* (Managua), March 27, 1847.

Santa Maria, Domingo. Inaugural Speech to Congress in 1883. Public Records Office, Kew, Foreign Office Archives, Chile, 16/223: 1883.

Santoni, Pedro, ed. *Daily Lives of Civilians in Wartime Latin America: From the Wars of Independence to the Central American Civil Wars*. Westport, Conn.: Greenwood Press, 2008.

Sarmiento, Emilio. *Memorias de un soldado de la Guerra del Chaco*. Buenos Aires: El Cid Editor, 1979.

Sarramone, Alberto, *Catriel y los indios pampas de Buenos Aires*. Azul: Editorial Biblos, 1993.

Sater, William. *Andean Tragedy: Fighting the War of the Pacific, 1879–1884*. Lincoln: University of Nebraska Press, 2007.

———. *Chile and the War of the Pacific*. Lincoln: University of Nebraska Press, 1986.

Sater, William, and Holger H. Herwig. *The Grand Illusion: The Prussianization of the Chilean Army*. Lincoln: University of Nebraska Press, 1999.

Scarano, Francisco A. "The Jíbaro Masquerade and the Subaltern Politics of Creole Identity Formation in Puerto Rico, 1745–1830," *The American Historical Review* 101, no. 5 (1996): 1398–431.

Schoo Lastra, Dionisio. *El indio del desierto*. Buenos Aires, Agencia General de Librería y Publicaciones, 1928.

Schwarcz, Lilia Moritz. *As barbas do imperador: Dom Pedro II, um monarca nos trópicos*. Sao Paulo: Companhia das Letras, 2000.

———. *O espectaculo das raças: Cientistas, instituões e questão racial no Brasil, 1870–1930*. Sao Paulo: Cia/Das Letras, 1993.

Scheina, Robert L. *Latin America's Wars*. 2 vols. Washington D.C.: Brasseys, 2003.

Schindler, Helmut. *Die Reiterstämme des Gran Chaco*. Berlin: Dietrich Reimer Verlag, 1983.

Schirmer, Jennifer. *The Guatemalan Military Project: A Violence Called Democracy*. Philadelphia: University of Pennsylvania Press, 1998.

Scott, James. *Domination and the Arts of Resistance: Hidden Transcripts*. New Haven, Conn.: Yale University Press, 1990.

Scott, Rebecca J. *Degrees of Freedom: Louisiana and Cuba after Slavery*. Cambridge, Mass.: Belknap Press, 2005.

Seelwische, José, O. M. I. *Las misiones Nivaclé en el vicariato Apostólico Pilcomayo: Una experiencia de inculturación*. Asunción: Equipo Nacional de Misiones, 1978.

———. "Los Misioneros y la autogestión de los pueblos indígenas, la evolución de su comprensión y práctica en el equipo nacional de misiones." Unpublished manuscript, Archives of the National Missions Team, Asunción.

———. *Sui papi catsinôvot p'alhaa na lhcootsjat, ti yisclansha'ne: Lecturas de Historia para el 5to Grado*. Asunción: Imprenta Makrografic, 1995.

Segall, M. "Esclavitud y trafico de Culíes en Chile." *Journal of Inter-American Studies* 10, no. 1 (1968): 117–33.

Sepúlveda, Rodríguez. *Patricio Lynch, vicealmirante y general en jefe*. Santiago: Editorial Nascimento, 1967.

Serra, Rafael. *La doctrina de Martí: Carta abierta al coronel José C. López y teniente coronel Julian V. Sierra*. New York, 1900.

Sharman, Russell Leigh. "The Caribbean *Carretara*: Race, Space and Social Liminality in Costa Rica." *Bulletin of Latin American Research* 20, no. 1 (2001): 46–62.

Shenk, Gerald Edwin. "'Work or Fight': Selective Service and Manhood in the Progressive Era." Unpublished PhD dissertation, University of California, San Diego, 1992.

Silva, Eduardo. *The Prince of the People: The Life and Times of a Brazilian Free Man of Colour*, translated by Moyra Ashford. London: Verso, 1993.

———. "O Príncipe Obá, um voluntário da pátria." In *Guerra do Paraguai 130 anos depois*, edited by Maria Eduarda Castro Magalhães Marques, 67–75. Rio de Janeiro: Relume Dumará, 1995.

Silveira, Mauro César. *A batalha de papel: A guerra do Paraguai atraveìs da caricatura*. Porto Alegre, Brazil: L & PM Editores, 1996.

Silveira de Mello, Raul. *Historia do Forte de Coimbra*. Vol. 4. Rio de Janeiro: Imprensa do Exército, 1961.

Siqueira, Jamie Garcia, Jr. "Esse campo custou o sangue dos nossos avos: A construção do tempo e espaço Kadiweu." Unpublished master's thesis, Universidade de Sao Paulo, 1993.

Skidmore, Thomas E. *Black into White: Race and Nationality in Brazilian Thought*, 2nd ed. Durham, N.C.: Duke University Press, 1992.

Skocpol, Theda. *Protecting Soldiers and Mothers: The Political Origins of Social Policy in the United States*. Cambridge, Mass: Belknapp Press, 1992.

Smith, Anthony D. "War and Ethnicity: The Role of Warfare in the Formation, Self-images and Cohesion of Ethnic Communities." *Ethnic and Racial Studies* 4, no. 4 (1981): 375–97.

Smith, Carol. "Race-Class-Gender Ideology in Guatemala: Modern and Anti-Modern Forms." *Comparative Studies in Society and History* 37 (1995): 723–49.

Smith, Ralph A. "Apache Plunder Trails Southward, 1831–1840," *New Mexico Historical Review* 37, no. 1 (January 1962): 20–42.

———. *Borderlander: The Life of James Kirker, 1793–1852.* Norman: University of Oklahoma Press, 1999.

———. "Indians in American-Mexican Relations before the War of 1846," *Hispanic American Historical Review* 43, no. 1 (February 1963): 34–64.

Sodré, Nelson Werneck. *A história da literatura brasileira.* Rio de Janeiro: Civilização Brasileira, 1964.

Soihet, Rachel. *Subversão pelo riso: Estudos sobre o carnaval carioca da Belle Epoque ao tempo de Vargas.* Rio de Janeiro: Fundação Getulio Vargas Editora, 1998.

Sommer, Doris. *Foundational Fictions: The National Romances of Latin America.* Berkeley and Los Angeles: University of California Press, 1993.

Sotomayor Roggero, Carmela, and Ramón Arando de los Rios. *Sublevación de campesinos negros en Chinca, 1879.* Lima: Universidad Nacional Mayor de San Marcos, 1979.

de Sousa Doria, João Antônio. *Estudos sobre a promoção nos exércitos.* Rio de Janeiro: Typ. Popular, 1871.

Souza, Paulo. *A Sabinada: A revolta separatista da Bahia, 1837.* São Paulo: Editora Brasiliense, 1987.

de Souza, Vincente. *O império e a escravidão: O parlamento e a pena de morte: conferência.* Sao Paulo: Centro de Memria Sindical, 1993.

Stab, Silke, and Kristen Hill Maher. "The Dual Discourse about Peruvian Domestic Workers in Santiago de Chile: Class, Race and a Nationalist Project." *Latin American Politics and Society* 48, no. 1 (Spring 2006): 87–116.

Stahl, Wilmar. *Escenario indígena chaqueño pasado y presente.* Filadelfia: ASCIM, 1982.

Stepan, Alfred C. *Rethinking Military Politics: Brazil and the Southern Cone.* Princeton, N.J.: Princeton University Press, 1988.

Stern, Steve, ed. *Resistance, Rebellion and Consciousness in the Andean Peasant World.* Madison: University of Wisconsin Press, 1987.

Stewart, Watt. *Chinese Bondage in Peru.* Durham, N.C.: Duke University Press, 1951.

Stokes, Susan Carol. "Etnicidad y clase social: Los afro-peruanos de Lima, 1900–1930." In *Lima obrera, 1900–1930.* Vol. 2., edited by Steve Stein, 171–252. Lima: Ediciones El Virrey, 1987.

Stoll, David. *Rigoberta Menchú and the Story of All Poor Guatemalans.* Boulder, Colo.: Westview Press, 1999.

Sulé, Jorge Oscar. *Rosas y sus relaciones con los indios.* Buenos Aires: Instituto Nacional de Investigaciones Históricas Juan Manuel de Rosas, 2003.

Súsnik, Blanislava. *Los aborígenes del Paraguay: Etnohistoria de los Chaqueños 1650–1910.* Asunción: Museo Etnografico Andrés Barbero, 1981.

Súsnik, Branislava, and Miguel Chase-Sardi. *Los índios del Paraguay.* Madrid: Editorial Mapfre, 1995.

Swayne y Mendoza, Guillermo. *Mis antepasados (genealogía de las familias Swayne, Mariategui, Mendoza y Barreda).* Lima, 1951.

Tamayo, Alfredo Espinosa. *Psicología y sociología del pueblo ecuatoriano*. Quito: Banco Central del Ecuador, 1979. (Originally published in 1918)

Tardieu, G. *Los negros y la iglesia en el Perú: Siglos XVI-XVII*. Quito: Centro Cultural Afroecuatoriano, 1997.

Taunay, Afonso d'Escragnolle. "Juca, o tropeiro." In *Historias Brazileiras*. Rio de Janeiro: B. L. Garnier, 1874.

———. *Memórias do Visconde de Taunay*. São Paulo: Melhoramentos, 1946.

———. "Relatório Geral da Comissão de engenheiros junto às forças em expedição para a província de Matto Grosso 1865–1866." *Revista do Instituto Historio e Geográfico Brasileira–RIHGB*. Tomo XXXVI, Parte Segunda, 1874.

———. *Scenas de Viagem*. São Paulo: Livraria do Globo, 1923.

Taunay, Alfredo d'Escragnolle, *A retirada da Laguna*. Traducción. São Paulo: Cia das Letras, 1997. Oringinally published as *La Retraite de Laguna*. Rio de Janeiro: Typographie Nationale, 1871.

Tax, Sol. "The Problem of Democracy in Middle America." *American Sociological Review* 10, no. 2 (1944): 192–99.

Tellez, I. *Una raza militar*. Santiago: Imprenta Sudamericana, 1944.

Terzaga, Alfredo, *Historia de Roca, de soldado federal a president de la República*. Buenos Aires: A. Peña Lillo, 1976.

Thomas, Hugh. *Cuba: The Pursuit of Freedom*. New York: Harper & Row, 1971.

Thomson, Guy. "Popular Aspects of Liberalism in Mexico, 1848–1888." *Bulletin of Latin American Research* 10 (1991): 121–52.

Thomson, Guy P. C., with David G. LaFrance. *Patriotism, Politics, and Popular Liberalism in Nineteenth-Century Mexico: Juan Francisco Lucas and the Puebla Sierra, 1854–1917*. Wilmington, Del.: SR Books, 1999.

Thrapp, Dan. *The Conquest of Apachería*. Norman: University of Oklahoma Press, 1967.

———. *Victorio and the Mimbres Apaches*. Norman: University of Oklahoma Press, 1974.

Thurner, Mark. "Historicizing 'the Postcolonial' from Nineteenth-Century Peru." *Journal of Historical Sociology* 9, no. 1 (March 1996): 1–17.

———. *From Two Republics to One Divided: Contradictions of Postcolonial Nationmaking in Andean Peru*. Durham, N.C.: Duke University Press, 1997.

Thurner, Mark, and Andres Guerrero (eds.) *After Spanish Rule: Postcolonial Predicaments of the Americas*. Durham, N.C.: Duke University Press, 2003.

Tilly, Charles, ed. *The Formation of National States in Western Europe*. Princeton, N.J.: Princeton University Press, 1975.

Tirado Mejía, Alvaro. *Aspectos sociales de las guerras civiles en Colombia*. Bogotá: Instituto Colombiano de Cultura, 1976.

Torres Cuevas, Eduardo. *Antonio Maceo: Las ideas que sostienen el arma*. Havana: Editorial de Ciencias Sociales, 1995.

Trazegnies Granda, Fernando. *En el país de las colinas de arena*. 2 vols. Lima: PUCP Fondo Editorial, 1994.

Treece, David. *Exiles, Allies, Rebels: Brazil's Indianist Movement, Indigenist Politics and the Imperial Nation State*. Westport, Conn.: Greenwood Press, 2000.

Troncoso, Julio C. *Vida anecdótica del General Eloy Alfaro: Nacimiento, juventud, campanas y cronología de los combates, administración, obras realizadas, y muerte sacrificada del notable estadista.* Quito: Editorial Santo Domingo, 1966.

Troncoso Barba, Elías. *La Campana de 1900 de Tulcán (capitulo olvidado en la historia del Ecuador y del sur de Colombia).* Quito: Talleres Gráficos de Educación, 1943.

Turner, Christina Bolke, and Brian Turner. "The Role of Mestizaje of Surnames in Paraguay in the Creation of a Distinct New World Ethnicity." *Ethnohistory* 41, no. 1 (Winter 1944): 139–65.

United States Department of State, *The Executive Documents of the House of Representatives for the Second Session of the Forty-Ninth Congress, 1886–1887.*

Unos Caucanos. *Los tratados con Mosquera.* Bogotá: Imprenta de "El Mosaico," 1860.

Uribe-Uran, Victor M. *Honorable Lives: Lawyers, Family, and Politics in Colombia, 1780–1850.* Pittsburgh: University of Pittsburgh Press, 2000.

Urrutia M., Miguel, and Mario Arrubla, eds. *Compendio de estadísticas históricas de Colombia.* Bogotá: Universidad Nacional de Colombia, 1970.

Utley, Robert M. *Frontier Regulars: The United States Army and the Indian, 1866–1891.* New York: McMillan, 1973.

Valdés Domínguez, Fermín. *Diario de un soldado.* 4 vols. Havana: Centro de Información Científica y Técnica, Universidad de la Habana, 1972–75.

Valdés Oliva, Arturo. *Fundación de la Escuela Politécnica.* Guatemala: Editorial "Jose de Pineda Ibarra," 1971.

Valdez, Ramón Sotomayor. *Historia de Chile bajo el gobierno de don Joaquín Prieto.* Santiago: Editorial Universidad Católica de Chile, 1962.

Valencia Llano, Alonso. *Estado Soberano del Cauca: Federalismo y regeneración.* Bogotá: Banco de la República, 1988.

Vanderwood, Paul. *The Power of God against the Guns of Government: Religious Upheaval in Mexico at the Turn of the Nineteenth Century.* Stanford, Calif.: Stanford University Press, 1998.

Vanegas, Juan de Dios. "El asesinato del jefe coronel José Zepeda y compañeros, 25 de Enero de 1837." *Revista de la Academia de Geografía e Historia,* 11, no. 2 (January–March 1952): 166–72.

Vangelista, Chiara. "Confines políticos y relaciones interétnicas." *Reflexiones en torno a 500 años de historia de Brasil,* edited by Elda González, Alfredo Moreno, and Rosario Sevilla, 115–36. Madrid: Ministerio da Educación y Cultura/ Embajada de Brasil en España, 2001.

———. "Los Guaikuru, Españoles y Portuguese en una región de frontera: Mato Grosso, 1770–1830. *Boletín del Instituto de História Argentina y Americana "Dr. Emilio Ravignani,"* no. 8, (1993):55–76.

Vega Bolaños, Andrés, comp. and ed. *Gobernantes de Nicaragua: Notas y documentos.* Managua: N.p., 1944.

Velázquez, José Luis. *La formación del estado en Nicaragua.* Managua: Fondo Editorial Banco Central de Nicaragua, 1992.

Versen, Max von. *Historia da guerra do Paraguai.* Traducción. Belo Horizonte: Itatiaia–São Paulo: EDUSP, 1976, translated from *Reisen in Amerika und der südamerikanische, Krieg.* Breslau: M. Mälzer, 1872.

Vicuña Mackenna, Benjamín. *Historia de la campaña de Lima, 1880–1881*. Santiago: R. Jover, 1881.

———. "Cuarto discurso sobre la pacificación de Arauco." National Congress, August 14, 1868. Reprinted in Jorge Pinto, *La formación del Estado y la nación, y el pueblo mapuche*. Santiago: DIBAM, 2003.

Vijil, Francisco. "El Licenciado don Francisco Castellón visto por el Señor Obispo Viteri." *Revista de la Academia de Geografía e Historia de Nicaragua* 3, no. 3 (1940): 289–99.

Villalobos, Sergio. *Historia del pueblo Chileno*. Santiago: Zig-Zag, 1980.

———. *Los pehuenches en la vida fronteriza: Investigaciones*. Santiago: Ediciones Universidad Católica, 1989.

Villalobos, Sergio, et al., eds. *Relaciones fronterizas en la Araucanía*. Santiago: Ediciones Universidad Católica, 1982.

Villegas, Jorge, and Antonio Restrepo. *Resguardos de indígenas, 1820–1890*. Medellín: Universidad de Antioquia, 1977.

Viñas, David. *Indios, ejército y frontera*. Buenos Aires: Siglo XXI Editores, 1983.

Vinson, Ben, III. *Bearing Arms for His Majesty: The Free Colored Militia in Colonial Mexico*. Stanford, Calif.: Stanford University Press, 2001.

Voelz, Peter M. *Slave and Soldier: The Military Impact of Blacks in the Colonial Americas*. New York: Garland Publishing, 1993.

Wade, Peter. *Blackness and Race Mixture in Colombia*. Baltimore: Johns Hopkins University Press, 1993.

———. *Music, Race, and Nation: Musica Tropical in Colombia*. Chicago: University of Chicago Press, 2000.

———. "Negros, indígenas e identidad nacional en Colombia." In *Imaginar la nación*, edited by François-Xavier Guerra and Monica Quijada, 257–88. Munster: Lit, 1994.

———. *Race and Ethnicity in Latin America*. London: Pluto Press, 1997.

Wagley, Charles. *Economics of a Guatemalan Village*. Menasha, Wis.: American Anthropological Association, no. 58, 1941.

Walker, Charles F. *Smoldering Ashes: Cuzco and the Creation of Republican Peru, 1780–1840*. Durham, N.C.: Duke University Press, 1999.

Walker, William. *The War in Nicaragua*. Mobile, Ala.: S. H. Goetzel, 1860; reprint Tucson: University of Arizona Press, 1985.

Walther, Juan Carlos. *La conquista del desierto*. Buenos Aires: Eudeba, 1974.

Warren, Kay. *Symbolism of Subordination: Indian Identity in a Guatemalan Town*. Austin: University of Texas Press, 1978.

Wells, William V. *Explorations and Adventures in Honduras*. New York: Harper & Brothers, 1857.

———. *Walker's Expedition to Nicaragua*. New York: Stringer and Townsend, 1856.

Whigham, Thomas L. *The Paraguyan War*. 2 volumes. Lincoln: University of Nebraska Press, 2002.

Whigham, Thomas L., and Barbara Potthast. "The Paraguayan Rosetta Stone: New Insights into the Demographics of the Paraguayan War, 1864–1870." *Latin American Research Review* 34, no. 1 (1999): 174–86.

Whitten, Norman E., and Rachel Corr. "Imageries of Blackness in Indigenous Myth, Discourse and Ritual." In *Representations of Blackness and the Performance of Identities*, edited by Jean Rahier, 213–34. Westport, Conn.: Bergin and Garvey, 1999.

Whitten, Norman, and Diego Quiroga. "Ecuador," in *No Longer Invisible: Afro-Latin Americans Today*, edited by Minority Rights Group. London: Minority Rights Group, 1995.

Wiener, Charles. *Perú y Bolivia: Relato de viaje seguido de estudios arqueológicos y etnográficos y de notas sobre la escritura y los idiomas de las poblaciones indígenas*. Lima: Instituto Francés de Estudios Andinos, Universidad Nacional Mayor de San Marcos, 1993.

Wilcox, Robert W. "Cattle Ranching on the Brazilian Frontier: Tradition and Innovation in Mato Grosso, 1870–1940." Unpublished Ph.D. dissertation, New York University, 1992.

Winkler, Norman. "The Sertão in the Romances of Four Brazilian Writers: José de Alencar, Bernardo Guimarães, Franklin Távora, and Alfredo d'Escragnolle Taunay." Unpublished Ph.D. dissertation, University of Pittsburgh, 1960.

Witt, Heinrich. *Diario y observaciones sobre el Perú: 1824–1890*. Compilado y traducido por Pablo Macera. Lima: COFIDE, 1987.

Wolf, Eric R. *Peasant Wars of the Twentieth Century*. New York: Harper & Row, 1969.

Wolfe, Justin. *The Everyday Nation-State: Community, and Ethnicity in Nineteenth-Century Nicaragua*. Lincoln: University of Nebraska Press, 2007.

Woodward, Franc R. E. *"El Diablo Americano" = The Devil American: Strange Adventures of a War Correspondent in Cuba*. New York: G. F. Burslem and Co., c. 1895.

Woodward, Ralph Lee, Jr. *Central America: A Nation Divided*. Oxford: Oxford University Press, 1985.

Wright, Winthrop. *Café con Leche: Race, Class, and National Image in Venezuela*. Austin: University of Texas Press, 1990.

Wu Brading, Celia. *Testimonios Británicos de la ocupación chilena de Lima (enero de 1881)*. Lima: Instituto Francés de Estudios Andinos, Universidad Mayor de San Marcos, 1993.

Yunque, Alvaro. *Calfucurá: La conquista de las pampas*. Buenos Aires: Ediciones Antonio Zamora, 1956.

Zambrana Fonseca, Armando. *Civiles y militares: 180 años en Nicaragua*. Managua, Nicaragua: PAVSA, 2001.

Zamora Castellanos, Pedro. *Vida Militar de Centro América*. Guatemala: Tipografía Nacional, 1924.

Zook, David. *La conducción de la Guerra del Chaco*. Buenos Aries: Ed. Policarpio Artaza, 1962.

———. *The Conduct of the Chaco War*. New Haven, Conn.: Bookman Associates, 1960.

Zuluaga Ramírez, Francisco. *Guerrilla y sociedad en el Patía: Una relación entre clientelismo político y la insurgencia social*. Cali: Universidad del Valle, 1993.

Contributors

Richard N. Adams is professor emeritus of anthropology at the University of Texas at Austin, and director of the Centro de Investigaciones Regionales de Mesoamerica in Antigua, Guatemala.

Peter M. Beattie is associate professor of history at Michigan State University and Acting Director of the University's Center for Latin American and Caribbean Studies.

David Carey Jr. is professor of history and women and gender studies at the University of Southern Maine.

Maria de Fátima Costa is professor of history at the Federal University of Mato Grosso in Brazil.

Joanna Crow is a lecturer in Latin American Studies at the University of Bristol, United Kingdom.

Nicola Foote is associate professor of Latin American and Caribbean history at Florida Gulf Coast University.

Aline Helg is professor of history at the University of Geneva in Switzerland.

René D. Harder Horst is professor of history at Appalachian State University.

Julia O'Hara is associate professor of history at Xavier University in Cincinnati, Ohio.

Vincent C. Peloso is professor emeritus of history at Howard University.

James E. Sanders is associate professor of Latin American History at Utah State University.

Carlos Martínez Sarasola is the director of the Fundacíon Desde América in Buenos Aries, Argentina.

Justin Wolfe is associate professor of Latin American history at Tulane University.

Index

www.ingramcontent.com/pod-product-compliance
Lightning Source LLC
Chambersburg PA
CBHW050331270326
41926CB00016B/3407